# Food Security for Developing Countries

## Also of Interest

*Food, Politics, and Agricultural Development: Case Studies in the Public Policy of Rural Modernization*, edited by Raymond F. Hopkins, Donald J. Puchala, and Ross B. Talbot

*Protein, Calories, and Development: Nutritional Variables in the Economics of Developing Countries*, Bernard A. Schmitt

*World Food, Pest Losses, and the Environment*, edited by David Pimentel

*The Challenge of the New International Economic Order*, edited by Edwin P. Reubens*

*International Trade and Agriculture: Theory and Policy*, edited by Jimmye S. Hillman and Andrew Schmitz

*Successful Seed Programs: A Planning and Management Guide*, compiled and edited by Johnson E. Douglas

*Small Farm Development: Understanding and Improving Farming Systems in the Humid Tropics*, Richard R. Harwood

*Animals, Feed, Food and People: An Analysis of the Role of Animals in Food Production*, edited by R. L. Baldwin

*New Agricultural Crops*, edited by Gary A. Ritchie

*Administering Agricultural Development in Asia: A Comparative Analysis of Four National Programs*, Richard W. Gable and J. Fred Springer

*World Economic Development: 1979 and Beyond*, Herman Kahn

*Agricultural Credit for Small Farm Development: Policies and Practices*, David D. Bathrick

*Rice in the Tropics: A Guide to Development of National Programs*, Robert F. Chandler, Jr.

*Green Revolution? Technology and Change in Rice-Growing Areas of Tamil Nadu and Sri Lanka*, edited by B. H. Farmer

*Available in hardcover and paperback.

# A Westview Special Study

*Food Security for Developing Countries*
edited by Alberto Valdés

Five years after the 1975 World Food Conference's call for a global food security system, not only does no such system exist, but there is no indication that one is to be established. The creation of the required system, able to meet the needs of poor people in poor countries, calls for substantial action in both low and high income countries. In this volume, policy advisers and researchers discuss the nature and magnitude of the security problem in the less-developed countries and assess the likely impact of national and international initiatives upon food security in these countries.

**Alberto Valdés** is currently a research fellow and program leader of the Trade Program for the International Food Policy Research Institute (IFPRI). He was formerly director of the Graduate Program in Economics and Agricultural Economics, Universidad Católica de Chile, and economist with the International Center for Tropical Agriculture (CIAT), based in Colombia. Dr. Valdés has contributed articles to leading economics journals.

# Food Security for Developing Countries

edited by Alberto Valdés

LONDON AND NEW YORK

First published 1981 by Westview Press

Published 2019 by Routledge
52 Vanderbilt Avenue, New York, NY 10017
2 Park Square, Milton Park, Abingdon, Oxon OX14 4RN

*Routledge is an imprint of the Taylor & Francis Group, an informa business*

Copyright © 1981 by Taylor & Francis

All rights reserved. No part of this book may be reprinted or reproduced or utilised in any form or by any electronic, mechanical, or other means, now known or hereafter invented, including photocopying and recording, or in any information storage or retrieval system, without permission in writing from the publishers.

Notice:
Product or corporate names may be trademarks or registered trademarks, and are used only for identification and explanation without intent to infringe.

**Library of Congress Cataloging in Publication Data**
**Main entry under title:**
Food security for developing countries.

Papers presented at a 1978 conference sponsored by the International Food Policy Research Institute and the International Maize and Wheat Improvement Center.

Bibliography: p.
Includes index.
1. Underdeveloped areas—Food supply—Congresses. 2. Food supply—International cooperation—Congresses. I. Valdés, Alberto, 1935- II. International Food Policy Research Institute. III. International Maize and Wheat Improvement Center.

| HD9000.5.F597 | 338.1'9'1724 | 80-18340 |
| --- | --- | --- |

ISBN 13: 978-0-367-01842-9 (hbk)
ISBN 13: 978-0-367-16829-2 (pbk)

# Contents

List of Figures and Tables . . . . . . . . . . . . . . . . . . . . . . . . . . ix
Foreword, *John W. Mellor* . . . . . . . . . . . . . . . . . . . . . . . . . xv
The Contributors . . . . . . . . . . . . . . . . . . . . . . . . . . . . . . . . xix
Abbreviations . . . . . . . . . . . . . . . . . . . . . . . . . . . . . . . . . . xxi

1  Introduction, *Alberto Valdés and Ammar Siamwalla* . . . . .1

**Part 1**
**Nature and Magnitude of Food Insecurity**
**in Developing Countries**

2  Assessing Food Insecurity Based on National
   Aggregates in Developing Countries,
   *Alberto Valdés and Panos Konandreas* . . . . . . . . . . . . . .25

3  Long-Term Consequences of Technological Change
   on Crop Yield Stability: The Case for Cereal Grain,
   *Randolph Barker, Eric C. Gabler, and*
   *Donald Winkelmann* . . . . . . . . . . . . . . . . . . . . . . . . .53

4  Security of Rice Supplies in the ASEAN Region,
   *Ammar Siamwalla* . . . . . . . . . . . . . . . . . . . . . . . . . . .79

5  Food Security: Some East African Considerations,
   *Uma Lele and Wilfred Candler* . . . . . . . . . . . . . . . . . .101

6  The Nature of Food Insecurity in Colombia,
   *Jorge García García* . . . . . . . . . . . . . . . . . . . . . . . . .123

*vii*

viii                                                                                    *Contents*

7   Food Security Program in Egypt,
    *Ahmed A. Goueli* .............................143

**Part 2**
**National and International Approaches**
**to Reduce Food Insecurity**

8   Price, Stock, and Trade Policies and the
    Functioning of International Grain Markets,
    *Timothy Josling* .............................161

9   Feasibility, Effectiveness, and Costs of Food
    Security Alternatives in Developing Countries,
    *Shlomo Reutlinger and David Bigman*..............185

10  The International Wheat Agreement and LDC
    Food Security, *Daniel Morrow* .................213

11  Insurance Approach to Food Security: Simulation
    of Benefits for 1970/71–1975/76 and for 1978–1982,
    *Barbara Huddleston and Panos Konandreas*.........241

12  Grain Insurance, Reserves, and Trade: Contributions
    to Food Security for LDCs, *D. Gale Johnson* .......255

13  Responsiveness of Food Aid to Variable Import
    Requirements, *Barbara Huddleston*...............287

14  Compensatory Financing for Fluctuations in the
    Cost of Cereal Imports, *Louis M. Goreux* ..........307

*Participants*...................................333
*Index*.......................................335

# Figures and Tables

## Figures

3.1 Moorman's model of the relation of land in use for
specific agricultural purpose and land quality . . . . . .61
3.2 Distribution of yields at low level of technology,
97 experimental observations on farmers' fields,
Plan Puebla, 1971-74 . . . . . . . . . . . . . . . . . . . . . . .67
3.3 Distribution of yields at high level of technology,
78 experimental observations on farmers' fields,
Plan Puebla, 1971-74 . . . . . . . . . . . . . . . . . . . . . . .68
5.1 Conceptual model of food grain production and
disposition. . . . . . . . . . . . . . . . . . . . . . . . . . . . . . .103
5.2 Increase in Zambian marketed maize production . . . .104
7.1 Wheat flow chart for Egypt, 1978. . . . . . . . . . . . . . .152
7.2 Maize flow chart for Egypt, 1978 . . . . . . . . . . . . . . .153
10.1 Model of determination of price and
ending stocks. . . . . . . . . . . . . . . . . . . . . . . . . . . . . .218
10.2 Relationship between ending stocks and
total supply. . . . . . . . . . . . . . . . . . . . . . . . . . . . . . .218
10.3 Relationship between price and ending stocks. . . . . . .219
10.4 Probability distribution of price . . . . . . . . . . . . . . . .219
10.5 WTC price indicator (annual average) . . . . . . . . . . . .224

## Tables

2.1 Composition of food consumption, in calorie
equivalents, for 94 developing countries, 1972-74 . .28
2.2 Variability in staple food consumption, 1961-76 . . . . .30

| | | |
|---|---|---|
| 2.3 | Ratio of food imports to total export revenue (1965–76 except as noted) | 32 |
| 2.4 | Variability in staple food production, 1961–76. | 34 |
| 2.5 | Variability of the food import bill, 1961–76. | 37 |
| 2.6 | Reduction in the variability of consumption and in the required imports under two alternative food security decision rules, 1961–76 | 40 |
| 2.7 | Shortfalls in export earnings with and without adjustments for food import bills (1965–76 except as noted) | 45 |
| 2.8 | Financial resources to cover fluctuations in cereal imports of LDCs (1965–76) | 47 |
| 2.9 | Food consumption variability (coefficient of variation). | 50 |
| 2.10 | Ratio of food imports to export earnings under Alternative Food Security Rules (1965–76 except as noted) | 51 |
| 3.1 | Linear regression results, yields on years, for two wheat-producing areas. | 59 |
| 3.2 | Change in yield variability accompanying increase in yield due to technological change for selected countries in Asia, 1955–67 vs. 1967–77. | 59 |
| 3.3 | Rice yield variability for selected locations in Asia ranked according to the percent area in irrigation. | 64 |
| 3.4 | Yield variability from trend for three countries in East Asia, 1955–56 to 1976–77. | 65 |
| 3.5 | Corn yield and variability of yield at high and low input levels, 97 and 78 experimental observations in farmers' fields, Plan Puebla, 1971–74 | 67 |
| 3.6 | Rice yield and variability of yield at high and low yield levels and for wet and dry season observations, survey data average of 29 Asian villages, 1971–72. | 69 |
| 4.1 | Importance of rice in the international trade of Indonesia, Malaysia, the Philippines, and Thailand | 81 |

*Figures and Tables*  xi

4.2 World rice production and world rice trade
(milled rice basis) . . . . . . . . . . . . . . . . . . . . . . . . . .81

4.3 Proportion of total rice area planted to modern
varieties, Southeast Asia, 1974–75 . . . . . . . . . . . . .82

4.4 Imports and exports of rice in ASEAN
countries. . . . . . . . . . . . . . . . . . . . . . . . . . . . . . . . .83

4.5 "Real" rice prices in Indonesia, the Philippines,
and Thailand . . . . . . . . . . . . . . . . . . . . . . . . . . . . . .86

5.1 Tanzania: Various production estimates of
principal cereals, 1965–66 to 1977–78 . . . . . . . . . .108

5.2 Estimates of sales of maize flour and rice
through official channels, Tanzania. . . . . . . . . . . . .110

6.1 Composition of food consumption in
Colombia in 1972 . . . . . . . . . . . . . . . . . . . . . . . . . .124

6.2 Food production and food availability in
Colombia, 1950–75. . . . . . . . . . . . . . . . . . . . . . . . .125

6.3 Output, supply, and consumption of calories in
Colombia, 1950–75. . . . . . . . . . . . . . . . . . . . . . . . .126

6.4 Probability of a given shortfall in trend production. . .127

6.5 Projections of food output and of imports of food
for a 5 percent shortfall in trend production. . . . . .128

6.6 Daily per-capita calorie consumption in
Colombia, 1972. . . . . . . . . . . . . . . . . . . . . . . . . . . .131

6.7 Population, per-capita income and expenditure
by household income bracket in the urban and
rural sectors of Colombia, 1972 . . . . . . . . . . . . . . .132

6.8 Expenditure on food as a proportion of income
and total expenditure in low-income groups
(in percentage terms). . . . . . . . . . . . . . . . . . . . . . . .134

6.9 Percentage rise in the price of food due to a
shortfall in supply . . . . . . . . . . . . . . . . . . . . . . . . . .135

6.10 Percentage fall in real expenditure due to
shortfalls in food supply . . . . . . . . . . . . . . . . . . . . .136

7.1 Food consumption in Egypt . . . . . . . . . . . . . . . . . . .145

7.2 Per-capita food consumption in Egypt . . . . . . . . . . .145

7.3 Food trade balance in Egypt: Net imports
in 1975 and projected for year 2000. . . . . . . . . . . .147

7.4 Exports and imports of commodities in Egypt . . . . . .148

xii

*Figures and Tables*

7.5  Effect of changes in volume and price on the value
     of food imports, 1969–75 . . . . . . . . . . . . . . . . . . .149
7.6  Sources covering the Egyptian current account
     deficit, 1974–76 . . . . . . . . . . . . . . . . . . . . . . . . . . .150
7.7  U.S. food aid shipments to Egypt, 1972–77,
     under PL480 . . . . . . . . . . . . . . . . . . . . . . . . . . . . . .151
8.1  Basic market identities . . . . . . . . . . . . . . . . . . . . . . .162
8.2  Change over previous year in selected variables:
     wheat, 1969/70–1976/77 . . . . . . . . . . . . . . . . . . . .166
8.3  Market identities and sector accounts . . . . . . . . . . . . .171
8.4  Policy-induced trade volume effects, selected
     developed countries, and stock changes:
     wheat, 1967/68–1976/77 . . . . . . . . . . . . . . . . . . . .173
9.1  Country demand parameters . . . . . . . . . . . . . . . . . . .192
9.2  Price elasticities of demand with and
     without subsidy payments. . . . . . . . . . . . . . . . . . . . .193
9.3  Country's price elasticities of demand with
     and without stabilizing trade. . . . . . . . . . . . . . . . . . .194
9.4  Stability of food policy-related variables:
     Probability (in percent) of specified event. . . . . . . .195
9.5  Expected annual gains and losses from
     different policies. . . . . . . . . . . . . . . . . . . . . . . . . . . .198
9.6  Expected annual gains and losses due to buffer
     stocks . . . . . . . . . . . . . . . . . . . . . . . . . . . . . . . . . . .199
9.7  Expected annual gains and losses due to
     stabilizing trade policy . . . . . . . . . . . . . . . . . . . . . .202
9.8  Expected annual gains and losses of program
     to subsidize consumption of low-income
     consumers . . . . . . . . . . . . . . . . . . . . . . . . . . . . . . . .203
9.9  Foreign exchange instability: Probability of
     import bill exceeding $700 million . . . . . . . . . . . . .205
9.10 Stability of country's foodgrain supply and
     foreign exchange account . . . . . . . . . . . . . . . . . . . .207
9.11 Stability of foreign exchange account from
     food trade with alternative policies . . . . . . . . . . . . .208
10.1 Ending stocks of wheat in excess of minimum
     working stocks . . . . . . . . . . . . . . . . . . . . . . . . . . . .227
11.1 Distribution of value of benefits of insurance

*Figures and Tables*                                                    *xiii*

scheme, by country, 1978–82 and
1970/71–1975/76 .........................247

11.2 Comparison of expected compensation for
historical and future periods and probability
associated with estimated actual compensation
required for 1970/71–1975/76 ................249

12.1 Optimal carryovers for selected countries and
regions, 1975. ..............................261

12.2 Supply and optimal carryovers, 1977 .............264

12.3 Supply and optimal carryovers, 1977a ............265

12.4 Insurance payments to developing countries
for different programs, 1955–73 ...............270

12.5 Optimal carryover levels for selected
developing countries and regions, 1975,
alternative insurance programs in effect .........273

12.6 Effects of carryover program on available
supply based on actual production,
India and Africa, 1968–75. ..................275

12.7 Effects of carryover program on available
supply based on actual production, 6 percent
insurance policy, India and Africa, 1968–75 ......275

12.8 Effects of carryover program on available
supply based on actual production, 4 percent
insurance policy, India and Africa, 1968–75 ......276

12.9 Estimates of total demand functions, log linear
form .....................................286

13.1 Insurance payments to developing countries for
different programs, cereal food aid, actual
and food security imports ...................290

13.2 Cereals food aid and hypothetical compensation
under IFPRI insurance scheme, 1970/71–
1975/76 totals, by country ..................294

14.1 Service exports: Dependence and variability,
1963–75 (IFS data, 46 countries) ..............320

14.2 Cereal imports: Dependence and variability,
1963–75 (IFS data, 46 countries) ..............322

14.3 Extending the scope of the facility to cover
fluctuations in earnings from services exports.....324

*xiv*                                                         *Figures and Tables*

14.4   Extending the scope of the facility to cover fluctuations in the cost of cereals imports........326

14.5   Extending the scope of the facility to cover fluctuations in the cost of cereals imports net of aid content.........................328

14.6   Simulated shortfalls in export earnings by commodity groups (1963–75, IFS data, 46 countries).............................331

# Foreword

The International Food Policy Research Institute (IFPRI) focuses its research on the low-income countries of the Third World and the low-income people who inhabit those countries. That emphasis leads IFPRI to study the problem of fluctuating food supplies. In high-income countries, much of the adjustment to fluctuating supplies is made by changes in livestock numbers. Contrastingly, in low-income countries it is the low-income people who must adjust to fluctuating supplies. In addition, as compared to the low-income countries, the high-income countries have a greater capacity to adjust imports and stocks to counter domestic production fluctuations. In the low-income countries, reduced consumption by low-income people is achieved directly through the income-depressing effect of higher prices or indirectly through lower employment arising from decreased economic activity induced by drought or public efforts to combat inflation.[1] No matter how low their initial food consumption levels, it is the poor who make the bulk of the adjustment to lessened food availability. They do so because food expenditure constitutes the bulk of their total expenditures. Although the more well-to-do can and do adjust to an increase in food prices or a decline in family employment by decreasing their consumption of other goods and services, the poor lack that option. Hence, no matter the privation, the long-term costs in physical and mental health, or even the short-term capability to work and earn, the poor reduce their consumption of food.

Because continued random fluctuations in weather effect

*xv*

large fluctuations in food supply, some means of dealing with those fluctuations is of vital concern to the poor. However, the fluctuations in various regions rarely occur in unison; therefore, fluctuations for the world are much less than for any one region. As grain storage is costly, there is considerable scope for increased efficiency and decreased costs through international trade. It should be noted that it follows that subsistence agricultures—by definition self-sufficient and nontrading—find it difficult and costly to adapt to fluctuations in production other than by fluctuations in consumption and consequent privation. The International Food Policy Research Institute's research program has given substantial attention to both aspects of this problem.

Defining the problem of fluctuating supplies of food in Third World countries as a problem of the poor emphasizes two major elements. First, it might be necessary and desirable to separate the problem of fluctuating food supplies to poor people from fluctuating feed supplies to livestock. Second, if the concern for food supply fluctuations is with its impact on the poor, the means of dealing with the problem must include mechanisms that enable the benefits to reach the poor.

Despite the interrelationship of policies for dealing with fluctuations in food supplies and of means of ensuring that the poor receive benefits from those policies, there has been a tendency toward division of concern and analysis between national schemes dealing with delivery of food to the poor and international schemes to stabilize availability. Consequently, the inhabitants of these two closets tend to deal unrealistically with their problems for lack of attention to their relationship to the other. A major contribution of the conference from which this volume grew was to bring these two groups together so that the relationship of international schemes to national needs could at least be seen and a start made at relating them. It will be apparent, however, that the task of relating the two aspects of the problem has a considerable distance to go before effective policy can be framed. The bulk of international schemes still fails to deal with the immense practical problems of implementation under the conditions of the countries they are meant to assist. Of particular note are the problems of data inadequacy at the national level for administering trigger prices

*Foreword*                                                                     *xvii*

and other mechanics of the sophisticated international schemes, and lack of adequate transport facilities to move supplies from points of abundance to points of scarcity—a particular problem for the rural poor. Understanding that these problems exist does not tax the technicians but the development of schemes that work under those constraints does.

If food security is viewed as a problem of the poor, then little purpose is served by separating the problem of fluctuations in food supplies from the problem of inadequate total supplies. That is particularly true of the search for policy solutions, because production-augmenting policies also affect fluctuations. Thus, one must consider the trade-off between the immense cost of buffer stocks and the cost of irrigation that may increase supplies and reduce fluctuations. It is also necessary to consider the future effects of the new production technologies—upon which future production growth is necessarily so dependent—on the size of fluctuations. It was the latter concern that brought IFPRI together with the International Maize and Wheat Improvement Center (CIMMYT) to sponsor the food security conference and this volume. I am very grateful to CIMMYT for joining with us in developing this venture and for collaborating with us in organizing and administering the Conference held at CIMMYT in November 1978. The CIMMYT staff was exceedingly helpful to our deliberations.

The United Nations Development Programme (UNDP) and its Division for Global and Interregional Projects financed the Conference. We are grateful for their help in this respect as well as for their thoughtful substantive suggestions. The Agricultural Development Council (ADC) in 1978 held a conference emphasizing the role of developed countries in food security, which was helpful to us in organizing this conference.

The Institute is following up the November 1978 Conference by research on various types of food delivery schemes, with emphasis on effects on nutrition, analysis of changes in fluctuations in food production over time, and analyses of various types of international programs. This and other research are being drawn together into a broad analysis of food security defined to include all the measures necessary to ensure adequate food to low-income people. That analysis thrust will culminate *xviii*                                                    *Foreword*

in a series of policy workshops to include policymakers in various relatively homogeneous groupings of countries.

*John W. Mellor*
Washington, D.C.

## Notes

1. The workings of these mechanisms are described in detail in John W. Mellor, "Food Price Policy and Income Distribution in Low-Income Countries," *Economic Development and Cultural Change* 27, no. 1 (October 1978).

# The Contributors

**Randolph Barker,** from the United States, is a professor at Cornell University and for twelve years served as an economist at the International Rice Research Institute (IRRI) in the Philippines.

**David Bigman,** an Israeli, formerly with the International Monetary Fund, is currently professor at the Hebrew University of Jerusalem.

**Wilfred Candler,** a New Zealander, previously a professor at Purdue University, is an economist at the World Bank.

**Eric C. Gabler,** from the United States, is a graduate student in agricultural economics at Cornell University.

**Jorge García García,** a Colombian, formerly deputy director of the National Planning Commission of Colombia, is a professor at the Universidad de los Andes (Bogotá) and a visiting researcher at IFPRI.

**Louis M. Goreux,** from France, is deputy director for research at the International Monetary Fund (IMF).

**Ahmed A. Goueli,** an Egyptian, is a professor at the Zagazig University in Egypt.

*The Contributors*

**Barbara Huddleston,** from the United States, is a research fellow at IFPRI. She was director of the Trade Negotiations Division, U.S. Department of Agriculture.

**D. Gale Johnson,** from the United States, is provost and a professor of economics at the University of Chicago.

**Timothy Josling,** from England, is a professor at the Food Research Institute, Stanford University.

**Panos Konandreas,** from Greece, was a research associate at IFPRI and is now an economist at the International Livestock Center for Africa, in Kenya.

**Uma Lele,** from India, is an economist at the World Bank.

**Daniel Morrow,** from the United States, is an economist at the World Bank. Previously he was special assistant to the Assistant Secretary for International Affairs and Commodity Programs at the U.S. Department of Agriculture.

**Shlomo Reutlinger,** a United States citizen, is an economist at the World Bank.

**Ammar Siamwalla,** from Thailand, was a professor of economics at Thammasat University in Bangkok and is now a research fellow at IFPRI.

**Alberto Valdés,** a Chilean, is now a research fellow at IFPRI. Previously he was an economist at the International Center for Tropical Agriculture (CIAT) in Colombia and a professor at the Universidad Católica de Chile.

**Donald Winkelmann,** from the United States, is an economist at the International Center for Wheat and Maize (CIMMYT), located in Mexico.

# Abbreviations

| | |
|---|---|
| ACP | African, Caribbean, and Pacific |
| ADB | Asian Development Bank |
| BSA | Buffer Stock Agency |
| BULOG | National Logistics Agency (Indonesia) |
| CIAT | Centro Internacional de Agricultura Tropical (Colombia) |
| CIMMYT | Centro Internacional de Mejoramiento de Maíz y Trigo (Mexico) |
| CSD | Consultative Sub-Committee on Surplus Disposal |
| CWRS | Canadian Western Red Spring |
| DANE | Departamento Administrativo Nacional de Estadística (Colombia) |
| EC/EEC | European Community |
| ESCAP | United Nations Economic and Social Commission for Asia and the Pacific |
| FAO | Food and Agriculture Organization |
| IBRD | International Bank for Reconstruction and Development |
| ICBF | Instituto Colombiano de Bienestar Familiar |
| IDA | International Development Association |
| IEFR | International Emergency Food Reserve |
| IFPRI | International Food Policy Research Institute |
| IFS | International Financial Statistics |
| IMF | International Monetary Fund |
| IRRI | International Rice Research Institute |
| IWA | International Wheat Agreement |
| IWC | International Wheat Council |

| | |
|---|---|
| LDCs | less-developed countries |
| MOF | Marketing Organization for Farmers (Thailand) |
| MSA | most seriously affected |
| MWS | minimum working stocks |
| NGA | National Grains Authority (the Philippines) |
| NMC | National Milling Corporation (Tanzania) |
| SDCs | selected developed countries |
| SDR | Special Drawing Rights |
| STABEX | Stabilization of Exports |
| UMRs | usual marketing requirements |
| UNCTAD | United Nations Conference on Trade and Development |
| UNDP | United Nations Development Programme |
| USAID | United States Agency for International Development |
| USDA | United States Department of Agriculture |
| WFP | World Food Programme |
| WTC | Wheat Trade Convention |

# 1
# Introduction

*Alberto Valdés*
*Ammar Siamwalla*

In 1974 the World Food Conference was convened in Rome to discuss the world food crisis. Food security was the dominant theme. Food security may be defined as the ability of food-deficit countries, or regions within those countries, to meet target consumption levels on a year-to-year basis. Agricultural prices had risen to record highs, carry-over stocks of grain were at precariously low levels, and concern was focused on the undernourished millions in the Third World suffering from the scarcity and high price of food. Fears grew that the world was irrevocably moving toward chronic food shortages, attributable to unfavorable long-term climatic changes and continued high rates of population growth.

The current global food situation is, fortunately, much improved. International prices of cereals have fallen in real terms, grain stocks have been rebuilt, and the crisis atmosphere has abated. World food security has ceased to be a major concern for the press and for the general public. Yet, the underlying causes of food crises such as the one in 1972–1974 have not disappeared; in fact, even though the developing countries have themselves made some important strides in dealing with food insecurity, on the international scene only limited progress has been made to help them in these efforts.

Discussions of potential remedies have tended to overlook the enormous differences in nature and magnitude of the food security problems in countries or regions in Asia, Africa, and Latin America. From these discussions, only a limited number of policy instruments were seen as relevant to the problem of food security. Often, the debates gave the impression that less-developed countries (LDCs) would surmount the problem if only larger grain reserves were available. Food security proposals often seemed to underestimate the complexity of the practical problems at the level of individual countries in designing and implementing policies for stabilization of food supplies, particularly for the rural areas. It was in light of these concerns that the Conference on Food Security for Developing Countries was organized.

There have been numerous food security proposals emanating from both international organizations and universities. In order to help assess the relative merits of these proposals both at the national and the international levels the International Food Policy Research Institute (IFPRI) and Centro Internacional de Mejoramiento de Maíz y Trigo (CIMMYT) invited participants from international agencies and developed countries and from among the researchers and policymakers in the LDCs.

The principal aim of the Conference was to help improve our understanding of the problem of food security in Asia, Africa, and Latin America and to assess the merits of alternative national and international interventions. A product of this effort is the identification of important economic issues currently not on the research agenda.

This chapter attempts to synthesize the papers that have been organized into a general framework in order to analyze food security issues. As the term *food security* has been used in many different contexts and has connoted different meanings, it is necessary first to define and discuss the concept and nature of food security. The discussion is partly a distillation of participants' ideas and partly our own expansion on those ideas.

## On the Concept of Food Security

Food security may be defined as the ability of food deficit countries, or regions or households within these countries, to meet target consumption levels on a year-to-year basis. What constitutes target consumption levels? Whose ability to maintain consumption is being referred to? These are the central issues of a country's food policy: therefore, we must expound

*Introduction* 3

upon these issues. The analyst has some choices of target levels; for instance, the minimum daily requirements level, employing nutritional criteria; the average level over the past $n$ years; or the trend level of consumption. Although we should never lose sight of the fact that the most severe impact of short-term food supply instability is felt by the poor, chronic malnutrition that is caused by persistent poverty constitutes a long-term problem whose dimensions and solutions lie beyond the question of food security, which we conceive as a problem of short-term variability. Thus, we do not adopt the nutritional basis for our target consumption, but instead use the trend level of consumption as the target. The second issue is the question of whose ability to maintain consumption is being referred to. We can analyze the problem in terms of the household's, the region's, or the nation's ability to attain food security. Stable food supplies in the aggregate—that is, for a nation as a whole—is not necessarily synonymous with consumption stability for large segments of the population. The nation must have some means to deliver food to the households that are exposed to food insecurity risks. A complete understanding of the repercussions of food insecurity would require us to analyze the problem at all these levels, which is what we intend to do.

Variability of food supply may have many causes. The focus of this book is on variability that is inherent in agriculture, namely that caused by the impact of fluctuating weather on the size of harvests. Superimposed on this there may be acute shortages of food as a consequence of natural disasters, such as earthquakes and floods, or of political conflicts, as in Bangladesh in 1972-1974 and in Cambodia in 1979. This second type of problem is distinct from the first one in that it involves disruption of the normal channels of delivery of food to the afflicted area in addition to the production shortfall. A resumption of the flow along those channels is the main priority in such a circumstance. This usually demands an engineering or a political solution rather than an economic one, in the sense that the quantities of food required are small, seldom more than a million tons (Sarris and Taylor, 1977), and the humanitarian grounds for providing it are so evident that an economic calculus becomes superfluous here. A further reason for concentrating on weather-induced variability of supplies is that with the accumulation of data (imperfect as they may be), we are beginning to have better quantitative information on the distribution of the supply fluctuations to guide any policy measures that might be undertaken. In contrast, with the second type of problem, for any given country we are dealing with either a small-probability risk, or with a situation of uncertainty where the distribution of risks is unknown.

The focus on the impact of fluctuating weather also implies that we are working with annual flows of supplies and annual movements of prices rather than with week-to-week or month-to-month fluctuations. This shorter term consideration raises a distinct analytical issue that involves an understanding of the quality and quantity of information flows to policymakers on domestic supplies, and the time lags in converting information into decisions, decisions into action, and action into actual inflows of food. Specifically, when we discuss stocks below, we exclude consideration of working stocks, which are necessary to bridge the time lags and the unreliability of information in situations where policies have to be devised to meet very short-term targets, such as within a few weeks to a few months. However, we do not wish to belittle issues related to working stocks. In fact, we suspect that a great deal of the concerns expressed by policymakers from the LDCs arise from their difficulties in coping with day-to-day operation of the food markets and the agencies involved in food supplies. As such, they raise management issues rather than the conceptual problems with which we are primarily concerned.

## The Nature of Food Insecurity

We naturally tend to associate food insecurity with either the fluctuations in food production or with changes in its price. Actually, fluctuations in nonfood production and prices also have considerable impact on food insecurity: for example, a cotton grower's consumption of wheat may be as much affected by the boll weevil that destroys his crop or by a sharp fall in cotton prices as by an increase in the price of wheat. Thus, from the analytical point of view, it is more useful to classify

*Introduction* 5

the causes of food insecurity as follows: (1) production fluctuations, regardless of whether the fluctuation is in the food or the nonfood sector; (2) price fluctuations, again regardless of whether it is the price of food or of nonfood that is affected.

These two causes lead directly to a fluctuation in real income within the community. The fluctuation may make its appearance to different members of the community in different ways. To a farm household it appears simply as a fluctuation in output and income; to a farm laborer it appears as a fluctuation in employment. In addition to this direct effect on the level of real income there is an indirect effect as a primary gain or loss in income affects other parts of the economy through increased or reduced spending by affected households. This is the familiar multiplier process, which may make the magnitude of these indirect effects much larger than the direct effects.

These fluctuations in real income, both direct and indirect, affecting the farmer, the agricultural laborer, as well as other members of the community, will ultimately have an impact on household food consumption, that of the poorer households being particularly sensitive. It follows that if the fluctuations in real income can be smoothed, food security could be attained. The conventional economist's solution to this problem is some sort of capital market mechanism to transfer income intertemporally. In most cases, the mechanism needs to operate only on the households and sectors directly affected, for if their incomes are raised, say in a bad year, this compensation will percolate to the other sectors, negating the multiplier effects of the original loss in income. As will be seen below, however, it is essential that the capital market mechanism be operative at all levels for the country as a whole as well as for individual households.

To achieve the aim of food security, the capital market mechanism must involve assets that possess a high degree of liquidity, as their conversion to food must be effected relatively quickly. The type of mechanism discussed is to hold assets in the form of either food stocks themselves or in the form of monetary instruments such as foreign exchange reserves or cash balances to be used to purchase food in the lean periods. The problem of which type of assets to hold is one of portfolio management and is amenable to solution using conventional economic criteria. For example, it has been found that for LDC importers that are price takers in the world market, food security can be achieved at lower cost through varying the levels of imports while operating a relatively small buffer stock. This implies holding liquid assets in the form of foreign exchange reserves rather than in the specific form of food.[1] This argument applies a fortiori in favor of households holding cash rather than storing food. However, regardless of the form in which they are held—to the extent that all these liquid assets have lower returns than, say, investment in plant and machinery, in land, or in education—attaining food security is a costly process, the cost essentially being measured by the difference in the rate of return in illiquid versus liquid assets multiplied by the volume of diversion in investment required.[2]

It may be argued that the country or the household suffering from food insecurity need not divert its own resources into liquid investments but can borrow as the need arises. As the overall ability to borrow is limited in the long term by the wealth of the country or of the household, the access to a particular line of credit will tend to be at the expense of credit for longer term investments, and the argument of the previous paragraph still applies in full force.

Although a correct measure of food insecurity would rest on real income fluctuations, if we confine our analysis to the national level an approximate measure may be obtained by looking at deviations from trend in foreign exchange earnings minus the excess expenditure over trend on food imports for the current year. This is referred to as deviations in "real" export earnings in Chapter 2 by Valdés and Konandreas. An analysis of optimal foreign exchange reserve policies could be based on this measure of real export earnings, although none of the chapters addressed themselves directly to this question.

Thus far, we have merely generalized the results available in the main body of the food security literature. As can be seen, the arguments rest rather heavily on the assumption of a frictionless world. Relatively unexplored are some of the issues that arise when such an assumption is removed. The following is an attempt to analyze some of these issues.

*Introduction* 7

## Inadequacies of the International Market for Cereals

Several writers have concluded that each country should become self-reliant on food and thus build its own system of national food security. Minhas (1976), for example, concluded that India should opt out of the world food security system, not depend at all on food imports, raise its level of self-sufficiency, and build its own reserve stocks.

The justification for such policy is that each nation faces highly unreliable international supplies. There are several strands to this argument. In many of the discussions, there is no distinction made between concessional and commercial supplies. The reliability of each source differs considerably. The general perception, which we fully share, is that concessional supplies are completely unreliable. Food aid was in fact cut back in 1973-1974. Worse still, in individual cases donors have used food aid to wring political concessions from the recipients. It seems to us that the only policy implication that we can draw from these incontrovertible facts is that national food policies relying on food aid supplies are highly risky. It is, however, quite unjustified to move from this position to advocacy of complete independence from all forms of food imports. To justify this latter position, one must show that commercial supplies are unreliable. Unreliability here can carry two meanings. One is that world prices are highly unstable but supplies are always available for the needs of the small and medium-sized countries. The second, and stronger, version is that there are periods, such as 1973-1974, when supplies are unavailable at any price. The first set of problems is within the framework just discussed. On the issue of sheer availability of supplies, we have not seen any documentation of the charge. We do not know of any point in time when it was not possible to obtain supplies of wheat at some price, even though the price may have been considered exorbitant by some LDC importers. The situation in the rice market is somewhat different. It is a thin market and therefore subject to sudden interruptions and shifts in trade channels. Thus, rice exports from Thailand, a major exporter, were banned in the second half of 1973. Even though the People's Republic of China stepped in with increased supplies, the delays in trade negotiations caused by the shift in sources led to major rice crises in many Asian cities.

## Barriers to Internal Trade

In most cases, the state has assumed the functions of trader in foodgrains. Either through the parastatal agency or through tariff policies, the government has attempted to ensure food security by insulating the domestic price from the international price. If the problem originates in a price shift in the world market, a policy of domestic price insulation implies that the burden of real income fluctuation caused by the terms of trade shift is borne by the public treasury. Because the public treasury has better access to the capital markets (both domestic and international) than does an individual household, a policy of price insulation in this circumstance is adequate to achieve domestic food security.[3] This price insulation policy, if backed by effective macroeconomic stabilization policies, would be sufficient to ensure stability of food consumption in the urban areas. It is for this reason that there has been, in the general perception, an association of food security with stability in the price of food. If we take a broader view, and if the cause of food insecurity lies in production fluctuations however, such a policy by itself would be insufficient, particularly for rural areas, as will be shown.

Another form of trade barrier is the high transport cost resulting from the geographical isolation of many areas. High transport costs mean that trade of foodgrains in and out of such regions is quite uneconomical. Consequently, most such regions are "self-sufficient" in the sense that production and consumption are the same, although this does not imply nutritional adequacy. Fluctuations of production away from the "normal" level would of course affect the real income level of the particular community and the requirements of liquidity would still have to hold. The only difference here is that because of the high transport cost, local storage of foodgrains may be preferred to other forms of assets, however liquid the latter may be.

## Imperfections in the Capital Market

This is a far more intractable problem. In a sense, this entire

*Introduction* 9

chapter rests on the argument that food insecurity is ultimately a problem that arises from real income fluctuations, for which the classical solution is a reliance on the capital market to smooth them out. It follows, therefore, that the failure of the capital market lies at the root of the food security problem. As will be seen in Part 2 of this book, a logical solution to the food security problem, at least at the national level, lies in the direction of introducing credit facilities to enable countries to tide over bad years. This proposal does not preclude the need for concessional aid for the poorest countries.

Critical as it is, the national-level problem is in fact conceptually the easiest part. Its "solution" is sufficient to ensure that the problem of food insecurity is solved at the household level, but only for those households that do not experience output or employment fluctuations, specifically those in urban areas. For them, food security is synonymous with price stability, which can be achieved if the country is able to adjust its imports of food or the level of stocks so as to compensate exactly for the aggregate fluctuations in domestic production. However, as a result of a large reduction in farm output, sales of manufactured goods could decline and thus indirectly reduce employment and income in the urban areas. In this case, stable food prices are no longer a sufficient condition for food security.

In the rural areas, when the real income of a household is directly affected as a result of fluctuations in its own production (of food or nonfood), stability of food consumption can no longer be achieved merely through domestic price stability, as this takes no account of the fall in real production and therefore the income level of the household. The problem now lies as much on the demand as on the supply side of the food market, as we can no longer be sure that the capital market will act to stabilize the effective demand for food of the household by meeting the shortfall in its income. The capital market facing the household (especially the poor household) in LDCs is either nonexistent or what capital is available is very expensive (see Morris, 1974, for a contrary view). Any attempt on the part of the government to introduce arrangements that act as substitutes for a capital market at this level would be administratively very costly. It appears that some outright income transfer mechanisms become unavoidable at times of shortages. Crop insurance is one such device, although it is administratively quite difficult to implement and does not address the question of the landless laborer. Another device is a public food distribution program that is focused on the poor agricultural households and adjusts its grant element to counter the effects of output fluctuations. Unfortunately, there are very few public distribution programs that reach extensively into the rural areas, where income fluctuations arising out of fluctuations in production are the most severe. The few pieces of research into this problem, useful as they are, are conditioned by institutional and geographic specificity and thus do not lend themselves to applications to other countries. Consequently, there is as yet no answer as to why there are so few public distribution programs in rural areas.

One alternative route is to operate through the labor market with a "food for work" type of program. Such a public works program may be introduced (or intensified) at times of shortages. The basic rationale is that a crop failure would reduce labor demand and lead to unemployment in the producing areas. To put the unemployed on the payroll without providing for the wage-good (food) at a time when that wage-good is particularly scarce would increase the local price of food. Hence, the combination of food and work.

Historically, most governments have remained powerless to deal with the complexities of the food insecurity problem in rural areas. The complexity arises not only from difficulties of transportation and other physical constraints, but also from the much more difficult economic problem of providing affected households with adequate purchasing power at times of crop failure. It is for this reason that government action on food security has historically been more often perceived in terms of meeting urban demands.

### The Conference Papers

The chapters derived from the Conference papers fall into two broad groups. The chapters in Part 1 describe the nature and magnitude of food insecurity in LDCs, stressing the various practical problems at the country level. Part 2 presents various

*Introduction*                                                                11

national and international approaches to coping with food insecurity.

## Part 1: Magnitudes and Nature of Food Insecurity in Selected Developing Countries

The chapter by Valdés and Konandreas, based on data between 1961 and 1976, demonstrates that most of the LDCs show little evidence of having effectively stabilized food consumption through changes in imports and stocks. In fact, more than half of the sample of 24 LDCs analyzed had an amazingly high degree of consumption variability. Part of this inadequacy in consumption stabilization may be caused by foreign exchange constraints. Although, on average, the ratio of food imports to total export receipts is not particularly large, it varies substantially and in some years food imports alone can absorb a very high fraction of a country's earnings.

Whereas the emphasis in Valdés and Konandreas was on a cross section of countries, the chapter by Barker, Gabler, and Winkelmann examines the change over time in production variability, with technological change as the main explanatory variable. Whether or not new food production technology that raises mean yields will lead to a greater production instability has been a long-standing controversy. Actually, new technology is not a unitary concept but is a package of many components, some stabilizing (such as extra irrigation) and some destabilizing (such as the increased susceptibility of new crop varieties to pests and diseases). Barker, Gabler, and Winkelmann present a thorough analysis of the potential stabilizing characteristics of water control, agronomic practices, and plant breeding on wheat, rice, and maize yields. On balance, they conclude that while absolute variability could have increased, variability relative to mean yields has remained unchanged or even declined. Unfortunately, it is not known how much of the observed yield variability is due more to the failure of the factor market—for example, irregularities in the supply of fertilizers, seeds, and other inputs in a productive system critically dependent on them—rather than to the new technology itself. If such market failure is the cause of the problem, the logical solution lies in correcting the factor market distortion rather than in redesigning technology to reduce variability at the cost of yields.

The next four chapters examine food security issues in four distinct geographical areas. In Southeast Asia, food security is associated exclusively with security in rice supplies. The peculiar characteristics of the world rice market, including a high degree of price instability, set the region apart from international discussions of food security that are framed in terms of the much more active wheat market. In spite of this world market instability, Siamwalla finds that trade occupies a more strategic role than stocks in domestic stabilization policies among members of ASEAN (in line with the analysis by Reutlinger and Bigman) but that the reliance on imports may well impose an additional burden on the international rice market. In light of Thailand's concern about the instability in its export revenues and Indonesia's preoccupation with security of supplies to meet its fluctuating import demand, Siamwalla argues that a regional commodity agreement on rice may contribute to a significant reduction in world price instability. If accompanied by security of rice trade among participants, a buffer stock for the region based on jointly controlled stocks seems feasible, although it is probably still quite far from actual implementation on any significant scale.

Rather than adopting the predominantly urban approach in the policies followed by governments elsewhere, Lele and Candler's chapter on East Africa eloquently raises the case for specific policy directions tailored to deal with rural food insecurity, but expresses some skepticism as to the effectiveness of consumption stabilization programs in reaching the rural poor. The authors point to a better understanding of the role of private trading and storage activities and their interactions with government operations, the promotion of drought-resistant crops such as millet and sorghum, and improving farm-level storage and market outlets as critical elements in alleviating food insecurity for the rural poor.

The case of Colombia is illuminating because it shows that malnutrition may be widespread even in a country where, in total, food supplies are adequate. Colombia has adequate foreign exchange resources, abundant agricultural land for its population, and a relatively low food production variability. However,

*Introduction* 13

the country is divided by high mountain barriers into different regions accessible to one another only at high transportation costs. Localized crop failures therefore tend to increase prices sharply within a region. Because of the uneven income distribution, even minor price increases could result in a significant reduction in food consumption among the poor. The chapters by Lele and Candler and by García García serve to stress that food security is not necessarily synonymous with stability in total food supplies.

In contrast with Colombia, Egypt relies to a large and increasing extent on food imports, the full market value of which now represents nearly 60 percent of total export revenues. Moreover, food subsidies account for a high fraction of the national budget. At such levels, the extent and magnitude of the adjustments in its overseas trading account and the government budget to stabilize food consumption may drain resources needed for economic development and the expansion of productive capacity in agriculture. As a consequence, efforts to deal with food insecurity may exacerbate the long-term food problem.

*Part 2: National and International Policy Approaches*

In current discussions, there are two different but related approaches to the problem of food security. One addresses itself to the question of world food security and, in particular, world price stabilization mechanisms. The other addresses issues of food security for a subsystem of the world, namely, food-deficit developing countries. For the latter, trade is an option that is less attractive the more prices fluctuate.

As pointed out earlier, food insecurity involves a fluctuation in real income. Josling (Chapter 8) shows how the stabilization of food consumption shifts the instability to other markets. The manner in which these adjustments occur, their efficiency, and the distributional consequences will all depend on the policies adopted. Josling provides a framework to analyze the implications for the variability of other elements in the economy, relating variability in food production and stocks with the concomitant adjustments required in government budgets and foreign accounts. The system of identities he develops to bring out the logic of stabilization schemes is sufficiently general to apply at the world level. He illustrates this by discussing the effect of developed country policies (including those of the USSR) on price instability in the world wheat market.

The chapter by Reutlinger and Bigman illustrates the magnitude of some of the adjustments that occur under alternative strategies, in a hypothetical developing country made to resemble India. They examine in particular the choice between a trade-oriented approach and domestically held reserves, concluding that, contrary to common belief, trade policies can be an efficient stabilization force for most countries. The burden of the adjustment must fall particularly on the foreign exchange market and the government budget, as recognized by Josling.

Greater price stability in the world food market is an important element in food security for some LDCs. However, as shown by Valdés and Konandreas, variability in the volume of imports explains much of the variability of the total food import bill. Only about one-quarter is explained by world price movements. Consequently, world price stabilization schemes cannot solve, but might alleviate, the burden of consumption stabilization in LDCs. In and of themselves these schemes do not address aspects of financing food imports.

Several international approaches are currently being discussed that could enhance food security in LDCs. These approaches include (a) greater reliance on an international grain reserve system, (b) consumption adjustments in developed countries, and (c) food aid and other financial approaches to alleviate the foreign exchange constraint. Political support for each of these initiatives is still, however, quite uncertain.

*International buffer stock systems.* Under the auspices of the UN Conference on Trade and Development (UNCTAD) and the International Wheat Council (IWC), considerable efforts have been devoted since 1977 to negotiations for a new Wheat Trade Convention (WTC) to create an internationally coordinated system of wheat reserves. Its primary purpose would be to reduce the short-term variability of the wheat price in international markets.

Undoubtedly, larger grain reserves could be managed to reduce world price variability. However, after two years of negotiations, the collapse of the IWA negotiations in February 1979

*Introduction* 15

confirms the suspicion that an agreement on the price issues that would simultaneously consider market realities and accommodate LDC requirements is most unlikely. What implications will this failure of the WTC have for food-deficit developing countries?

For observers of these negotiations it has been hard to develop a clear position on this issue, due, to a large extent, in our opinion, to the lack of an explicit conceptual framework and the relevant parameters to analyze the potential impact on price stability of the proposals for reserve accumulation and price trigger mechanisms.

The chapter by Daniel Morrow offers such a framework, which he then uses to analyze the consequences of particular price trigger levels and reserve stock capacity on world price variability, taking into account the specific policies in various countries that were not in themselves subject to the WTC. Even if the mechanism envisioned for the WTC had been agreed upon and functioned well, Morrow concludes it would have had a modest impact on world price variability. There would have been little or no additional stock accumulation during the life of the agreement.[4] Especially if the price band were too broad or too low and the reserve obligations too small, the major wheat exporters could have fulfilled their WTC reserve stock obligations with stocks that they would have held anyway. Furthermore, by the time the agreement would have come into effect, the opportunity for accumulating reserve stocks during the period of low prices might have passed.

However, although its tangible effect on stocks and prices might have been questionable, a new agreement would have allowed an active periodic review of market conditions and national wheat policies by senior policymakers, perhaps avoiding a repeat of the 1972/73 situation. In this sense, the collapse of the wheat negotiations is a setback to LDC food security and increases the need to explore alternative policy instruments relevant to food security for LDCs.

*Food aid.* The experience of the early seventies highlighted the lack of responsiveness of food aid to cover widespread production shortfalls, aggravated by high world market prices and the weaknesses of domestic food systems to distribute larger volumes of grain. In years of high world prices, some donors were not willing to divert supplies from commercial markets to food aid, as reflected in the cutback of food aid in 1973–1974.

In her chapter, Barbara Huddleston documents the lack of correspondence between past food aid flows and import needs in LDCs, which clearly aggravate the burden of imports, particularly in years of high world prices. This is apart from strictly emergency relief efforts, which she concludes involve volumes on the order of one half million to one million tons per year. A different orientation of food aid, by incorporating a variable component in aid flows, could greatly enhance food security in LDCs, and she concludes that this could be achieved without jeopardizing the ability of donor countries to commit substantial volumes of aid for purposes other than food security, such as for overall economic development. In fact, for the entire 1970–1975 period, aid flows substantially exceeded the variable requirement of LDCs to achieve stability of supplies. However, food aid flows would not have been sufficient to cover needs in an occasional but widespread bad harvest year.

On the aggregate basis, concessional food sales have been dependent until now upon erratic surpluses in donor countries and hence can hardly be considered a dependable base for food security in LDCs. Unlike the pattern for food aid in the past, the aggregate volume of food aid should increase when the prices are high. But to enhance the food security of individual countries, the given quantity of food aid can be allocated among LDCs according to their individual needs in that year. That means that bilateral flows would be variable.

A variable food aid model operating through a grain insurance program is presented by D. Gale Johnson. The United States, alone or in cooperation with other donors, would "guarantee to each developing country that in any year in which grain production declines more than a given percentage below trend production that the shortfall in excess of that amount would be supplied." He argues that a substantial degree of internal price stability could be achieved with this proposal at a low cost to each developing country. His results indicate that food security could be achieved by modifying the distribution of food aid without significant increases in the average long-run volume, which in any case is relatively small and concentrated in a few recipient countries.[5]

*Introduction* 17

Food aid programs modified along the lines of Johnson's "grain insurance program" and Huddleston's "variable component" of food aid would represent a major adjustment in present programs. It seems probable that such adjustments would greatly enhance food security in poor countries. However, the provision of food aid would be very closely linked to the availability of grain reserves. As a consequence, the burden of food aid would fall largely on the grain-exporting countries, an aspect that must surely affect the political feasibility of variable food facilities, not to mention the loss to the current major recipients. A further politically relevant point is that donor countries would have to give up their discretionary power on the quantity of food aid on a year-by-year basis.

*A financial food facility and an insurance scheme.* Another approach to reducing food insecurity is to enlarge the scope of existing compensatory financing schemes to include the cost of cereal imports. Existing schemes are the IMF facility, the Stabilization of Export Receipts (STABEX) scheme, administered by the European Community for some fifty countries in the African, Caribbean, and Pacific regions, and the Arab Monetary Fund.

The financial facility has the advantage of simplicity. It protects member countries against fluctuations in the cost of cereal imports by providing foreign exchange in years of above-trend food imports. As shown by Louis Goreux, "it would be technically possible to extend coverage of the IMF facility so as to protect members against fluctuations in the cost of imports; this could be done by subtracting the cost of imports from the value of export earnings before calculating the net shortfalls on which the drawings would be based." For a sample of 46 countries, Goreux concludes that the cost of expanding the scope of the facility to cover food imports does not raise the sum of compensation for shortfalls under the existing scheme. Its cost would be significantly below the cost of establishing a separate facility dealing exclusively with (actual food) imports, because of the positive correlation of export earnings with cereal imports for several LDCs observed during 1963–1975. Moreover, this financial food facility would have benefited particularly the lower income countries. Working with rules for a "food security level of imports" rather than with the actual level of cereal imports,

Valdés and Konandreas conclude that the cost of expanding the IMF facility would have involved somewhat larger withdrawals. Their calculations illustrate the sensitivity of the expected withdrawals from the facility with respect to the country coverage—all LDCs or only the most seriously affected (MSA) countries—and to whether or not the facility is adjusted by export earnings.

The study by Huddleston and Konandreas analyzes an international food insurance scheme, projected for the years 1978–1982. The scheme could either serve as a purely financial mechanism that would provide LDCs with funds to cover overruns in their cereal import bill or it could be supported with a limited grain reserve, in the latter case deliberately restricted to high-price years so as to avoid rapid depletion of the reserve. For the period 1978–1982, Huddleston and Konandreas proposed creating a reserve of 20 million tons and a compensatory financing capacity of $5 billion.

The existence of these schemes would tend to reduce the elasticity of LDC import demand with respect to the world price as well as to increase the need and the profitability of holding stocks. There is as yet no research that examines whether the increased profitability would by itself induce sufficient stock accumulation to match the need.

A limitation common to the variable food aid scheme and the food facility scheme (to the extent that the latter has a concessional element) is that both rest on the availability of accurate information on production shortfalls. Although many claim that this is an insurmountable problem, particularly for the poorest LDCs, the authors share the optimistic belief that the existence of such schemes will in itself induce greater effort at overcoming problems whose solution, after all, is not technically difficult.

## Conclusions

The solution to the food insecurity problem must begin at the national level, and every country can take important initiatives to reduce food insecurity. The analysis indicates that these will probably include large investment in food distribution systems, transport and communications, early warning systems,

*Introduction* 19

and a mix of stock and trade policies. Although there is considerable scope in many LDCs for larger investment in working stocks, one clear generalization that can be made on the basis of past research is that relying mainly on domestic grain reserves to cover year-to-year fluctuations is an expensive solution when trade is a real possibility. Beyond this, the design of food security policies would have to consider specific country situations.

Given their food consumption stabilization objectives, LDCs seek to minimize the resource cost of managing the short-term variation in real income. The three implications of these food consumption stabilization policies are (1) the incentive for private domestic stockholding would be reduced, (2) the foreign trade balance and the government budget would have to absorb the instability, and (3) the loss in purchasing power or real income of farmers and farm laborers due to the crop failure must be compensated for. Otherwise, stabilizing national food supply per se would be insufficient to offset declines in effective demand in the rural areas. This last implication, which could be resolved only at very high financial cost if followed, has not been discussed much in the literature. Part of the unfinished business is a more explicit recognition of the connections among the markets for food, nonfood products (agricultural and others), and foreign exchange, which could open for consideration a wider range of policy instruments for managing the real income adjustment. The manner in which a country copes with short-term instability may well influence the longer term performance of its agricultural sector, and specifically the mean levels of food consumption.

The international initiatives discussed in this chapter include an international grain reserve system, consumption and production adjustments in developed countries, and food aid and financial approaches to alleviate the foreign exchange constraint. Empirical analysis clearly demonstrates that these initiatives do reduce the costs of national solutions in LDCs, although they do not replace the role of national policies. Numerous opportunities exist for donor countries and multilateral action to help alleviate food insecurity in LDCs, such as the lifting of foreign exchange constraint of food imports, technical and financial assistance to improve food delivery systems in LDCs, and agricultural policies that are less disruptive to world grain trade. Insofar as instability in the import bill is concerned, there is nearly professional consensus that compensatory financing schemes are the most effective approach, far better than international grain reserves. Creating such a financial facility for food is highly desirable. With such an approach the focus is where it should be: on the import bill rather than on import prices. This proposal may be implemented by liberalizing the existing scheme of compensatory financing to take into account fluctuations in "real" export earnings—that is, compensating for unexpected or excess imports of food.

An unexpected increase in the food import bill will result in a larger than usual current account deficit. Given the temporary nature of this excess demand for foreign exchange, painful macroeconomic policy adjustment would not be required if the country has access to additional financing at normal borrowing rates. The argument in favor of a food financial facility is based on the premise that (a) downward consumption adjustment of food is undesirable and often not feasible; (b) the country must act rapidly to assure the additional imports of food, and thus cannot wait for the results of an overall evaluation as required in general balance of payment support; and (c) for many poor countries, borrowing on short notice in the international capital market is not a feasible possibility. Thus, a multilateral financial scheme that offers rapid processing based on clear, predetermined rules seems an effective instrument. In addition to the advantage that it is less subject to political criteria—such as those prevailing in food aid—a liberalized financial facility is likely to help the poorest of the developing countries.

## Notes

The authors gratefully acknowledge the comments of Anne del Castillo, John W. Mellor, Daniel Morrow, and Grant M. Scobie on an earlier draft of this article.

1. Even if food is available to a country on concessional terms, to the extent that these imports must be supplemented by commercial imports

# Introduction

and thus represent "inframarginal" transfers—which is the case for all countries—that food aid should be used to replace current commercial imports rather than to build reserve stocks.

2. This above conclusion is determined by assuming that the nation or the household does not have a consistently better access to market information, thereby enabling it "to play the market" and to expect to win. Under the opposite assumption, they should become regular "speculators," trading in volumes not necessarily connected to their food security requirements.

3. This statement is strictly correct for a country considered alone. As Josling (Chapter 8) has pointed out, a policy of price insulation has an adverse impact on the functioning of the world market as a whole.

4. This conclusion disregards the complexities of cost sharing (given uncertainty about the distribution of benefits of such reserves) and implementation of the Wheat Trade Convention proposals.

5. During 1970 and 1977, food aid represented less than 13 percent of the total volume of cereal imports by all LDCs. Of this volume of food aid approximately 70 percent was received by five LDCs and the balance, approximately 2.4 million tons per year, was received by the remaining LDCs.

## References

Minhas, B. S. "Toward National Food Security." *Indian Journal of Agricultural Economics* 30, no. 4 (1976):8.

Morris, David M. "What is a Famine?" *Economic and Political Weekly* 9, no. 44 (India, Nov. 2, 1974).

Sarris, A. H., and L. Taylor. "Cereal Stocks, Food Aid, and Food Security for the Poor." *The New International Economic Order: The North-South Debate*, edited by J. Bhagwati. Cambridge, Mass.: M.I.T. Press, 1977, p. 286.

# Part 1

## Nature and Magnitude of Food Insecurity in Developing Countries

# 2
# Assessing Food Insecurity Based on National Aggregates in Developing Countries

*Alberto Valdés*
*Panos Konandreas*

For developing countries there are basically two distinct food supply problems. The major one is the large and growing long-term deficits in domestic food supply. The second problem, referred to more specifically as food insecurity, is the uncertain ability to finance needed imports to meet immediate targets for consumption levels.

There are two main causes of food insecurity. The first is shortfalls from domestic production trends, which are usually weather induced and can be quite substantial. The second cause is sudden increases in world prices for food imports (and other imports) and/or decreases in the prices of exports used to cover the cost of food imports. Domestic production shortfalls occurring in a year of adverse world prices (as in 1974 for many African and South Asian countries) devastate the ability of LDCs to meet target consumption levels. It is unacceptable to allow food consumption in the LDCs to rise and fall according to weather and/or world price changes, yet these changes are largely beyond the control of the LDCs.

The consequences of food insecurity for developing countries are disturbing. In a given year, per-capita consumption levels are likely to be forced downward from already unacceptably low levels. The burden of adjusting to consumption levels is likely to fall on the poorest families in the country. Food insecurity also has an adverse impact on scarce foreign exchange and capital resources. To pay high food import bills, developing countries must often forego other needed imports and/or cut back on investments, including investments designed to reduce long-run food supply deficits or expand export earnings.

This chapter attempts to present a broad quantitative assessment of the magnitude of the food insecurity problem of LDCs in terms of national aggregates. It is based on a quantitative description of the situation for a sample of LDCs during the period 1961–1976.

The first section deals with the extent of food insecurity, discussing food consumption patterns and consumption variability in developing countries. As a device that assesses the foreign exchange constraint, this section emphasizes the weight and variability of food imports in developing countries' balances of trade. The second section discusses the two sources of variability in the food import bill, namely, domestic production variability and fluctuations in world prices. The third section estimates the volume of food imports that would have been required at the country level to achieve food security under two alternative decision rules and the potential reduction in the variability of food consumption achieved. Finally, food insecurity is examined in terms of its importance to and correlation with the country's export revenues. Fluctuations of a country's food import bill may coincide with fluctuations of its export earnings, and thus some of the countries should have no problem financing the excess food import bill.

Individual computations were done for 24 developing countries, with the exception of the analysis of food consumption found in Table 2.1, which was based on a wider coverage (94 countries) available from the FAO. These 24 countries include 6 each from the regions of Asia, North Africa and the Middle East, sub-Sahara Africa, and Latin America. This sample of countries was selected to represent different situations among food-deficit countries with respect to dependence on food imports, variability in consumption and production, size, and geographic distribution.

The country approach analyzed in this chapter could lead to three dangerous misinterpretations. The sum of the countries' import needs cannot be a global supply goal to be achieved by eliminating world food insecurity. If many countries simultaneously changed their import behavior following the import requirement rules suggested in this chapter, the result would

*Food Insecurity in Developing Countries* 27

undoubtedly be an upward pressure on world prices. At best, the estimates are guides to the magnitude of the physical and financial resources involved in the establishment of a food security scheme for LDCs. Second, one cannot assume that food insecurity would disappear even at the national level should the calculated deficits be satisfied. Within each country, a myriad of obstacles exists that hampers an even distribution of available food supply. In some countries, inadequate transportation networks—including poor roads and insufficient storage facilities—create formidable barriers to food distribution. In other countries, severe imbalance in levels of income precludes the participation of some sectors of the population in the commercial grain markets. Moreover, political priorities frequently dictate that supplies be concentrated in some localities (usually metropolitan) at the expense of others. Third, measurement errors are a very real problem for some countries. This problem is dramatically illustrated in this chapter by comparing results that use different reputable sources.

### Assessing Food Insecurity: The Problem

Most studies on food security (Reutlinger, 1977; Konandreas et al., 1978) have defined food solely as cereals. Although the average share of cereals in total food consumption (measured in calorie equivalents) is very high, the range across countries is considerable. The proportion of cereals in total food consumption for 1972-1974 ranges from an average of 85 percent in Afghanistan to only 16 percent in Zaire.[1] For 50 of the 94 countries studied, the share of cereals is above 50 percent of total calorie consumption. Cereals are clearly the dominant staple in Asia. In Africa and Latin America, however, the role of noncereals in consumption is very important and must be incorporated into any meaningful consumption equation.

As shown in Table 2.1, the proportion of other major staples, sugar, and livestock products increase as the share of cereals declines. In 26 of the 94 countries studies for which cereals constitute less than 40 percent of the calories consumed, variability in production of noncereals cannot be overlooked as a source of food insecurity. Countries for which this is particu-

## 28  *Alberto Valdés and Panos Konandreas*

Table 2.1 Composition of Food Consumption, in Calorie
Equivalents, for 94 Developing Countries, 1972-74

| Share of cereals in total | Number of countries | Average percentage share of | | | |
|---|---|---|---|---|---|
| | | Cereals | Other major staples[a] | Sugar | Livestock products and fish[b] |
| (percent) | | | | (percent) | |
| above 60 | 30 | 70.1 | 8.5 | 6.3 | 6.2 |
| 40 - 60 | 38 | 50.8 | 13.5 | 10.9 | 10.1 |
| below 40 | 26 | 29.5 | 37.8 | 9.5 | 10.6 |

a/  Root crops, pulses, nuts, oilseeds, plantains, bananas, dates.

b/  Meat, eggs, milk and seafood.

larly true include most Latin American countries, several in
Africa (Mali, Ethiopia, Morocco, and others), and Singapore.
  Although all food items should be included in an analysis of
consumption variability, it is not appropriate to aggregate
simply by calorie equivalents. This is particularly true in the
case of livestock products and some legumes. Moreover, consistent data for a wide selection of products are not available for
several countries. The availability and quality of data are a
serious limitation on analyzing consumption variability, particularly if the noncereal component is a high portion of the diet.
  However, most governments concerned with food security
focus on grains. Grains compose an average of more than 70 percent of total calorie intake in LDCs; thus, they constitute a
reasonable approximation by which to measure the variability
of food consumption in most situations. Assuming that substi-

*Food Insecurity in Developing Countries* 29

tutability in consumption between cereals and other major staples is relatively high, and considering that the latter are nontraded goods for developing countries, one can conclude that in years of shortfalls in noncereal production cereal imports could stabilize total consumption levels beyond the "average" share of cereals in the diet.

In this study, staple food consumption for a given year $t$ is calculated as production $(Q_t)$ of cereals and other major staples (pulses, groundnuts, root crops, and plantains), plus net cereal imports $(M_t)$, and changes in cereal stocks $(\Delta S_t)$.[2] It is assumed that noncereal imports are significant only for a few countries (for example, in Central America) and that carryover stocks for noncereals are negligible compared to the volume of cereal imports and stocks. A time series for total staple food consumption for the period 1961–1976 was devised in which FAO production figures were combined with USDA figures on cereal imports and changes in stocks.

Consumption may fluctuate from year to year depending on the degree of production variability and the extent to which this variability has been compensated by changes in cereal imports and stocks. The extent to which such adjustments were made is discussed in the next section. Here we want to measure the degree of past consumption variability experienced by each country regardless of the causes of this variability.

Indicators of the observed variability of consumption from trend levels during 1961–1976 are presented in Table 2.2. In this analysis consumption instability is measured around the long-term trend $(\hat{C}_t)$, using the coefficient of variation as a measure of variability.[3] The observed trend refers to actual food consumption rather than nutritional requirements; thus, even meeting the deficits would not necessarily result in a nutritionally satisfactory level of per-capita consumption.

As observed in column 2 of Table 2.2, the coefficient of variation ranges from a low of 3 to 4 percent (the Philippines and Peru) to a high of 20 to 25 percent (Morocco and Algeria). Among countries where consumption of cereals constitutes over 40 percent of total food consumption, variability levels of 15 percent or more (which, in our opinion, are extraordinarily high) are concentrated in North Africa and the Middle East.

# Table 2.2 Variability in Staple Food Consumption, 1961-76

| | Staple food consumption instability | | Probability of actual consumption falling below 95 percent of trend |
|---|---|---|---|
| | Standard deviation[a/] | Coefficient of variation | |
| | (1) | (2) | (3) |
| | (thousand metric tons) | (percent) | (percent) |
| **Asia** | | | |
| Bangladesh | 1,013 | 7.6 | 26 |
| India | 5,570 | 5.3 | 17 |
| Indonesia | 1,204 | 6.1 | 21 |
| Korea, Rep. of | 531 | 6.5 | 22 |
| Philippines | 192 | 3.3 | 6 |
| Sri Lanka | 163 | 8.3 | 27 |
| **North Africa/Middle East** | | | |
| Algeria | 667 | 24.6 | 42 |
| Egypt | 1,164 | 12.6 | 34 |
| Jordan | 88 | 21.2 | 40 |
| Libya | 115 | 16.2 | 38 |
| Morocco | 933 | 19.3 | 40 |
| Syria | 360 | 18.7 | 39 |
| **Sub-Sahara Africa** | | | |
| Ghana | 134 | 6.1 | 21 |
| Nigeria | 965 | 5.6 | 19 |
| Senegal | 319 | 15.7 | 37 |
| Tanzania | 517 | 14.6 | 37 |
| Upper Volta | 126 | 9.5 | 30 |
| Zaire | 172 | 4.1 | 11 |
| **Latin America** | | | |
| Brazil | 1,955 | 5.8 | 20 |
| Chile | 386 | 14.4 | 36 |
| Colombia | 147 | 4.7 | 14 |
| Guatemala | 69 | 6.9 | 24 |
| Mexico | 757 | 5.3 | 17 |
| Peru | 110 | 3.9 | 10 |

Sources: Cereals and other major staples from FAO *Production Yearbook*; net cereal imports from FAO *Trade Yearbook*, and cereal stocks from US Department of Agriculture data base. Sensitivity of results according to different sources and to the exclusion of stocks; see Annex 1.

a/ Defined as the standard deviation of the variable $C_t - \hat{C}_t$.

High levels are also observed in Senegal, Tanzania, and Chile. One is struck by the generally high degree of consumption variability; in 44 of 67 countries, the observed consumption variability is equal to or above 7 percent.

Column 3 of Table 2.2 presents the probability of actual consumption falling below 95 percent of trend consumption, given the actual level of imports. In 51 of 67 countries, a consumption

# Food Insecurity in Developing Countries

shortfall below 95 percent of trend occurred once in every five years. In most of the Arab countries, it occurred approximately twice every five years.

## Foreign Exchange Constraints

In addition to adequate domestic infrastructure to cope with unforeseen import demand in years of production shortfalls—including adequate statistical reporting systems for the planning of grain imports—foreign exchange availability is critical if a country is to be able to stabilize food consumption through imports. To what extent do food imports burden the balance of trade, and by how much can the food import bill increase in years of unfavorable production and/or world prices, given fixed supplies of foreign exchange in any particular year? To what extent is the fact that the observed fluctuations in grain imports have been substantially smaller than fluctuations in grain production (Sarris, 1976) due to lack of foreign exchange?

As an indicator of these relationships, the average ratio of the actual value of food imports to total export revenues (including services) for the period 1965–1976 and the upper limit of this ratio during the same period are presented in Table 2.3. The food import/export ratio is used as an indicator of the pressure put on foreign exchange supplies to finance food imports. Except for three of the 24 cases (Bangladesh, India, and Sri Lanka), during 1965–1976 the mean ratio was less than 15 percent, which, in the opinion of the authors, does not indicate a severe constraint during normal years. However, more pertinent to food insecurity is the degree to which this ratio can reach significantly higher levels in unfavorable years. In column 2 of Table 2.3, one observes that for some countries with "low" average ratios, such as Tanzania, Syria, and Mexico, exceptionally unfavorable years can raise this ratio by a multiple of three to four. This ratio becomes intolerably high for several countries, particularly in Asia, but also in Egypt, Tanzania, and Senegal. The ratio remains remarkably low even at its maximum values in some countries, such as Nigeria, Libya, and Colombia. The sharp contrast in country situations often is not fully recognized in international forum discussions on food security.

32

**Table 2.3    Ratio of Food Imports to Total Export Revenue (1965-76 Except as Noted)**

|  | Mean (1) | Maximum (2) |
|---|---|---|
|  | (percent) | |
| **Asia** | | |
| Bangladesh[a] | 88.4 | 119.4 |
| India[b] | 22.4 | 44.5 |
| Indonesia | 9.5 | 19.9 |
| Korea, Rep. of | 13.5 | 21.4 |
| Philippines | 4.9 | 9.1 |
| Sri Lanka | 27.2 | 49.2 |
| **North Africa/Middle East** | | |
| Algeria[c] | 6.0 | 9.3 |
| Egypt[d] | 14.0 | 27.0 |
| Jordan[d] | 10.6 | 15.4 |
| Libya[d] | 1.4 | 2.3 |
| Morocco | 7.0 | 13.4 |
| Syria[d] | 5.7 | 18.4 |
| **Sub-Sahara Africa** | | |
| Ghana[d] | 3.7 | 5.4 |
| Nigeria[d] | 1.9 | 2.5 |
| Senegal[b] | 12.2 | 17.8 |
| Tanzania[d] | 5.5 | 22.2 |
| Upper Volta[e] | 7.4 | 13.0 |
| Zaire[b] | 3.1 | 6.9 |
| **Latin America** | | |
| Brazil | 3.9 | 8.5 |
| Chile | 5.3 | 13.9 |
| Colombia | 2.8 | 4.9 |
| Guatemala | 2.4 | 3.3 |
| Mexico | 0.4 | 9.3 |
| Peru | 6.6 | 10.5 |

a/  Time period of analysis 1973-76.

b/  Time period of analysis 1965-75.

c/  Time period of analysis 1966-76.

d/  Time period of analysis 1967-76.

e/  Time period of analysis 1968-75.

# Food Insecurity in Developing Countries

## Causes of Food Insecurity

Historically, annual food consumption has varied considerably. For most LDCs, changes in stock levels are not sufficient to balance the interyear consumption variability. Thus, with few exceptions, fluctuations in consumption result from fluctuations in the levels of production and/or imports.

### Production Variability

Production has been relatively stable in most large low-income countries, as measured by the coefficient of variation of production presented in column 2 of Table 2.4. These include Bangladesh, Egypt, India, Indonesia, and the Philippines. For these countries, the coefficient of variation of production is around or below 6 percent. In contrast, in almost half of the countries—mostly small countries—this figure is 10 percent or more, and in seven Arab countries it is above 20 percent. Expressed in terms of the probability of production falling below 95 percent of trend (column 3 of Table 2.4), in 30 of the 67 countries shortfalls occur in one of every three years. For planning the operation of an international food security scheme, the absolute magnitude of the shortfall (column 1 of Table 2.4) is critical. A country such as India may have a relatively low level of instability (6.4 percent) but a high value of absolute variability (6.6 million tons); in contrast, Morocco has relatively high instability (27.2 percent) but an absolute variability only one sixth that of India (1.2 million tons). Hence, a scheme could very well become dominated by the withdrawal of the large countries, many of which have relatively low production variability.

Results in Table 2.4 suggest that production variability has been high in most of the smaller countries, particularly the Arab countries. A policy of consumption stability requires that imports reflect a highly negative correlation with production. Conversely, if imports did not cover production shortfalls, consumption would display a high positive correlation coefficient with production. Our analysis shows a significant correlation (column 4 of Table 2.4) consistent with the observed instability in consumption presented in Table 2.2. Thus, as a general rule

Table 2.4   Variability in Staple Food Production, 1961-76

| | Staple food production instability | | Probability of actual production falling below 95% of trend | Correlation coefficient between total staple food production and consumption | Correlation coefficient between cereal production and total staple food production |
|---|---|---|---|---|---|
| | Standard deviation[a]/ (000's m.t.) (1) | Coefficient of variation[b]/ (%) (2) | (%) (3) | (%) (4) | (5) |
| | (thousand metric tons) | (percent) | (percent) | | |
| **Asia** | | | | | |
| Bangladesh | 765 | 6.4 | 22 | .90 | .99 |
| India | 6,653 | 6.4 | 22 | .89 | .99 |
| Indonesia | 1,040 | 5.4 | 18 | .92 | .94 |
| Korea, Rep. of | 445 | 7.1 | 24 | .20 | .96 |
| Philippines | 346 | 5.7 | 19 | .03 | .99 |
| Sri Lanka | 107 | 9.3 | 29 | .56 | .91 |
| **North Africa/Middle East** | | | | | |
| Algeria | 531 | 28.9 | 43 | .78 | 1.00 |
| Egypt | 282 | 4.5 | 13 | .29 | .96 |
| Jordan | 119 | 65.6 | 47 | .63 | 1.00 |
| Libya | 56 | 28.0 | 43 | .62 | 1.00 |
| Morocco | 1,156 | 27.2 | 43 | .98 | .96 |
| Syria | 702 | 38.8 | 45 | .92 | 1.00 |
| **Sub-Sahara Africa** | | | | | |
| Ghana | 121 | 5.8 | 20 | .98 | .93 |
| Nigeria | 958 | 5.7 | 19 | .99 | .92 |
| Senegal | 325 | 18.6 | 39 | .99 | .81 |
| Tanzania | 430 | 12.7 | 35 | .98 | .09 |
| Upper Volta | 128 | 9.8 | 30 | .95 | .99 |
| Zaire | 190 | 4.9 | 15 | .96 | -.21 |
| **Latin America** | | | | | |
| Brazil | 1,600 | 5.2 | 17 | .92 | .60 |
| Chile | 215 | 11.1 | 33 | .54 | .99 |
| Colombia | 126 | 4.4 | 13 | .51 | .85 |
| Guatemala | 56 | 6.5 | 22 | .51 | .99 |
| Mexico | 1,060 | 7.7 | 26 | .53 | 1.00 |
| Peru | 197 | 9.8 | 30 | .37 | .97 |

a/ Defined as the standard deviation of the variable $Q_t - \hat{Q}_t$.

b/ Defined as the standard deviation of the variable $\dfrac{Q_t - \hat{Q}_t}{\hat{Q}_t} \cdot 100$

# Food Insecurity in Developing Countries

for most countries, fluctuations in staple food consumption follow closely the fluctuations of domestic staple food production. This is particularly true for sub-Sahara Africa but not generally so for Latin America.

Moreover, although production included cereal and noncereal staples, it is the variability in cereal production that explains most of the variance in total food production. The correlation coefficient between cereal and total production is 90 percent or more, and there are very few exceptions (see column 5 of Table 2.4). This reflects the high share of cereals in total production and/or the relatively higher variability of production of cereals. Thus, for most countries, consumption of total staples fluctuates with cereal production, and the relationship is a proportional one.

## Variability of the Price of Imports

In the previous discussion, food insecurity was measured as the observed fluctuation in total food consumption. To compensate for the variability in domestic production, some countries could have created an unmanageable food import bill. Moreover, fluctuations in volumes are compounded by the world-price instability of cereals. What proportion of the variability in the cost of food imports is explained by world price instability, and what proportion by fluctuations in the volume of imports? This question is critical to price stabilization schemes currently under international negotiation.

With the dollar value of the food import bill defined as $V$, the volume of cereal imports as $M$, and the import price as $P$, the following identity holds:

$$V = MP \tag{1}$$

Expanding the above identity as a first order Taylor Series, taking expectations and expressing variances (Burt and Finley, 1968), we obtain:

$$\text{Var}(V) = \bar{P}^2 \cdot \text{Var}(M) + \bar{M}^2 \cdot \text{Var}(P) + 2\bar{P} \cdot \bar{M} \cdot \text{Cov}(P,M) \tag{2}$$

where the first term on the right-hand side represents the contribution of the import volume alone to the variance of the import bill, the second term represents the contribution of import price alone, and the third term represents the joint impact of both volume and price. If the import demand has some elasticity with respect to price, then the interaction effect should be negative.

The relative contribution of volume and price to the variance of actual import bill can be obtained by dividing Equation 2 by the first two terms of the right-hand side:

$$\frac{\bar{P}^2 \cdot \text{Var}(M) + \bar{M}^2 \cdot \text{Var}(P) + 2\bar{P} \cdot \bar{M} \cdot \text{Cov}(P,M)}{\bar{P}^2 \cdot \text{Var}(M) + \bar{M}^2 \cdot \text{Var}(P)} = R_M + R_P + R_{MP} \quad (3)$$

where $R_M$ and $R_P$ are the relative contributions of import volume and price, respectively, and $R_{MP}$ their interaction.

It is clear from Table 2.5 that during the 1961–1976 period, the variability of the import volume explains most of the variability of the import bill. Generally, only one-quarter of the variability of the import bill is explained by import price variability. The picture of the interaction effect is rather mixed, however, with more negative cases than positive ones. Closer examination of the interaction effect reveals a negative interaction for all the major importers except Egypt and Iran. This observation is consistent with a negative price elasticity of imports, that is, *ceteris paribus*, a reduction of imports when prices rise and vice versa. However, this elastic import demand can imply a conflict with consumption stabilization goals, unless either cereal consumption represents a low proportion of total food consumption or the country has a grain stock system capable of alleviating domestic production shortfalls in years of high world prices.

One must qualify the above analysis by two important observations. First, during the period of our analysis, particularly before 1972, policies of major exporting countries kept world grain prices relatively stable for a long period. Many analysts believe that this situation is unlikely to reappear. Second, in the past a considerable portion of imports to developing countries has been in the form of food aid. The quoted price of

# Food Insecurity in Developing Countries

Table 2.5   Variability of the Food Import Bill, 1961-76

| | Portion of the variability of import bill due to | | |
|---|---|---|---|
| | Volume | Price | Interaction |
| | (2) | (2) | (3) |
| | | (percent) | |
| **Asia** | | | |
| Bangladesh | 84 | 16 | -10 |
| India | 96 | 4 | -19 |
| Indonesia | 92 | 8 | -13 |
| Korea, Rep. of | 80 | 20 | -13 |
| Philippines | 68 | 32 | - 7 |
| Sri Lanka | 40 | 60 | 13 |
| **North Africa/Middle East** | | | |
| Algeria | 88 | 12 | 4 |
| Egypt | 69 | 31 | 66 |
| Jordan | 79 | 21 | -26 |
| Libya | 57 | 43 | 3 |
| Morocco | 93 | 7 | 30 |
| Syria | 100 | -- | -- |
| **Sub-Sahara Africa** | | | |
| Ghana | 65 | 35 | 9 |
| Nigeria | 62 | 38 | -34 |
| Senegal | 55 | 45 | -20 |
| Tanzania | 96 | 4 | 20 |
| Upper Volta | 85 | 15 | -29 |
| Zaire | 40 | 60 | -19 |
| **Latin America** | | | |
| Brazil | 85 | 15 | 21 |
| Chile | 88 | 12 | 24 |
| Colombia | 83 | 17 | -29 |
| Guatemala | 55 | 45 | 38 |
| Mexico | 100 | -- | - 4 |
| Peru | 45 | 55 | 15 |

imports used here does not represent the true price of food aid imports to the importer. However, the results of recent research suggest that with very few exceptions (e.g., India), food aid imports have not represented a net addition to food supply over and above that which would have been imported through commercial imports (see Abbot, 1976). Hence, import volumes including food aid can be treated as the minimum "desired" level that LDCs would have imported even in the absence of food aid.

The above analysis, showing that it is the variability in the import volume that explains most of the variability in the import bill, suggests that successful world price stabilization schemes could help mitigate food insecurity, but price stabilization alone is clearly insufficient for the task at hand.

## Reducing Food Insecurity

### Food Security Decision Rules

Food security, as defined above, aims at balancing the year-to-year variability in aggregate consumption around a long-run trend. Food security does not imply an increase in the average levels of consumption above trend levels. Rather, it is designed to prevent consumption levels from falling below trend values. Indirectly, food security resources could contribute to an increase in the long-run average level of consumption, by assuring governments of needed grain supplies in crisis years and thus making national food distribution schemes more politically and financially feasible.

Depending on the symmetry of the adjustments required to offset deviations from the trend, there is some scope for modifying the average levels of consumption. For example, if no ceiling is imposed on consumption in years when food availability is above trend, and if the scheme allows a country to cover all of its shortfalls in bad years, then consumption will rise above the long-run trend. Conversely, a scheme that allows for some downward adjustment in consumption in years of production shortfalls or high import prices and imposes some ceiling on consumption in years of exceptionally high levels of availability will not increase the average level of consumption.

Two rules regarding the maximum permissible adjustments in consumption were evaluated. We do not claim that the suggested rules are optimal for any individual country. These rules were designed to allow a quantitative assessment of the approximate magnitude of the resources needed to stabilize consumption on a country basis. The two rules are:

*Rule I.* For a particular year $t$, food security consumption $(C_t^I)$ is maintained at trend level $(\hat{C}_t)$ when there is a shortfall in actual consumption $(C_t)$, and when food consumption is set equal to other actual consumption. Symbolically,

$$\text{when } C_t < \hat{C}_t \text{ then } C_t^I = \hat{C}_t; \text{ and}$$

$$\text{when } C_t > \hat{C}_t \text{ then } C_t^I = C_t.$$

# Food Insecurity in Developing Countries

*Rule II.* Food security consumption $(C_t^{II})$ is maintained at trend levels when there is a shortfall in actual consumption, but is adjusted downward if actual consumption levels rise above trend levels through planned commercial imports. Symbolically,

when $C_t < \hat{C}_t$ then $C_t^{II} = \hat{C}_t$;

when $C_t > \hat{C}_t$ and $M_t > C_t - \hat{C}_t$ then $C_t^{II} = \hat{C}_t$; and

when $C_t > \hat{C}_t$ and $M_t < C_t - \hat{C}_t$ then $C_t^{II} = C_t - M_t$.

In some years, countries have imported more than they needed to stabilize consumption, as defined by Rule II. These excess imports are not included in our calculation of import requirements for consumption stabilization.

Moreover, even if trend consumption levels are accepted ex ante as a true reflection of desired levels, the actual level could be above the trend level because of an unexpected good harvest or food aid obtained under exceptionally favorable conditions.

## Estimate of Required Food Imports

Table 2.6 compares the results for the 24 countries in relation to Rules I and II, shows the variability of food security consumption vis-à-vis historical levels, and indicates the volume of imports required to achieve consumption stabilization.

As expected, actual food consumption levels were below food security levels in all selected countries.[4] This is consistent with Sarris's analysis (1976) on wheat import demand in LDCs. However, under Rule II, actual consumption is closer (than under Rule I) to food security consumption levels as defined above. This fact implies that, in general, countries have achieved consumption above the trend through "excess" imports, and as such imports are not allowed under Rule II, average consumption levels are below those under Rule I.[5]

As expected, under Rule I consumption variability in several countries is reduced to about one half or less of actual consumption variability. This reduction occurs because under Rule I shortfalls in consumption are completely eliminated and no

# 40 Alberto Valdés and Panos Konandreas

Table 2.6 Reduction in the Variability of Consumption and in the Required Imports Under Two Alternative Food Security Decision Rules, 1961-76

| | Variability of food security consumption, as a percentage of actual consumption variability | | Comparison between food security and actual imports (1976 trend values) Food Security Imports | | Actual Imports |
|---|---|---|---|---|---|
| | Rule I (1) % | Rule II (2) % | Rule I (3) | Rule II (4) (thousand metric tons) | (5) |
| **Asia** | | | | | |
| Bangladesh | 50 | 0 | 2,582 | 2,085 | 2,084 |
| India | 40 | 20 | 5,442 | 4,029 | 3,563 |
| Indonesia | 50 | 17 | 1,953 | 1,558 | 1,674 |
| Korea, Rep. of | 50 | 0 | 3,881 | 3,601 | 3,601 |
| Philippines | 33 | 0 | 1,070 | 1,015 | 1,015 |
| Sri Lanka | 75 | 0 | 1,098 | 1,054 | 1,054 |
| **North Africa/Middle East** | | | | | |
| Algeria | 68 | 32 | 1,967 | 1,556 | 1,700 |
| Egypt | 38 | 0 | 2,619 | 1,855 | 1,855 |
| Jordan | 52 | 5 | 275 | 255 | 255 |
| Libya | 75 | 0 | 819 | 739 | 739 |
| Morocco | 55 | 44 | 1,135 | 920 | 907 |
| Syria | 53 | 42 | 527 | 334 | 271 |
| **Sub-Sahara Africa** | | | | | |
| Ghana | 50 | 33 | 241 | 163 | 135 |
| Nigeria | 50 | 33 | 1,002 | 748 | 583 |
| Senegal | 44 | 25 | 569 | 406 | 336 |
| Tanzania | 67 | 50 | 260 | 188 | 203 |
| Upper Volta | 33 | 33 | 119 | 92 | 46 |
| Zaire | 75 | 50 | -- | -- | -- |
| **Latin America** | | | | | |
| Brazil | 50 | 33 | 2,289 | 1,853 | 1,335 |
| Chile | 71 | 0 | 1,255 | 997 | 997 |
| Colombia | 50 | 0 | 446 | 335 | 335 |
| Guatemala | 57 | 0 | 177 | 142 | 138 |
| Mexico | 80 | 60 | 2,146 | 1,934 | 1,814 |
| Peru | 50 | 0 | 1,172 | 1,102 | 1,102 |

downward adjustments are made when consumption is above the trend. In contrast, under Rule II (for which there is some adjustment when consumption is above trend), consumption variability is always smaller than under Rule I, except when a country has achieved the above-trend consumption level solely through its own production. This is true, for example, for Upper Volta. Under Rule II, consumption variability is eliminated altogether for several countries (indicated by values of 0 in column 2). This implies that for those countries food security consumption corresponds to the trend level of actual consumption.

Thus, comparing consumption stabilization Rules I and II, one notes that the former allows an average level of consumption

# Food Insecurity in Developing Countries

that is above the average historical level but with some instability in consumption. Rule II, on the other hand, reduces or eliminates instability but at a lower average level of consumption than under Rule I.

The trend imports required to achieve consumption stabilization as defined by Rules I and II and the actual trend imports for the last year of our analysis (1976) are presented in Table 2.6, columns 3, 4, and 5, respectively. As anticipated, import levels required under Rule II are equal to or below the actual trend import levels for several countries. This implies that these countries could use their "excess" imports to compensate their consumption shortfalls during low consumption years.

If consumption obtained through Rule I is accepted as the target level, the comparison of required imports (column 3) and the trend level of actual imports (column 5) implies that for several countries actual imports are considerably below the targeted consumption trend levels. For example, India's actual trend imports are only 65 percent of the target import volume, Egypt's 71 percent, and Nigeria's 58 percent. For the 67 countries analyzed, food security consumption at 1976 trend values would have been achieved with an aggregate level of cereal imports on the order of 47.7 million tons a year, in contrast to actual imports of 36.6 million tons in 1976. These calculations are made on the basis of trend values (for 1976) of production and import volumes.

The food security level of imports presented in Table 2.6 should be interpreted as the expected annual volume of supplies required for imports, if consumption stabilization is to be achieved. Under both rules, the model adheres to the historical trend in food consumption during 1961–1976. Although the food security rules reduce and often eliminate consumption instability, they do not alter the long-term consumption trend, even when negative.

## The Variability of Food Import and Export Earnings

The food insecurity problem of developing countries should be analyzed within the context of their foreign exchange position. A large food import bill could be small relative to a country's total export earnings. Similarly, the fluctuations of a country's food import bill may coincide with fluctuations in its export earnings. In both of these cases the country should have no problem in financing needed food imports. Obviously, the food security problem of a country is more severe the higher the food import bill relative to total export earnings and/or the lower the correlation between the food import bill and foreign exchange earnings.

Virtually any country can finance food security imports in any given year. However, drawing heavily on foreign exchange reserves or destabilizing other essential imports to afford adequate food supplies may hamper economic development plans.

Thus, we redefine food insecurity to be the reduction in a country's total export earnings adjusted for by the value of imports (which, according to the analysis, will consist of changes in the volume and/or the price of imports) that guarantee food security. To facilitate this analysis, we define

$V_t, \hat{V}_t:$ actual and trend food import bill, respectively, in year $t$;

$V_t^I, V_t^{II}:$ import bills in year $t$ to finance food imports needed to meet alternative consumption levels under Rules I and II, respectively;

$X_t, \hat{X}_t:$ actual and trend export earnings (goods and services), respectively;

$NX_t = X_t - V_t:$ actual net export earnings in year $t$, adjusted by subtracting the cost of actual cereal imports from actual export earnings;

$NX_t = X_t - V_t^I; NX_t^{II} = X_t - V_t^{II}:$ net export earnings in year $t$, adjusted by subtracting the cost of cereal imports needed to meet alternative consumption levels under Rules I and II, respectively.

We assume that actual and trend values are related in the following manner:

$$V_t = \hat{V}_t + v_t$$
$$X_t = \hat{X}_t + x_t$$
$$NX_t = \hat{X}_t - \hat{V}_t = X_t - V_t + w_t,$$

Food Insecurity in Developing Countries

where $w_t = x_t - v_t$ and where the random disturbances $v_t$ and $x_t$ are assumed normally distributed with

$$E(v_t) = E(x_t) = 0,$$
$$E(v_t^2) = \sigma_v^2, \text{ and}$$
$$E(x_t^2) = \sigma_x$$

and the random disturbance of $NX_t$ has the following properties:

$$E(w_t) = 0$$
$$E(w_t^2) = \sigma_x^2 + \sigma_v^2 - 2\sigma_x\sigma_v r_{xv} \equiv \sigma_{nx}^2$$

Thus, the variability of net export earnings ($\sigma_{nx}^2$) is a function of the variability of actual export earnings ($\sigma_x^2$), the variability of the actual food imports bill ($\sigma_v^2$), and the correlation coefficient between export earnings and the food import bill ($r_{xv}$).[6] *Ceteris paribus*, the variability of net export earnings decreases as the variability of the food import bill ($\sigma_v^2$) decreases and as the correlation coefficient ($r_{xv}$) becomes larger. Thus, a country can maintain its ability to import nonfood goods when its food import bill variability is low and/or in years when high import bills coincide with high export earnings.[7] In general, the absolute variability of the food import bill is smaller than the variability of export earnings (in 16 of the 24 countries, $\sigma_v < \frac{1}{4}\sigma_x$). Only in three countries (Bangladesh, India, and Sri Lanka) is $\sigma_v > \sigma_x$. In general, as evinced by the correlation coefficient $r_{xv}$, food import bills are positively correlated to export earnings. This result is consistent with a high positive correlation between world prices of food imports and major export commodities, which implies that in years when the food-import bill is higher as a result of higher import prices of food and/or higher import volumes, foreign exchange earnings are also higher. Thus, most countries can afford a higher import bill. For half the countries included here, net export revenues fluctuated more than un-adjusted export revenues. This fact implies that in these cases, nonfood imports must be adjusted in order to accommodate the variable food import bills.

In order to measure the national food insecurity problem

in terms of the diversion of net export earnings used to meet target consumption levels, define

$$D_x = \sum_t \{-x_t = \hat{X}_t - X_t | x_t < 0\} \text{ and}$$

$$D_n = \sum_t \{-n_t = \hat{V}_t - V_t | n_t > 0\},$$

which represents the sum of a country's shortfalls of actual export earnings from trend;

$$D_{nx} = D_x - D_n = \sum_t \{-w_t = (\hat{X}_t - X_t) - (\hat{V}_t - V_t) | w_t < 0\},$$

which represents the sum of a country's shortfalls of net export earnings from its trend;

$$D_{nx}^I = \sum_t \{-w_t^I = (\hat{X}_t - X_t) - (\hat{V}_t - V_t^I) | w_t^I < 0\}$$

under Rule I; and

$$D_{nx}^{II} = \sum_t \{-w_t^{II} = (\hat{X}_t - X_t) - (\hat{V}_t - V_t^{II}) | w_t^{II} < 0\}$$

under Rule II, which represents the sum of a country's shortfalls of net export earnings after adequate food imports to meet food security consumption levels.

In Table 2.7, column 1 presents the sum of shortfalls in export earnings and column 2 represents the sum of excess values in the food import bill, both in reference to trend values. Shortfalls in the adjusted (or net) export earnings presented in column 3 correspond to the sum of the shortfalls in export earnings and excesses in food imports in year $t$.

The comparison of columns 1 and 3 indicates that shortfalls in net export earnings are significantly higher than unadjusted shortfalls in 8 to 9 of the 24 selected countries. This increase is particularly significant for India, Bangladesh, and Tanzania. However, it does not seem to be significant for several countries, which reflects some positive correlation between export earning and actual food import bills. For example, in the Philippines an export shortfall of $1,441 million and an excess food import . bill of $149 million, when analyzed to take this correlation into

Table 2.7 Shortfalls in Export Earnings With and Without Adjustments for Food Import Bills (1965-76 except as noted)

| | Sum of shortfalls in gross export earnings $(D_x)$ (1) | Sum of excessive actual food import bills $(D_v)$ (2) | Sum of shortfalls of net export earnings, adjusted by import bills | | | Difference between shortfalls of net export earnings and shortfalls in gross export earnings | |
|---|---|---|---|---|---|---|---|
| | | | actual $(D_{nx})$ (3) | Case I $(D_{nx}^I)$ (4) | Case II $(D_{nx}^{II})$ (5) | Case I (6)=(4)-(1) | Case II (7)=(5)-(1) |
| **Asia** | | | | | | | |
| Bangladesh[a/] | 84 | 135 | 443 | 532 | 305 | 448 | 221 |
| India[b/] | 1,123 | 1,197 | 2,714 | 8,884 | 7,784 | 7,761 | 6,661 |
| Indonesia | 2,699 | 508 | 2,970 | 3,551 | 3,433 | 852 | 734 |
| Korea, Rep. of | 2,154 | 605 | 2,220 | 2,318 | 2,106 | 164 | -48 |
| Philippines | 1,441 | 149 | 1,344 | 1,322 | 1,261 | -119 | -180 |
| Sri Lanka | 182 | 208 | 269 | 248 | 174 | 66 | -8 |
| **North Africa/Middle East** | | | | | | | |
| Algeria[c/] | 2,716 | 202 | 2,546 | 2,748 | 2,729 | -31 | 13 |
| Egypt[d/] | 953 | 651 | 1,255 | 1,059 | 463 | 106 | -490 |
| Jordan[d/] | 342 | 41 | 342 | 339 | 313 | -3 | -29 |
| Libya[d/] | 3,458 | 68 | 3,483 | 3,503 | 3,423 | 45 | -35 |
| Morocco | 798 | 312 | 721 | 991 | 898 | 193 | 100 |
| Syria[d/] | 372 | 158 | 410 | 825 | 825 | 453 | 453 |
| **Sub-Sahara Africa** | | | | | | | |
| Ghana[d/] | 257 | 33 | 271 | 364 | 314 | 107 | 57 |
| Nigeria[d/] | 3,429 | 51 | 3,464 | 3,932 | 3,609 | 503 | 180 |
| Senegal[b/] | 137 | 61 | 166 | 321 | 286 | 184 | 149 |
| Tanzania[d/] | 162 | 45 | 355 | 386 | 318 | 224 | 156 |
| Upper Volta[e/] | 22 | 6 | 23 | 122 | 120 | 100 | 98 |
| Zaire[b/] | 985 | 50 | 981 | 1,051 | 1,027 | 66 | 42 |
| **Latin America** | | | | | | | |
| Brazil | 1,789 | 451 | 2,762 | 1,812 | 3,173 | 1,022 | 384 |
| Chile | 1,437 | 159 | 1,329 | 1,452 | 1,406 | 15 | -31 |
| Colombia | 578 | 69 | 629 | 606 | 484 | 28 | -94 |
| Guatemala | 213 | 22 | 208 | 231 | 215 | 18 | 2 |
| Mexico | 1,480 | 1,381 | 1,200 | 1,789 | 1,701 | 309 | 221 |
| Peru | 604 | 91 | 596 | 596 | 522 | -8 | -82 |

a/ Time period of analysis 1973-76.   c/ Time period of analysis 1966-76   e/ Time period of analysis 1968-75.

b/ Time period of analysis 1965-75.   d/ Time period of analysis 1967-76.

account, result in a shortfall in adjusted export earnings equal to $1,344 million (column 3), lower than the unadjusted value in column 1.

If countries were to defend consumption levels (according to the food security decision rules defined earlier), it can be observed in column 4 of Table 2.7 that Rule I implies a significant increase in adjusted export shortfalls in all except 3 of the 24 countries, and the results for Rule II vary. However, even under Rule II, significant increases in adjusted shortfalls result for India, Indonesia, Bangladesh, and sub-Sahara Africa. Nevertheless, declines are observed for 9 of the 24 countries.

Table 2.10, as a complementary analysis, emphasizes the importance of the food security import bill to total export earnings (including both merchandise and services), stressing the differences between mean and maximum values. Under Rule I, in 7 of 24 countries, the mean ratio of food security imports to exports is above 15 percent, but under the same rule, in 15 of 24 countries the maximum can be significantly above 15 percent, as shown in column 4. To illustrate, in Syria a mean ratio of 9.5 percent rises to a maximum of 47.6 percent; in Upper Volta, a mean ratio of 24.4 percent reaches a 60 percent maximum level. Thus, although the mean value of this ratio is a good guide for what would be the constant pressure for financing adequate levels of food imports, a maximum value gives a more vivid picture of the extraordinary adjustment in nonfood imports necessary to stabilize food consumption.

To approximate the financial resources that would have been required to compensate for excessive food imports during the 1965–1976 period, or alternatively for shortfalls in export earning after adjusting for the excess cost of food imports, we calculated sums of the columns of Table 2.7, which are presented in Table 2.8.

Part A in Table 2.8 presents results for an international facility operating independently of the export-earning situation. A facility that compensated each country for its actual excess food import bill would have needed a total of $12 billion for the 1965–1976 period for the 67 LDCs, or an average annual payment of approximately $1 billion. If, instead, one applies Rule II to those 67 countries, the annual average expected value is approximately $2 billion. If the country cover-

*Food Insecurity in Developing Countries*  47

Table 2.8 Financial Resources to Cover Fluctuations in Cereal Imports of LDCs (1965-76)

| | 67 countries[1] | 34 MSA countries[2] |
|---|---|---|
| | (US billions, constant 1975 prices) | |
| A. Sum of excess food imports | | |
| actual food imports | 12.0 | 6.8 |
| consumption stabilizing imports | | |
| under rule I | 27.6 | 15.9 |
| under rule II | 22.9 | 13.2 |
| B. Sum of increase in compensatory financing for export earnings adjusting for variability in the cost of cereal imports | | |
| actual imports | 2.9 | 3.0 |
| consumption stabilizing imports | | |
| under rule I | 17.0 | 12.0 |
| under rule II | 12.6 | 9.5 |

1. Excludes major oil exporters as defined by IMF, namely Algeria, Sudan, Iran, Iraq, Libya, Nigeria, Saudia Arabia, and Venezuela.
2. Most seriously affected countries (MSA) as defined by FAO.

age is reduced to include most seriously affected (MSA) countries only, these figures are reduced by approximately one-half, as shown in Table 2.8.

Alternatively, as shown in Part B of Table 2.8, if the compensation for the variability in export earnings were made after adjusting for the excess cost of actual food imports, the increment in the compensation for the 67 LDCs would be approximately $263 million annually (or a sum of $2.9 billion during 1965-1976) or approximately $1.1 billion annually if Rule II is followed.[8]

The results suggest the extreme sensitivity of our calculations with respect to (a) whether actual imports or consumption stabilizing rules are used, (b) the country coverage, and (c) whether or not the food facility is adjusted by export earnings (Parts A and B, respectively).[9] Restricting the coverage to MSA countries significantly reduces the financial resources required, except when actual imports are used instead of Rules I or II in the adjusted scheme based on export earnings variability.

## Concluding Remarks

This chapter presents empirical evidence, based on national aggregates, regarding the magnitude of food insecurity in selected countries. It shows that production instability varies considerably among countries and that imports and stocks have generally not been used very effectively to stabilize food consumption. In analyzing the sources of the variability in the food import bill, we find that the variability in the import volume explains most of the historical variability of import costs for most developing countries.[10] On average, only about one-fourth of this variability is explained by world price variability.

The analysis of the constraint on foreign exchange—designed to finance imports that will stabilize food consumption—suggests that, except for 3 of the 24 countries, during 1965–1976 the mean ratio of food import to total export revenues does not indicate a severe constraint during normal years. However, this ratio becomes intolerably high in unfavorable years, particularly in Asia and parts of Africa. Basing our opinion on normative food security rules, we conclude that in order to have stabilized domestic consumption, the volume of cereal imports would have been considerably higher than the historical levels of food imports.

Finally, in the context of the overall balance of the trade position of 64 LDCs and alternatively for the poorest LDCs only, the authors quantitatively assess the increase in the compensatory financing flows required to finance consumption stabilizing imports, adjusting for fluctuations in export revenues and for their correlation with the variability in the food import bill. The results suggest the extreme sensitivity of overall financial flows that are required, according to the country coverage and to the decision rules followed.

## Notes

The authors thank Wilfred Candler for his comments and Robin Donaldson, Pat Tillman, and Joachim Zietz for their assistance in programming the model and processing the data.

*Food Insecurity in Developing Countries*        49

1. Composition of food consumption was taken from the FAO's *Food Balance Sheet* series.

2. Defined as $C_t = Q_t + M_t + \Delta S_t$.

3. The coefficient of variation is defined as the standard deviation of the percentage fluctuations from trend, i.e., the standard deviation of the variable:

$$\frac{C_t - \hat{C}_t}{\hat{C}_t} \cdot 100.$$

4. Among countries, actual consumption fell within a range of 89 to 98 percent of food security consumption for 1976 trend values. For the 1961–1976 average the mean value was about 96 percent. Because of space limitations, these results are not reported here.

5. "Excess" should not be taken literally; trend consumption levels alone are not objective yardsticks from a welfare point of view. In fact, some countries' trend consumption levels are well below nutritional requirements.

6. If $r_{xv}$ is positive, then the variability of net export earnings is less than $\sigma_x^2 + \sigma_v^2$. In the extreme case of perfect correlation between $X$ and $V$ ($r_{xv} = 1$), then $\sigma_{nx}^2 = (\sigma_x - \sigma_v)^2$, where $\sigma_{nx}^2 = (\sigma_x - \sigma_v)^2 < \sigma_x^2, \sigma_v^2, \sigma_x, \sigma_v > 0$. Alternatively, if $r_{xv}$ is negative, then $\sigma_{nx}^2$ is greater than $\sigma_x^2 + \sigma_v^2$. In the extreme case of perfect negative correlation between $X$ and $V$, where ($r_{xv} = -1$), then $\sigma_{nx}^2 = (\sigma_x + \sigma_v)^2$.

7. The relationship between $\sigma_{nx}$, $\sigma_x$, $\sigma_v$, and $r_{xv}$ is available upon request from the authors.

8. For a detailed analysis including food imports in the IMF compensatory financing facility, based on actual food imports, see Chapter 14.

9. If instead of covering 100 percent of the excess food import bill, one wants to cover a fraction of the excess imports, a simple linear adjustment may be applied to the values in Table 2.8.

10. But for some LDCs with a low food–self-sufficiency ratio, world price instability is the major concern.

## References

Abbot, P. C. "Developing Countries and International Grain Trade." Ph.D. dissertation, Massachusetts Institute of Technology, 1976.

Burt, O. R., and R. M. Finley. "Statistical Analysis of Identities in Random Variables." *American Journal of Agricultural Economics* (August 1968):734–744.

Huddleston, Barbara, and Panos Konandreas. "Insurance Approach to

50            *Alberto Valdés and Panos Konandreas*

Food Security: Simulation of Benefits for 1970/71-1975/76 and for 1978-82." See Chapter 11, this book.

Reutlinger, Shlomo. *Food Insecurity: Magnitudes and Remedies.* World Bank Working Paper No. 267. Washington, D.C.: World Bank, 1977.

Sarris, Alexander. "The Economics of International Grain Reserves Systems." Ph.D. dissertation, Massachusetts Institute of Technology, 1976.

## ANNEX 1

### Estimated Coefficient of Variation in Food Consumption According to Different Sources and Definitions

In this chapter FAO sources are used for data on production and imports, and USDA sources for data on changes in cereal stocks. Our calculations show that the variability of consumption for a few countries is higher than the variability of production, which is contrary to what one expects. With this fact in mind, a comparison was made using USDA data for imports and ignoring changes in stocks. A sample of this comparison appears in Table 2.9. In this sample, the difference in consumption variability is particularly significant for Egypt; based on USDA import figures (without the influence of changes in stocks) the results show a consumption variability lower than production variability.

Table 2.9  Food Consumption Variability (coefficient of variation)

|  | With changes in stocks | | Ignoring changes in stocks | |
|  | FAO imports | USDA imports | FAO imports | USDA imports |
| --- | --- | --- | --- | --- |
| Egypt | 12.6 | 7.6 | 8.6 | 4.7 |
| Morocco | 19.3 | 15.0 | 20.8 | 17.1 |
| Bangladesh | 7.6 | 4.9 | 7.3 | 4.9 |
| Chile | 14.4 | 14.7 | 12.2 | 13.9 |
| Tanzania | 6.1 | 5.0 | 6.1 | 5.0 |

Sources: Production from FAO and changes in stocks from USDA, imports from FAO or USDA as shown.

Table 2.10    Ratio of Food Imports to Export Earnings[f]/Under Alternative Food Security Rules (1965-76 except as noted)

| | Actual Values | | Rule I | | Rule II | |
|---|---|---|---|---|---|---|
| | Mean (1) | Maximum (2) | Mean (3) | Maximum (4) | Mean (5) | Maximum (6) |
| **Asia** | | | | | | |
| Bangladesh[a]/ | 88.4 | 119.4 | 99.2 | 130.4 | 77.8 | 130.4 |
| India[b]/ | 22.4 | 44.5 | 32.7 | 85.6 | 27.7 | 85.6 |
| Indonesia | 9.4 | 19.9 | 15.5 | 53.6 | 13.7 | 53.6 |
| Korea, Rep. of | 13.5 | 21.4 | 13.6 | 30.8 | 11.8 | 27.2 |
| Philippines | 4.9 | 9.1 | 4.9 | 11.7 | 4.1 | 10.8 |
| Sri Lanka | 27.2 | 49.2 | 27.9 | 48.7 | 26.4 | 46.6 |
| **North Africa/Middle East** | | | | | | |
| Algeria[c]/ | 6.0 | 9.3 | 7.5 | 12.4 | 6.4 | 12.4 |
| Egypt[d]/ | 14.0 | 27.0 | 14.3 | 27.0 | 10.5 | 18.6 |
| Jordan[d]/ | 10.6 | 15.4 | 12.2 | 26.7 | 11.3 | 26.7 |
| Libya[d]/ | 1.4 | 2.3 | 1.5 | 2.3 | 1.3 | 1.9 |
| Morocco[d]/ | 7.0 | 13.4 | 9.2 | 26.1 | 8.1 | 26.1 |
| Syria[d]/ | 5.7 | 18.4 | 9.5 | 47.6 | 9.2 | 47.6 |
| **Sub-Sahara Africa** | | | | | | |
| Ghana[d]/ | 3.7 | 5.4 | 5.1 | 12.0 | 3.5 | 12.0 |
| Nigeria[d]/ | 1.9 | 2.5 | 4.6 | 14.5 | 3.9 | 14.5 |
| Senegal[b]/ | 12.2 | 17.8 | 18.7 | 28.2 | 14.9 | 28.2 |
| Tanzania[d]/ | 5.5 | 22.2 | 7.2 | 23.9 | 5.5 | 23.9 |
| Upper Volta[e]/ | 7.4 | 13.0 | 24.4 | 60.0 | 20.8 | 60.0 |
| Zaire[b]/ | 3.1 | 6.9 | 4.0 | 9.3 | 3.2 | 9.3 |
| **Latin America** | | | | | | |
| Brazil | 3.9 | 8.5 | 6.2 | 14.8 | 4.6 | 10.4 |
| Chile | 5.3 | 13.9 | 6.3 | 15.9 | 4.8 | 11.9 |
| Colombia | 2.8 | 4.9 | 2.8 | 4.1 | 2.2 | 4.1 |
| Guatemala | 2.4 | 3.3 | 3.1 | 5.6 | 2.5 | 5.6 |
| Mexico | 0.4 | 9.3 | 2.5 | 8.1 | 2.3 | 6.7 |
| Peru | 6.6 | 10.5 | 6.6 | 9.7 | 6.2 | 9.7 |

[a]/  Time period of analysis 1973-76.

[b]/  Time period of analysis 1965-75.

[c]/  Time period of analysis 1966-76.

[d]/  Time period of analysis 1967-76.

[e]/  Time period of analysis 1968-75.

[f]/  Merchandise and services.

# 3

# Long-Term Consequences of Technological Change on Crop Yield Stability: The Case for Cereal Grain

*Randolph Barker*
*Eric C. Gabler*
*Donald Winkelmann*

National governments are confronted with the problem of maintaining adequate food supplies to meet domestic demand. The problem has two elements: (1) maintaining an upward trend in food production that will allow per-capita levels of food consumption to be maintained or preferably increased and (2) maintaining adequate year-to-year supplies of food to meet domestic requirements given the high degree of variation around the trend in domestic production caused by weather, pest damage, and other factors. This book is concerned principally with the latter issue of food security and examines strategies to manage annual supply fluctuations. Our chapter focuses on the long-term effect of the introduction of new crop technology on the magnitude of the deviations around the production trend. Does technological change result in greater stability or greater instability in crop yields?

The first section of this chapter summarizes the current views on the projected long-term trend in foodgrain production and demand. The next four sections discuss the factors that influence variability in yield with emphasis on the role of technological change. The chapter concludes with a brief examination of policy issues related to yield stability.

Our discussion deals with rice, wheat, and maize. These cereals are major sources of energy and protein in developing countries and are the dominant commodities being bought and sold in international trade.

## Prospects for Increasing Foodgrain Production

Much has been written recently about the widening gap between projected trends in consumption and production in the developing countries of the world. The projections of IFPRI (1977), the World Bank (1976), and the Asian Development Bank (1978) all estimated a substantial widening in the gap between foodgrain production and demand in the decade ahead. For example, the IFPRI study concludes that the production shortfall of staple food crops in the developing market economies will range from 120–145 million metric tons by 1990. This is more than three times the shortfall of 37 million metric tons that occurred during the relatively good production year of 1975 (IFPRI, 1977, p. 17).

The "gap" analyses described above are not predictions, but indications of the pressures that are likely to occur in the system. Supply will always equal demand. The "shortfall" will be eliminated either through (1) increased imports, (2) more rapid growth in production, (3) a decline in the level of consumption, (4) drawing from stocks, or (5) some combination of the first four. Herdt, Te, and Barker (1977) estimated that input requirements for Asian rice production will keep pace with the growth in demand. They concluded that increased production was possible through not only an intensification in irrigation and the use of modern inputs, but further investment in new technology research. These conclusions probably apply to other cereal grain crops as well. The conclusions suggest that in order to maintain or enhance production growth rates, greater emphasis must be placed on use of modern inputs and the expansion of infrastructure. The development plans of a number of countries are beginning to expand investments in modern agricultural technology and research.

Yields will continue to increase if farmers use even more intensive production strategies: more fertilizer, more careful husbandry, better moisture control, denser stands, and higher yielding varieties. What effect will intensive practices have on the annual variation in yields? Will the practices increase stability or will they be a source of additional variability? This question is examined in the sections that follow.

## Factors Influencing Variability in Yield

Yield variability over time can be divided into trend, cyclical, and year-to-year components. Year-to-year yield variability is measured in this analysis in terms of the deviation of yield from a trend. Methods for determining the trend will be discussed subsequently. The standard deviation of the distance of observations from the trend is calculated and this term is divided by the mean to determine the coefficient of variation. The standard deviation (or standard error of the regression) is a measure of absolute variance and the coefficient of variation is a measure of relative variance. In situations where the relative variance is reduced, the absolute variance may actually increase. Both measures are important. Policymakers planning national food security are concerned with the actual volume of grain that can be imported and stored. But as production and yield trends move upward along with population it is useful to know the relative change in yield variability.

Individual countries, like individual farmers, are apt to be concerned with major downward deviations from trend or years of serious crop loss. However, they may exhibit different risk preference. For example, if there is a trade-off between greater stability and higher yield, some countries may be more inclined than others to accept a greater degree of instability for a higher yield.

### Climatic Change over Time

Many environmental factors influence yield variability. Climatic factors such as temperature and rainfall have both a direct and an indirect (through disease and pests) impact. Technological changes can either enhance or mitigate yield variability.

Long-term climatic changes may have a major impact on the magnitude of yield variability. Abnormal temperatures can affect yield variability. Thompson (1969), for example, argued that the difference between U.S. maize yields in the 1930s and the 1940s was due to the unusually high temperatures of the 1930s. Greater variability in precipitation tends to be associated with a long-term cooling trend. Experts do not agree as to whether we are in a global cooling or warming trend. A recent study conducted jointly by a number of U.S. government agencies (National Defense University, 1978) has worked out five possible scenarios for climatic change to the year 2000. These range from a severe global cooling to a severe global warming change. Each scenario would have a considerably different impact on regional grain production. However, the impact on total world production would be slight with gains in some regions offsetting losses in others.

The potential impact of a large global cooling trend (by the year 2000 the mean northern hemisphere temperature would be about $0.6°C$ cooler than in the early 1970s) would be to increase the annual variability in the length of the growing season in the middle latitudes. It would increase the probability of droughts and severe cold spells in the higher middle latitudes, particularly in Canada. The frequency of droughts in the Sahel region would also increase (National Defense University, 1978, p. 20). This scenario, perhaps the most unfavorable in terms of the effect on yield variability, is given a probability of only one in ten. The experts surveyed generally agree that there will be no radical change in global temperature by the year 2000.[1] There was a slight group bias toward global warming. Yield change due to weather is expected to be much smaller than the change due to technology.

*Technology*

Simply stated, as yields approach zero the range over which they can vary necessarily declines. Yield-increasing technology should then be associated with increasing annual variability, particularly absolute variability.

These conclusions, which appear to be conventional wisdom, have been challenged in recent years. Analysis of U.S. data shows that yields were more stable in the decades of the 1950s and 1960s than in the 1930s and 1940s. During the same periods yields have increased notably and, in the case of maize, dramatically. The U.S. Department of Agriculture made the following statement (Thompson, 1975, p. 535):

> A comprehensive study published by this Department in 1965 evaluating the effects of weather and technology on corn yield for

## Consequences of Technological Change

the years 1929 through 1962 concluded that through the use of better varieties and improved cultivation and fertilizer practices, man has reduced variation in yield in both good and bad weather.

However, others argue that the change in weather accounted for more stable yields. Thompson's (1969) observations of the effects of weather changes with respect to corn yields has already been noted. Later, Thompson (1975) commented that co-efficients showing the effects of weather on wheat yields would have been more heavily influenced by weather had the coefficients been developed during periods of high yields. In a personal communication, Thompson observed that it cannot be concluded that more intensive production practices have reduced yield variation. Rather, it appears that for any given environment, weather-induced variability could increase as production strategies become more intense.

The argument that new technology stabilizes yields is found in literature of the "green revolution." Swaminathan (1972, p. 14) observed the reduced likelihood of the recurrence of crop losses of the magnitude of 1965–1967:

> Besides the advantages gained in infrastructure and programme development, the most significant factors which provide room for optimism that a drop in production of the magnitude witnessed during 1965–67 need not be permitted again even if the rainfall fails to the same or even greater extent, stem from recent scientific advances.

The Conference on Climate Change, Food Production, and Interstate Conflict sponsored by the Rockefeller Foundation (1976, p. 27) concluded:

> To a great extent the human impacts of reduction in crop yields caused by climatic anomalies such as those that occurred in 1972 tend to be most severe in regions that have one or more of these characteristics:
>
> 1. Crops are produced under conditions that are marginal at best in terms of precipitation and/or temperature;
> 2. Modern agricultural technology has not been applied to an optimum extent;

3. Crops are produced for local consumption by a large population;
4. The nation is not in a favorable financial position to compete in world food markets.

These statements are not substantiated with evidence. In contrast, a well-documented study of the impact of technology on wheat production in Turkey by Mann (1977, p. 44) concluded: "It is important to note that while technology has raised yields, the possibility remains of substantial production variation due to weather. The range of this variation in terms of wheat is likely to expand considerably under improved technology."

In an effort to resolve the conflict between the above-cited statements and Mann's findings, we conducted further analyses. Three procedures for examining trend and estimating the variability of the deviation from the trend are: (1) fitting a trend line, (2) taking first differences or alternatively fitting a regression equation with yield lagged one year as the dependent variable, and (3) calculating moving averages. Because of the short length of time series available for most countries, we chose to apply the first two methods. A linear trend was fit to yields for the period 1955–1977 for rice and for a slightly different time duration in wheat in several localities. Rice trends were fit separately for the periods 1955–1967 and 1967–1977. The trend variable used in the latter period was $1/t$ instead of $t$ to reflect the initial rapid increase and gradual leveling off in yield growth. The standard error of the regression and coefficient of variation were calculated for both time periods.

A regression was fit for the two time periods using rice yield as the dependent variable; yield lagged one year as the independent variable. Measures of standard deviation and coefficient of variation using this method compared very favorably with the results based on trends.[2] Estimates of variability based on deviation from trend are presented in Tables 3.1 and 3.2.

The regions chosen for wheat were the Yaqui Valley, Mexico, and the state of Nebraska. Intensive production practices, involving improved varieties and greater use of chemicals, led to higher yields in both areas. Yields more than doubled (from a three-year average of 2.14 tons per hectare in 1956–1958 to

# Consequences of Technological Change

Table 3.1 Linear regression results, yields on years, for two wheat-producing areas

|  |  | $R^2$ | Mean | SDR[1/] | Coefficient of variation |
|---|---|---|---|---|---|
|  |  |  | (t/ha) | (t/ha) | (percent) |
| Nebraska: | 1954-76 | .45 |  |  |  |
|  | 1954-64 |  | 1.38 | 0.31 | 22.5 |
|  | 1966-76 |  | 2.01 | 0.31 | 15.3 |
| Yaqui Valley: | 1956-78 | .87 |  |  |  |
|  | 1956-66 |  | 2.52 | 0.29 | 11.2 |
|  | 1968-78 |  | 4.12 | 0.42 | 10.2 |

1/ $[\Sigma (Di)^2/n-1]^{\frac{1}{2}}$ where Di is the deviation from trend.

Table 3.2 Change in yield variability accompanying increase in yield due to technological change for selected countries in Asia, 1955-67 vs. 1967-77.

|  |  | $R^2$ | Mean | Standard error of regression | Coefficient of variation |
|---|---|---|---|---|---|
|  |  |  | (t/ha) | (t/ha) | (percent) |
| Indonesia: | 1955-67 | 0.69 | 1.74 | 0.03 | 1.7 |
|  | 1967-77 | 0.89 | 2.43 | 0.10 | 4.3 |
| Pakistan: | 1955-67 | 0.70 | 1.35 | 0.05 | 3.6 |
|  | 1967-77 | 0.85 | 2.13 | 0.12 | 5.8 |
| Philippines: | 1955-67 | 0.66 | 1.22 | 0.06 | 4.9 |
|  | 1967-77 | 0.39 | 1.64 | 0.15 | 8.8 |
| Sri Lanka: | 1955-67 | 0.47 | 1.54 | 0.09 | 5.6 |
|  | 1967-77 | 0.85 | 2.19 | 0.11 | 5.0 |

4.42 tons in 1976-1978) in Mexico's irrigated Yaqui Valley and increased by 60 percent (from a three-year average of 1.19 tons per hectare in 1954-1956 to 1.91 tons in 1974-1976) in the Nebraska rain-fed wheat area. In Nebraska, the standard deviation was constant while yields increased. There was a substantial increase in the standard deviation in the Yaqui Valley.

Table 3.2 makes similar comparisons for rice production in

four countries in South and Southeast Asia that have experienced rapid yield increases following the introduction of modern varieties. In all cases the standard error of the regression coefficient increased with the introduction of the new technology. Since the introduction of modern varieties, in some years severe crop loss has resulted from insect damage in Indonesia, Pakistan, and the Philippines, from drought in Sri Lanka and the Philippines, and from floods in Pakistan and the Philippines.

Given the limited available time-series data, only the most cautious conclusions can be drawn. Furthermore, we are considering yield and not total production, one crop and not total food, and in some cases only one small region in a country. But the limited evidence does suggest very strongly that the introduction of new technology results in greater yield variability, particularly in absolute terms. It is useful to examine the effects of the specific technological elements to determine what steps could be taken to enhance yield stability.

Moorman (1975) provided a useful framework for conceptualizing the various types of technological change. He ranked environment or "land" according to its suitability for rice production. Here we generalize his framework to include cereal grains. Land, in his terms, is "a specific area of the earth's surface, the characteristics of which embrace all reasonably stable or predictable cyclical attributes related to atmosphere, soil, topography, and hydrology, the plant and animal population, and the results of human activity." Most of Class I land in Figure 3.1 is already cultivated with highly productive cereal grains including new semidwarf varieties of rice and wheat. Class II land is suitable for crop production, but with increasing limitations. The difference between Subclass II-A and II-B is that the productivity in II-B is too low to yield a profitable return to purchased inputs.

Technological change results in the improvement from Class II-B to Class II-A or I where it becomes profitable to use recurrent inputs such as fertilizer and chemicals. Moorman identified basic plant and land amelioration as the means of achieving such a transfer. Land amelioration can be achieved through factors that improve soil, moisture, or temperature conditions: for example, soil conservation measures, irrigation and drainage,

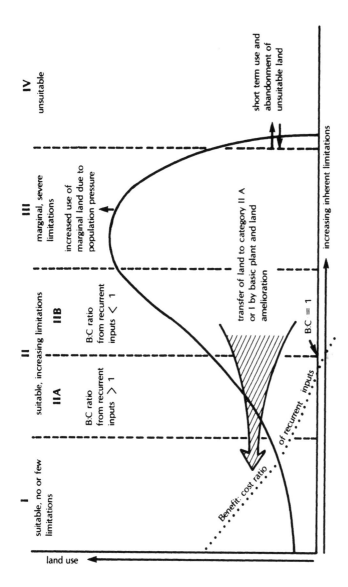

Figure 3.1 Moorman's model of the relation of land in use for specific agricultural purpose and land quality

and the construction of vinyl seedbeds. Plant amelioration, carried on by the breeders, can produce plants suited to existing on II-B land so that such land is shifted to II-A. Land classes (environments) can differ by season. The development of new rice varieties in many cases resulted in a shift from II-B to II-A land in the dry season, but not in the wet.

The transition from II-B to II-A or I land implies a higher level of technology inputs and higher yields, but not necessarily greater stability in yields. For example, the development of irrigation facilities would reduce crop losses due to moisture stress, but the accompanying intensification of cropping practices may result in greater crop loss due to insects and diseases. Further, improvements in rice and wheat varieties have not only raised yields, but have allowed rice and wheat to move into formerly marginal areas. This movement is very evident in South Asia and China.

Using the above framework, we have singled out in the sections that follow three components of technology: (1) water control, (2) agronomic practices including the application of recurrent inputs, and (3) plant breeding. What are the potentially stabilizing and destabilizing characteristics of these components?

## Water Control

There are several classes of infrastructure that affect the stability of cereal grain yields. The most obvious is water control, including both irrigation and drainage. Other types of infrastructure include roads, electrical power, and grain storage facilities. This section focuses on irrigation.

The world's irrigated area will substantially increase over the next decade. Massive projects are now scheduled in China, India, and Pakistan. Smaller projects will be implemented throughout Asia and in other regions where the expansion of cultivated land area is very costly. Over the next two decades it is estimated that more than half of the expected growth in rice production in South and Southeast Asia will be due to the application of technology in the irrigated area (see Barker and Herdt, 1978). For some countries (e.g., Indonesia, Pakistan, the Philippines,

# Consequences of Technological Change 63

and Sri Lanka) this figure will exceed 75 percent.

What impact does irrigation have upon the variability in crop yields? Although irrigation may potentially reduce moisture stress, it is frequently associated with an intensification of crop production and input use that is destabilizing. Thus, one cannot say a priori that irrigation development results in greater yield stability. In fact, we have already seen in Table 3.1 that in the past decade wheat yields have been higher but more variable in the irrigated Yaqui Valley of Mexico than in rain-fed Nebraska.

Further analysis was conducted to determine the impact of irrigation on rice-yield variability. A linear trend was fit to time-series data for: (1) selected countries in Asia from 1955/56 to 1976/77, (2) selected states in India from 1960/61 to 1975/76, and (3) rain-fed and irrigated yields in the Philippines from 1960/61 to 1974/75. The mean, the standard error of the regression, and the coefficient of variation were calculated and data for countries and states were ranked according to the percent of the rice area irrigated (Table 3.3).

Among 10 countries analyzed, there was a tendency for the percent area in modern varieties, yield, standard error, and coefficient of variation to increase with a rise in the percentage of irrigated rice area. The percentage of area in modern varieties and yield also increased with irrigation in the Indian states, but the standard error showed no trend and the coefficient of variation declined. Essentially the same pattern prevailed for irrigated rice in the Philippines.

It is interesting to compare the states of Bihar and Tamil Nadu in India. Bihar, in eastern India, has one of the most difficult environments for rice production and the high variability of rice yields reflects the frequency of severe floods and droughts. Most of the rice land in the south Indian state of Tamil Nadu is irrigated. The average yield is more than twice as high as in Bihar, but the absolute variability in yield is essentially the same.

The results in Tables 3.1 and 3.3 indicate that expansion of irrigation does not result in greater yield stability. One reason may be that irrigation development in South and Southeast Asia does not permit substantial control of water. Most of the irrigated area is still subject to flooding, droughts, and salinity.

## Table 3.3 Rice yield variability for selected locations in Asia ranked according to the percent area in irrigation

| | Percent area irrigated 1973-75 | Percent area in modern varieties 1974-75 | $R^2$ | Mean | Standard Error | Coefficient of Variation |
|---|---|---|---|---|---|---|
| | | | | (t/ha) | (t/ha) | (percent) |
| **Selected Countries in Asia (1955-56/1976-77)** | | | | | | |
| Bangladesh | 11 | 15 | 0.56 | 1.64 | 0.11 | 6.4 |
| Burma | 16 | 6 | 0.46 | 1.60 | 0.11 | 7.0 |
| Nepal | 17 | 18 | 0.52 | 1.88 | 0.10 | 5.5 |
| Thailand | 24 | 7 | 0.16 | 1.80 | 0.13 | 7.2 |
| India [a/] | 39 | 28 | 0.61 | 1.55 | 0.11 | 7.0 |
| Indonesia [a/] | 39 | 40 | 0.99 | 2.07 | 0.04 | 1.9 |
| Philippines [a/] | 40 | 62 | 0.98 | 1.40 | 0.10 | 7.1 |
| Sri Lanka [a/] | 50 | 67 | 0.95 | 1.88 | 0.09 | 5.0 |
| Malaysia [a/] | 63 | 37 | 0.85 | 2.57 | 0.13 | 5.0 |
| Pakistan [a/] | 100 | 39 | 0.87 | 1.75 | 0.06 | 3.5 |
| **Selected States in India (1960-61/1975-76)** | | | | | | |
| Uttar Pradesh | 16 | 30 | 0.25 | 1.13 | 0.16 | 13.8 |
| Bihar | 24 | 12 | 0.03 | 1.26 | 0.22 | 17.3 |
| Orissa | 26 | 7 | 0.25 | 1.13 | 0.16 | 14.4 |
| West Bengal | 26 | 17 | 0.15 | 1.74 | 0.14 | 7.9 |
| Tamil Nadu | 87 | 69 | 0.68 | 2.56 | 0.22 | 8.5 |
| Andhra Pradesh | 100 | 77 | 0.65 | 2.10 | 0.14 | 6.5 |
| **Rainfed and Irrigated Area in the Philippines (1960-61/1974-75)** | | | | | | |
| Rainfed rice | 0 | 50 | 0.41 | 1.27 | 0.11 | 9.3 |
| Irrigated rice | 100 | 79 | 0.78 | 1.78 | 0.11 | 6.0 |

a/ In these countries the following function was fit to account for the non-linear trend due to the rapid introduction of new technology:

$$Y = a + bT + cV - dTV$$

where: Y = national yield
T = straight line trend, T = 1 in 1955-56, 2 in 1956-57, etc.
V = 1 until the year prior to the introduction of modern varieties (year 5). Thereafter, V = 1/T - S - 1 (i.e. if modern varieties are introduced in 1967, 1966 = 1, 1967 - 1/2, 1968 - 1/3, etc.).
TV = interaction term
a,b,c,d = constants

By comparison with the straight line trend this function increases the $R^2$ and lowers the variability.

It might be hypothesized that with a more intensive development of infrastructure, yields would be less variable. In the case of Asian rice, the most highly developed infrastructure and the highest yields are found in East Asia. The likelihood of crop damage due to either flood or drought has been virtually eliminated. Roads, rural electricity, and grain storage facilities link the farmer more closely with the consumer. This has encouraged

# Consequences of Technological Change

65

Table 3.4  Yield variability from trend for three countries in East Asia, 1955-56 to 1976-77[a]

|  | Percent area irrigated 1973-75 | $R^2$ | Mean | Standard error | Coefficient of variation |
|---|---|---|---|---|---|
|  |  |  | (t/ha) | (t/ha) | (percent) |
| Japan | 96 | 0.78 | 5.12 | 0.23 | 4.6 |
| S. Korea | 92 | 0.82 | 4.40 | 0.35 | 7.9 |
| Taiwan | - | 0.86 | 3.90 | 0.20 | 5.1 |

[a] Based on exponential instead of linear trend.

the use of more intensive production practices. One needs to be cautious in comparing yield variability in East Asia with that in South and Southeast Asia. The former region lies almost entirely in the temperate zone where temperature is the main source of yield variability, whereas the latter regions lie in the tropics where moisture and pests are the main sources of yield variability. Nevertheless, it is interesting to observe that the standard error of the regression for the East Asian countries (Table 3.4) is higher than that for the South and Southeast Asian countries (Table 3.3) while the coefficient of variation falls in about the same range for both. This again suggests that higher yields and more intensive use of modern technology increases the absolute yield variability. However, there is less concern over the variability in crop production in East Asia as these countries are relatively well-equipped with infrastructure to deal with food security problems.

## Agronomic Practices

A wide range of agronomic practices falls under the heading of new technology and can have either a stabilizing or destabilizing effect on yields. The effect depends upon the combination of practices used at any one location at a given time. In general, those practices that demand more of the environment will tend to make yields less stable and those practices that add to the environment's capacity to support a crop will add to stability. However, the issue is more complex. Initially stabilizing activities may encourage subsequent practices that introduce instability.[3] The recent introduction of modern varieties in developing nations has resulted in an increased use of fertilizer and modern inputs, and it is therefore important to examine the effect of all these practices on yield stability.

A note of caution is warranted concerning the use of the standard deviation to measure yield variability. Day (1965) and Roumasset (see Barker, Cordova, and Roumasset, 1976), using experiment station data, demonstrated that field-crop yield distributions are generally nonnormal and nonlognormal. The degree of skewness and kurtosis depends on the specific crop and the amount of fertilizer applied. However, there seems to be a tendency for the skewness to be more positive (median yield below mean yield) at low levels of fertilizer input and more negative (median yield above mean yield) at high levels of input. Thus, the increase in standard deviation due to the higher level of input may overstate the increase in risk involved. In this section we have included in our analysis the standard skewness coefficient, $\sqrt{\beta} = \mu_3/\mu_2^{3/2}$ where $\mu_2$ and $\mu_3$ are the second and third population moments about the mean.

In the Puebla Project in Mexico, farmers were advised that to obtain higher yields they should increase the number of plants per hectare (from roughly 30,000 to 50,000) and at the same time increase the application of fertilizer (from 30 kg N/ha to 120 kg N/ha and from essentially no $P_2O_5$ to 40 kg $P_2O_5$/ha). Data from experiments conducted in farmers' fields between 1971 and 1974 show that this recommendation would increase the absolute variability in yields even though the coefficient of variation is lowered (Table 3.5). But as the yield level increases with the application of technology, our results confirm the earlier findings of Day and Roumasset (1965 and 1976, respectively) that the skewness changes from positive to negative (Figures 3.2 and 3.3). Not only are yields higher, but the probability of being below the average yield is much lower. This could place the farmer in a more favorable risk situation, depending on costs. National food security models based on mean yields would tend to overestimate predicted yields for countries or regions with low use of modern technology and

Table 3.5 Corn yield and variability of yield at high and low input levels; 97 and 78 experimental observations in farmers' fields, Plan Puebla, 1971-74.

| Input land | N | P | Density | Mean yield | Standard deviation | Coefficient of variation | Skewness |
|---|---|---|---|---|---|---|---|
| | (kg/ha) | (kg/ha) | (plants/ha) | (t/ha) | (t/ha) | (percent) | $\sqrt{b_1}$ |
| Low | 0-50 | 0-25 | 20-35,000 | 1.68 | .92 | 54.8 | .76 |
| High | 90-150 | 30-70 | 40-55,000 | 3.17 | 1.17 | 36.9 | -.71 |

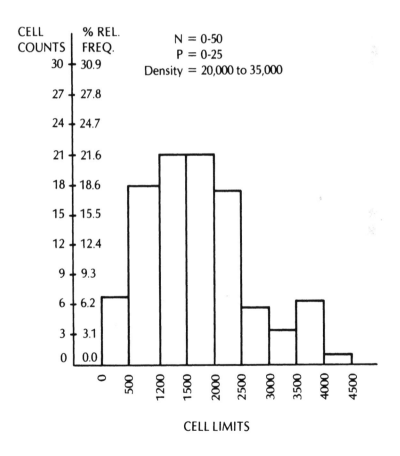

**Figure 3.2** Distribution of yields at low level of technology, 97 experimental observations on farmers' fields, Plan Puebla, 1971-74

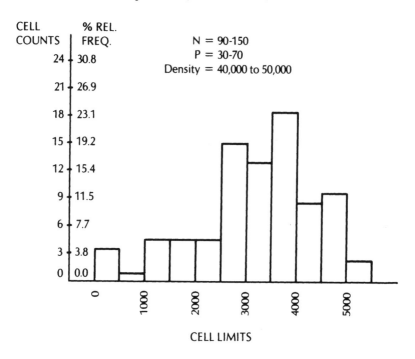

Figure 3.3  Distribution of yields at high level of technology, 78 experimental observations on farmers' fields, Plan Puebla, 1971-74

underestimate predicted yields for the very advanced regions.

According to the rice data from a survey of villages conducted in 1971-1972 (IRRI, 1975), out of a total of 36 villages, 29 were irrigated and grew two crops of rice (see Table 3.6). There was considerable variability among villages in the quality of irrigation. The 58 total observations were classified into "low" and "high" based on yield level, standard deviation, coefficient of variation, and skewness computed for each of the village observations and averaged for the two groups. The corresponding average fertilizer (NPK) input was also calculated.

The results are similar to those found for corn at Plan Puebla in Mexico. The standard deviation increased with high yields and input levels but the coefficient of variation declined. The degree of skewness is highly variable among villages. Those villages with low yield and low levels of fertilizer input show a strong positive skewness in yield distribution and those vil-

# Consequences of Technological Change

Table 3.6 Rice yield and variability of yield at high and low yield levels and for wet and dry season observations, survey data average of 29 Asian villages, 1971-72

|  | NPK | Mean Yield | Standard deviation | Coefficient of variation | Skewness |
|---|---|---|---|---|---|
|  | (kg/ha) | (t/ha) | (t/ha) | (percent) | $\sqrt{b_1}$ |
|  |  |  | Yield level[a] |  |  |
| Low | 45 | 2.14 | 0.99 | 46.3 | 0.95 |
| High | 148 | 4.89 | 1.33 | 27.2 | 0.22 |
|  |  |  | Season |  |  |
| Wet | 87 | 3.36 | 1.13 | 35.7 | 0.79 |
| Dry | 111 | 3.67 | 1.19 | 32.4 | 0.38 |

a/ 58 observations for wet and dry season were divided at the median based on yield.

lages with high yield and high levels of fertilizer input have an almost normal yield distribution. The pattern of change is consistent with previous findings. In the high technology villages, it is reasonable to expect that the level of technology is not as high as that under experimental conditions. On average, skewness remains slightly positive, although 10 out of 29 observations showed negative skewness.

The relative stability of yields between wet and dry seasons was also examined. The Indian government is now emphasizing in its development plans the expansion of the dry-season cropped area, not only to raise production but also ostensibly to increase yield stability. Our results suggest that this strategy will not increase yield stability,[4] although it could improve annual stability of food supplies.

The difference in risk preference among farmers and among countries should be emphasized. If the familiar E-V frontier is used to conceptualize the trade-off between high yield and low variance, countries will almost certainly prefer to operate at different points on the frontier. The most important considerations, of course, are the frequency and magnitude of severe crop losses.

Higher yield and fertilizer input levels enhance the potential loss due to insect and disease damage. This problem seems to be particularly acute in the tropics and monoculture areas. Rice farmers considered diseases, insects, and other pests to be the most important constraints to higher yield (IRRI, 1975, p. 23). Several serious incidents of loss due to insect and disease damage have followed the introduction of modern varieties. For example, in Central Luzon, the Philippines, yields in 1971–1972 declined by about 30 percent from the previous two-year average due principally to tungro virus damage. In Indonesia rice crop loss due to the brown planthopper in 1976 was estimated to exceed 1 million metric tons or 4 percent of the total crop.

Use of insecticides has increased rapidly with the introduction of modern varieties, but for rice there is little evidence to suggest that the farmers' levels and methods of application have been very effective. The higher recommended level of insecticides may be more effective in controlling insects, but the additional costs frequently outweigh the additional benefits (IRRI, 1977, p. 78). Benefit-cost ratios for chemical control of diseases tend to be even less favorable. Attempts to reduce yield variability due to insects and diseases will depend fairly heavily on the ability of plant breeders to develop and disseminate resistant varieties.[5]

## Plant Breeding

Plant breeders have long been concerned with problems of yield stability. Breeding rust resistance was recognized as essential for increasing wheat yields in the Rockefeller Foundation's first endeavor in Mexico in the 1940s. Considerable research has been conducted on downy mildew in corn and on blast disease in rice. Recently, interest has focused on fertilizer-responsive wheat and rice varieties. For rice especially, new varieties create new problems of crop protection. Increased input of fertilizer and more vigorous plant growth seem to have increased the incidence of severe insect and disease attack. Yield stability in the less favorable environments where the new varieties have made little headway is also a problem. For example,

# Consequences of Technological Change

in a recent survey of the predominantly rain-fed rice-growing areas of eastern India, a joint Indian Council of Agricultural Research–IRRI team recommended as follows (Swaminathan, 1977, p. 12):

> Since the performance and profit of existing high-yielding varieties with costly inputs are uncertain, scientists should develop a technology which combines good yield with reliability and security of profit to farmers. In other words, we need a high yielding and high stability technology, if small and marginal farmers are to be helped to take such a technology.

Developing varieties with greater yield stability involves two steps. The first step is to identify and incorporate genes into the plant that will result in greater resistance to insects and diseases or tolerance to adverse environments. The second step is to test the relative stability of the new lines and varieties.

Evenson et al. (1978, p. 4) observed that there is considerable confusion in the recent literature over the concepts of stability and adaptability. Stability, as we have used it in this chapter, refers to the performance of a genotype with respect to changing environmental factors over time within a given location. Adaptability refers to the performance of a genotype with respect to changing environmental factors across locations. It has been erroneously presumed that adaptability and stability are highly correlated. But Evenson et al. (1978, pp. 12–17) presented evidence to suggest that this might not be the case. This evidence is important for crop improvement strategies. The breeder can achieve greater crop yield stability usually by sacrificing other plant qualities. (Crop yield stability is a result of genetic characteristics.) Thus, in breeding for stability it becomes important to specify the environment and to identify the trade-offs between stability and other traits in order to establish priorities in breeding objectives. In the remainder of this section we will describe some of the lines of investigation being explored that offer promise for improving yield stability in the coming decade.

Three diseases are important to maize in various parts of the developing world: streak virus in Africa, downy mildew in

Southeast Asia, and stunt in tropical South America. Progress is being made in developing resistant varieties for these areas. Breeding strategies are also aimed at developing varieties with a greater capacity to accommodate moisture stress. The efforts involve several national and some international programs.

Wheat has a persistent problem with rusts as mutating pathogens ensure that first one variety and then another falls to this set of diseases. Strategies are being followed to gain an advantage over the pathogens. One strategy follows classical breeding principles and seeks to develop greater disease resistance by incorporating various sources of resistance. Multilocation testing is used to verify the degree of resistance.

New research avenues offer great promise of reducing the impact of the rusts. The first, an old idea recently reintroduced, is the development of multilines. Each multiline variety combines several lines of wheat that have many virtually identical characteristics—e.g., maturity, height, grain type—but have different sources of resistance to rust. It is unlikely that all of the isogenic lines will succumb to any given set of mutant pathogens. Moreover, the different lines tend to buffer one another against the spread of rust's spores. One investigation shows that with as many as one line in three susceptible to a particular family of rusts, yield damage will be slight. The resistant lines buffer the susceptible ones from the encroachment of the disease. Several countries are pursuing the multiline idea. India's wheat improvement program announced the release of three such varieties in 1978.

"Slow rusting" is another approach to the problem of disease in small grain. Here, varieties are developed that succumb to rust so slowly that little damage is done to the plant's grain production capacity. This contrasts with the classical strategy of seeking complete resistance.

Spring-wheat scientists (and most of the developing world's wheat is spring wheat) seek varieties that show greater capacity to accommodate moisture stress. The early results of crossing spring wheats with winter wheats have been promising. Some of these crosses display remarkable hardiness, indicating that this breeding strategy could be exploited for many characteristics not usually found in spring wheat.

## Consequences of Technological Change

Recently, tungro virus has been a serious problem in rice production. It is transmitted by the green leafhopper and brown planthopper. Efforts to control the virus through plant breeding increased after a serious outbreak in the Philippines. Varieties were developed with resistance to both the insects and disease and considerable success has been achieved in forecasting tungro virus outbreaks.

A 1973 issue of *The IRRI Reporter* announced that "IR-26 is resistant to brown planthopper" (IRRI, 1973). Shortly thereafter, it was discovered that the brown planthopper had developed several biotypes. These biotypes vary not only in their ability to attack different varieties, but in their susceptibility to control by pesticides.

Control methods other than host plant resistance are now being sought, including the use of the pesticides and biological control. A new breeding strategy might include the development of moderately resistant varieties or varieties similar to the multilines. The objective would not be the elimination of the brown planthopper but control against epidemic outbreaks. For the present, varieties are being developed with resistance to the various biotypes of brown planthopper.

A new rice disease, ragged stunt, was found in 1977 in both Indonesia and the Philippines and subsequently in several other areas. Breeding for insect and disease resistance is an important "maintenance" research cost essential for maintaining yield potential and stability. There is little likelihood that any significant increase in stability will be accomplished through breeding, although we have yet to witness the impact of multiline breeding.

Rice breeding for adverse environmental conditions includes developing varieties that are drought resistant, flood tolerant, tolerant to adverse soil conditions, and tolerant to low temperatures. The research involves making crosses to incorporate these characteristics with other desirable traits such as high yield potential. The development of varieties with abbreviated growth cycles (90 to 100 days from transplanting to harvest) allows the rice variety in many areas to escape drought. There is evidence that this can lead to a significant increase in yields in the rainfed rice-growing areas (Barker and Herdt, 1978). Research of this nature will increase the stability of rice production in those areas now regarded as marginal. However, the consequence may be to permit greater crop intensification on existing land or to allow the spread of the rice crops to areas now thought to be submarginal, resulting in lower yields. Therefore, it is difficult to predict the effect of such research on yield stability.

The final decision on the desirable level of uncertainty or yield stability rests with the farmer. Much has been written to suggest that small and marginal farmers in the developing countries are averse to risks, but the evidence on this point is not conclusive. For example, the government of India has been attempting, without visible success, to convince farmers in eastern India to switch from rice to millet in the drought-prone upland areas. For any given crop there must be some limit to the degree of instability that farmers in a given location are willing to tolerate. This probably is higher for preferred staples such as rice, wheat, and corn than for other crops.

## Policy Implications

Economists frequently measure the impact of various policies on the adoption of new technology and growth in food production. However, the understanding of the impact of technological change on yield variability, and hence which policies might lead to greater yield stability, is much less clear. It is almost implicitly assumed that the adoption of modern technology leads to greater yield stability. We have found no evidence to support this contention. On the contrary, our results show a tendency for the absolute variability to increase even though relative variability may in some cases remain unchanged or even decline. These results confirm the earlier findings of Mann (1977) for wheat in Turkey.

The belief that variability will decline is perhaps related to the fact that several components of the modern technology are ostensibly yield-stabilizing. For example, plant- and land-ameliorating activities, including breeding for insect and disease resistance and tolerance to adverse environments, and irrigation expansion, taken independently, should be yield-stabilizing. But these changes have the effect of raising the marginal pro-

*Consequences of Technological Change* 75

ductivity of recurrent inputs such as fertilizer. Hence, stabilizing technology is almost invariably accompanied by destabilizing technology and, on balance, absolute variability in yield tends to increase.

However, there is consistent evidence to show that as new technology is introduced, the skewness in yield distribution shifts from being strongly positive to negative, perhaps creating a more favorable risk environment. It would be useful to improve our understanding of the nature of the yield distribution around the trend. Does the distribution change with an increase in the level of technology, and if so, how? It almost goes without saying that a country would accept instability on the high side if it didn't have to worry about instability on the low. The use of modern inputs to raise yield levels will intensify in the developing countries in the years ahead. The fact that yield variability is likely to increase should not act as a deterrent to the use of modern inputs, but does suggest the need for precautionary measures to insure food security. In order to minimize the inherent instability associated with new technology, it will be necessary to increase the investment in maintenance research. Increased efforts to develop insect- and disease-resistant varieties are needed to realize the yield potential of the new varieties. Because of the sharply rising costs of irrigation development, it also will be useful to increase research designed to develop varieties tolerant to moisture stress.

The development of transportation, storage facilities, and buffer stocks can reduce the problems resulting from yield variability. These are the subjects of other chapters in this book. However, it is important to recognize that the introduction of new technology in the absence of appropriate policies and programs can aggravate the food security problem. The recent fertilizer crisis is an excellent example. In anticipation of a severe shortage, many developing countries imported large quantities of fertilizer in 1974, driving fertilizer prices to unrealistically high levels. The direct cost to these governments for fertilizer imports as well as the indirect cost in terms of higher fertilizer prices and lower farm production has been very substantial.[6]

In summary, we believe that crop losses of the magnitude

# 76                Randolph Barker, Eric C. Gabler, and Donald Winkelmann

experienced during the unfavorable weather years of 1965 and 1972 can recur. In fact, according to some weather experts, increased sunspot activity will destabilize the weather in the decade ahead. Advances in the use of modern technology notwithstanding, annual variability in grain yields could increase, and planning for food security could be even more difficult in the future than it has been in the past.

## Notes

We are indebted to D. Byerlee and B. F. Stanton for criticism of an earlier draft and to coparticipants in the Conference for their constructive comments.

1. It should be pointed out that in this investigation, the experience of the panel of experts (nearly all of whom are from the Western world) with the impact of climatic change on crop production, trade, and prices in developing countries appears to be extremely limited.

2. Results available from the authors upon request.

3. In the Pacific Northwest of the United States in the early 1940s, a new method of handling soil was introduced. The result was a notable increase in wheat yields and an initial reduction in variability. But this made it possible to increase the level of fertilizer and other modern inputs.

4. D. Gale Johnson called to our attention the fact that this statement is predicated on the assumption that wet and dry season yields are correlated. In years of heavy flood, low wet-season yields are offset by higher than normal dry-season yields. But the most serious cause of yield loss is drought and under these circumstances wet and dry season yields are highly correlated.

5. N. Borlaug emphasized the complexity of the problem of integrated pest management, citing some cases where chemical control has been highly effective. Monoculture rice presents one of the most difficult situations with respect to insect and disease control.

6. In this same context, D. A. Khan called to our attention the adverse effect on yields of the inadequate fertilizer procurement and distribution program in Pakistan.

## References

Asian Development Bank. *Rural Asia Challenge and Opportunity.* New York: Praeger, 1978.

## Consequences of Technological Change

Barker, R., V. Cordova, and J. Roumasett. "The Economic Analysis of Experimental Results in Nitrogen Response to Rice." *Farm Management Notes for Asia and the Far East* (July 1976):28–41.

Barker, R., and R. W. Herdt. "Rainfed Lowland Rice as a Research Priority." Paper prepared for the International Rice Research Conference, IRRI, Los Baños, Philippines, April 17–21, 1978.

Day, R. H. "Probability Distributions of Field Crop Yields." *Journal of Farm Economics* 47, no. 3 (August 1965):713–741.

Evenson, R. E., J. C. O'Toole, R. W. Herdt, W. R. Coffman, and H. E. Kaufmann. "Risk and Uncertainty as Factors in Crop Improvement Research." *IRRI Research Paper Series*, no. 15 (March 1978).

Hadler, S. "Developing Country Food Grain Projections for 1985." International Bank of Reconstruction and Development, Bank Staff Working Paper No. 247. Washington, D.C., November 1976.

Herdt, R. W., and R. Barker. "Multi-Site Tests, Environments, and Breeding Strategies for New Rice Technology." *IRRI Research Paper Series*, no. 7 (March 1977).

Herdt, R. W., A. Te, and R. Barker. "Prospects for Asian Rice Production." *Food Research Institute Studies* 16, no. 3 (1977).

International Food Policy Research Institute (IFPRI). *Food Needs of Developing Countries*. Research Report No. 3. Washington, D.C., December 1977.

International Rice Research Institute (IRRI). "IR-26 Is Resistant to Brown Planthopper." *The IRRI Reporter*, no. 4 (1973):1–2.

_____. *Changes in Rice Farming in Selected Areas of Asia*. Los Baños, Philippines, 1975.

_____. *Research Highlights for 1976*. Los Baños, Philippines, 1977.

Mann, Charles K. "The Impact of Technology on Wheat Production in Turkey." *Studies in Development* 14 (1977):30–47.

Moorman, F. R. "Agricultural Land Utilization and Land Quality." Unpublished mimeo. International Institute of Tropical Agriculture, Ibadan, Nigeria, 1975.

National Defense University. *Climate Change to the Year 2000*. Washington, D.C.: Fort Lesly J. McNair, February 1978.

The Rockefeller Foundation. "Climate Change, Food Production, and Interstate Conflict; A Bellagis Conference, 1975." New York, February 1976.

Swaminathan, M. S. "Can We Face Widespread Drought Again Without Food Imports." Dr. Rajendro Prasad Memorial Lecture, Indian Society of Agricultural Statistics, March 26, 1972.

_____. "Indian Agriculture at the Crossroads." Presidential address, Indian Society of Agricultural Economics, December 27, 1977.

Thompson, L. M. "Weather and Technology in the Production of Corn in the U.S. Corn Belt." *Agronomy Journal* 61 (May–June 1969):453–456.

___. "Weather Variability, Climatic Change, and Grain Production." *Science* 188 (May 9, 1975):535–541.

# 4
# Security of Rice Supplies in the ASEAN Region

*Ammar Siamwalla*

The five countries composing the Association for Southeast Asian Nations (ASEAN)—Indonesia, Malaysia, the Philippines, Singapore, and Thailand—are dependent on rice as their staple food. Although possibilities for substitution do exist to some degree,[1] rice is the central item in consumption,[2] and "food security" has tended to be thought of in terms of rice supply security in these countries. In this chapter, accordingly, rice supply security will be regarded as synonymous with food security. This assumption accords well with the observed behavior of the ASEAN countries' governments, whose fixation on rice is well known.

Table 4.1 presents some data on the role of international trade in rice in the domestic economies of these countries. As a factor affecting total domestic supply of rice, it is significant only in Malaysia and Thailand; as a factor affecting foreign exchange, it is significant only in Thailand. This marginality of rice trade is characteristic of Asia as a whole. Of a total world production in 1975 of some 235 million tons (milled rice), 95 percent of which grew in Asia, only 7 to 8 million tons, or just over 3 percent, was involved in international trade. If anything, the figures of Table 4.1 tend to show a somewhat heavier dependence on foreign trade than is the norm for the rest of Asia.

Further examination into the peculiarities of the rice trade reveals the operation of a vicious circle that keeps the traded volume low. Most governments argue that they cannot rely on international trade as a secure source of rice. Because it is a very thin market to begin with, recourse to it at times of shortage has a tendency to drive prices up very sharply. Governments therefore have a tendency to adopt policies that lessen their countries' dependence on foreign trade—in other words, they aim for "self-sufficiency." These policies keep traded volumes low, the market thin, and prices unstable, thus providing further justification for less reliance on imports—and so the vicious circle continues.

Table 4.2 provides estimates of production and trade in rice. A steady decline in the proportion of exports to production starting around the early 1960s may be observed. Even more dramatic is the comparison with the traded volume in the prewar period, when the absolute value of rice traded was not much different from that during the postwar period.

Apart from the antitrade bias of the policies alluded to above, it must be recognized that the trend of technology in the period since 1965 has shown a similar bias. If one looks at the traditional rice exporters in Asia, their comparative advantage was based on the ready supply of land provided by the vast deltaic plains of Southeast Asia. These areas have relatively poor water control compared to the insular countries of Southeast Asia whose topography allows the development of smaller projects and a higher degree of water control with less capital investment (Trung, 1978). The modern technology associated with high-yielding varieties has been used most extensively in the latter group of countries, as can be seen from Table 4.3.

The antitrade thrust of government policies is supported by a ready availability of technology. The desire for self-sufficiency is to be achieved through production drives such as the Bimas Program in Indonesia or the Masagana 99 Program in the Philippines. These drives rely on the ready availability of technology for their success. Thus, policy and technology aid each other in causing the decline of the trade ratio observed in Table 4.2.[3]

Technology and policy have played important roles in moving many importing countries, notably Malaysia and the Philippines, closer to self-sufficiency and have also considerably enhanced production in Indonesia. These are developments on the "trend" line, as it were. To cope with fluctuations, the main

Table 4.1 Importance of Rice in the International Trade of Indonesia,
Malaysia, Philippines and Thailand

|  | 1970-72 | 1973-75 |
|---|---|---|
| A. Rice imports or exports as percent of domestic production (tonnage basis) | | |
| Indonesia (imports) | 5.5 | 7.6 |
| Malaysia (imports) | 24.1 | 22.6 |
| Philippines (imports) | 8.4 | 5.5 |
| Thailand (exports) | 18.2 | 9.6 |
| B. Value of rice imports or exports as percent of total value of merchandise imports or exports | | |
| Indonesia (imports) | 3.0 | 7.2 |
| Malaysia (imports) | 2.1 | 2.9 |
| Philippines (imports) | 1.7 | 1.5 |
| Thailand (exports) | 18.0 | 14.8 |

Source: Part A - IRRI, World Rice Statistics, 1978.

Part B - United Nations, Yearbook of International Trade Statistics.

Table 4.2 World Rice Production and World Rice Trade (milled rice basis)

|  | Production | Trade (total exports) | Percent export to production |
|---|---|---|---|
|  | (million metric tons) | | |
| 1936-1940 | 109.3[a] | 5.7[b] | 5.2 |
| 1950-1954 | 122.0 | 4.7 | 3.9 |
| 1955-1959 | 147.3 | 6.1 | 4.1 |
| 1960-1964 | 163.5 | 6.8 | 4.2 |
| 1965-1969 | 184.2 | 6.7 | 3.7 |
| 1970-1974 | 208.6 | 7.3 | 3.5 |

Sources: 1936-1940: Wickizer and Bennett (1941), for production in all countries excluding China (see note below). For China, the estimate of 80 million tons paddy for 1933 (see Liu and Yeh, 1965) was taken. This was probably on the high side.
After 1950: IRRI, 1978. Conversion from paddy to milled rice basis is based on a "world" milling rate of 0.66.

a/ 12 countries in Asia only (Burma, French Indochina, Thailand, Korea, Taiwan, Japan, India, Malaya, Ceylon, Java and Madura, the Philippines and China). These countries produced about 91 percent of world production in 1950.

b/ Three countries only (Burma, French Indochina, and Thailand). Trade between Japan and its colonies (Korea and Taiwan) is specifically excluded, because it does not cross political boundaries.

# 82
*Ammar Siamwalla*

Table 4.3 Proportion of Total Rice Area Planted to Modern Varieties, Southeast Asia, 1974-75

| | |
|---|---|
| Importers | |
| Indonesia | 40.3 |
| Laos | 7.3 |
| Malaysia (peninsular only) | 37.5 |
| Philippines | 61.5 |
| Traditional exporters | |
| Burma | 6.4 |
| Thailand | 6.6 |

Source: IRRI, 1978.

substitution role for trade is not so much domestic production as stockholding. Trade still occupies a strategic role in domestic stabilization for many countries, as fluctuations in trade volumes witness (Table 4.4). This is particularly true for Indonesia and Thailand, two major actors in international rice trade. Domestic policies that affect the choice between relying on trade and relying on stock variations have evolved over a long period and, although constantly in transition, merit our attention.

## The Evolution of Rice Policies as They Affect the Choice Between Relying on Trade or on Stocks

Trade and buffer stocks are merely the instruments of overall rice policies. Thus, to understand how these instruments are deployed we must first examine the objectives of overall policy. These objectives are by no means engraved in stone and pursued consistently through the years. It is more fruitful to regard them as evolving gradually over time, in response to both external events and their own internal logic.

Among the four countries that are the subject matter of this chapter (Singapore being excluded), Malaysia is unique in that it has had a rather consistent rice policy ever since it became

*Rice Supplies in the ASEAN Region*  83

Table 4.4 Imports and Exports of Rice in ASEAN Countries[a]

| | Indonesia (imports) | Malaysia and Singapore (imports) | Philippines (imports) | Thailand (exports) |
|---|---|---|---|---|
| | (thousand tons) | | | |
| 1970 | 955.6 | 551 | 0 | 1,064 |
| 1971 | 502.9 | 420 | 367.8 | 1,576 |
| 1972 | 748.0 | 480 | 444.9 | 2,112 |
| 1973 | 1,663.8 | 419 | 311.4 | 849 |
| 1974 | 1,070.4 | 377 | 169.9 | 1,000 |
| 1975 | 720.3 | 360 | 145.3 | 951 |
| 1976 | 1,300.0 | = | 55.2 | 1,973 |

Source: IRRI, 1978.

a/ Includes all rice traded between each of the countries regardless of whether or not the trade is with other ASEAN countries.

independent in 1958. This policy is designed primarily to enhance producer welfare, achieved by means of a high level of protection for domestically produced rice. Because of its uniqueness and consistency we shall not examine it here but refer the reader to the excellent account by Goldman (1975).

The other three countries—Indonesia, the Philippines, and Thailand—make an interesting case for comparative study, because they have followed a rather similar set of objectives, have seen these objectives evolving in similar fashion almost simultaneously, and yet, because they face different circumstances, have translated these objectives into quite different policy measures. The effect on trade and stock policies, in particular, is related to the issues raised by Reutlinger and Bigman (Chapter 9).

A proper understanding of the objective of rice policies in Indonesia, the Philippines, and Thailand can only be obtained if we look at the formative years during and immediately following World War II. The most acute problem then was the need to provision the cities at a time when rice supplies were extremely scarce both domestically and internationally, and domestic transport and marketing networks had broken down. Further, there was a need to control price inflation (which in Indonesia and the Philippines was to become endemic), and a need to protect the real incomes of government employees in the face of such inflation (Mears, 1961; Mears et al., 1974; and Siamwalla, 1975). In the case of Thailand, a surplus producer, there was the need to procure and deliver to the Allies 1.5 million tons of rice as war reparations.

These problems preoccupied governments at the time and they dealt with them as best they could. We need not concern ourselves with the details of those responses except to note that the circumstances caused the governments to set up institutions and incentive (or disincentive) structures that long outlasted the problems that gave rise to them. These new structures dominated rice policies for the next two decades, are of major importance to this day, and therefore merit attention here.

Specifically, these governments began to develop marketing structures, such as the organizations that are today (after many metamorphoses) known as the National Logistics Agency (BULOG) in Indonesia and National Grains Authority (NGA) in the Philippines. These organizations were expected to provision the cities and serve the requirements of particular groups within the citizenry.[4] Once these specialized state agencies were set up,[5] ultimately they, as well as the governments that were in control at the time, were held accountable for their actions. Failure to live up to objectives was easily monitored, particularly by the urban-based mass media. Eventually these branches of the government came to have an overwhelming impact on policy. The objective of ensuring the flow of food to the cities acquired strong political support through the pressures exerted by those agencies, with all other aspects of rice policy being subordinated to their needs.

In contrast, although lip service was paid to the need of farmers to obtain "adequate returns," by means of price-support policies, floor prices for paddy were set so low that either the free market prices exceeded them without much effort by the government or else, in years when they could have affected the prices, the capacity of the government procurement was puny.[6] BULOG and NGA both found reliance on imports a better

*Rice Supplies in the ASEAN Region*　　　　　　　85

means of ensuring continuous flow of food to their clientele than domestic procurement. It is certainly no accident that these agencies acquired monopoly rights over import trade before any other branch of the rice distribution system. With such readiness to draw on imports to counter year-to-year production variations, a cost-effective approach according to the findings by Reutlinger and Bigman (Chapter 9), it is not surprising to find that these agencies invested little in holding stocks to achieve the same end.[7] This approach to rice policies received a minor shock in the years 1967-1968[8] and a major one in 1973-1974, but by the latter time, rice policy in these countries had already evolved away from the picture presented above.

To decide what policy objectives are in fact followed by governments is an exercise fraught with difficulties. Although we do have confidence in the judgments made above in the context of the technologically static world of the 1950s and most of the 1960s, with the technological dynamism that characterized rice production in Asia from about 1970 onward, the picture has become more complex.

Thus, it is often alleged that policy objectives in the 1970s are less clearly biased against producers than in the previous two decades. One way of checking on this is to look at output price policies. This is precisely the method adopted by the Asian Development Bank (ADB) in its second agricultural survey for Asia (ADB, 1978). Examining the terms of trade between agriculture and nonagriculture and between food and nonfood, the ADB survey team concluded that the agriculture/food sector was a major beneficiary of the price changes[9]—changes that were not necessarily consciously policy-designed, but which merely reflected various market pressures to which policies had to adapt themselves.

Confining ourselves to the factual issues, first, we see from Table 4.5 that the real price of rice has moved up in the 1970s in the Philippines (somewhat uncertainly) and Thailand (definitely), but has declined in Indonesia. The Indonesian situation is striking, not just because of its importance in the region, but also because it has been pursuing the most aggressive price policy among the three countries under study. We cannot

Table 4.5 "Real" Rice Prices in Indonesia, Philippines and Thailand

|  | Indonesia (Sept. 66 = 100) | Philippines (1970 = 100) | Thailand (1970 = 100) |
|---|---|---|---|
| 1965 | n.a. | 97 | 86 |
| 1966 | 112 | 115 | 114 |
| 1967 | 117 | 113 | 129 |
| 1968 | 165 | 104 | 107 |
| 1969 | 89 | 96 | 117 |
| 1970 | 99 | 100 | 100 |
| 1971 | 84 | 113 | 80 |
| 1972 | 92 | 124 | 91 |
| 1973 | 115 | 130 | 131 |
| 1974 | 80 | 123 | 146 |
| 1975 | 84 | n.a. | 139 |
| 1976 | 82 | n.a. | 137 |
| 1977 | 70 | n.a. | n.a. |

Notes and sources: Indonesia: Jakarta rice price deflated by 62 commodity Jakarta Cost of Living Index excluding rice, as calculated in Leon A. Mears and Sidik Moeljono (1977); Philippines: Wholesale Rice Price Macan First Class, Manila (reported in IRRI, World Rice Statistics, 1978, Table 38), deflated by non-food Price Index (reported in Asian Development Bank, Rural Asia, p. 414); Thailand: Wholesale Rice Price 5/broken, Bangkok (reported in IRRI, loc. cit.), deflated by non-food component of Consumer Price Index, Bangkok (food and all items indexes reported in IRRI, op. cit., Table 42, non-food index being computed using 49 percent weight for food, as reported in Bank of Thailand, Monthly Review, December 1978).

explain away this country's uniqueness in Table 4.5 as a response to a specific market situation peculiar to Indonesia alone. True, the growth rate in production in Indonesia has been rather high,[10] but the growth in demand has been even more rapid, fed in part by a high income elasticity reckoned to be about 0.5 to 0.7, leading to a strong upward trend in imports. Ultimately, it is this willingness to bring in rice from abroad that allows prices to be kept down. Low rice prices are thus clearly a matter of policy.

Yet, the general observation that rice policies in general have shifted in favor of supporting producers' welfare can hardly be disputed even for Indonesia. Using the rice price as the indicator of the direction of policies presupposes that it is the only instrument used by the government to attain its objectives. Such was the case in the 1950s and 1960s, as explained above. The coming of high-yielding varieties has added a new instrument to rice policies, that is, programs of input subsidies in which credit and fertilizers play central roles. These programs were known as "Perfected BIMAS" in Indonesia,[11] and "Masagana 99" in the Philippines.

In a situation where fertilizers are underutilized relative to a profit-maximizing level—an assumption that appears quite reasonable in the technologically dynamic situation of the first half of the 1970s in the Philippines—there are sound economic reasons why input subsidies should be preferred to an output price-support program.[12] We shall not look at the rationale of this choice, but rather its implications. These are particularly noteworthy as far as the government's procurement and stock-holding policies are concerned.

It is clear that, to the extent that a price-support program in many cases involves stock accumulation, a weak program on price support would involve necessarily less year-to-year stock accumulation, requiring a reliance on imports to counter the production fluctuations.[13] A country such as the Philippines that has allowed the rice price to rise can do so largely by accumulating stocks. The Philippine level of stocks in the last ten years is particularly striking, rising from about 0.5 million tons in 1970 to about 1 million tons now—the same as that of Indonesia, whose production level is thrice that of the Philippines. This stock accumulation is a result of a combination of a rather high rate of growth in production—3.9 percent per annum between the 1969-1971 average and the 1975-1977 average (IRRI, 1978)—a fortuitous lack of bad weather and pests in the last few years, and a rather poorly developed capacity to export.

Indonesia, a country continuously in deficit, can only accumulate stocks by importing more. Using imports to build up stocks is not unknown (India did it between 1975-1978) nor is it irrational—if world prices are expected to go up by more than the storage cost, it is quite rational to store more rice. BULOG has, however, chosen not to accumulate stocks, allowing its import volume to fluctuate quite considerably (see Table 4.3).[14]

Although Thailand joined her two neighbors in the shift towards a more producer-oriented strategy, the physical environment of her rice production areas is not conducive to the adoption of modern technology (see Table 4.3). Consequently, there was little attempt to use input subsidies as a tool, although the burdensome protection policy for domestic fertilizers was done away with. It is precisely because it cannot follow the route of input subsidization that Thailand has followed most strongly the policy of increasing output prices relative to the levels prevailing in the 1960s. This it did merely by the traditional mechanism of relaxing the level of the export premium much more steeply and rapidly in the post–1974 period.[15] Thus, unlike the Philippines, Thailand raised the real price of rice without a massive increase in the level of stocks; as with Indonesia, this high price level is sustainable only if Thailand is willing to allow the traded volume to fluctuate.

The conclusion to be drawn from this survey of the domestic policies followed by the three countries in the 1970s is somewhat paradoxical in the sense that the stock and import strategies of the various countries are somewhat at variance with what we would expect from considering the external conditions they face. One would expect that the Philippines, as a "small" country in the world rice market, would rely more heavily on trade variation rather than stock variation as a stabilization tool. The opposite strategy would be expected of Indonesia and Thailand, both major actors in that market. As shown above, the actual situation is the reverse of our expectations. We have described the purely domestic reasons why this particular situation has arisen. It remains for us to examine whether it is possible to understand the problem from an international angle.

## Policies at the International Level

There have been two attempts by Asian countries to arrange methods of cooperation to achieve stability in the international rice market. The first, which may be quickly passed over, is the

Asian Rice Trade Fund created under the auspices of the United Nations Economic and Social Commission for Asia and the Pacific (ESCAP) and FAO. It was designed to finance and refinance rice trade among members, which at the moment consist of five importing countries (Bangladesh, India, the Philippines, Sri Lanka, and the former Republic of South Vietnam) and no exporting country. Despite its name, it has as yet no capital funding. Not surprisingly, it has not been a factor in world rice trade.[16]

A second attempt, associated with the five-member Association of Southeast Asian Nations, has as its aim the achievement of supply security in food and energy. "Food" was later explicitly taken to mean rice and "energy" to mean petroleum. A very small step was taken in the direction of greater intra-ASEAN trade when the member countries recently initialed an agreement which committed them to give fellow members the right of first refusal. More importantly, they have asked Thailand to study the feasibility of an ASEAN stock to be held both nationally and regionally. In light of this, ASEAN decided in November 1978 on a modest effort to build up an emergency rice-stock reserve totaling 50,000 tons to be held by various member nations. Like most other activities of ASEAN, extreme caution is the hallmark of this agreement. Thus, the agreement "provides for the release of rice from the Reserve after notification of need, with the price, tons, and conditions to be negotiated bilaterally."[17] It was expected that this cautious start would be merely the beginning of something more ambitious.

At the international level, although rice was proposed at the UNCTAD IV meeting in Nairobi by the Secretariat as one of 17 commodities slated for an integrated commodity program, it was not featured as one of the items in the final resolution, presumably because it is an item on which the developing countries are somewhat ambivalent, most of them being importers of the commodity.

## The Proposed Schemes and the ASEAN Countries

Most of the schemes proposed for food security are largely couched either in terms of the wheat market or for the aggregated foodgrain markets. An insurance-type scheme specifically for rice, which is meant to economize on buffer stocks required, faces many obstacles in implementation, given the structure of the present world market for rice. Apart from the more general implementation problems that beset schemes like this, such as difficulties of finding the correct level of production in any given year, there are a couple of problems peculiar to the rice market.

The first set of problems is practical in nature. It is normally assumed in most literature on stabilization policies that there is such a concept as an internationally quoted rice price. Unfortunately, rice is not a commodity traded in commodity exchanges where information on transacted prices is in the public domain. The most commonly used price indicator for rice is f.o.b. Bangkok, which is issued on a weekly basis by the Rice Committee of the Board of Trade of Thailand. According to Usher (1967) in his account of the genesis of this price series:

> Every week there is a meeting of the exporters' representatives, called the Rice Committee of the Board of Rice Trade. They draw up a price list for all grades of rice. The list is submitted for approval to the Ministry of Economic Affairs. If the Ministry approves the price list, and it has never failed to do so, then the prices become official and the Ministry of Economic Affairs undertakes to forbid the export that week of rice priced at less than 97 percent of the official quotation. The Board of Trade arrives at its price list by adding up the wholesale price of rice, the export taxes (including the rice premium), the cost of sacks, and a much inflated estimate of the exporters' costs. The apparatus of officially sponsored prices is a facade ignored in practice by the exporters who accept prices well below the officially sponsored limits wherever competition forces them to do so.

In short, the prices that have been used as indicators of the world price are nothing more than "posted prices."[18] This would affect the feasibility of those schemes that proposed compensation not only for production shortfalls but to cover high prices as well.

Furthermore, rice is not of uniform quality. If the different qualities of rice, substitution among which is less than perfect, are taken into account, provisions of any security scheme would

# Rice Supplies in the ASEAN Region

have to be complicated further. If a pooled buffer stock scheme is to be implemented, it would have to be large to enable it to cope with variations of individual qualities.[19]

The second set of problems is more basic and arises because the proportion of rice that is traded internationally is a very small proportion of world production and consumption. The payment of money in order to shift the fluctuations from the domestic economies to the world market would be unrealistic without an adequate level of buffer stocks. Again, because of the wide extent of the production fluctuations, buffer stocks to be held at the international level would be a very large proportion of the total volume of world trade. There is no rice-exporting country that dominates the world market as strongly as the United States does in wheat and maize. The result is that much of the buffer stocks would have to be held at the domestic level. Unless strong international control is exerted on these stocks, most of the alleged savings through an insurance scheme would be lost.

Given these problems plus the fact that the major exporters in rice (the United States, the People's Republic of China, and Thailand) have such divergent capacities and political interests, a worldwide insurance scheme specifically for rice would have to be out of the question for the time being. There are two alternatives: one is to stay within the "rice only" framework and consider the problem in the context of a joint effort among a subset of countries, in this case the five ASEAN countries, and the other is to explore the feasibility of a food insurance scheme that pays for rice production shortfalls or high rice prices in terms of alternative crops, e.g., wheat and maize. An intra-ASEAN buffer stock scheme would have considerable possibilities for implementation, at least from a crude assessment of the calculations made by Johnson.[20]

The section in this chapter on the evolution of rice policies suggests that, within the ASEAN countries, the cleavage of interests may not be between the importers and Thailand,[21] but between "small" traders such as Malaysia and the Philippines on the one hand, and large traders such as Indonesia and Thailand on the other. For the small countries, international instability in rice prices does not adversely affect their welfare. The former pair of countries, being price takers in the world market, are unlikely to be interested in international action to stabilize world prices,[22] although they may be interested in implementing, and indeed have initiated, national reserve stock programs designed to offset domestic production fluctuations. Indonesia and Thailand, being price makers in the world market, have sufficient interest in ensuring that fluctuations of their harvests do not add to international price instability.[23] The question is whether they have anything to gain from a joint action.

One possible scenario is for the two countries to agree to give first priority to the import needs or export availability of the other in their rice trade (as was partly agreed to by ASEAN) and to pool their buffer stocks so that the joint excess supply or demand vis-à-vis the rest of the world is stabilized. The constraint to this solution is that both Indonesia and Thailand would prefer to diversify their source of supply or market. The scenario outlined above would create undue dependence on one another, an outcome that is, despite talk of the "spirit of ASEAN," premature.

It is possible that some compromise between the above scenario and go-it-alone national buffer stock schemes that minimize import (or export) variability for each country could be worked out. This would involve a joint buffer stock scheme that would supplement national buffer stocks and could be drawn on to serve as a partial offset to production fluctuations, it being understood that primary reliance would have to be placed on the regular markets where the two countries would pursue their separate interests as before.

The second alternative is for each of the ASEAN countries to subscribe to one of the proposed insurance schemes with the understanding that the compensation would be paid in wheat or maize.[24] In such a case, the key element is the degree of substitutability of these two crops for rice. This can be given a more precise expression as follows: if $Q_R$ and $Q_W$ are the "normal" volumes of rice produced and wheat imported, then the long run equilibrium rice and wheat prices $P_R$ and $P_W$ may be solved by the following pair of simultaneous equations:

*Rice Supplies in the ASEAN Region*

$$Q_R = f_R (P_R, P_W, \ldots Z)$$

$$Q_W = f_W (P_W, P_R, \ldots Y)$$

where $f_R$ and $f_W$ are the demand functions for the two cereals with $Z$ and $Y$ representing factors that are extraneous to the consideration at hand. If there is no shortfall of production in rice, the proportionate increase in wheat imports necessary to maintain rice price would be given by the following expression:

$$\Delta Q_W = \frac{\epsilon_{WW}}{\epsilon_{RW}} \cdot \frac{Q_W}{Q_R} \Delta Q_R$$

where

$\Delta Q_R$ and $\Delta Q_W$ are the deviations of actual production of rice and import of wheat from $Q_R$ and $Q_W$ respectively;

$\epsilon_{RW}$ is the cross elasticity of demand for rice with respect to the wheat price, and

$\epsilon_{WW}$ the own price elasticity of demand for wheat.

Thus, using parameters that have been estimated for Indonesia, we have used the above formula to calculate that every ton of rice shortfall in that country would have to be compensated by approximately 2.5 tons additional import of wheat.[25] This would stabilize domestic rice price, but the domestic wheat price may decline substantially, perhaps requiring a heavy subsidy.

There are a few important caveats[26] to be borne in mind in using alternative cereals, particularly wheat, to stabilize rice prices. The first is that the above formula is calculated on the basis of small percentage changes in supplies. Although the approximation probably holds good for rice supply and rice demand functions, the kind of volume changes in wheat consumption that may be necessary may be very large and the approximation may no longer hold, except in the special case where we can be confident that the demand function for wheat is log-linear.

Secondly, when we use a commodity such as wheat to stabilize rice prices in a society where wheat is consumed or is thought to be consumed largely by well-to-do people, the political repercussions of the implied income redistribution of such a policy may be unacceptable.[27] It is perhaps for this reason that the policy of using wheat imports to stabilize rice prices has not been adopted by Southeast Asian governments.

Another reason for this reluctance may be that consumption shifts may be very difficult to achieve because in the short run cross elasticities of demand may be very low, particularly if it involves a shift into exotic items such as wheat. It may be better to manipulate the supplies of alternative cereals for which (a) there is a fairly active demand in the domestic market already, and (b) the commodity is one for which there is a fairly active international market. A good example would be maize in the Philippines and Indonesia.[28]

In any case, intervention in alternative crops appears infeasible for Thailand, where the dominance in rice is particularly strong. Thailand's interest appears much more clearly to lie in increasing the level of its own stocks to stabilize the level of its exports to the rest of the world, and thereby participate more extensively in stabilizing the international market in rice in which it has a significant share.

## Conclusions

It has been argued in this chapter that traditional policies in the Asian countries towards the international rice market have been to draw upon it in times of shortage while insulating domestic prices from world price movements. This has been accompanied by inadequate stocks within the exporting countries, for the countries that dominate the export trade in rice do not dominate in production and consumption. There is one exception, namely the People's Republic of China, whose role has been very flexible and responsive to world price. However, it appears that this flexibility arises from its ability to shift consumption rather than from the volume of stock it holds.

Given this structure of world rice trade, the policies to be

*Rice Supplies in the ASEAN Region*

adopted by ASEAN countries must be ones by which they increase the level of their own rice stocks, preferably jointly as they are proposing to do. Because of the presence within this grouping of two important traders in the world market, namely, Indonesia and Thailand, such a proposal, if carried out, would also help stabilize the world market.

A possible fallback position, at least for the importing countries, is for them to rely on alternative foodgrains, particularly maize, to achieve the objective of rice price stabilization.

## Notes

1. In the Philippines there are some regions where maize is the staple food, but in some areas there is some "lower-end substitution" of maize for rice. In Indonesia, there is also similar lower-end substitution of maize, sorghum, and cassava for rice. In all countries, there is an upper-end substitution of wheat for rice, which is becoming significant for all the countries except Thailand. Average wheat imports for July/June crop years of 1974/75–1976/77 are as follows (in metric tons):

| | |
|---|---|
| Indonesia | 884,000 |
| Philippines | 538,000 |
| Thailand | 96,000 |
| Malaysia | 377,000 |
| Singapore (net of re-exports) | 150,000 |

There is no domestic production of wheat in any of these countries.

2. The percentage shares of rice and other cereals in the total calorie supply of the ASEAN countries are as follows:

| Country | Rice | Wheat | Other staples[a] | Nonstaples |
|---|---|---|---|---|
| Indonesia | 56.2 | 1.8 | 25.8 | 16.2 |
| Malaysia | 45.9 | 10.6 | 5.8 | 37.7 |
| Philippines | 44.6 | 5.1 | 20.2 | 30.1 |
| Singapore | 33.3 | 12.8 | 4.8 | 49.1 |
| Thailand | 71.2 | 0.8 | 7.1 | 20.9 |

*Source:* FAO Food Balance Sheets, 1972–1974.

[a] Includes other cereals, root crops, pulses, nuts, and seeds.

96                                                                                                  *Ammar Siamwalla*

3. Also see the section on the evolution of rice policies in this chapter.

4. See Mears (1961, p. 156); Mangahas (1972); and Siamwalla (1975). In this respect, these organizations had the same origins as the public food distribution systems of South Asia, even though they never retained a full-fledged rationing system characteristic of the South Asian systems. See George (1979) and Ahmed (1979).

5. Although no specialized distribution agency equivalent to BULOG and NGA was set up in Thailand, the Ministry of Commerce, which regulated closely the Thai export trade and less closely the domestic trade, is "responsible" for keeping rice prices down. The role of the Agricultural Ministry and its creature, the Marketing Organization for Farmers (MOF), has been minimal.

6. See Mears et al. (1974, pp. 289–293). For Thailand, see Siamwalla (1975, p. 244). In Indonesia, there was no clear policy on floor prices for farmers until 1971. See Afiff and Timmer (1971).

7. Thailand's policies are a mirror image of the policies followed by Indonesia and the Philippines: little stocks were held, the adjustment burden being placed on the export volumes.

8. See Timmer (1975, pp. 197–231, and particularly pp. 212–215).

9. The agriculture-versus-nonagriculture terms of trade for Indonesia moved against agriculture, but this may be because of the presence of a large petroleum component in the nonagricultural sector. Indonesia's food/nonfood price ratio moved in favor of food in the 1970s.

10. At 3.3 percent between 1968–1970 (three-year average) and 1975–1977, as against 4.0 percent in the Philippines and 2.1 percent in Thailand for the same period.

11. As the name implies, the BIMAS program has had a long history in Indonesia, but prior to 1970, it was either a pilot project or, when enlarged, an unsuccessful program. For a history of these programs, see Afiff and Timmer (1971, pp. 137–143).

12. For an analysis of this choice for the Philippines, see Barker and Hayami (1976).

13. It does not necessarily involve less government procurement from domestic sources within any given year. Thus, the yearly average of domestic procurement during the First Plan Period in Indonesia (1969/70–1973/74) was 348,616 tons per year, as against 469,985 tons per year during the Second Plan (1974/75–1977/78) (BULOG, 1978). The reason for the increase was the narrowing gap between the floor price for paddy and the ceiling price for rice declared by the government.

14. I am omitting here the quite considerable short-term accumulation à la Russe that took place when BULOG entered the international market quietly and purchased rice extensively in 1977/78 before the rest of the

*Rice Supplies in the ASEAN Region* 97

market became aware of the large Indonesian shortfall and began to bid up the price.

15. See the postscript in Siamwalla (1975).

16. This account is largely based on Setthawong (1976).

17. FAO (1979).

18. In fact, the parallel with the petroleum case goes further, for these "posted prices" are largely used for the purpose of calculating export taxes.

19. If the stocks were to be held in Thailand, where the markets for various grades are well articulated, the size could be reduced as the buffer stock manager would be able to readily substitute one quality for another.

20. See his chapter in this book, Table 12.1. Although the table did not show the calculation specifically for rice or for the ASEAN countries, the estimates of the level of stocks for the individual ASEAN countries add up to a figure considerably higher than that for the optimal level of stocks for the combined Far East.

21. The Philippines is still included as an importing country, even though it has been exporting modest amounts of rice for the past few years. As will be seen, this does not affect the argument unduly.

22. This follows from the well-known theorem that price takers (whether on the import or the export side) lose from price stabilization.

23. The problem of welfare gains and losses from stabilization—usually employed as predictors of the countries' interest in price stabilization—has a vast literature. For price takers, the results tend to be unambiguous: they do not benefit from stabilization. For the others, the results are somewhat more ambiguous, particularly when free trade is not assumed (Just et al., 1977).

24. If cash is to be paid out, it must be calculated as if the subscribing countries will meet their shortfalls by imports of wheat or maize necessary to stabilize domestic rice price. The imported wheat or maize may, in tonnage terms, be much larger than the size of rice production shortfall (see equation below).

25. Details of the calculation are available upon request from the author.

26. I am indebted to James Gavan of IFPRI for raising these issues.

27. Note from the editor: In the discussion of this chapter, Dr. A. T. Birowo pointed out that at least in Indonesia, "wheat has been used more and more in consumption, and imports have been increasing." He added this his impression was that wheat for rice is no longer an upper-end substitution; in fact, it is common to find villagers eating bread for breakfast and no longer cassava or rice.

28. Government intervention in the maize market has been extensive

in the Philippines for a long time, although it is not clear whether the government has followed an integrated approach in its intervention in the two markets. In Indonesia, BULOG has moved into the maize market only recently, and the government is more explicit about using the intervention in the maize market to lighten its task in the rice market.

## References

Afiff, S., and C. P. Timmer. "Rice Policy in Indonesia." *Food Research Institute* 10, no. 2 (1971):131–159.

Ahmed, R. *Foodgrain Supply, Distribution and Consumption Policies with a Dual Pricing Mechanism: A Case Study of Bangladesh.* Research Report No. 8. Washington, D.C.: International Food Policy Research Institute, 1979, P. 22.

Asian Development Bank (ADB). *Rural Asia: Challenge and Opportunity.* New York: Praeger, 1978. Pp. 159–162, 265, and 412–415.

Barker, Randolph, and Yujiro Hayami. "Price Support versus Input Subsidy for Food Self-Sufficiency in Developing Countries." *American Journal of Agricultural Economics* 58, no. 4 (November 1976):617–628.

BULOG. *Rice Stabilization in Indonesia: Annual Report 1977/78.* Jakarta: June 1978. Table 2.

Food and Agricultural Organization, Committee on Commodity Problems. *Report of the Twenty-Second Session of the Intergovernmental Group on Rice.* CCP 79/4 (CCP:RI 79/10). Rome: FAO, May 1979. P. 10.

George, P. S. "Public Distribution of Foodgrains in Kerala—Income Distribution Implications and Effectiveness." *Research Report No. 7.* Washington, D.C.: International Food Policy Research Institute, 1979. P. 20.

Goldman, R. H. "Staple Food Self-Sufficiency and the Distributive Impact of Malaysian Rice Policy." *Food Research Institute Studies* 14, no. 3 (1975):251–293.

International Rice Research Institute (IRRI). *World Rice Statistics.* 1978.

Just, R., E. Lutz, A. Schmitz, and S. Turnovsky. "The Distribution of Welfare Gains from International Price Stabilization Under Distortions." *American Journal of Agricultural Economics* 59, no. 4 (November 1977):652–661.

Liu, T. C., and K. C. Yeh. *The Economy of the Chinese Mainland: National Income and Economic Development 1933–1959.* Princeton, 1965.

Mangahas, Mahar. "Philippines Rice Policy Reconsidered in Terms of Urban Bias." *Philippines Review of Business and Economics* 9, no. 1 (June 1972):57–77.

Mears, Leon. *Rice Marketing in the Republic of Indonesia.* Jakarta: P. T.

# Rice Supplies in the ASEAN Region 99

Pembangunon, 1961. Chapter 2, particularly sections E and F.

Mears, Leon, et al. *Rice Economy of the Philippines*. Quezon City: University of the Philippines Press, 1974. Chapter 2.

Mears, Leon, and Sidik Moeljono. "Food Policy." Mimeo., November 28, 1977.

Setthawong, Phisit. "Evaluation of the Asian Rice Trade Fund from the Developing Rice-Exporting Country's Point of View." BSCAP, AD/RCR/ARTF/R.4. December 1976.

Siamwalla, Ammar. "A History of Rice Policies in Thailand." *Food Research Institute Studies* 14, no. 3 (1975):233–249.

Timmer, C. Peter. "The Political Economy of Rice in Asia: Indonesia." *Food Research Institute Studies* 14, no. 3 (1975).

Trung, Ngo Quoc. "Economic Analysis of Irrigation Development in Deltaic Regions of Asia: The Case of Central Thailand." In International Rice Research Institute, *Irrigation Policy and Management in Southeast Asia*. Los Baños, Philippines, 1978.

Usher, Dan. "The Thai Rice Trade." In T. H. Silcock (ed.), *Thailand: Social and Economic Studies in Development*. Canberra: Australian National University Press, 1967.

Wickizer, V. D., and M. K. Bennett. *Rice Economy of Monsoon Asia*. Stanford: Food Research Institute, 1941.

# 5
# Food Security:
# Some East African Considerations

*Uma Lele*
*Wilfred Candler*

This chapter is based on the authors' experience with food production and food security issues in eastern and southern African countries including the Sudan, Ethiopia, Kenya, Tanzania, Zambia, Malawi, and Lesotho. But we believe that the points made have a broad validity for countries in sub-Sahara Africa.

Viewed from this perspective, much of the discussion of food security in the international literature seems unrealistic and nonoperational (see, for example, Johnson, Chapter 12 of this book; Reutlinger, 1977; and Konandreas et al., 1978). This chapter first reviews the realities of the food supply and supply reporting system in these countries and then considers the working of the various food marketing channels. These are compared to the assumptions made in the literature. The review leads us to conclude that official food trade is only the visible portion of a much larger total trade; and although the government is responsible for food security, it has no power to control major components of the food distribution system. These facts suggest that consideration of an official food reserve, and/or financial reserve, is probably necessary—mainly, to deal with the urban problem and thus indirectly with the rural problem. But such a consideration does not address the total problem of food insecurity adequately, as is often implied in the literature. Nor is it the most efficient way of dealing with this problem overall. Further, the proposed solutions are especially unsuited for the problems of rural areas, which require a different set of solutions. Our view of the production

## Underdevelopment

Most discussions of food security start with the following implicit assumptions: (1) that there is an efficient, price-responsive agricultural industry; (2) that essentially all food passes through commercial marketing channels; (3) that there is a price for grain, at which one can buy or sell at will; (4) that the influence of trading activity in one part of the market is quickly and effectively transmitted to all parts of the market; and (5) that reliable information on production and market performance is instantly and freely available.

Essentially, none of these implicit assumptions apply in sub-Sahara Africa. Figure 5.1 illustrates the marketing channels characteristic of most East African countries. Frequently, there are two production sectors: large scale and traditional. The large-scale sector may be predominantly expatriate as in Zambia, or may consist of state farms as in Tanzania and more recently in Ethiopia. Typically, the large-scale sector sells only through official channels and, typically, to a monopsonistic parastatal (a semiautonomous public-sector entity, which usually has a commercial function). Traditional producers, in contrast, retain some food for self-consumption, use some food for barter, and sell on the official and the unofficial markets. Although the marketing parastatal will sell to consumers and undertake official exports, in the unofficial market, sales are made to consumers or produce is exported informally, either for barter or, more usually, for differentially overvalued foreign currency.

Three features of this marketing system deserve special emphasis:

1. Frequently only the transactions of the marketing parastatal are known with any certainty (and our experience indicates that even this may be suspect). Thus, analyses

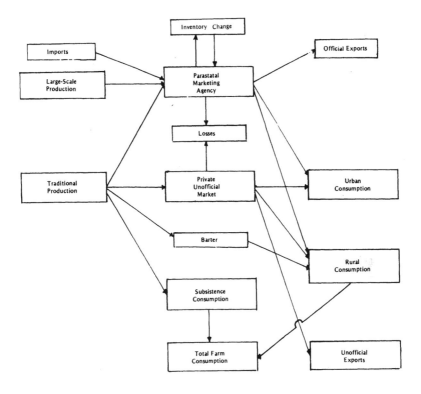

Figure 5.1 Conceptual Model of Food Grain Production and Disposition

that assume that production, consumption, or stocks can be ascertained simply misstate the problem.

2. Most food transactions—and hence private "food security" decisions—take place without passing through the marketing parastatal; hence, they are beyond direct government control.

3. Transfers between marketing channels are frequent. There is no necessary correlation between changes in the activity of the marketing parastatal and changes in production.

This latter point is well illustrated in Figure 5.2, which gives purchases and sales by Namboard (Zambia's marketing parastatal). During the period 1964–1976, purchases grew at an

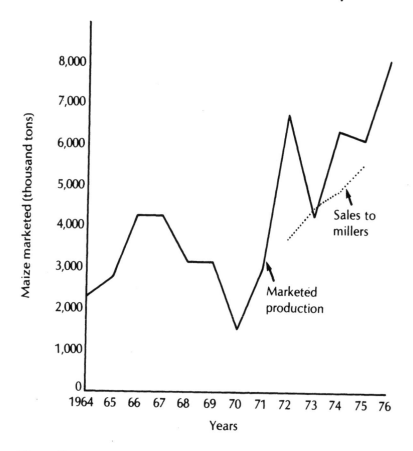

**Figure 5.2** Increase in Zambian marketed maize production

annual compound rate of 8.5 percent. Between 1972 and 1975, sales grew at the rate of 14 percent compounded. It is inconceivable that changes in population or incomes accounted for the rapid rise in Namboard sales. It is more likely that during these four years Namboard's market share increased and, as a corollary, the market share of the informal channels fell. And yet, literature on food security in the international circles does not address the issue of the growth of public distribution systems, which have become national objectives in many African countries.

Because of this dual marketing structure, the parastatal tends to become overburdened or hit with a "double whammy" during food shortages. The parastatal faces both declining inventories and additional consumers who are unable to purchase

# Food Security: East African Considerations

their requirements at reasonable prices from the unofficial market. Sales of milled products, i.e., maize flour, wheat flour, and rice, by the National Milling Corporation in Tanzania, nearly reached 300,000 tons in 1973/74, compared to 190,000 in 1970/71, and fell to 238,000 in 1977/78. Purchases were 170,000 of the same three unmilled grains in 1973/74 compared to 320,000 tons in 1970/71 and 300,000 tons in 1977/78. National food administrators must deal with the simultaneous halving of available supplies and doubling of official demand. Again, this is a problem not dealt with in the literature.

Not only does the parastatal handle only a small percentage of the crop, but the parastatal's price applies for only a part of the season. After the main harvest period, farmers can sell stored crop at higher prices—frequently up to twice the official price—on the unofficial market. Thus, studies that rely on the official price fail to take into account the actual situation that the farmer and consumer face.[1]

We should reiterate that information on the informal markets is imperfect and often nonexistent. We should also emphasize that the parastatal statistics may be imperfect (i.e., parastatal statistics on stocks may refer to amounts put into storage, not the net amount after allowing for losses and pilferage). The existence of an unofficial market usually indicates a high cost structure of the parastatal where its procurement costs represent typically only half of the sale price of crops handled by the parastatal.[2]

Thus, any realistic approach to national food security policies in East Africa must be a combined exercise in "planning without facts," within the context of a complex marketing system and particular national policies. As shown later, we do not believe that the exercises of economists in the international agencies are inherently futile; but we do warn that such analyses should not start with the facile assumptions that all the required data are readily available and that the system is totally commercial.

## Domestic Food Reserve

The issue of a best form for food security, i.e., whether a reserve should be international, regional, or national; whether it should consist of food or be a monetary reserve; or whether it should simply be a food insurance scheme, has been debated in the international circles for some time.[3] After the food crises of 1973/74, some East African countries such as Kenya and Tanzania began building a national food reserve. This chapter assumes these national reserves exist.[4,5]

At any time, a domestic food reserve has three major components: (1) the official "national food reserve," (2) stocks held by the official food marketing organization for its routine purchase and sale activities, and (3) stocks held by the private sector, predominantly farmers. Except just prior to harvest, the private stocks—principally held by individual farmers—will generally exceed all other stocks. Thus, to think in terms of public stocks as the only component to food security is to overlook the single most important contributor to food security: the private sector.

Many cultural practices, e.g., mixed cropping, planting of cassava and drought-resistant cereals, and timing of planting, are explicitly designed to offset the yield fluctuations of a monoculture in a marginal climatic environment. In addition to the stocks of harvested crop held in the farm household, many East African farmers carry an inventory of unharvested food reserves in the form of cassava.

**Production Levels**

*Food*

Food security is frequently conceived in terms of reducing fluctuations in domestic supply around a trend line by a certain percentage. Conceptualization of the problem in this manner is of little operational significance.

Data on domestic agriculture in most African countries are too unreliable to ascertain the level of production in any given year. Further, year-to-year production fluctuations in reported statistics are often too large to estimate a trend with any degree of confidence. Judgments about deviations from a trend by amounts as small as 5 or 10 percentage points would be nearly impossible.

It is instructive to consider the available production estimates

*Food Security: East African Considerations* 107

for Tanzania. Table 5.1 presents the various series of crop production over the 1965/66–1977/78 period published by Tanzania's Ministry of Agriculture and various international agencies. Maize is an important crop in Tanzania. The table indicates that USDA's and FAO's estimates of maize production for the year 1974/75 are 2.3 times greater than the estimate published by the Tanzanian Ministry of Agriculture. The Ministry and USDA/FAO series for maize production in Tanzania have a correlation coefficient of only .59! The series have a higher correlation with time than they do with each other. Which series would be used to estimate food reserve requirements? For the same year, the USDA estimate of sorghum and millet production is 3.5 times that of the Ministry of Agriculture, whereas FAO's estimate is 88 percent of the Ministry's. Incidentally, while the Ministry's estimate of maize production in 1973/74—a drought year—shows a decline from the previous year's level by 26 percent, the USDA series shows an increase of 30 percent over the previous year! The Ministry's maize series shows an annual growth of 19,527 tons per year over the 1966/67–1976/77 period. The USDA series for the same years shows an annual growth of 91,020 tons. The standard deviation of each "b" coefficient is highly significant. There is no a priori reason to believe that any one of these series is more accurate than another or that any rate of growth is more representative than another.[6]

Which production series should be used in the management of a food security scheme? Despite the recognition of these problems by national governments and international agencies involved in compiling statistics, only recently have small amounts of international development funds been made available to develop methods and institutions to generate reliable statistics.[7] Too much effort is devoted to instant fabrication and mechanistic analyses of meaningless numbers.

### Marketed Production

Because production statistics are known to be unreliable, "marketed" production is used as the proxy for decision making about food security by many national agencies. Further, it

Table 5.1 Tanzania: Various Production Estimates of Principal Cereals, 1965-66 to 1977-78[*]

| Year | Maize | | | Paddy | | | Wheat | | | Millet and sorghum | | |
|---|---|---|---|---|---|---|---|---|---|---|---|---|
| | Min. Agr. | USDA | FAO | Min. Agr. | USDA | FAO | Min. Agr. | USDA | FAO | Min. Agr. | USDA | FAO |
| | (thousand metric tons) | | | | | | | | | | | |
| 1965/66 | 532 | - | - | - | - | - | - | - | - | 265.4 | - | - |
| 1966/67 | 752 | 1,127 | - | - | 140 | - | - | 39 | - | 299 | 1,122 | - |
| 1967/68 | 630 | 549 | 560 | - | 114 | 115 | - | 31 | 35 | 254 | 1,145 | 292 |
| 1968/69 | 647 | 664 | 678 | 125 | 136 | 136 | - | 44 | 40 | 284.5 | 1,150 | 275 |
| 1969/70 | 663 | 525 | 530 | 139 | 144 | 136 | 79.8[a/] | 39 | 39 | 282 | 1,155 | 236 |
| 1970/71 | 746 | 637 | 650 | 184 | 182 | 182 | - | 61 | 61 | 322.6 | 1,180 | 245 |
| 1971/72 | 730 | 715 | 715 | 193 | 193 | 193 | - | 84 | 84 | 276.9 | 1,200 | 279 |
| 1972/73 | 856 | 681 | 863 | 171 | 171 | 171 | - | 98 | 98 | 319.1 | 1,220 | 319 |
| 1973/74 | 624 | 888 | 800 | 184.9 | 204 | 152 | 79.8 | 78 | 80 | 333.4 | 1,165 | 295 |
| 1974/75 | 623 | 1,446 | 1,446 | 134.3 | 310 | 293 | - | 45 | 46 | 189.6 | 950 | 324 |
| 1975/76 | 825 | 1,350 | 1,354 | 150 | 385 | 430 | 46.1 | 56 | 56 | 339.2 | 1,200 | 615 |
| 1976/77 | 897 | 1,619 | 1,619 | 172 | 400 | 430 | 57.6 | 56 | 60 | - | 1,200 | 1,190 |
| 1977/78 | 968 | 1,700 | - | 194 | 400 | - | 70.8 | 50 | - | - | 1,000 | - |

* Ministry of Agriculture: Report on Price Recommendations of the Marketing Development Bureau, 1978/79, pp. 53, 72,79,90.
USDA: Indices of Agricultural Production in Africa and the Near East 1956-75. The authors were informed by a USDA staff member that these were revised down considerably subsequent to our discussions with USDA Headquarters staff about discrepancies among various series.
FAO: *Production Yearbook*.

a/ 1968-72 average.

# Food Security: East African Considerations

is the production marketed through "official" channels rather than total marketings that influences policymaking as it determines the supply of food to cities and major towns. Government distribution efforts are largely concentrated in urban areas. The reasons for this include (1) the desire for political and economic stability—if food prices rise, urban populations can organize to demand both higher wages and/or a different government; (2) the administrative imperative—the limited manpower and management cannot be spread adequately to deal with both urban and rural distribution needs, and the civil service that makes and benefits from these decisions is largely concentrated in the cities; (3) the inadequate transport, storage, and handling facilities in rural areas frequently frustrate official distribution efforts; and (4) the high unit cost of public sector distribution of grain to rural areas that require large subsidies if extensive rural distribution is undertaken.

Data are not available by sectors but are recorded by administrative regions. In 1977/78, a relatively good crop year, 77 percent of the Tanzanian National Milling Corporation's sales of rice, maize flour, and wheat flour were concentrated in 6 regions (Dar es Salaam, Morogoro, Tanga, Arusha, Dodoma, and Mwanza) that have major urban population concentrations, out of a total of 22 regions. Urban demand is more predictable than other variables that influence "national" food security, i.e., rural demand, production, or marketed quantities. However, even urban demand is not completely met by official sources, as offtake from official channels increases in bad crop years and declines in good crop years (see Table 5.2).

The remaining 23 percent of the official distribution in Tanzania in 1977/78 was sold in 16 mostly rural regions. Field observations suggest the distribution occurred largely in major towns rather than in the countryside. There are always pockets of shortage in rural areas as official distribution is thin and traditional rural markets are highly fragmented. Welfare and political considerations have prompted an improved distribution effort to the rural areas in years of extreme food shortages. Despite these improvements, the amount of rural demand satisfied by official distribution is still limited.

Although the problem of food security pervades the whole

Table 5.2 Estimates of Sales of Maize Flour and Rice Through Official Channels,[1] Tanzania.

| Year | Maize Flour | Rice |
|---|---|---|
| | (thousand metric tons) | |
| 1965/66 | 78.8 | 16.0 |
| 1966/67 | 65.8 | 21.6 |
| 1967/68 | 81.9 | 23.4 |
| 1968/69 | 92.0 | 23.9 |
| 1969/70 | 108.6 | 28.4 |
| 1970/71 | 102.6 | 35.4 |
| 1971/72 | 140.8 | 51.5 |
| 1972/73 | 135.5 | 59.8 |
| 1973/74 | 184.5 | 59.5 |
| 1974/75 | 175.4 | 39.4 |
| 1975/76 | 114.6 | 38.8 |
| 1976/77 | 121.3[2] | 56.1[2] |
| 1977/78 | 110.0[2] [3] | 57.0[3] |

Source: Coopers and Lybrand, Final Report (1976).

[1] Refers to sales of the National Agricultural Produce Board and the National Milling Corporation.

[2] Preliminary estimates based on data supplied by the National Milling Corp.

[3] Preliminary.

nation, government action is perceived in terms of meeting (1) urban demand plus (2) the share of rural demand that the governments feel obliged to meet especially in bad crop years.[8] Defined in this way, the maize reserve requirements for Tanzania may be about 100,000 tons, compared to 34,000 tons and 68,000 tons if conceived in terms of offsetting production fluctuations by 5 percent and 10 percent, respectively, based on the Tanzanian official cereal production series. The figures will vary if USDA's estimates are used. In Zambia, as shown in Figure 5.2, the rapid market penetration by Namboard requires

# Food Security: East African Considerations

an extra 45,000 tons per year, quite apart from any food security considerations. No direct estimates are available of either production or consumption variability in Zambia.

The conceptualization of food security requirements has substantial implications not only on the size but also on the composition and the cost of the food reserve. Rural and urban consumption patterns may markedly influence whether the source of the supply of the reserve is imported or produced domestically. Different food security schemes will also influence domestic pricing and other agricultural production and trade policies differently. The standard international models of food security assume that a 5 percent reduction in production would lead to a corresponding percentage decline in consumption across the board. Our observation, however, suggests that the rural population, 80 percent of whose production is for subsistence, would attempt to maintain their consumption level in the face of a production decline. Thus a 5 percent decline in production is more likely to lead to a 25 percent decline in the marketed production (i.e., in the 20 percent of production that is marketed).[9] This is significant in the conception of the problem and would lead to different sizes and compositions of buffer stocks than those arrived at on the basis of overall production fluctuations.

## Composition of Urban and Rural Demand

The urban cereal consumption pattern in many African countries is relatively more homogeneous than the rural, consisting largely of maize and some wheat and rice. (In Ethiopia, teff is also important.) International food assistance is, however, frequently influenced by the particular cereal that donors can spare. This can lead to a radical shift in the urban consumption patterns away from domestically produced cereals (i.e., maize) to imported grain (as can be documented in the case of some East African countries).

Rural food consumption patterns are substantially more diverse and involve consumption of several different crops including cassava, sorghum, millets, rice, bananas, and maize depending on local production. This diversity aggravates the problems of ensuring rural food security through official channels, as it complicates (if not makes impossible) the problem of management and distribution of stocks in different regions. Thus neither national nor international food distribution programs directly assist the rural sector. By absorbing rural surpluses for urban consumption, these distribution programs do help the rural areas indirectly.

## Production Marketed Through Official Channels

It is essential to identify the consumption requirements of the rural and urban sector. These specific commodity requirements for national food security will have important implications on domestic food production strategy and efficient resource use in the long run. The simplistic formulation of the food security problem in the international literature, in contrast, is formulated in terms of "tonnage" and "calories." For instance, a shift in the domestic consumption pattern that tended to substitute wheat and rice for maize would increase import dependence unless domestic production of those crops increased or domestic consumption could be curbed. Increasing consumer prices and/or reducing imports are politically awkward options. Rather than control consumption, a country may attempt to increase domestic production of imported cereals to meet future urban demand. In the short run, however, an increase in the official purchases of domestic crops beyond levels of domestic needs may result in subsidized exports. A subsidy may be needed just to cover the producer prices and costs of transport and handling their extensive rural distribution. For instance, the average margin required by the National Milling Corporation in Tanzania to cover costs of official domestic distribution amounts to approximately U.S. $100 per ton. Without a subsidy, consumer prices would be too great for the effective demand in rural areas. In most of these countries, the domestic market for livestock feed is very limited. Although this can be developed, it would involve a radical change in the livestock sector's practices. The scarce and poor storage facilities incur enormous losses for stocks stored longer than one year.[10] The only option left to these countries to minimize short-run costs is to subsidize exports of minor crops.

If the objective of domestic food self-sufficiency is to be achieved without sacrificing overall agricultural growth, careful

# Food Security: East African Considerations

attention to relative crop pricing, production, and trade policy is required. This is especially true if the crops requiring subsidized exports are not to be generated at the cost of the stagnation (or decline) of traditional export crops that contribute to the fiscal revenues.

## Determinants of "Official" Marketed Surpluses

The relationship of production to "official marketings" is not clear, although figures of 10 to 30 percent of the production are usually quoted. The proportion seems to vary considerably among crops (depending on their importance in home consumption) and from one year to another. A small increase in production often appears to lead to a more than proportionate increase in official marketings, implying elasticity of domestic consumption to change in production of less than one. The situation is complicated by three factors. First, marketed production may often be greater than rural consumption levels would suggest because of the tendency among farm families to sell grain during the season to meet cash requirements and buy grain in the market for consumption in the off-season. An attractive postharvest price obviously facilitates early sales. Correspondingly, grain shortfalls or a very high price in the off-season can have an adverse impact on the food supply of rural families and hence on rural food security.

Second, apart from the level of production, the amount sold in the official channels is a function of the relative prices in the official and the "unofficial" market, the payment terms used by the official marketing agency (the official tendency being not to make prompt cash payments), and the accessibility of an official purchasing center. It is difficult to isolate the effect of policy changes and of production changes on the increase or decrease in official marketings.

Third, trading patterns in the unofficial market are not confined to the national boundaries. This exacerbates the problem of estimating the extent to which it is the production increase rather than the sealing of national borders, relative changes in exchange rates or availability of consumer goods across national boundaries that has caused changes in unofficial exports and domestic official purchases.

A number of hypotheses can be advanced concerning levels

and changes in production and marketing. But any formal analysis is made difficult by a variety of factors including (1) the lack of reliable farm-level data, (2) the factors that affect local farming decisions, (3) the extremely diverse farming systems precluding aggregation and generalization, and (4) the low and in some cases decreasing level of monetization, especially in the case of low-income subsistence farmers, which creates difficulties in carrying out formal analysis based on the concepts of exchange and specialization.

*Food Pricing*

Although official agricultural prices are known, actual prices that are faced by the majority of rural producers and consumers are not known. Not only do they seem to differ from official prices, they also differ from one rural area to another. These discrepancies are caused by the fragmentation of grain markets, the varying conditions that influence them, and the differing levels of prices of other goods and services that influence food pricing.

The conclusion that can be drawn from this phenomenon is that little is known or predictable about the factors that influence food production and marketing, making it immensely difficult to plan a "national" food security program. The governments' strategy under these circumstances is usually twofold: (1) to meet commercial demand through a strategic reserve and (2) to increase availability of supplies in rural areas through increased production.[11]

## Policy Directions

As indicated above, the food grain markets in East Africa are fragmented, with an urban sector supplied mainly by the parastatal and the rural market supplied mainly by the unofficial system. This is important to any discussion on food security policies. Increasing the supplies available to the marketing parastatal may merely tend to increase the urban supplies, with very little, if any, trickle back into the rural areas.

Rural food security is very largely a question of rural self-sufficiency. This point is well appreciated by rural producers,

# Food Security: East African Considerations

and indeed is widely recognized as the primary consideration in the determination of cropping pattern and amounts to be marketed. This point may not be as well appreciated by urbanized policymakers.[12] Given this perspective, four policy directions suggest themselves.

1. The promotion of drought-resistant food crops to achieve self-sufficiency at the farm household and the village or a small area level is critical. In many cases, the more drought-resistant crops of sorghum and finger and bulrush millet have been downgraded by policymakers in comparison with crops such as maize.

2. The provision of a market for surpluses of drought-resistant crops is another important aspect. The major food crops of maize, wheat, and rice have substantial commercial markets, and cassava has a minor domestic and a potential export market. However, the drought-resistant crops have essentially no market. Without government intervention, excess production of these crops in good years would be valueless and thus the incentive to produce them would be reduced. In Tanzania, a conscious policy of subsidizing these crops is being pursued as a means of encouraging self-sufficiency at the village level.[13] This may well be cheaper than providing famine-relief supplies at the village level in years of low yield. Further analysis of this issue is needed.

3. The private cash market for foodgrains in rural areas needs explicit recognition and promotion. At present the parastatals provide a market in which farmers can sell their excess foodgrain. However, to buy foodgrain, farmers have to rely on the informal market, at prices often well above the official price offered by the parastatal. Furthermore, in the rainy season it may not be possible to buy foodgrain from outside the village. This essentially forces self-sufficiency at the village level, with all of the associated losses in economic efficiency that come from a closed rather than an open economic system. Increasing the efficiency of rural markets is not easy or cheap. It involves improving transportation and communications and a tolerant attitude to the activities of the private sector.

4. Research and extension are needed on improved methods of farm-level storage. Despite some efforts in this direction, farm-level storage would seem to involve losses of from 10 to

30 percent over a 12-month period. (Certainly, food prices may double at the village level from the post- to preharvest periods; and physical considerations also confirm these loss estimates.) As not all grain is held for the full year, farm-level losses on average may be no more than 15 to 20 percent. This would appear to represent the single most promising direction for a quantum jump in available food supplies. A program of research on new farm storage methods and extension is desirable.

We consider urban food security the tail, not the dog. There are some parallels between the food security problem in East Africa and the problem as it is discussed in international economic fora. However, the East African problem differs from the assumptions underlying the discussions on international food security in several respects.

1. The variance of demand as well as that of supply poses a problem for the marketing parastatal. When the price of maize flour in the informal market rises, consumers substitute with maize flour produced by the parastatal (a product with lower consumer acceptability) and with wheat flour and rice. Thus, at fixed prices a low maize crop, with lower supplies to the informal market, will increase urban demand for all the major foodgrains. This variation in demand is a primary source of urban food insecurity. As shown in Table 5.2 the sales of the National Milling Corporation (NMC, the Tanzanian grain-marketing parastatal) were 61 percent higher in 1973/74 than 1975/76.

2. As seen in the previous paragraph, official sales fluctuate by much more than 5 to 10 percent. Therefore, stocks to protect against fluctuation in demand would be much greater than stocks needed to protect against production fluctuations.[14]

3. A food security program that guarantees foodgrains in essentially the proportion consumers would demand at normal prices and one that guarantees the supply of a single grain have different commodity requirements. In Kenya and Tanzania, strategic grain reserves are being accumulated with funding both of the grain reserve and the necessary stores from donor countries. The intended composition of the grain reserve has therefore immediate operational significance. If the composition of the reserve is immaterial, then wheat or rice donated for the

*Food Security: East African Considerations* 117

reserve can be sold on the domestic market for immediate consumption and can be replaced by domestic maize or cassava.[15] On the other hand, if the composition is important, then only wheat would be rotated with wheat.

4. There are technical limits to the size of the strategic reserve. Maize can be stored for two years before becoming unfit for human consumption. Therefore, even with 100 percent rotation of the strategic reserve, only one year's normal sales could be stored (i.e., the first year after harvest the maize would be in the strategic reserve, the second year it would be sold before becoming unfit for human consumption). Thus, high rates of deterioration for stored grain may pose technical limits to the amount that can be stored. These limits are quite apart from the economic and political questions of how much should be stored. As this technical constraint is approached, the management of the food reserve would pose increasingly severe problems. Grain not milled within a year of going into strategic store would have to be downgraded to animal feed. It seems likely that substantially higher transport bills would have to be incurred with a central strategic national reserve than without it. If the reserve is a small percentage of annual marketings, its turnover can be expected to be arranged at very little extra cost. At the point where all purchases have to pass through the strategic reserve, the costs of this extra constraint could mount substantially. As a corollary to this line of thought, minor crops with little or no sale in a normal year are unsuitable candidates for the reserve. As there is no scope for turnover, there is no possibility of maintaining high quality grain in the reserve.

### Conclusion

This chapter describes some of the major considerations that should enter into the formulation of national food security strategies in the East African context. It contrasts these considerations with the assumptions made in the standard global models of food security. These latter are expected to be applicable not only across countries but across continents and across a range of different—and changing—policy objectives (i.e., role of public distribution), institutional development

# 118

(i.e., the extent and efficiency of the private and public marketing systems), infrastructure, data availability, and cereal demands.

Some of the inferences of our presentation are self-evident. First, if international schemes are to be effective and responsive to the needs of the recipient, then such schemes have to be tailored to the individual countries. This requires designing schemes suited for a group of countries similar in terms of economic development, policy objectives, cereal demands, and so on, rather than one global scheme applicable to all.

Second, it should be recognized that a food security scheme in most East African countries based on public distribution will inadequately solve the problem of rural food security. Rural food security will be achieved through increased research and extension on the production of drought-resistant crops, improved input supply, produce marketing, an improved communication network, and an effective farm household storage program. An effective farm household storage program will have to use local and inexpensive materials.

Third, we stress the impact of subsistence consumption maintenance as a cause of urban food supply instability. This feature leads to a markedly different perspective on the problem than does a model that implies that an across-the-board reduction in consumption is the result of a supply decrease.

The final conclusion is the vital need for additional data on total crop production and distribution in order that the basic statistics for effective national food security schemes be available.

## Notes

The views expressed are those of the authors and do not necessarily reflect those of the World Bank.

1. Furthermore, the effectiveness of this price may be in question. In some regions the parastatal may shorten the procurement season and in others payment may be delayed. The existence of an official price does not mean that farmers can necessarily sell at this price for cash whenever they wish to. Further, villagers typically have difficulty exchanging cash

Food Security: East African Considerations 119

for consumer goods. If the parastatal really wished to increase market share, it would take basic consumer products to the village to sell for the grain being bought.

2. It is widely recognized that per-ton transport costs are often much higher in most African than Asian countries because of poor infrastructure and the greater mileage relative to the volume of trade. The costs should thus apply equally to the public and private sector. However, in practice, the cost of public-sector distribution frequently tends to be higher due to unnecessary transport of grain, i.e., from the rural to urban center, before it is shipped to the distant rural areas again. This is partly a result of centralized processing facilities and management. Partly it is a result of pan-territorial official pricing, which results in relatively more being sold to and bought from the official sources in distant areas where the official prices are competitive vis-à-vis the unofficial market prices. The reverse is the case in the areas close to the centers of urban consumption.

3. See Part 2 in this book.

4. Tanzania's import bill in 1974 went up to U.S. $133 million from U.S. $34 million in the previous year. To avoid such situations in the future, Tanzania plans to build a reserve of 100,000 tons. Assistance from bilateral and international agencies in the form of storage facilities and grain are expected to cover all capital costs, which are expected to be about U.S. $30 million. Management expertise is also being provided by donors. Tanzania is typical of a small country to which international assistance for national food reserves is readily forthcoming because of the small amounts involved.

5. The debate on the best form of food security may still be essential if all countries have not proceeded to build a domestic reserve. This is especially true if large countries such as India, Indonesia, and Bangladesh—whose demand for food in the international market is significant—do not have their own reserves. Further, even in the East African countries that are proceeding with national reserves, there is a possibility that either domestic food production may not be able to replenish the reserve or that the composition of the domestic production increase may not be suitable for meeting the objectives of the reserve as seen by national policymakers (more is said on this later). Therefore, analysis as to how to keep the national reserve operating at minimum cost to the country may be necessary. However, it is evident that a different analytical focus is needed than that noted in much of the international literature on the question of food security.

6. An analysis of the rate of growth of food production carried out for India has documented the other obvious fact that the growth rate obtained is highly dependent on the choice of base- and end-year production levels,

i.e., a poor crop in the base year and an excellent crop in the end year exaggerates the growth rate and the reverse understates it. See for instance Uma J. Lele and John W. Mellor (1964).

7. Notably, the United Nations Development Programme's (UNDP) early warning, crop-yield forecasting project in Tanzania. Though useful expenditures have also been made by the Ford Foundation in Zambia and by the World Bank in several countries in a farm management context, these expenditures are not sufficient to provide a picture of the overall production situation even in a limited project area. At this stage, obtaining a national picture from these data is thus completely out of the question.

8. The recognition of the impracticality of dealing with the rural food security problem through distribution may prompt governments to promote production of drought-resistant food crops. The official policy of promoting production of cassava, sorghum, and millets since 1973/74 in Tanzania is prompted by such a concern for "national" food security.

9. The precise percentage change in the marketed surplus would, of course, depend on the distribution of production. For producers already on the verge of subsistence in normal years, decline in production would mean a net requirement for purchased foods. Whether this requirement is fulfilled would depend on (1) whether supplies are available in rural markets for purchases and (2) whether the rural population has the income to purchase the food.

10. Especially given the existence of a strategic reserve of 100,000 tons, i.e., roughly equivalent to eight months of urban consumption requirements, it is unlikely that the turnover period of "excess" domestic stocks, especially of the less preferred minor crops, would be less than one crop year.

11. It should be emphasized that an increase in average yield ($y$), with no change in the coefficient of variation, may have little effect on the level of food security (defined as the probability of having to draw down stocks to meet current consumption), i.e., the variance would have to increase correspondingly. An extensive analysis of policy options in Zambia showed that while expected production could be substantially increased, the probability of meeting annual requirements in any one year was essentially unchanged.

12. For instance, in Lesotho, even though research results and farmers' experience shows an attractive return only at very low levels of fertilizer use, much too high dosages of fertilizer are promoted by the Ministry of Agriculture. In Tanzania, there is evidence that in the recent past, arbitrary policy decisions have included exclusive reliance on monoculture (where farmers' experience suggests that consortia of crops have more

*Food Security: East African Considerations* 121

reliable yields) and indiscriminate promotion of fertilizer even in areas where its marginal productivity is very low. A less monolithic approach is now being taken, with the encouragement of drought-resistant crops such as millets and sorghum in areas of unreliable rainfall. It is not clear, however, that at the local level sufficient appreciation exists of the adverse effects coercive efforts are likely to have on the individual farmer's efforts to assure food security for himself and his family.

13. Augmented by restriction of seed supply for other crops that farmers may wish to produce, but which are not currently in demand in urban areas.

14. Because the international literature refers to fluctuations relative to total production and not official sales, the absolute level of stock requirements may be of the same general order of magnitude. But, at the same time, the parastatal might be required to hold stocks equivalent to 100 percent of its sales in order to cope with a 5 percent variation in total production.

15. Again, the acceptability of cassava, or even sorghum or millets, as a component of the strategic reserve should be the result of a conscious decision.

## References

Coopers and Lybrand Associates Limited, Management and Economics Consultants. "Grain Storage and Milling Report" (final draft). London, England, 1977.

Johnson, D. Gale. "Grain Insurance, Reserves, and Trade: Contributions to Food Security for LDCs." Chapter 12, this book.

Konandreas, Panos; Barbara Huddleston; and Virabongsa Ramangkura. "Food Security: An Insurance Approach." Research Report No. 4. Washington, D.C.: IFPRI, 1978.

Lele, Uma, and John W. Mellor. "Estimates of Change and Causes of Change in Foodgrains Production: India, 1949–50 to 1960–61." *Cornell University International Development Bulletin* No. 2. Ithaca, New York. August 1964.

Reutlinger, Shlomo. "Food Insecurity: Magnitude and Remedies." Abstract, World Bank Staff Working Paper No. 267. July 1977.

# 6
# The Nature of Food
# Insecurity in Colombia

*Jorge García García*

This chapter discusses what "food security" means in the particular context of Colombia. First, it assesses to what extent the variability in aggregate food production and the availability of foreign exchange could represent serious sources of insecurity in food consumption in Colombia, concluding that these are not major concerns. However, there seems to be widespread malnutrition in Colombia because of uneven distribution of income: even minor increases in food prices can induce significant real income losses that increase the incidence of malnutrition in both urban and rural sectors. This chapter continues by discussing policy options for coping with the deterioration of nutritional levels for vulnerable groups.

## Food Situation in Colombia

Most discussions on food security consider foodgrains only. An inadequate definition of food can lead to an incorrect assessment of the magnitude of insecurity and the resources needed to reduce or eliminate it.

According to a survey conducted in 1972 by the Instituto Colombiano de Bienestar Familiar (ICBF), 12 products account for almost 90 percent of the weight of food consumption and contribute 76 percent and 77 percent, respectively, of the calorie and protein consumption of the average Colombian. This average food consumption basket of white- and blue-collar workers of Colombia, presented in Table 6.1, has remained unchanged throughout the last 25 years.[1] As shown in

# 124 Jorge García García

Table 6.1 Composition of Food Consumption in Colombia in 1972

|  | Share in consumption | |
| Food Item | Protein | Calorie |
|  | (percent) | (percent) |
| Potato | 5.4 | 6.2 |
| Milk | 8.5 | 3.6 |
| Plantain | 2.0 | 5.8 |
| Non-centrifugal sugar | 0.8 | 12.1 |
| Rice | 12.7 | 13.6 |
| Meat | 23.5 | 6.8 |
| Wheat | 12.5 | 8.5 |
| Cassava | 0.6 | 3.0 |
| Sugar | --- | 7.5 |
| Maize | 6.8 | 7.1 |
| Bananas | 0.2 | 0.5 |
| Beans | 4.0 | 1.3 |
| Others[a/] | 23.0 | 24.0 |
| Total | 100.0 | 100.0 |

Source: Departamento Nacional de Planeacion *Plan Nacional de Alimentacion y Nutricion: Seleccion de Alimentos,* Documento DNP-UDS-DPN-011, Octubre 18 de 1974, Tables No. 3,4 and 5, quoting ICBF, *Encuesta Nacional de Dietas 1972.*

a/ Others comprises vegetables and animal oil, oil, eggs, fish, onions, tomatoes, carrots, orange, guavas, lentils, green beans, broad beans, "arracacha," and cabbage.

Table 6.1, an analysis of food security in Colombia that only considers cereals could be misleading.[2]

## Food Production and Availability in Colombia

Colombia has been a net exporter, though very small, of food products (see Table 6.2). Almost all total food output goes to satisfy internal consumption needs. This relation has been

# The Nature of Food Insecurity in Colombia

Table 6.2 Food Production and Food Availability in Colombia, 1950-1975

| Period | Total Production | Total Availability | Per capita Production | Per capita Availability | Availability Production |
|---|---|---|---|---|---|
| | (thousand metric tons) | | (kilograms per year) | | |
| 1950 - 1955 | 6,614 [a] | 6,511 | 560 | 552 | .984 |
| 1956 - 1960 | 7,472 | 7,385 | 526 | 520 | .988 |
| 1961 - 1965 | 8,518 | 8,427 | 507 | 501 | .989 |
| 1966 - 1970 | 10,076 | 9,793 | 515 | 501 | .972 |
| 1971 - 1975 | 12,313 | 12,225 | 549 | 545 | .992 |

Reference: García García (1979).

a/ The figures are an average for the period.

relatively stable, implying that food production and availability have grown at about the same rate during the 1950–1975 period. However, per-capita output and availability of food have fallen during this period. Despite a substantial recovery in production in the last five years, per-capita availability is still below the levels existing at the beginning of the second half of this century. Between 1961 and 1970, this decline is particularly notorious, with per-capita consumption stagnating at an annual level of 501 kilograms. This decrease might be indirect evidence that the nutritional status of the Colombian population deteriorated throughout the study period.[3] The high rate of population growth, particularly between 1950 and 1964,[4] more than offset any reasonable increase in agricultural output. The severe shortage of foreign exchange during the 1958–1969 period[5] did not permit imports needed to maintain constant per-capita consumption. The situation was exacerbated by the diversion of some food commodities to the international markets to earn badly needed foreign exchange.

The behavior of gross per-capita output, gross per-capita supply, and net per-capita supply (consumption) of calories (Table 6.3) also indicates that the nutritional well-being of Colombians has deteriorated. Only in the mid-1970s did daily

126 *Jorge García García*

Table 6.3 Output, Supply and Consumption of Calories in Colombia: 1950-1975

| Period | Gross Output | Gross Supply | Net Supply (Consumption) | Availability Production |
|---|---|---|---|---|
| | | (per capita per day) | | |
| 1950-1955 | 2,859[a] | 2,863 | 2,171 | 1.004 |
| 1956-1960 | 2,603 | 2,654 | 1,996 | 1.010 |
| 1961-1965 | 2,574 | 2,590 | 1,944 | 1.006 |
| 1966-1970 | 2,622 | 2,591 | 1,943 | .988 |
| 1971-1975 | 2,895 | 2,926 | 2,170 | 1.010 |

Reference: García García (1979).
a/ The figures are an average for the period.

per-capita calorie consumption reach the levels of the early 1950s. Nevertheless, given the recommended minimum daily per-capita consumption of 1,970 calories per day,[6] there has not been, on the average, a serious nutritional problem in Colombia. These aggregate average figures may be hiding a serious nutritional problem, particularly among the poor.

*Is There an Aggregate Food Insecurity Problem in Colombia?*

Food production in Colombia for the 1950-1975 period has been remarkably stable. The trend growth rate of food output has been 2.99 percent per year with a variability around trend of 3.71 percent.

Output in the last 16 years (1959-1975) has displayed even greater stability.[7] The rate of growth of annual food output reaches 3.43 percent and the variation drops to around 2.61 percent. This implies that the annual rate of growth of food output from 1950 to 1959 was less than 2.99 percent and the variability around trend was greater than 3.10 percent.

Mean production is 8.67 and 9.87 million for the 1950-1975 and 1959-1975 periods with standard deviations around trend production of 322 and 295 thousand tons, respectively, and the mean food supply is 8.55 million tons and 9.73 million tons for the 1950-1975 and 1959-1975 periods, with standard devia-

# The Nature of Food Insecurity in Colombia

Table 6.4 Probability of a Given Shortfall in Trend Production

| Adjusted | Shortfall | | | |
|---|---|---|---|---|
| trend line | 1 percent | 3 percent | 5 percent | 10 percent |
| 1950 - 1975 | 0.39 | 0.215 | 0.10 | 0.002 |
| 1959 - 1975 | 0.36 | 0.14 | 0.04 | 0.001 |
| 1961 - 1975 | 0.33 | 0.09 | 0.02 | 0.005 |

tions of 333 and 311 thousand tons, respectively. We can conclude that both the relative and absolute variability of food production and food availability in Colombia were reduced during the 25-year span considered in this study.[8]

Initially, one could examine food insecurity just by concentrating on food production variability, regardless of whether or not financial or foreign exchange resources to eliminate the deficit are available. The percentage shortfalls chosen are 1 percent, 3 percent, 5 percent, and 10 percent. Table 6.4 shows the probability of shortfalls based on trend lines adjusted for the 1950–1975, 1959–1975, and 1961-1975 periods. If the production trends continue, a shortfall of 1 percent in trend production will occur in 1 out of every 3 years; of 3 percent in 1 out of every 5 or 10 years; of 5 percent in 1 out of 10 or 50 years, and a 10 percent shortfall in trend production in 1 out of 500 years.[9] Likewise, the probability of having a 3 percent shortfall in trend output during two consecutive years (assuming these are independent events) is 1.96 percent (1959–1975 trend) and around 0.03 percent during three consecutive years. The event of a 1 percent shortfall in trend output during 3 consecutive years will have a 1.7 percent probability of occurring, and less than 1 percent (0.6 percent) probability for 5 consecutive years. Cases of a 5 or 10 percent shortfall in trend production for more than one year are extremely unlikely.

If cereal production had been used as an indicator of food output, the degree of food insecurity, as measured by the probability of a given shortfall in trend production, would have been greater. A 1 percent, 3 percent, 5 percent, and 10 percent

128                                                                   *Jorge García García*

shortfall in trend production would have meant a probability of around 50 percent, 37 percent, 28 percent, and 13 percent for the occurrence of each event respectively.[10] Since cereal production represents around 17 percent of total food production, the absolute value of the shortfall would have been underestimated. Therefore, the actions necessary to meet that deficit would probably also have been underestimated.

Though the size of food insecurity is very small in Colombia, it is instructive to determine the magnitude of the foreign exchange needed to meet any shortfall in food production in excess of 5 percent for any given year through imports of wheat. (See Table 6.5.) It is assumed that the imported wheat is to be consumed during that same year and therefore the cost of storage can be neglected.[11]

In the unlikely case of a consecutive shortfall of 5 percent in trend production for the next 5 years, wheat imports would require $123 million for 1979 and $141 million for 1983 of foreign exchange. This represents between 6.6 percent and 7.5 percent of imports of goods and services and 4.8 percent and 6.6 percent of exports of goods and services for 1976 respectively. As imports and exports of goods and services for the 1979–1983 period grow, the burden of having food security through increased imports on the balance of payments decreases.

Food insecurity at the aggregate level is a very small problem in Colombia.[12] However, a problem might occur at the regional

Table 6.5 Projections of Food Output and of Imports of Food For a 5 Percent Shortfall in Trend Production[a]

| Year | Trend food production | 5 percent shortfall | Cost of imports |
|------|------|------|------|
| | (thousand metric tons) | | (US $ million) |
| 1979 | 14,892 | 745 | 123 |
| 1980 | 15,411 | 771 | 127 |
| 1981 | 15,948 | 797 | 132 |
| 1982 | 16,504 | 825 | 136 |
| 1983 | 17,079 | 854 | 141 |

a/ Projections based on the adjusted trend line for the 1959-1975 period.

level due to inadequacies of the food distribution system and physical infrastructures. Colombia may not yet be equipped with the port and transport facilities required by a security scheme based on imports. Also, considering that food imports have been relatively small, consisting primarily of wheat, the importation of large quantities of certain foodstuffs might be difficult in the short run because of unfamiliarity with the mechanics of the international markets for some commodities and the lag inherent in all import decisions.

Thus, Colombia has neither a high probability of substantial shortfall in trend production of food output nor insufficient foreign exchange earnings to meet the food import bill necessary to cover such a shortfall. However, even in the case of small shortfalls of food trend production, an insecurity problem might arise because imports may not be capable of meeting the food gap due to infrastructure and institutional problems.

## Nutritional Situation of the Colombian Population

### The Overall Nutritional Situation

Based on national averages, comparison between required calorie consumption (1,970 calories per day) and actual consumption reveals only a very slight nutritional problem in the country.[13] Calorie consumption is approximately 98.5 percent adequate. Yet, as is evident to an observer in the rural and urban areas, malnutrition is a widespread phenomenon in Colombia.

To explore this issue further, we estimated the effects of income distribution on calorie consumption for the country as a whole and for the rural and urban sectors for 1972, which is the most recent year for which information on household distribution of income and expenditure exists. This analysis was done by computing calorie consumption as a function of income and alternatively as a function of expenditure. Several specifications of the estimating equation were computed, but finally a semilog specification was used because it yields a declining calorie-income (or expenditure) relationship.

The estimated equations used to calculate daily per-capita calorie consumption for each income bracket in Table 6.6 are:

$$C = -4707.1 + 773.05 \ln X \qquad R^2 = 0.64$$
$$(-3.475)\ (4.9648) \qquad\qquad \text{D.W.} = 1.48$$

$$C = -3087.5 + 609.31 \ln E \qquad R^2 = 0.60$$
$$(-2.7629)\ (4.5688) \qquad\qquad \text{D.W.} = 1.36$$

where ln stands for natural logarithm, $C$ for calorie consumption per day, $X$ for income per capita per year, and $E$ for private consumption expenditure per capita per year. Figures in parentheses are the $t$-statistics of the estimated coefficients.

In Table 6.7 data on population, per-capita income, and expenditure are shown for 1972. Using these results and the per-capita daily calorie requirement established by ICBF of 1,970 calories per day, one concludes that between 28 and 52 percent of the Colombian population is undernourished—columns (2) and (1) in Table 6.6 respectively—for the following reasons: first, the estimates of calorie consumption of column (1) are too low to maintain human body weight; second, the distribution of income within each class is uneven and, certainly, some people in Group III in column (2) are consuming less than the estimated 1,970 calories per day. However, as argued by Sukhatme (1977), we could be overestimating the degree of malnutrition because of the downward adjustment of requirements necessary to allow for variations in individual calorie requirements. Nevertheless, the level established by ICBF is low enough to be considered a minimum, rather than an average.[14]

The data in the last row of Table 6.6 provide the implicit caloric consumption (unadjusted) if incomes were evenly distributed. According to these figures, the caloric requirements for the whole country would be more than satisfied with the available food supply.

The consumption of low-income groups could be raised by increasing imports, domestic production, or their income. If incomes were increased by one and two percent per year, Group I would have to wait between 75 and 47 years, respectively, to achieve the required consumption of calories! The comparison of consumption by income bracket with the minimum requirements reveals that the calorie gap for the total population in income Groups I-III, expressed in cereal equivalents, adds up to between 141,300 and 407,000 tons of cereal per annum.

Table 6.6 Daily Per Capita Calorie Consumption in Colombia: 1972

| Household income bracket | National total | | Urban | | Rural | |
|---|---|---|---|---|---|---|
| | (1)[a/] | (2)[b/] | (1)[a/] | (2)[b/] | (1)[a/] | (2)[b/] |
| I | 1,049 | 1,530 | 1,119 | 1,592 | 1,012 | 1,511 |
| II | 1,497 | 1,796 | 1,598 | 1,786 | 1,440 | 1,773 |
| III | 1,846 | 1,974 | 1,944 | 2,074 | 1,758 | 1,896 |
| IV | 2,109 | 2,116 | 2,175 | 2,201 | 2,014 | 1,990 |
| V | 2,425 | 2,292 | 2,469 | 2,359 | 2,367 | 2,191 |
| VI | 2,713 | 2,441 | 2,771 | 2,536 | 2,582 | 2,155 |
| VII | 2,984 | 2,577 | 3,008 | 2,609 | 2,936 | 2,478 |
| VIII | 3,371 | 2,810 | 3,434 | 2,881 | 3,147 | 2,544 |
| IX | 3,732 | 3,045 | 3,765 | 3,086 | 3,286 | 2,479 |
| X | 4,463 | 3,325 | 4,493 | 3,344 | 4,484 | 3,596 |
| X[c/] | 1,973 | 2,089 | 2,180 | 2,236 | 1,478 | 1,755 |

a/ Derived from equation $C = -4707.1 + 773.05 \ln X$.

b/ Derived from equation $C = -3087.5 + 609.31 \ln E$

c/ This line shows the unadjusted calorie consumption corresponding to the average per capita real income or expenditure of the survey.

Note: The consumption of calories has been adjusted according to the method explained in García García, 1979.

132                                                                    *Jorge García García*

Table 6.7  Population, Per-Capita Income, and Expenditure by Household Income
Bracket in the Urban and Rural Sectors of Colombia, 1972.

| Household annual income bracket | Urban sector | | | Rural sector | | |
|---|---|---|---|---|---|---|
| | Cumulative distribution of population | Income | Expenditure | Cumulative distribution of population | Income | Expenditure |
| Pesos 1970 (000s) | % | | Pesos 1970 (000s) | % | | Pesos 1970 (000s) |
| I 0-6.8 | 4.3 | 1.4 | 1.7 | 9.8 | 1.2 | 1.5 |
| II 6.8-13.7 | 19.1 | 2.2 | 2.3 | 43.0 | 1.9 | 2.2 |
| III 13.7-22.7 | 38.9 | 3.2 | 3.5 | 72.3 | 2.6 | 2.7 |
| IV 22.7-31.8 | 56.7 | 4.0 | 4.2 | 86.7 | 3.4 | 3.1 |
| V 31.8-40.9 | 65.8 | 5.4 | 5.3 | 92.2 | 4.9 | 4.2 |
| VI 40.9-54.6 | 74.8 | 7.4 | 6.9 | 96.4 | 6.1 | 3.9 |
| VII 54.6-72.8 | 84.0 | 9.3 | 7.8 | 97.4 | 8.7 | 6.4 |
| VIII 72.8-109.2 | 91.2 | 14.4 | 11.6 | 99.5 | 10.8 | 7.0 |
| IX 109.2-182.0 | 96.2 | 20.2 | 15.8 | 99.7 | 12.4 | 6.4 |
| X 182.0- | 100.0 | 42.2 | 23.2 | 100.0 | 41.8 | 33.8 |
| Average income and expenditure | | 7.4 | 6.2 | | 2.9 | 2.8 |
| Total population | 12,264,167 | | | 7,951,036 | | |

Source: Derived from DANE 1977b, *Ingresos y Gastos de los Hogares en Colombia:* 1972
(Bogota: Division de Edicion del DANE, 1977),Tables 3.1, 3.2, and 4.1.
See García García (1979).
Note: The average real exchange rate for 1972 (at 1970 prices) is 17.35 pesos
per US dollar.

## *The Nutritional Situation in the Urban and "Rural" Sectors*

Table 6.6 presents the implicit daily per-capita calorie consumption for the average of each income per-capita bracket in the urban and rural sectors of the country. The estimates of column (1) are far lower than those of column (2) for the low-income groups and far higher for the high-income groups. The estimates of column (1) illustrate what occurs when income from national accounts is used as an explanatory variable in the estimation of calorie-income relationships (which are used later with household survey data) and not necessarily to reflect the "true" calorie consumption of different income groups in the country.

# The Nature of Food Insecurity in Colombia

If estimates of column (1) were used, the extent of malnutrition would be approximately 52 percent of all the Colombian population. However, these estimates of calorie consumption seem to be too low. The column (2) estimates indicate that malnutrition affects about 19 percent of the urban and 72 percent of the rural population, or 2.3 million and 5.8 million people in the urban and rural sectors, respectively (8.09 million people for the country). This represents 40 percent of the national population.[15] This percentage could be higher, since income is not equally distributed within Group IV of the rural sector.

Malnutrition is more serious in the rural than in the urban sector. Even if income were evenly distributed within each sector, the rural sector would still have a serious problem although malnutrition in the urban sector would disappear. These results suggest that the inequality in the distribution of income between the urban and rural sectors, rather than the inequality within each sector, is more relevant to explaining the existing malnutrition problem in Colombia.

Colombia suffers a calorie gap of between 1.6 and 3.8 billion calories per day,[16] of which approximately 68 percent occurs in the rural sector. The total deficit is equivalent to 165 and 400 thousand tons of cereal per year. To fill this gap by imports implies an increase in the annual food import bill of approximately U.S. $38 to $92 million, which, for example in 1972, represents between 3.8 and 9.3 percent of total exports of goods and services—a relatively small burden on the current account balance.

## Food Insecurity for Whom?

Food insecurity in Colombia arises from the fact that the poor spend a high proportion of their income on food. A relatively small shortfall in the supply of food that causes an increase in food prices will reduce their real income. This could generate a decrease in food consumption and a deterioration in an already impaired nutritional status.

As shown in Table 6.8, income groups I, II, III, and IV spend more than 50 percent of their incomes and total expenditures on

Table 6.8 Expenditure on Food as a Proportion of Income and Total Expenditure in Low-Income Groups (in percentage terms)

| Income bracket | Total national | | Urban | | Rural | |
|---|---|---|---|---|---|---|
| | Income | Expenditure | Income | Expenditure | Income | Expenditure |
| I | 80.0 | 65.0 | 73.0 | 59.0 | 85.0 | 69.0 |
| II | 73.0 | 62.0 | 67.0 | 58.0 | 77.0 | 66.0 |
| III | 67.0 | 58.0 | 58.0 | 53.0 | 66.0 | 65.0 |
| IV | 53.0 | 52.0 | 51.0 | 48.0 | 57.0 | 63.0 |

Source: Derived from DANE, op. cit., table 4.1.

food, with the exception of income group IV in the urban sector. Assuming a calorie expenditure elasticity of 0.35 and an initial per-capita daily calorie consumption of 1700 calories, if food prices rose 10 percent, daily average consumption would drop to 1670 calories.

## The Real Income Effect of Shortfalls in Food Trend Production

Imports of food, except for a brief period, have rarely been used to offset production shortfalls in Colombia. Therefore, decreases in trend output are fully reflected in price rises with the consequent negative effects on low-income groups.

Because the estimates of calorie consumption with income as explanatory variable are unrealistically low, expenditure was used instead. Based on elasticity estimates (available on request from the author), Table 6.9 shows the rise in the price of food resulting from shortfalls of 3 and 5 percent in supply. These values, together with the values on the proportion of total expenditure for food (Table 6.8), are then used to calculate the fall in real expenditure shown in Table 6.10.

We observe that a relatively small percentage shortfall in food supply causes substantial increases in prices and large reductions in the purchasing power of money income, particularly for low-income groups. The inelasticity of the demand for food causes an increase in food prices to increase total expenditure on food, thus reducing expenditure on other commodities. The most

# The Nature of Food Insecurity in Colombia

Table 6.9 Percentage Rise in the Price of Food Due to a Shortfall in Supply

| Price elasticity of demand for food | Food production shortfall | |
|---|---|---|
| | 3 percent | 5 percent |
| -.27 | 11.00 | 18.6 |
| -.34 | 8.8 | 14.6 |
| -.44 | 6.8 | 11.4 |

Note: The procedure followed to derive the demand elasticity for food is available on request from the author.

vulnerable groups are those in the rural sector. As shown in Table 6.10, the highest percentage fall in real expenditure occurs in Groups I through IV of the rural sector.

Within the rural sector, of course, real income of the wage earners falls with a rise in the price of food, while this is not necessarily the case with the small farmer, who consumes part of his own production. The small farmer is often a part-time farmer, complementing his income by working outside his farm. Thus, the effect of a rise in the price of food on the real income of these groups is indiscernible. As information on income sources within the rural sector is not available, we cannot determine with certainty the effect on real income for the rural sector as a whole. The information from the Departamento Administrativo Nacional de Estadística (DANE) household survey covers mainly salaried workers in the rural sector and thus the results in Table 6.10 should be interpreted as such.[17]

For income groups I and II, a 5 percent reduction in food supply implies a reduction in food consumption (expressed in caloric intake) equivalent to 40 to 67 calories per day in the urban sector and 40 to 62 calories per day in the rural sector. In these income groups, in both sectors, the initial level of food consumption is estimated at approximately 1,600 calories per day. These results show that small percentage shortfalls in food production may have significant effects on the nutritional status of relatively large groups that are already malnourished.

Table 6.10 Percentage Fall in Real Expenditure Due to Shortfalls in Food Supply

| Income bracket and sector | Food supply shortfall[a/] | | | | | |
|---|---|---|---|---|---|---|
| | 3 percent | | | 5 percent | | |
| | (1) | (2) | (3) | (1) | (2) | (3) |
| Urban | | | | | | |
| I | 6.5 | 5.2 | 4.0 | 11.0 | 8.6 | 6.7 |
| II | 6.4 | 5.1 | 3.9 | 10.8 | 8.5 | 6.6 |
| III | 5.8 | 4.7 | 3.6 | 9.9 | 7.7 | 6.0 |
| IV | 5.3 | 4.2 | 3.3 | 8.9 | 7.0 | 5.5 |
| Rural | | | | | | |
| I | 7.6 | 6.1 | 4.7 | 12.8 | 10.1 | 7.9 |
| II | 7.3 | 5.8 | 4.5 | 12.3 | 9.6 | 7.5 |
| III | 7.2 | 5.7 | 4.4 | 12.1 | 9.5 | 7.4 |
| IV | 6.9 | 5.5 | 4.3 | 11.7 | 9.2 | 7.2 |

a/ Columns (1), (2), and (3) correspond to the fall in real expenditure caused by price rises calculated using demand elasticities of -.27, -.34, and -.44, respectively.

It has been shown that food insecurity defined as either a highly unstable food supply around the trend or as a serious burden on foreign exchange earnings does not exist in Colombia. However, a large proportion of the population is malnourished. A relatively small shortfall in food trend production will worsen their nutritional status. At the core of the Colombian food insecurity is poverty, especially rural poverty.

*Policy Options*

Aside from the question of income redistribution to attack the poverty problem, Colombia has several policy options. These are a domestic buffer stock supplied with either domestic or imported commodities, trade liberalization, and target-oriented programs designed to assist the most vulnerable groups and to encourage the efficient operation of the marketing of food in the hands of the private sector.

The accumulation of food stocks for release during shortfalls is a frequently posited solution. However, as shown by

*The Nature of Food Insecurity in Colombia* 137

Reutlinger and Bigman in Chapter 9, to depend on domestic buffer stocks alone could be a very expensive and inefficient solution.

A more efficient approach would be to rely on imports to meet production shortfalls. This could be accomplished through more liberal trade policies. However, the development of a distribution and transport system, especially in the rural sectors, is obviously very costly in Colombia.

Nevertheless, in the long run the food distribution network for the rural sectors will have to be improved to reduce food insecurity. This could include improving the transport system and perhaps implementing a dual price system for the benefit of the poor. This program would be most effective if it is targeted at only the most vulnerable groups of the rural sector.

## Conclusions

This chapter has shown that Colombia does not have an aggregate food insecurity problem. In fact, food production and food supply are very stable around trend and the probability of a shortfall in trend output or in trend supply is negligible. Should such a shortfall occur, it can be easily met through imports, placing little burden on foreign exchange earnings. However, a decision to use imports to smooth out production variability requires ports to handle increasing food imports, new storage facilities and roads, an efficient distribution system, and, most importantly, efficient institutions. This effort represents an additional cost to the pure foreign exchange cost of making imports.

The need for food security in Colombia arises from the country's widespread poverty. Currently, 40 percent of the population can be said to suffer from light to severe malnutrition. A small shortfall in the trend supply of food can impair the nutritional level of large segments of the nutritionally vulnerable population. The insecurity problem is not caused by absolute poverty for the country as a whole, but rather by poverty for specific groups. If income were equally distributed, people would be consuming calories in excess of the minimum requirements, and the internal production of food would still

138                                    Jorge García García

be larger than the demand.

The problem of food insecurity can be solved by eliminating the underlying cause of insecurity—poverty—or by preventing shortfalls in food trend supply. The elimination of poverty is a long-run solution and the prevention of shortfalls in food supply is something that can be tackled rather quickly, with short-run measures that imply the building of certain infra-structure facilities.

The short-run solution is supplying food either through imports or release of stocks accumulated by storing excesses over trend of past production or imports. No excessive burden on foreign exchange earnings should be expected from relying on imports for immediate consumption. Accordingly, Colombia would have little interest in participating in a purely financial scheme to assure food security. Moreover, schemes suggesting that countries can draw food from the scheme if production falls by 4 or 5 percent or more from trend production are not attractive for Colombia because, as we saw in the text, these shortfalls are very unlikely to occur in Colombia. But a food security scheme that guarantees the supply of cereal imports could be attractive.

Another "short-run" solution is to provide income transfer to the vulnerable groups that experience income losses from increased food prices, although this could involve the establishment of an expensive bureaucratic system. A cost-effective system could take the form of direct nutrition interventions targeted for the most vulnerable groups. In the long run, the solution is a permanent increase in the income of the poor through a continued process of economic growth in the Colombian economy.

## Notes

Helpful comments on the manuscript by Alberto Valdés and by participants during the Conference are gratefully acknowledged.

1. For the importance of each of the different food items in the food consumption basket of white- and blue-collar workers see Departamento Administrativo Nacional de Estadística (DANE 1977a). The products

*The Nature of Food Insecurity in Colombia* 139

used for analysis in this chapter (12 listed individually in Table 6.1 plus barley) were chosen because of their representativeness in the Colombian food consumption basket as well as by the availability of information necessary to deal with a sufficiently long span of time.

2. It can be argued that when studying cereals, the production of meat and dairy products is being implicitly counted, since cereals are used also as animal feedstuffs. However, this is not the case in Colombia, where cattle-raising activities rely mainly on pastures for animal feed.

3. We do not know the proportion of food used for human consumption and the distribution of consumption among different income groups for each of those years.

4. That is, 3.4 percent for the years 1950–1964 and 2.8 percent for the years 1964–1973. See Departamento Nacional de Planeación, "La Economía Colombiana 1950–1975," *Revista de Planeación y Desarrollo* 9, No. 3 (October-December 1977).

5. For an account of these balance of payments problems, see Jorge García García (1976).

6. ICBF (1977).

7. The trend lines adjusted are:

1950–1975 $\ell$n Food Output = 8.69461 + 0.02989T    $R^2$ = 0.975 D.W. = 0.849
(30.78)    S.E.E. = 0.0371
1959–1975 $\ell$n Food Output = 8.92364 + 0.03425T    $R^2$ = 0.978 D.W. = 1.32
(26.425)    S.E.E. = 0.0261
1961–1975 $\ell$n Food Output = 8.9733 + 0.03631T    $R^2$ = 0.984 D.W. = 1.95
(28.43)    S.E.E. = 0.0213

The values in parentheses are the *t*-statistics of the estimated coefficients and S.E.E. stands for standard error of the regression.

8. One could say that the magnitude of food insecurity is determined by the growth and variability in calorie supply rather than food supply because output does not reflect correctly the nutritional content of a given quantity of food. To determine the growth and variability of calorie supply, we adjusted trend lines with the following results:

1950–1975 $\ell$n Calorie Supply = 3.1274 + 0.030433T    $R^2$ = 0.95 D.W. = 0.78
(155.87) (22.11)    S.E.E. = 0.0526
1959–1975 $\ell$n Calorie Supply = 3.3441 + 0.036609T    $R^2$ = 0.95 D.W. = 1.29
(171.22) (17.58)    S.E.E. = 0.042
1961–1975 $\ell$n Calorie Supply = 3.3958 + 0.038956T    $R^2$ = 0.95 D.W. = 1.58
(169.77) (16.02)    S.E.E. = 0.0406

The values in parentheses are the *t*-statistics of the estimated coefficients.

140                                              *Jorge García García*

9. The intervals given in the text correspond to the minimum and maximum interval of years in which a given percentage shortfall is expected to occur; they are obtained with the trend lines adjusted for the 1961–1975 and 1950–1975 periods, respectively. If the magnitude of the insecurity were measured as the probability of a given shortfall in trend supply, the size of the insecurity would be slightly higher than the one calculated in the text.

10. These figures are derived from an adjusted trend line for cereal output for the 1950–1975 period.

11. This calculation assumes that port facilities plus all the required infrastructure to distribute food to the final consumer are already available. An average c.i.f. price of $165 per ton of wheat is assumed.

12. The magnitude of the food insecurity problem might not be negligible in probability terms if a 1 percent shortfall in trend production is considered the insecurity level; however, its effect on balance of payments is very small.

13. For an explanation of the reasons to use calorie consumption as an indicator of nutritional achievement, see Reutlinger and Selowsky (1976).

14. On the need to allow for variations in requirements see Sukhatme (1977). On whether the requirements for Colombians are an average or a minimum, FAO had established an average requirement of 2,320 calories per day, and ICBF had established 2,150 calories per day for 1972, a requirement that has been reduced by ICBF to 1,970 calories per day since 1974. In view of these divergencies I have assumed that 1,970 calories per day gives the minimum daily calorie consumption for an active and healthy life; this corresponds to a 17 percent and 9 percent reduction in relation to the higher values established by FAO and ICBF and can be considered as the minimum value of the confidence interval suggested by P. V. Sukhatme.

15. The 40 percent figure found here is very similar to the one suggested by the National Planning Office of Colombia. See Departamento Nacional de Planeación (1974a).

16. The gap is as follows:

|       | Urban | | Rural | | Total | |
|-------|-------|-------|-------|-------|-------|-------|
|       | (1) | (2) | (1) | (2) | (1) | (2) |
| I     | 452   | 201 | 749   | 359 | 1,201 | 560 |
| II    | 675   | 334 | 1,400 | 520 | 2,075 | 854 |
| III   | 63    | –   | 493   | 172 | 556   | 172 |
|       | 1,190 | 535 | 2,642 | 1,051 | 3,832 | 1,586 |

# The Nature of Food Insecurity in Colombia

The figures of columns (1) and (2) are derived from columns (1) and (2) of Table 6.6 and information on population presented in Table 6.7.

17. See Urrutia and Berry (1975).

## References

Departamento Administrativo Nacional de Estadística (DANE). *Indice de Precios al Consumidor 1954-Junio 1977*. Bogotá: División de Edición del DANE, 1977a.

____. *Ingresos y Gastos de los Hogares en Colombia: 1972*. Bogotá:División de Edición del DANE, 1977b.

Departamento de Nacional Planeación. "La Economía Colombiana 1950-1975." *Revista de Planeación y Desarrollo* 9, No. 3 (October-December 1977).

____. *Plan Nacional de Alimentación y Nutrición*. Mimeo. Bogotá, October 1974a.

____. "Plan Nacional de Alimentación y Nutrición: Selección de Alimentos." Documento DNP-UDS-DPN-011. Mimeo. Bogotá, October 1974b.

García García, Jorge. "A History of Economic Policies in Colombia: 1953-1970." Ph.D. dissertation, Department of Economics, The University of Chicago, Fall 1976.

____. "Es Importante la Seguiridad del Suministro de Alimentos en Colombia?" *Revista de Planeación y Desarrollo* 11, No. 3 (September-December 1979).

____. "La Incidencia de la Desnutrición en Colombia." Forthcoming in *Desarrollo y Sociedad* (1980).

Huddleston, Barbara, and Panos Konandreas. "Insurance Approach to Food Security: Simulation of Benefits for 1970/71-1975/76 and for 1978-1982." Chapter 11, this book.

Instituto Colombiano de Bienestar Familiar (ICBF). *Encuesta Nacional de Dietas 1972*. As quoted by Departamento Nacional de Planeación, *Plan Nacional de Alimentación y Nutrición: Selección de Alimentos*. Documento DNP-UDS-DPN-011. Bogotá, October 1974. Tables 3, 4, and 5.

____. *Recomendación de Consumo de Alimentos para la Población Colombiana*. Revision 1977. Bogotá, March 1977.

Johnson, D. Gale. "Increased Stability of Grain Supplies in Developing Countries: Optimal Carryovers and Insurance." *World Development* 4, no. 12 (1976):977-987.

Reutlinger, Shlomo. "Food Insecurity: Magnitude and Remedies." World Bank Staff Working Paper No. 267. July 1977.

Reutlinger, Shlomo, and David Bigman. "Feasibility, Effectiveness and

Costs of National Food Security Alternatives in Developing Countries." Chapter 9, this book.

Reutlinger, Shlomo, and Marcelo Selowsky. "Malnutrition and Poverty: Magnitude and Policy Options." World Bank Staff Occasional Paper No. 23. 1976. P. 9.

Sukhatme, P. V. "Incidence of Undernutrition." *Indian Journal of Agricultural Economics* (July/September 1977):1-7.

Urrutia, Miguel, and Albert Berry. *La Distribución del Ingreso en Colombia.* Medellín: Editorial La Carreta, 1975.

# 7
# Food Security Program in Egypt

*Ahmed A. Goueli*

Egyptian concern with food security began in ancient times. The wheat stores of the prophet Joseph are an early example of building reserve stocks in good years to compensate for short production in bad years. At that time, Egypt could produce enough wheat to meet the needs of its relatively small population.

Today the situation is different: Egypt relies heavily on the international market for satisfying its food needs. The population has increased at a relatively high rate compared with the growth rate of its agricultural land and cropped area. The Egyptian population, which totaled 5.1 million in 1897, reached 38.2 million in 1976.[1] With an anticipated growth rate of 2 percent, the population will increase to 63 million by 2000.

The agricultural land area, which covered 5.1 million feddans in 1897, grew to only 6.0 million feddans by 1976.[2] Available cropped area, as a result of multiple cropping, increased from 6.8 million feddans in 1897 to 11.2 million in 1976.

The limited land base per capita has declined. In 1897, one half of a feddan of agricultural land was available for every Egyptian. By 1976, this amount had decreased to one sixth of a feddan per capita. Available cropped area per capita is equivalent to 0.75 and 0.29 feddans in 1897 and 1976, respectively. The decline in the per-capita productive agricultural land, indicative of an increasing reliance on food imports, is accentuated by the rapid growth of the urban population. The rural population, which composed 81 percent of the total population in 1897, declined to 56 percent of the total in 1976. The higher level of urban incomes has increased consumption

## Food Composition

Cereals are the most important food item in Egypt. Bread consumed in urban areas is made with wheat. A blend of predominantly maize and wheat is used to make bread in the countryside. In upper Egypt, sorghum is an important food. Rice is consumed throughout Egypt and barley is used to manufacture beer and animal feeds. Table 7.1 shows the importance of food groups relative to the total food consumption during the periods of 1950/51-1954/55 and 1970/71-1974/75.

Annual per-capita food consumption rose from 376 to 482 kilograms between 1950/51 and 1974/75. More than one half of the increase is a result of a rise in cereal consumption (i.e., from 174 to 234 kilograms) and over a third is due to an increase in vegetable consumption (i.e., 50 to 87 kilograms) (Table 7.2). Cereals account for one half of total per-capita food consumption.

Daily calorie intake has increased over the period 1950/51-1974/75, from 2383 to about 3119 calories. Cereals provide about 70 percent of the calories and protein consumed, and animal proteins contribute about 12.5 percent of total protein intake per capita.

Wheat is the most important commodity in the Egyptian diet. Its share of total quantity consumed is 22 percent, followed by maize (15 percent) and rice (7 percent). Sorghum's share is only 4 percent. Annual per-capita consumption was about 104 kilograms of wheat, 73 of maize, 36 of milled rice, and 20 of sorghum during 1970/71-1974/75.

According to family budget surveys,[3] food expenditures account for about one half of total consumption expenditure in urban areas, and about two thirds in rural areas. Because of urban price subsidies, per-capita expenditure on cereals is low compared with the quantity of cereals consumed. In urban areas, the proportion of total expenditure on cereals and starches

Table 7.1 Food Consumption in Egypt

| Food group | Annual average 1950/51-1954/55 | | Annual average 1970/71-1974/75 | |
|---|---|---|---|---|
| (thousand metric tons) | | | | |
| | quantity | percent | quantity | percent |
| Cereals | 4680 | 47.4 | 10429 | 47.6 |
| Starchy roots & tubers | 228 | 2.3 | 682 | 3.1 |
| Sugar & sugar products | 548 | 5.6 | 927 | 4.2 |
| Pulses | 368 | 3.7 | 469 | 2.1 |
| Vegetables | 1194 | 12.1 | 4018 | 18.4 |
| Fruits | 1315 | 13.3 | 2739 | 12.5 |
| Meats | 248 | 2.5 | 413 | 1.9 |
| Fish | 65 | 0.7 | 106 | 0.5 |
| Eggs | 21 | 0.2 | 56 | 0.3 |
| Milk & dairy products | 1119 | 11.3 | 1713 | 7.8 |
| Oils and fats | 88 | 0.9 | 340 | 1.6 |
| Total | 9874 | 100 | 21892 | 100 |

Source: From Ministry of Agriculture, Agricultural Economics Bulletin, various issues, Food Balance Sheet, Cairo, Egypt.

Table 7.2 Annual Per-Capita Food Consumption in Egypt

| Food groups | Average 1950/51-1954/55 | | Average 1970/71-1974/75 | |
|---|---|---|---|---|
| (kilograms) | | | | |
| | quantity | percent | quantity | percent |
| Cereal grains | 174.4 | 46.4 | 233.7 | 48.5 |
| Starchy roots & tubers | 7.7 | 2.0 | 11.8 | 2.4 |
| Sugar & sugar products | 16.2 | 4.3 | 22.5 | 4.7 |
| Pulses | 10.1 | 2.7 | 10.0 | 2.1 |
| Vegetables | 50.1 | 13.3 | 86.9 | 18.0 |
| Fruits | 51.8 | 13.8 | 47.3 | 9.8 |
| Meats | 10.6 | 2.8 | 9.6 | 2.0 |
| Eggs | 0.8 | 0.2 | 1.4 | 0.3 |
| Fish | 2.8 | 0.8 | 2.7 | 0.6 |
| Milk & dairy | 48.2 | 12.8 | 48.8 | 10.1 |
| Oils | 3.5 | 0.9 | 7.4 | 1.5 |
| Total | 376.2 | 100 | 482.1 | 100 |

Source: Computed from the Ministry of Agriculture, same as Table 7.1.

146 Ahmed A. Goueli

is around 11 percent, and about 12.5 percent is spent on meats, fish, and eggs. In rural areas, expenditure on cereals and starches represents around 20 percent of total expenditure.[4]

The general composition of food consumption has been consistently dominated by cereal grains. It is expected that this pattern will prevail and that Egypt will increasingly rely on imported cereal grains.

## Food Imports

At present, food imports provide about half of Egypt's consumption needs. About two thirds of the wheat, two fifths of the oils and fats, and one fifth of the maize consumed are imported. The proportion of food imports to total consumption has increased dramatically since 1950. In 1975, Egypt imported around 3.2 million tons of wheat and half a million tons of maize and exported only 150 thousand tons of rice. Exports of rice have declined and exports of fruits and vegetables have remained marginal.

Between 1976 and 2000, Egypt will import about half of its total cereal grain needs and around 80 percent of its wheat needs. Table 7.3 shows the trade balance of food in Egypt in 1975 and the projected food gap for the year 2000.

The Egyptian commodity exports, valued at £E 188 million in 1959-60, increased to about £E 548 million in 1975.[5] Agricultural exports grew from £E 148 million to £E 271 million during the same period (Table 7.4). Cotton exports represented about 80 percent of total agricultural exports in 1975, and rice and fruit exports represented about 9 percent and 7 percent, respectively.

After 1973, total imports increased substantially, growing from £E 226 million in 1959-60 to £E 1530 million in 1975 (Table 7.5). The share of imported consumption goods has increased at the expense of capital and intermediate goods. Between 1969-70 and 1975, the proportion of consumer goods to the total import bill had increased from 20 to 35 percent, while that of capital goods had declined from 30 to 19 percent and of intermediate goods from 50 to 46 percent. It is apparent that this expansion of imports—explained to a large extent by the

*Food Security Program in Egypt* 147

Table 7.3 Food Trade Balance in Egypt: Net Imports in 1975 and Projected
for Year 2000

| Food groups | 1975 | 2000 |
|---|---|---|
| (thousand metric tons) | | |
| Cereal grains: total | 3514 | 10386 |
| wheat | 3247 | 7232 |
| maize | 418 | 1639 |
| rice (paddy) | -151 | 1062 |
| Starchy roots & tubers | -65 | -101 |
| Pulses | 151 | 330 |
| Oils and fats | 265 | 446 |
| Sugar | 121 | -355 |
| Vegetables | -185 | -119 |
| Fruits | -195 | -325 |
| Meats | 86 | 528 |
| Milk & dairy products | 97 | 84 |
| Fish | 39 | 114 |

Source: The Arab Organization for Agricultural Development, *The
Future of Food in the Arab Countries*, Khartoum, October 1978.

increasing value of cereals imports—has been detrimental to
the balance of payments and economic development.

The analysis of the Ministry of Planning cited below explains
that the increase in price of consumption goods, largely wheat
and other food commodities, has contributed up to 80 percent
of the rise in the import bill for consumption goods (Table 7.4):

This vast increase in the value of imports was the main cause of the
economic problem elucidated in the financial analysis, particularly
as the value of exports did not increase at a similar rate. The result
was disequilibrium in Egypt's foreign balances, and the weakness of
her standing abroad—what really happened was an increase in value
rather than additions in quantity. The amount of £E 1213 million
(difference in import value between 1969/70 and 1975) represents
an actual increase in the quantity of imports of £E 312 only, and a

148 *Ahmed A. Goueli*

Table 7.4 Exports and Imports of Commodities in Egypt

| Items | 1959/60 | 1964/65 | 1969/70 | 1975 |
|---|---|---|---|---|
| | (million Egyptian pounds) | | | |
| Imports: | 225.9 | 400.8 | 324.8 | 1530.0 |
| Consumption goods | 55.7 | 112.3 | 64.4 | 538.7 |
| Percent | 24.6 | 28.0 | 19.8 | 35.0 |
| Of which grains & flour* | 26.5 | 66.2 | 36.0 | 286.6 |
| Intermediate goods | 102.5 | 166.0 | 161.8 | 705.5 |
| Percent | 45.4 | 41.4 | 49.8 | 45.8 |
| Capital goods | 67.7 | 122.5 | 98.6 | 295.1 |
| Percent | 30.0 | 30.6 | 30.4 | 19.2 |
| Exports: | 188.1 | 263.5 | 327.9 | 547.8 |
| Of which agricultural goods | 147.6 | 185.1 | 220.7 | 270.7 |
| Percent | 78.0 | 70.0 | 67.0 | 50.0 |
| Deficit | -37.8 | -137.3 | + 3.1 | -982.2 |

Source: Ministry of Planning: various annual reports (Follow-up Reports).

*Funds for food aid are valued at the quoted price of imports and do not represent the true cost of food aid to the importer.

price increase of £E 901 million in 1975—specifically, the £E 471 million increase in the value of imports (consumption goods) represents an increase in prices of £E 379 million and only £E 92 million of an increase in the quantity of imports (Five Year Plan, 1977, pp. 10 and 12).

The long-run policy for food security is the achievement of self-sufficiency in all products but wheat. Self-sufficiency in wheat would require doubling the present land commitment to wheat at the expense of other export crops such as cotton.

Food security is of prime concern to President Sadat. Agencies involved include the Ministries of Agriculture, Land Recla-

## Food Security Program in Egypt 149

Table 7.5 Effect of Changes in Volume and Price on the Value of
Food Imports, 1969-75

| Item | 1969/70 | 1970/71 | 1971/72 | 1973 | 1974 | 1975 | Total |
|---|---|---|---|---|---|---|---|
| | | | (millions of pounds) | | | | |
| Consumption commodities: | | | | | | | |
| Value in current prices | 68 | 111 | 99 | 207 | 500 | 539 | 1455 |
| Value in 1969/70 prices | 68 | 101 | 79 | 148 | 153 | 160 | 640 |
| Change from 1969/70 | -- | +43 | +30 | +139 | +432 | +471 | +1115 |
| Quantity change | -- | +33 | +11 | +80 | +85 | +92 | +300 |
| Price change | -- | +10 | +19 | +60 | +347 | +379 | +815 |
| Total imports: | | | | | | | |
| Value in current prices | 325 | 409 | 380 | 542 | 1247 | 1538 | 447 |
| Value in 1969/70 prices | 325 | 374 | 337 | 445 | 516 | 637 | 2309 |
| Change from 1969/70 | --- | +85 | +56 | +217 | +922 | +1214 | +2492 |
| Quantity changes | --- | +49 | +13 | +120 | +192 | +312 | +685 |
| Price change | --- | +35 | +43 | +79 | +731 | +901 | +1807 |

Source: Ministry of Planning: The Five Year Plan 1978-1982, vol. 1, The
General Strategy for Economic and Social Development, Cairo, Aug. 1977,
p. 11.

mation, Planning, and New Communities, and a newly established organization for the "Green Revolution." The Ministry of Supplies and Domestic Trade is the responsible agency for short-run food security, acting through the autonomous General Agency for Commodities Supplies. All imported food commodities are handled and distributed through the General Agency. At the start of the fiscal year, the budget for food imports is negotiated with the Ministry of Finance based on expected demand and prices. The national budget can adjust to increases in the import food bill.

First priority is given to securing sufficient imports of wheat to meet urban demands. Pulses, oils and fats, and sugar each carry equal secondary importance; meats and fish are less important. Maize is imported for feed; domestic maize production

150                                                          Ahmed A. Goueli

is adequate for human consumption requirements. Locally produced rice is procured and distributed by the government for the urban sector.

**Current State of Public Policy**

In the Egyptian economy, crisis is always imminent. The increase in price levels in international markets in recent years, especially in 1975, has contributed to its economic difficulties. The current account deficit as a percentage of national product increased from 22 percent in 1974 to 27 percent in 1975 and 24 percent in 1976. The deficit was met through the means described in Table 7.6. Under such conditions, Egypt cannot finance a reserve grain stock. The country is limited to following a policy of hand to mouth.

Food aid continues to play an important role in financing food imports. Currently, the largest donor is the United States, which contributes chiefly wheat and wheat flour (Table 7.7). Food aid from the United States—which stopped after the 1967 war and started again in 1973—amounts today to approximately one half of the Egyptian wheat flour imports. Egypt also receives food aid from the European Community (EC) and its members. In 1976, it received 132 thousand tons of wheat equivalent from France, of which 100 thousand tons was national aid and the remainder was distributed through the EC aid program.

Table 7.6  Sources Covering the Egyptian Current Account Deficit, 1974-76

| Source (in millions of £E) | 1974 | 1975 | 1976 |
|---|---|---|---|
| Arab subsidies | 405 | 421 | 245 |
| Foreign loans | 498 | 893 | 1106 |
| Total | 903 | 1314 | 1351 |

Source:  Ministry of Planning, The General Strategy for Economic and Social Development, p. 4.

Food consumption is regulated by several stabilization policies. Domestic food production is fairly stable due to permanent irrigation systems. However, there are some fluctuations in production caused by variations in yield and area cultivated. The consumer food price policy offers basic commodities, bread (wheat), rice, and pulses at prices below market value. The administered prices are well enforced in the cities. However, in rural areas where there is less supervision, prices tend to reflect regional scarcity. Frequently, merchants and rural people, when in urban cities for business, buy subsidized commodities either for their own consumption or for profitable resale in rural markets.

Until 1976, local wheat procurement was carried out through a quota procurement policy. Farmers had to deliver 25 percent of their production to the government for prices usually below the international price. The quota system of wheat was abolished in 1977 and the delivery of wheat to the government is presently voluntary. It was argued that the insignificant quantity procured relative to total wheat consumption did not justify the

Table 7.7  U.S. Food Aid Shipments to Egypt, 1972-77, under PL 480.

| Year | Wheat | | Flour | |
|---|---|---|---|---|
| | volume | value | volume | value |
| | thousand tons | US$ million | thousand tons | US$ million |
| 1972/73 | 291 | 25,629 | 1 | 102 |
| 1973/74 | 709 | 121,035 | 89 | 8,648 |
| 1974/75 | 740 | 121,754 | 10 | 1,996 |
| 1975/76 | 972 | 134,042 | 253 | 35,847 |
| 1976/77 | 1,535 | 174,228 | 523 | 65,362 |

Source: U.S. Embassy in Cairo.

trouble or costs of the program. Also, as the procurement price now is above the international price, the quota system was unnecessary. Wheat imports are now channeled to the consumer largely through government mills that distribute flour to bakeries at the subsidized price (Figure 7.1). Thus, the price of bread to the consumer is only one fifth of its real cost to the government.

Maize is traded freely in the village markets. Imports are handled through the Ministry of Supplies and Domestic Trade; imported yellow feed maize is managed by the Ministry of Agriculture. Maize imported for human consumption is distributed at fixed prices through a controlled distribution system (Figure 7.2).

Rice is the only exported grain crop, and its market is par-

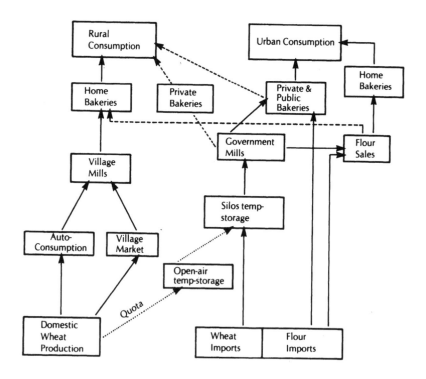

**Figure 7.1** Wheat flow chart for Egypt, 1978

(.....) Cancelled since 1976
(---) New Trends

tially controlled. Growers must deliver about half of their production to the government at prices below both international and prevailing local rural prices. This rice is milled by the government. Some is sold to the consumer at a very low price compared to the costs incurred by the government. The domestic rice consumption has increased at the expense of exports: exports are expected to disappear. The other half of production is consumed by the farm household or sold in the rural markets. The price of milled rice in rural areas is considerably higher than in the cities.

At present, sugar, tea, and oils are rationed. Rice is occasionally rationed when supply is short. Rationing is used to insure the supply of basic food commodities for the poor.

Consumer subsidies continue to increase with the rise in international prices. In 1975, the total subsidy amounted to about £E 642 million (Five Year Plan, 1977, p. 24). In addition to

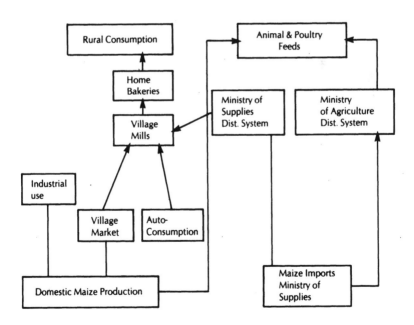

Figure 7.2 Maize flow chart for Egypt, 1978*

*There is an urban consumption of maize flour in special type of cakes, and also there is consumption of roasted maize in both urban and rural areas.

direct price subsidies, Egypt has a price stabilization fund of £E 224 million, financed through an incentive exchange rate below the official rate, which acts as a reserve against increased costs of certain imported commodities.

The subsidized price policy to urban consumers, which forces the farmer to buy dear and sell cheap, has discouraged farmers from producing strategic crops like cereal grains and pulses. As an income redistribution measure, the system of consumer subsidies in Egypt has proven to be ineffective and, instead, the program has created an undesirable disequilibrium. Thus, reforms are needed in Egypt's domestic price and food distribution policies.

### The Long-Run Policy of Food Security

Egyptian food insecurity does not stem from fluctuations in domestic food production, but from the uncertainties of the international market. Even the realization of the goal of sufficiency in food commodities except wheat would not guarantee food security. Egypt imports two-thirds of its wheat needs. By the turn of the century, it may import an even greater proportion. Reliance on the international market for wheat is risky. Building a reserve wheat stock from year to year is very costly. Participation in an international or regional program for food security could be to Egypt's advantage if the program could provide Egypt imported wheat at a stable price.

Egypt has taken many steps to increase its capacity to produce, import, and store food. These steps are summarized as follows:

*1. Improvement in the Performance of the Existing Land Base*

Egypt has undertaken, with the IBRD, a large-scale project for tile drainage to solve acute waterlogging and salinity problems. There are several programs to improve water management, institutional, and pricing policies. Projects to promote livestock, fishery, and poultry production exist. An agricultural program with international support is involved in agricultural mechanization and improvement in seed variety and fertilizer.

The proposed five-year plan for 1978–1982 has allocated about £E 184 million for vertical expansion. Over £E 453 million have been earmarked for drainage projects to be executed by the Ministry of Irrigation.

## 2. Reclamation of New Land

The Egyptian experience with land reclamation has been useful, but very costly. Since 1952, 912 thousand feddans have been reclaimed at a cost of about £E 600 million. The contribution of the new land is low relative to its area and expense. Targeted reclamation for the year 2000 is for 2.8 million additional feddans. These areas will produce mainly fruits, vegetables, and livestock products. A Sinai utilization program will begin after the Israeli withdrawal.

## 3. Arab Economic Cooperation

Food security has been an important issue to the Arab League and its agricultural development organization. The agricultural sector of the Arab countries has been studied to identify projects that can increase production. The Arab Food Security Declaration issued by the Arab Ministries of Agriculture recommended agricultural production programs and an Arab food reserve stock.

Joint agricultural projects in the Sudan are intended to increase Egypt's food supply. Potential commodities include meat, sorghum grains for feed, and oil crops. Progress has been made in a sorghum and oil crop production project in the Blue Nile province.

## 4. Expansion of Grain Storage Facilities

At present there are two wheat silos in Egypt, one in Cairo with a capacity of 106 thousand tons, and another in Alexandria with less than half that capacity, which represent a total storage capacity sufficient for 25 days' consumption. These silos cannot absorb the 3.5 million metric tons of imported wheat, and thus most imports are transferred to open-air storage facilities and transported in sacks. Sacks alone cost about £E 8 million, about 3 percent of the wheat is damaged in storage, and the slow process of unloading sacks is costly in terms of ship delays.

A program is aimed at expanding the country's storage capacity to hold enough wheat to meet the consumption needs of at least three months and flour for two months by 1990. The following has been proposed and is expected to be capable of handling the estimated 6.4 million tons of imported wheat needed in 1990:

1. New silo construction (100,000 tons) in Alexandria, in addition to the existing one (48,000 tons). This facility can receive 2.5 million tons of wheat.
2. A silo in Safaga on the Red Sea, the first phase is 50,000 tons and the second phase is 50,000 tons. This facility can receive 1.5 million tons.
3. Adabia port (Suez) (100,000 tons) to receive 1.5 million tons.
4. Improvement of Port Said to receive 0.9 million tons.

In addition to port wheat silos, the program includes the construction of two silos in Tanta and south of Cairo, and 40 silos (2000 tons) for distribution.

Investment allocated to port facilities and to silos in the current five-year plan is £E 89 million, of which £E 34.6 million is in foreign currency covered by loans (Five-Year Plan, 1977).

## Conclusions

Egyptian food insecurity does not stem from fluctuations in domestic food production, but from instability in the international market. Egypt has used food aid and loans and has adjusted the composition of its imports to cope with its food problem. The food crisis has weakened its balance of payments position, and has adversely affected economic growth. Foreign exchange has been spent on food imports at the expense of imports of intermediate and investment goods.

Wheat is the main cereal crop and food item in Egypt. At present, Egypt is importing two thirds of its wheat requirement, and increased reliance on the international market is expected.

Given the existing economic difficulties and the infeasibility of expanding total wheat production or building a reserve stock,

*Food Security Program in Egypt* 157

it may be to Egypt's advantage to join an international or regional program of food security. The program should guarantee sufficient wheat imports at a stable price. Until the Egyptian economy recovers, it will rely on the regular flow of food aid from the developed countries.

The issues raised in this chapter require further study by the Egyptian and international institutions. Several food policy issues deserve particular consideration. These include agricultural and consumer price policies, food rationing and distribution, and the impact of income distribution on the consumption of food and nutrition. Long-run considerations may include the relationship between food consumption, production, and agricultural trade policy and their linkage with the rest of the economy under alternative development strategies for Egypt.

## Notes

1. The Central Agency for Mobilization & Statistics, Egypt.
2. One feddan = 1.038 acres = 0.42 hectares.
3. Egypt conducted three national family budget surveys in 1958–1959, 1964–1965, and 1974. Before 1958–1959, these were limited surveys.
4. Salah El-Din Mansour, "The Role of Future Demand on Agricultural Crops in the Formulation of the Egyptian Agricultural Policy," MSc dissertation, Department of Agricultural Economics, Zagazig University, 1978.
5. One Egyptian pound = $1.42.

## References

The Five Year Plan 1978-82. Vol. 1. *The General Strategy for Economic and Social Development.* Cairo: Ministry of Planning, August 1977.

# Part 2

## National and International Approaches to Reduce Food Insecurity

# 8
# Price, Stock, and Trade Policies and the Functioning of International Grain Markets

*Timothy Josling*

Food security is greatly influenced by the structure of the distribution system. Although the nature of the underlying structure and the policies that have been suggested to improve it will only change slowly, it seems worthwhile to explore in some detail the reaction of the world wheat market to shocks on the production side, particularly its impact on supply stability in developing countries. The relevance of the issues becomes apparent in periods of scarcity, but the policies need to be operative before such events propel the issue into prominence.

## The Fundamentals of Market Stability

Market instability arising from inevitable production fluctuations can be explored by means of a simple conceptualization. Imagine a market for a staple food crop with naturally induced production yield fluctuations from a relatively static land area. All production moves either into consumption or into storage. If there is some "carry-in" from previous years then total availability (new production plus carry-in) must equal consumption plus carry-out. This ex-post identity for a closed market holds equally for changes from year to year. Variation in production levels must show up as offsetting changes in consumption and/or stock levels. The identity is also retained when put in value form, ignoring, for the moment, government activity. Producer receipts and revenue from stock sales will equal expenditure plus the cost of stock renewal—defined appropriately to reflect the two sides of the same set of financial

*161*

162                                                                          *Timothy Josling*

transactions. Table 8.1 records these identities.

Because the world as a whole is a "closed system," even this basic identity has some merit in organizing one's thoughts about stability. First, it becomes clear that there is a significant limitation to government policy in this area. If instability in production exists, its implications cannot be willed away. Either stocks or consumption (or both) must vary. The extent of trade liberalization, commodity price agreements, food aid, and the like are all essentially powerless to alter the reality. They "merely" influence the distribution of changes within and between the categories of consumption and stocks.[1] This approach highlights the obvious but nevertheless fundamental observation that only by reducing production instability itself can other variables in the system be made in aggregate more stable. If instability has a net social (global) cost—which is presumably

Table 8.1   Basic Market Identities

---

a) Closed system: volume identity

| Production | | Consumption |
| Carry-in | | Carry-out |
| Total Available | = | Total Used |

b) Closed system: value identity

| Producer receipts | | Consumer spending |
| Revenue from stock sales | | Cost of stock purchases |
| Total Receipts | = | Total Expenditure |

c) Open sub-system: volume identity

| Production | | Consumption |
| Carry-in | | Carry-out |
| Imports | | Exports |
| Total Available | = | Total Used |

d) Open sub-system: value identity

| Producer receipts | | Consumer Expenditure |
| Revenue from stock sales | | Cost of stock purchases |
| Import costs | | Export revenue |
| Total Receipts | = | Total Expenditure |

---

# Price, Stock, and Trade Policies

true if the unstable element is yield, implying similar resource costs for large and small harvests—then the returns from stabilizing production may be substantial even if all of the mechanisms for distributing instability are of debatable merit.

The value identity for the closed system also has some intuitive relevance for approaching the instability problem. The difference between revenue from stock sales and spending on stock replacement can be thought of as the cash-flow position of the storage sector.[2] If storage activities require an injection of cash, then producer receipts are enhanced relative to consumer spending. If producer receipts vary with output, then either stock financing or consumer spending (or both) will vary accordingly. Steady profits over time from storage reduces producer receipts relative to consumer expenditure, at least in the absence of government activity to offset these effects.

The closed system can itself contain closed subsystems. The implications hold for each of the parts of the system. Many agricultural markets in the world are essentially closed, whether by policy or natural isolation. This has the immediate implication that they are "responsible" for making internal adjustments to production variability. Many countries, for example, rarely use trade to counterbalance their own production changes. Food insecurity, in these conditions, is basically the outcome of the choice between stock and consumption changes. Such closed markets are, however, unaffected by instability in other areas. It would be worthwhile, though not attempted in this chapter, to identify sources of instability according to their degrees of isolation. No amount of manipulation at the level of international commodity markets will bring stability to an isolated region with negligible market links to the outside world. But these regions themselves may have in some cases fewer instability problems than if more fully integrated with commercial life.[3]

The more traditional security and instability questions relate to open subsystems of the world market, where trade is an option. Table 8.1 also presents the simple identities in this case. Variability in production levels must now be balanced by a combination of changes in stock levels, consumption, and trade balance. The value identities also hold where stock changes are those on the domestic market rather than speculation on transactions overseas. The individual country can thus make use of trade as a device to stabilize, for example, consumption levels, even though that option is not open to the world at large. Economic, if not necessarily political, logic would suggest that such stabilizing trade flows represent an improvement in "security."

Trade possibilities may appear to reduce the need for national stocks. But to complete the picture, the implications for the rest of the market must be considered. Extra imports into one country must be matched by changes in either stocks or consumption (if production is predetermined in a particular year) in other countries. Thus, in the world as a whole, production variations must still show up either as stock or consumption changes even if trade were unhindered. The major impact of trade flows in this respect is to influence the distribution of such changes. The advantage is that production variability is "shared" among countries; the major disadvantage is the other side of the same coin, that such adjustments will be required of a country even if its own production does not vary. The ambivalence of trade policy arises from the conflict between these stabilizing and destabilizing influences of trade flows on individual countries. In the present context, the implication of the simple identity approach is that the question of trade flows is logically distinct from that of stock adjustments in the trading system as a whole. For instance, if the degree of trade liberalization, or the extent to which countries will allow trade flows to vary, is itself otherwise determined, then the question of adjustments within that trade structure is still relevant.

This analysis suggests that a straightforward approach to assessing the overall level of world food security is to explore what has, in fact, happened in the past as a result of instability in production. As mentioned above, the "closed economy" case reflects the situation in the world as a whole. One would expect therefore, given adequate data, that one could plot the relationship between global production variations on the one hand and changes in total consumption and stocks on the other. Consumption series for both specific and aggregate food groups tend to be more stable than those of production—implying that stocks

## Price, Stock, and Trade Policies

do vary in a stabilizing way. The more significant question is how such instability is distributed. In which countries do stocks or consumption or both vary in response to world production changes? Unfortunately, the data to explore this crucial question are not readily available. Stock data are published only for a small number of countries and convincing consumption series are not much easier to find. Trade and production series, presumably the two most reliable of the basic market data sets, do not in themselves clarify this issue.

### An Illustration: the Wheat Market

Since the object of this chapter is to elaborate a framework for approaching these issues, no attempt will be made to fill this empirical gap. However, a convenient illustration of this approach is given by one set of relationships, that between developed countries, the Soviet Union, and developing country food importers in the market for wheat. Table 8.2 shows the variation from year to year in production, consumption, and stocks for selected developed countries (SDCs) and the USSR and, for comparison, the net imports by developing market economies. Production varies considerably in both the major developed countries and the Soviet Union. Changes in consumption are more modest, as one might expect both from low price elasticities of demand and also from various policies designed to offset the impact of food prices on inflation. The stock figures represent the change relative to the previous year in the amount by which stocks increased or decreased.

Thus, for instance, in 1969/70 developed countries suffered a decrease in production from the previous year of about 8 million tons, and increased consumption by 5.5 million tons. The stock accumulation, the difference between carry-out and carry-in, dropped by 17 million tons—implying a release of reserves relative to a continuation of the previous year's stock "policy." This resulted in a 3.5 million ton increase in the trade surplus. In this case, changes in stock decisions absorbed the production fall and the consumption increase, and released an extra amount of wheat for export.[4]

The downturn in Soviet production in 1972/73 was met

Table 8.2 Change Over Previous Year in Selected Variables, Wheat, 1969/70 - 1976/77

|  | 1969/70 | 1970/71 | 1971/72 | 1972/73 | 1973/74 | 1974/75 | 1975/76 | 1976/77 |
|---|---|---|---|---|---|---|---|---|
|  | | | | (million tons) | | | | |
| **Selected developed countries[a]** | | | | | | | | |
| Production | -8.4 | -16.1 | 17.2 | -2.4 | 12.1 | 2.6 | 5.2 | 12.3 |
| Consumption | 5.5 | -0.1 | 2.3 | 0.4 | -2.6 | -1.4 | -2.3 | 7.3 |
| Stock increase | -17.4 | -18.0 | 15.1 | -17.0 | 11.9 | 8.1 | 2.7 | 10.7 |
| Trade surplus | 3.5 | 2.1 | -0.2 | 14.2 | 2.8 | -4.1 | 4.8 | -5.8 |
| **USSR** | | | | | | | | |
| Production | -13.5 | 19.8 | -0.9 | -12.8 | 23.8 | -25.9 | -17.7 | 30.7 |
| Consumption | 7.7 | 7.4 | -7.5 | 4.8 | -3.0 | -1.9 | -9.6 | 4.6 |
| Stock increase | -21.0 | 11.0 | 11.0 | -1.0 | 12.0 | -25.0 | 3.0 | 20.0 |
| Trade deficit | 0.2 | -1.4 | 4.4 | 16.6 | -14.8 | -1.0 | 7.4 | -6.1 |
| **Less developed countries[b]** | | | | | | | | |
| Net trade deficit | 1.0 | 2.4 | 1.9 | 0.4 | 4.4 | 2.9 | 2.6 | -4.1 |
| **SDCs & USSR** | | | | | | | | |
| Net trade surplus | 3.3 | 3.5 | -4.2 | -2.4 | 17.6 | -3.1 | -2.6 | 0.3 |

a/ Includes Australia, Canada, Japan, European Community, and the United States.

b/ Developing market economies, as classified by IFPRI.

# Price, Stock, and Trade Policies

effectively by a reduction in developed country accumulation stock (primarily in the United States) and a consequent increase in trade between these countries. Only a small net decrease in the surplus available for other countries was noticeable. The next year, 1973/74, an exceptional harvest in the USSR allowed stock rebuilding and a reduction in imports. Stocks also responded in developed countries to higher production, but the result was still an increase in the trade surplus over the previous year—even without Soviet demand. The net surplus (SDCs and the USSR) thus increased significantly.[5]

The relatively high degree of food security for the developed countries and the USSR is evidenced by the small consumption changes on a year-to-year basis. From the viewpoint of other countries, the extent to which stock policy changes offset production fluctuations in this situation determines the external impact through trade. Over the period as a whole, changes in the export surplus have been relatively small. There does, however, appear to be a difference between the market economies and the USSR with respect to the incidence of production changes. In the developed market economies, production and consumption changes have the same sign in only three of the eight sets of year-on-year changes shown. By contrast, in the Soviet Union production and consumption move together in five of the eight years. Thus it does appear that the link between domestic production and consumption is weaker in the SDCs, indicating again a potential destabilizing force in world markets. The actual impact on other countries has to take into account stock changes. From the table it would appear that stocks changes carry the same sign as do production variations in every year for the SDCs; net exports vary with production changes in only two of those eight years. For the Soviet Union, stock changes follow production variations in six years out of eight, whereas the net trade balance for wheat varies with production in seven of these years.

The picture, then, is one of developed market economies running domestic policies that appear to obscure price signals to the users and consumers of wheat in part through stocks policies that reflect strongly the changes in production. Such production variations do not appear to be imposed on overseas markets. The stocks are responsive to trade demands as well as to changes in consumption. The question for food security in other countries is to what extent this responsiveness is enough to provide a positive stabilizing influence. The Soviet Union, although holding stocks that vary somewhat with domestic production, uses the trade system to make up much of the harvest variability while imposing on its own consumers more variation in availability than do the market economies.

This example illustrates that questions of food security on a world-wide basis can be phrased in terms of the basic relationships between production, consumption, trade, and stocks for the major countries or groups. With more complete data on stocks and trade, it would be possible to trace the impact of supply variations at a global level on individual country consumption patterns. Introducing production, consumption, and trade values would lead to further conclusions on the incidence of instability. Clearly the incidence of instability is itself determined in large part by the activities of governments.

### National Policy Options and Instability

The discussion of the previous section suggests an approach to policy options to deal with food insecurity both at a national and international level. If one retains the assumption that instability in production is the underlying cause of insecurity then it is possible to frame the question in the following way. Given that this instability will have implications for variables throughout the system, which subset of those variables should be made more stable and which, by implication, should be allowed to become less stable? The answer will clearly differ among countries and may change over time. It is also true that one country's answer will be contingent upon the resolution in other countries. Moreover, a collective agreement may not correspond to the individual choices of any nation separately. Nevertheless the various types of solutions can be illustrated.

For this, it is convenient to turn again to the value identities given in Table 8.1 but now to introduce government action in a more explicit manner. For any subpart of the global market, production value, import cost, and revenue from stock sales will

## Price, Stock, and Trade Policies

equal consumption expenditure, export revenue, and stock purchases. The trade deficit or surplus on this commodity will therefore show up as cash flows on stock transactions and the difference between producer income and consumer spending. Once again this constrains the system and connects the various objectives and concerns that governments might have. So as not to leave the government sector impotent, assume that it can intervene with import taxes and export subsidies to change the private cost of trading. The identity now includes import tariff revenue as a part of import cost and export subsidy payments as a part of trade receipts. The difference between these two amounts represents a surplus or deficit to the government account. This difference must therefore equal the sum of the private sector surplus (or deficit) and that of the overseas trading account. Thus while the government cannot interfere with the volume identity (even if it participates in the stocks function), it can, by running a surplus or deficit on account of this commodity, influence the private storage cash flow, the trade balance, and the gap between current consumption expenditure and producer receipts. These relationships are reproduced in Table 8.3. For completeness, government tax and subsidy policies on the domestic market have been included: many of these items will of course be zero in any particular instance.

For an individual country, and in particular a developing country without a large, grain-consuming livestock sector, the first imperative of a food security policy is presumably to stabilize food consumption levels. This may conveniently be done by stabilizing food prices—indeed this latter objective may become an aim in itself. If food demand itself does not change then stable prices will control food expenditure and, more importantly, prevent the transmission of instability to nonfood markets. Control of food prices could be accomplished by adjusting trade barriers, as would occur automatically if import levies and subsidies were tied to the difference between world and (stable) domestic price levels. More usually, control will be through state purchasing and distribution of imports and possibly the domestic crop. We would expect two implications to follow from these devices. First, the incentive for domestic stock-holding would be much reduced as prices on the internal market were stabilized.[6] Second, the foreign trade balance (in this product) and the government program cost will have to absorb the instability arising from production either at home or abroad.

If the instability occurs abroad, the foreign exchange and government revenue accounts may move together: an improvement in the trade balance (other import costs and export revenue remaining constant) will coincide with an increase in the government surplus (assuming no change in taxation and other government programs). Similarly, an increased deficit on external account may be linked with a similar deficit in the budget. If, however, the instability is in domestic production, government deficits may coincide with foreign exchange surpluses and vice versa. These impacts are made more severe by the depressing effect on private stockholding, since government-owned stocks would have to take up some of that function.

Similar problems arise with respect to developed countries, though the emphasis is more likely to be on stabilization of consumer prices than on consumption quantities per se. Those countries that allow private trade to conduct much of the business of marketing and storage will tend to use border taxes and subsidies to control prices. Central-plan countries and those with a structure of state trading will absorb instability directly into the government account. The end result will be similar, with the willingness to allow instability in the budget and the foreign exchange account being the quid pro quo for domestic price stability. Precisely the same problems arise with respect to stabilizing producer incomes, though it is much more normal for policies to aim at preventing rapid changes in producer prices, leaving incomes to fluctuate broadly with production variations.

If countries find that consumption-stability policies destabilize foreign exchange flows and government accounts, it follows that attempts to make these items more stable will clash with consumption objectives. For developing countries with a small tax base and severe payments constraints, this dilemma may be harsh. In the light of domestic production variations and a fixed amount of foreign exchange for use to purchase imports, domestic consumption can only be stabilized by stockholding extensive enough to cover all production changes. The private sector is unlikely to find such arbitrage profitable and govern-

*Price, Stock, and Trade Policies*

Table 8.3  Market Identities and Sector Accounts

---

Value identity for open sub-system, with government.[a]

| Private sector receipts | Private sector expenditures |
|---|---|
| Producer receipts | Consumer expenditure |
| Revenue from private stock sales | Cost of private stock accumulation |

| Government sector receipts | Government sector expenditures |
|---|---|
| Import tax receipts | Export subsidy costs |
| Producer tax receipts | Producer subsidy costs |
| Consumer tax receipts | Consumer subsidy costs |
| Sales of government stocks | Cost of government stock accumulation |

| Foreign sector receipts | Foreign sector expenditure |
|---|---|
| Import cost in foreign exchange | Export revenue in foreign exchange |

| Total Above Receipts | = | Total Above Expenditure |
|---|---|---|

---

[a] Value identity for a closed system is as above, but without the foreign sector.

ment costs will be high and erratic. Moreover this dilemma is evident also when world prices vary, as government stocks held when world prices rise will have a high opportunity cost and those held when prices fall will represent a more costly supply source than imports. Consumer price changes may be forced on a country simply because its fiscal and foreign exchange accounts cannot take the strain. In this respect, developed countries are more likely to be able to pursue single-minded consumption stability policies.

## Developed Country Policies and Stability

This discussion of national policy choices is well illustrated in the chapters drawn from the Conference that deal with the situation in individual developing countries. The types of policy choices faced by developed countries differ in degree rather than kind. Since developed country policies have not been discussed in detail in the previous chapters, it may be appropriate to consider them here—both as illustration of the types of policy response to instability and with respect to their implications for world food security. As suggested above, the primary focus of developed country policies has been on the extension of mechanisms designed primarily to protect producers from price fluctuations to include a degree of protection for consumers against inflation. The mechanisms have included export taxes and embargoes on one side and import and domestic subsidies on the other.

The results of such policies have been widely noted. They have the effect of achieving domestic stability at the expense of world markets and hence of other countries. The analysis of this chapter suggests that the role of stocks is crucial in this process. If adequate stocks are held, then impacts on other countries through trade of the domestic policies can be offset. Unfortunately, countries with stable domestic prices are unlikely to carry large stabilizing stocks unless such reserves are a conscious part of government policy. Importers, in particular, have no reason to store significant quantities unless they fear physical supplies may be unavailable. Japan and the European Community, among developed countries, have been particularly reluctant to engage in extensive stockholding of grain.

In the present context, the reaction of each individual developed country government is probably less important to a discussion of world food security than is the total impact of these countries together. If the net result of policies, both with respect to farm income and consumer food prices, is to exacerbate price swings by increasing supplies when prices are low and reducing them when prices rise, then an important obstacle to food security has been identified. A straightforward test is possible, using results from the study mentioned in Footnote 4. Table 8.4 summarizes the implied impact of the farm and food policies of the major developed countries on the wheat market in recent years.[7] For each country studied, an estimate was made of the likely production and consumption

Table 8.4 Policy-Induced Trade Volume Effects, Selected Developed Countries, and Stock Changes: Wheat, 1967/68 to 1976/77

| | 1969/70 | 1970/71 | 1971/72 | 1972/73 | 1973/74 | 1974/75 | 1975/76 | 1976/77 |
|---|---|---|---|---|---|---|---|---|
| | | | | | (million tons) | | | |
| Trade volume effect[a] | | | | | | | | |
| in SDCs | 13.3 | 13.4 | 13.2 | 13.7 | 1.9 | -4.6 | -1.0 | 5.2 |
| Change in stocks | | | | | | | | |
| in SDCs | -2.8 | 15.3 | 0.2 | 17.2 | 5.3 | -2.8 | -5.6 | -16.3 |
| Change in stocks in USSR[b] | 19.0 | 8.0 | -3.0 | -2.0 | -14.0 | 11.0 | 8.0 | -12.0 |
| Total stock and policy | | | | | | | | |
| effect in SDCs | 10.5 | 28.6 | 13.4 | 31.0 | 7.2 | -7.4 | -6.6 | -11.1 |
| Total effect including | | | | | | | | |
| USSR stock change | 29.5 | 36.7 | 10.4 | 29.0 | -6.8 | 3.6 | 1.4 | -23.1 |
| Change from previous year[c] | | 7.2 | -26.3 | 18.6 | -35.8 | 10.4 | -2.2 | -24.5 |

a/ Trade volume effect of policies as defined in text.

b/ Positive numbers refer to stock rundown.

c/ Change in total stock and policy effect: positive numbers indicate an increase in supplies due to stock and policy changes.

volume that would have been generated in the absence of the major price support programs. Production impacts were assumed to follow policy changes by one year, with consumption effects instantaneous. Stocks policies were defined as variations from a constant (or zero) level of stocks, even where such stocks were not under direct government control. A positive "trade volume effect" can be interpreted as the additional trade surplus in wheat generated by policy-induced production and the accompanying reduction in consumption due to price supports. This trade volume effect became negative during 1974–1976, as a result of policies designed to hold down domestic prices.

The rationale for adding stock changes to these policy impacts is to indicate whether these had the effect of offsetting the policy impact or of reinforcing such policies. Increasing stock levels at times of high prices accentuates the effect of domestic stabilization policies on world markets: when markets are adequately supplied, such stock accumulation removes from the market the extra net exports implied by price supports. If these net stocks-plus-policy effects are reasonably constant, the impact on world markets is confined to resource allocation rather than stability. The notable feature of the last few years, as illustrated in Table 8.4, is the extent to which this "total" policy effect switched from generating extra supplies in the period up to 1972/73 to creating extra demands on the market in 1973/74. Comparing these two years alone, one can see from the table that the price policies were "responsible" for the effective removal of nearly 12 million tons of wheat from the market: adding stock changes in the developed countries to this increased the figure to 24 million tons, and including Soviet stocks as well gave a total market "squeeze" of nearly 36 million tons.[8]

This total stock-and-price-policy impact reached its peak in 1972/73, with an estimated 31 million tons of wheat generated by stock rundown and price policy surpluses. By 1974/75 the corresponding figure was −7.4 million tons, with price policies reducing net availability and stocks beginning to be accumulated once again. The table also shows these total figures as changes from the previous year. Over the two-year period 1972/73 to 1974/75 the total policy impact was a reduction in net avail-

# Price, Stock, and Trade Policies

ability of 38.4 million tons. This should not be taken to mean that nearly 40 million tons was in fact held off the market: rather that with no price support policies in these countries and with constant stock levels the situation on world markets would have been the same as if 40 million more tons of wheat had been available over these two seasons.

Though this figure is considerable when seen in the context of the wheat market over these years, it should be interpreted with care. The charge cannot be sustained that the developed countries "created" a shortage by means of stock and price-support policies. In the absence of those policies it appears that wheat prices would have been somewhat higher over the period up to and including 1973/74, when the actual world price reached $170 per ton. Stock release and price protection in that year were still generating perhaps 7 million tons "extra" wheat over the situation that might have held if there were free markets and constant stocks in developed countries. Since 1974/75, wheat prices would have been somewhat lower in the absence of developed country policies. The high price in 1973 was not "caused" by the policies as such, but the change in prices from those prevailing before 1972 would have been much less, as they would have started from a higher base, and the duration of the "crisis" would have been diminished.

This can be put in another way. The Soviet purchase of 14 million tons of wheat (net of exports) in 1972/73 came at a time both when stocks were adequate and price-supported surpluses existed. The opportunity afforded by the intervention in the market of the USSR as an importer was welcomed by those countries with stocks and with expensive domestic programs. Soviet stocks had already been run down in previous years. Without the developed country stock release, market prices in 1972 would have risen considerably. But this action rebounded the next year. The Soviet Union built up stocks from a good harvest, more than absorbing the further stock depletion in the SDCs and their remaining surplus production. The net effect of Soviet and SDC stocks policies (and price policies in the SDCs) was to reduce supplies by nearly 7 million tons in 1973/74. Again it is the difference between this effect and that in the previous year that indicate the impact on price changes. This difference is nearly 36 million tons between 1972/73 and 1973/74. Coming at a time when developing country production was down (and when the cost of other imports, notably energy) was sharply up, this "squeeze" on the market was clearly a major reason for a 70 percent increase in the average export price over the year. The impact on prices in 1974/75 would have been worse if the Soviet Union had not released 11 million tons from stocks, indicating a combined stock-and-policy effect of an additional 4 million tons, an improvement of 10 million tons over the previous year as far as other countries were concerned.

This leads to the conclusion that developed country policies inadvertently exacerbated the problems in this period which arose from production variability. Stocks policies did not offset the impact of domestic policy changes. Instead they tended to reinforce these changes, moving in the same direction in every year from 1970/71 to 1975/76, inclusive. This is at the heart of the problem. For world price stability, stocks have to accumulate when domestic policies are generating overproduction until such policies can be changed, and have to be run down when domestic price stability objectives dictate that an increase in home supplies is necessary. Over the first half of the decade, policies were not responding in this fashion. Stocks were released onto markets as a way of exporting domestic overproduction and were accumulated just when consumption was higher and production lower than would have been the case under freer markets. This is the major impact of domestic policies on world market price stability.

These results illustrate the interrelationships that are crucial to an examination of food security. They indicate that even though stocks policies may over time appear to offset actual production changes and hence minimize the transmission of production variations (as in Table 8.2, above), a closer look suggests that they often reinforce the tendency of policies in domestic markets to shift the burden of instability or to avoid the "importation" of such instability from abroad. The international discussion of food security must grapple both with the problem of aggregate instability in production and with the mechanisms that operate to shift the burden of such instability onto markets that may be less able to cope with their effects.

## International Policy Alternatives

International schemes and initiatives regarding the problem of instability in markets have not been lacking. Support at a political level for any particular scheme has been less forthcoming. Three broad approaches have been discussed in recent years. The first is to increase the level and/or the price responsiveness of stocks in the system. This has taken several forms including financial and technical assistance in the construction of storage facilities in developing countries, coordination of stock management among governments, and the ownership of reserves by an international body. The second has been to increase the variability of consumption in developed countries, again by various means ranging from abstinence during scarcity to reform of domestic farm and food-price policies. The third has tackled the problem from a financial viewpoint, advocating some form of payments aid or food aid to alleviate foreign exchange problems. Each of these approaches has its own characteristics of political attractiveness, of economic impact, and of the distribution of costs and advantages. In keeping with the aims of this chapter, none of these will be discussed in detail here. But the analysis of the preceding pages may help to put them into perspective.

The stocks option has its own attractions. At a domestic level, adequate stocks appear to give a degree of autonomy over food supplies that may be missing when resort to world markets must always follow poor harvests at home. Even discounting the fact that stocks will seem much more desirable in high price periods, the recent interest shown by countries in increasing storage capacity would indicate that this aspect of marketing may have been neglected in the past. Storage policies could also have an important role in some cases of reducing (or capturing for the government) the arbitrage rents of various "middlemen." In addition, they can facilitate the development of internal distribution systems and provide more stable seasonal supplies. But as a food security instrument greater reserve levels as such have their limitations. Since holding and managing stocks is expensive, a general attempt at the international level to impose an undue burden on developing countries in the form of increased stockholding may be regressive. The profits from stockholding for an individual importing country, particularly if its market is small in size, are derived from speculating against world market price changes. The amount of information needed and the ability to move into and out of stocks as conditions dictate place limits on the wisdom of such a policy, but such a strategy will not always require substantial physical holdings of grain by the country concerned. Other alternatives are available that might give the same degree of security at a lower cost.

What is true for the individual small country may not be the case for the large grain trader. Two situations can be distinguished. The large importer of grain may feel constrained to carry reserves if there is the likelihood that greater-than-average purchases will push up the import price considerably. The marginal import cost might be high relative to the marginal cost of grain from storage—an economic justification for the political feeling that supply security can be enhanced by stocks. The same arguments with respect to internal transportation and marketing as mentioned above hold a fortiori for the geographically large and populous developing country. The significant grain exporter will have other motives for holding reserves, in particular to retain credibility as a supply source. In this sense, exporter reserves assist the food security objectives of importing regions. As was indicated by the analysis above, for any given set of trading conditions the ability of developing (and developed) importing countries to use trade rather than domestic stocks to offset production variability rests on the existence of variable stocks elsewhere in the world and in particular in the developed exporting countries. Other countries have a direct interest in the way these exporter stocks are managed.[9]

Much of the discussion of reserves has recently revolved around the international coordination of stock policies. This gives rise to the question as to whether such coordination brings benefits over and above those arising from the existence of stocks held under national initiative. There is a strong presumption that just as private stocks within a country may be inadequate from a national point of view so national stocks may not be sufficient from an international perspective.[10] This arises from the fact that a risk shared is a risk reduced. A government may wish to indemnify private traders from large losses (possibly in return for a

# Price, Stock, and Trade Policies

share in abnormal profits). Similarly trading partners may wish to bear some of the risks to individual countries in return for greater security. But, as one would expect, the negotiation of such a system has proved to be difficult, as each participant has pressed for a higher degree of risk taking and cost bearing by the others.

The second kind of solution to instability is to increase consumption adjustments in developed countries. The analytical approach of this chapter suggests this as a direct alternative to the manipulation of stocks in terms of evening out production variability. State trading and central plan countries can adjust world market purchases, should they wish, to avoid putting strain on available supplies in times of world shortage. They could increase imports when supplies are more than adequate. In doing so, their own foreign exchange costs might be made more stable. Countries that rely more on the price mechanism— whether or not distorted by trade barriers—for deciding on imports would be expected to allow price changes to stimulate consumption adjustments directly. The somewhat weaker mechanisms of moral suasion and voluntary abstinence have also been suggested. There are two problems with the consumption adjustment approach. First, it clashes with strong stability motives in these countries not just in terms of the consumer price level but also with respect to the cyclical behavior of the livestock sector. Secondly, it does not entirely solve, though it might somewhat alleviate, the foreign exchange problem of developing country importers. Nevertheless, this approach does bring into the open the interrelationship in the world food economy between developing and developed country policies. The extent to which such policies can be reconciled in this way determines the need for other measures such as stock management and foreign exchange facilities.

The various plans that address the foreign exchange problem come under two headings. The first group relates foreign exchange assistance directly to developing country import patterns. It envisages either a set of financial transfers linked to the variability of food import costs designed to improve the balance of payments of the importer and reduce that country's budget burden, or an additional line of credit to enable commercial imports to be paid for at a later date. It will be apparent from the analysis above that this type of solution is of a different nature than those involving stock and consumption adjustments. It does not in itself address the problem of global variability. To the extent that it allows countries to continue and strengthen policies that insure domestic consumption it increases the need for (and the profitability of holding) stocks. It aggravates the global adjustment problem and, without more flexible stocks or adjustments in developed country consumption, tends to destabilize prices. Such comments are not meant to reflect on the merits of these schemes but merely put them into perspective. Their objective is to reconcile the conflict noted earlier between the interest of a country in maintaining consumption patterns and stabilizing prices and the uncomfortably destabilizing implications of this for the foreign exchange account. They enable countries to participate in trade to a greater extent. Combined with more flexibility in stocks or with developed country consumption adjustments, they allow for both international stability and domestic food security; alone, they might promote the latter at the expense of the former.

The second group of foreign exchange–related policies is analytically similar, though with different connotations. Concessional food sales, both bilateral and multilateral, might be considered as the "traditional" approach to world food security. The recent emphasis has been to attempt to untie the link that has existed between food aid flows and domestic farm policies. Food aid that is dependent upon erratic surpluses in developed countries is not considered to be a sound basis for food planning in developing countries.[11] Food aid should therefore be made more directly a function of developing country needs, such as result from domestic harvest fluctuations. A guarantee of supplies to cover such needs would ensure that the developing country could avoid holding large domestic reserves—either of grain or of foreign exchange. The stocks necessary to underwrite such an "insurance" policy would presumably be held by the exporter, and the impact on global security would depend on whether the net change in stock flexibility was adequate to allow greater consumption stability. A policy of this type therefore has implications for the commercial as well as the conces-

# Price, Stock, and Trade Policies

sional market. Again, as with more direct import-assistance schemes, the greater level of consumption stability engendered by the policy, or the reduction in recipient stock level changes, will impose a somewhat greater burden on the rest of the trading system in terms either of consumption adjustment or stock management. The objective—to remove some degree of security cost from the developing country—must be met by assuming corresponding responsibilities elsewhere in the market.

What is important to the importer or food aid recipient is the implicit price level: the degree of concession in the aid, relating to conditions of payment as well as nominal price. A lower import price is tantamount to reducing foreign exchange costs for a particular import volume, but does not necessarily reduce foreign exchange costs if import quantities are elastic with respect to price changes. This depends on the way in which the importing government disposes of the food aid on the domestic market. The difference between this type of policy and that concerned directly with foreign exchange cost is that concessional sales have a price effect, at least for the government concerned. The granting of a line of credit or the transfer of compensatory finance would be expected to have a more general impact on the economy and on trading patterns as a whole. One might say that nonfood security is enhanced by such policies. The price effect of concessional sales will have such a wealth effect too, but its more direct impact will be on the decision as to how much of the favored foodstuff to import.

The intent of this chapter is to raise questions and suggest a structured approach to food security problems. The main argument has been built around a simple set of identities regarding trade volumes. Such elementary observations seem occasionally to be overlooked. There has been a tendency for some commentators, for instance, to view the variability of stocks levels per se as a cause for concern, leading to suggestions that governments stabilize stock levels either individually or collectively. This is tantamount to insuring that consumption be made as variable as production. Happily, governments have resisted the lure of stock-level stabilization. But international discussions on the appropriate level of stocks to be accumulated under particular stability and security schemes suggest that the paramount need for stocks to vary is not universally recognized. The relationship between stock management, price stability, and trade is complex: the link between production, consumption, and stock quantities involves only basic accounting identities. The policy questions thus revolve around the political desirability of imparting additional stability to particular magnitudes, such as consumption levels, and the use of various instruments to perform this task. The examination of such policies requires that the corresponding increase in instability in other variables also be discussed. If all stability schemes made clear the implication for the variability of other elements in the system, the economic and political nature of the choice would be that much clearer.

## Notes

1. It is sometimes implied that because variability in world production is less than the sum of variations in each country, freer trade reduces the need for offsetting consumption or stock changes. This is misleading, if not actually false. Aggregate production changes imply the same aggregate stock and consumption changes irrespective of the degree of freedom of trade. But whereas with no trade one country might be forced to consume (or store) less while another was consuming (or storing) more in a particular year, with trade these changes would be unnecessary. This is the sense in which trade influences the distribution of instability but not the total magnitude.

2. This is, of course, not the same as the "profit" from storage in that year arising from the difference between acquisition and sales prices of stocks (adjusted for costs and forgone interest). But over a period of years cash flows and gross profits will equate. In the present context, cash flow is emphasized mainly because of its relevance in discussions of the funding of reserve programs.

3. This situation is quite distinct from the other types of market isolation, arising from fixed domestic prices and variable trade barriers, as discussed below. A closed submarket "exports" none of its instability, whereas a price-unresponsive submarket "exports" all of its instability. The closed submarket "imports" no instability, whereas the fixed-price market absorbs instability in foreign exchange and government sector accounts without adjusting trade volumes. The implications for the world market as a whole differ considerably.

# Price, Stock, and Trade Policies
183

4. The concept of a change from the previous year of the level stock accumulation may seem unduly obscure, but its relevance is confirmed by the identities in Table 8.1. It is not sufficient to combine the actual stock change in a particular year with the production and consumption changes to obtain the trade surplus change. In 1969/70 for example, stocks actually increased by 2.8 million tons. But this did not imply a drop of 16.7 million tons in the export surplus. It was the difference between the stock increase of 20.2 million tons in 1968/69 and the 2.8 million tons in 1969/70 that effectively "released" 17.4 million tons to enable consumption to rise by 5.5 million tons, trade by 3.5 million tons, while production was down by 8.4 million tons relative to the previous year. The data presented here are from Josling (1980).

5. As developing market economies appeared to take only an extra 4.4 million tons of this surplus, the remainder presumably went to replenish reserves in countries not included in the table and to meet any higher import requirements that they may have had that year.

6. Some speculation on overseas trade might still be possible, but apart from the foreign exchange benefits of any profits this will not be relevant to the domestic market.

7. No attempt was made to estimate USSR policy impacts, though stock changes are included in Table 8.4. The difficulty in estimating Soviet output and consumption in the absence of government policies is obvious in a country where no clear market price mechanism is established. Since it is very likely that the effect of Soviet policy is similar to that in countries where farm support systems operate through market interventions, the figures in the table undoubtedly understate the impact on markets.

8. Soviet stock rundown in the next year (1974/75) more than offset the continued pressure from the developed countries on the wheat market.

9. Some of the most important developments in policy in recent years have, in the present context, been changes in internal stocks and reserve programs of major exporters and in the price conditions for their accumulation and release.

10. The differing attitudes of economists as to the appropriate management of stocks provides a further illustration of divergencies in objectives rather than a contest of alternative research methods. Stocks held for economic motives, matching a cost and a rate of return, may be very different in size and behavior from those designed to provide a particular path of prices or adequate to ensure a certain level of consumption. Added to the diversity of private, public, and international objectives, this makes the definition of an optimal stocks policy as much a political as an economic exercise.

11. In the light of the analysis of the relationship between production,

# 184

*Timothy Josling*

consumption, and stocks presented above, this criticism has to be modified somewhat. Farm product surpluses are not a readily identifiable item in the market balance identity: they are subsumed in the relationship between consumption, stocks, and trade. Thus the analysis of consumption, stocks, and trade changes incorporates concessional flows as well as those on commercial terms. Aid appropriations might be more forthcoming when commodities are in surplus and governments may make use of aid channels to divest embarrassing stocks. But the net availability of a commodity for export is not in itself changed by the existence of food aid outlets, just as the import requirements of developing countries per se are not related to the existence of surpluses. Surpluses will be disposed of somewhere, through trade or aid, and developing country governments will attempt to satisfy import needs on the best available terms. The natural ex-post link between food aid and surpluses does not seem to warrant excessive international concern.

## References

Josling, Timothy. "Developed Country Agricultural Policies and Developing Countries Food Supplies: The Case of Wheat." *IFPRI Research Report No. 14*. Washington, D.C.: IFPRI, April 1980.

# 9
# Feasibility, Effectiveness, and Costs of Food Security Alternatives in Developing Countries

*Shlomo Reutlinger*
*David Bigman*

Authors in this book have provided some useful empirical evidence about the diversity of symptoms associated with the variability in food production within and outside the boundaries of developing countries. As we now begin to consider the consequences of remedial interventions, we would do well to keep in mind the full range of symptoms that must be addressed. Unfortunately, both policymakers and theoretical economists have generally paid far too little attention to the multiplicity of adverse consequences associated with unstable food production. Further, proposed remedies and models have generally not addressed the diversity of important food-related concerns for developing countries.

Our second introductory observation is that discussions of remedies for food insecurity in national and international forums are still too panacea oriented. They usually fail to consider the whole range of policy instruments available for alleviating the ills of food production instability. Specifically, we have in mind the still very popular notion that the only solution to interyear variability in production is a large buffer stock operation. This notion derives, of course, from a failure to fully comprehend the opportunities in today's world for reallocating existing food supplies within and between countries. With high average levels of per-capita food production occurring under a great diversity of ecological and technological conditions, with highly developed channels of communication and transportation, and with much food normally going toward feeding the palate rather than the stomach, there are now real opportunities to prevent hunger by

*185*

reallocating food from low- to high-priority uses, even without the costly storing of food. Economists are less guilty of failing to recognize the opportunities of attaining stabilization through trade. Yet, they often do wear blinders of a different kind, for they fail to appreciate the full extent of deprivations arising from financial constraints on low-income people and countries.

Our main objective in this chapter is to present in broad brush strokes a method that any LDC can use—with suitable modifications—to analyze (a) the magnitude of its food insecurity problems and (b) the effectiveness and costs of pursuant remedial actions. Clearly, the simulation approach advocated here is not the only approach nor is the model nearly as developed as it could be. However, the approach does address the many concerns arising from instability in foodgrain production: the probability of shortfalls in food consumption to unacceptably low levels among vulnerable segments in the population, the probability of high and low food prices, and the probability of incurring high fiscal costs and foreign exchange requirements to the extent that governments intervene in the allocation of available food supplies and sanction high levels of imports. Moreover, the approach can easily accommodate itself to a comparative analysis of a whole range of policy options: buffer stocks, trade policies, and internal price subsidy and support programs for specific segments of the population.

The approach is illustrated by reference to data approximating conditions in India, an estimated variability in worldwide wheat production, and a simple model translating production variability to variability in world foodgrain prices. Results are reported in terms of stability parameters and in terms of long-run gains and costs to the overall economy, to specially vulnerable consumers, to farmers, and to the government.

The major conclusion, based on simulation experiments, is that in order to achieve a reasonably satisfactory level of food security LDCs ought to pursue stabilizing trade policies. To facilitate implementation of such policies, it will be necessary, however, to have available large foreign exchange and fiscal resources in years of poor harvests or high import prices. In this context, suitable financial and food aid arrangements or an international insurance fund have an important role to play.

*Food Security Alternatives* 187

### The Model

The model is of an open economy engaged in trade with the rest of the world. The sources of fluctuations in the domestic market are assumed to be random disturbances in domestic supply and the international price. The model can accommodate both a "small" country, for which the terms of trade are given, and a country that is significant enough in the world market to have an effect on the world price. The country is assumed to be "self-sufficient" in the sense that in a "normal" year, when both the country's production and the world price are at their mean level, there is no price differential between the country and the world and thus no incentive for trade. In other years, however, uncorrelated random fluctuations in domestic supply or in the world price may create price gaps sufficiently large to trigger imports or exports by the free market.

The main components of the model are:

1. A world grain price model that estimates the world price on the basis of (randomly distributed) world production and an estimated world demand function.
2. A country grain market model that estimates grain consumption, exports and imports, inventories in stock, and domestic grain price for each level of country production and world market price and in accordance with the policies implemented by the government.
3. A system of decision rules that represent the government policies in the grain market.
4. A procedure for the calculation of gains or losses to the various consumer groups, to producers, and to the government, due to stock, price, and trade policies.

For every given level of grain production in the world and in the country, the model estimates (a) world price; (b) price and quantity of grain consumed, stored, and traded in the country; (c) economic and financial gains to the various sectors; and (d) the balance of trade. The estimates are generated for a large sample of grain production events and aggregated into frequency distributions. The essential features of the model and the decision rules associated with each policy are described briefly below.

### Market Structure

*World price.* In the absence of sufficient historical evidence on the variability of world price for the purpose of estimating future world prices, a simple model was designed that transforms world grain production into a world price on the basis of an estimated world demand function. World production is assumed to be randomly distributed according to a specified probability distribution.

*Country's production.* Grain production in the country is subject to random disturbances with a specified probability distribution. The model can accommodate year-to-year serial correlation and correlation between the country's production and world production (and therefore the world price).

### Policy Decision Rules

*Subsidy program.* A food subsidy program aimed at maintaining consumption of low-income urban consumers is carried out by making foodgrains available to them at a price that is lower than the market price. The program becomes active only when the food grain price in the domestic market rises above its median level. The subsidized price is determined each year according to the actual market price in that year. To permit reducing the government's fiscal burden, the model assumes that the subsidized price can be increased with an increase in the market price, though at a lower rate.

*Support price program.* The model specifies a program of monetary compensation to producers whenever the market price falls below a specified floor price. The government does not constrain production to avoid surplus, nor does it extract any excess from the market. Therefore, the market price to consumers is not directly affected by this program. The floor price can either be fixed or can be determined each year on the basis of the actual market price that year. In the latter case, the model assumes that the floor price decreases monotonically with the market price so that the budget needed for the program is smaller than in the fixed floor price scheme.

*Storage rules.* Stabilization by means of buffer stocks is assumed, in the present version of the model, to take the form of a quantity band policy. Within prespecified boundaries, supply is allowed to fluctuate freely. When the actual quantity available for consumption falls short of the lower boundary, grain is released from storage up to that level—if sufficient grain is available in storage from the previous year. When domestic production exceeds the upper limit of the band, the excess above that limit is put into storage—if sufficient vacant storage capacity is available. The actual amount stored cannot, obviously, exceed the available storage capacity. Likewise, the amount of grain released from storage cannot exceed the amount available in storage in that year. Thus, the parameters of the storage rules are the intervention bands and the capacity of the storage facility.

*Trade policy.* Trade activities between the country and the world are carried out by the free market within limits of a specific trade policy implemented by the government. Thus, grain is imported when the domestic price exceeds the import price, and grain is exported when the export price exceeds the domestic price. The import and export prices are determined by the world price, transportation costs, and tariffs. The instruments for enforcing government goals with respect to trade are tariffs and quantity constraints. In order to diminish the potential destabilizing effects of trade, export is not permitted when the quantity available for domestic consumption is below a prespecified lower level and import is restricted so that the domestic price level does not fall below a specified lower limit.

Alternatively, the model can accommodate a trade policy specifically designed to increase stability in the domestic market by means of a complex tax-subsidy system. The principles of this policy are as follows: in times of shortfall in domestic production and high world prices, the government pays a subsidy on each ton of imported grain; alternatively, the government itself can purchase grain from abroad and sell it in the domestic market at a lower price.[1] In times of excess in domestic production and low prices, the government pays a subsidy on each ton of exported grain in order to avoid a large price drop for domestic producers. In times of above-average domestic production but very high world prices, the government imposes a tax on exports in order to prevent the domestic price from rising to the high levels of the world market.

*Trade and storage.* Trade and storage activities could be substituted for each other on occasion to achieve stabilization objectives. When production is low, world price is low, and stored-up grain is available, then grain can be either imported or withdrawn from storage. Likewise, when production is plentiful, export prices are high, and there is vacant storage capacity, then grain could be either exported or stored. It is assumed here that the authorities emphasize the food security aspect of stocks and thus grain is imported prior to releasing from storage whereas excess supply is first put into storage and only the remaining quantity is released for exports. When the stabilizing trade policy is active, the storage operations are more sensitive to fiscal and balance of payments considerations in the following sense: if the import price is too high to permit imports via the free market, but at the same time the target price is such that additional quantity is required over and above the quantity produced domestically to achieve the target, the authorities will release from storage prior to importing at the high world price. In that case, the storage operation will mostly affect government expenditures in foreign exchange and subsidy payments on the imported grain.

## The Calculation of Gains and Losses

Welfare gains from the various stabilization policies are measured in terms of the conventional consumers' and producers' surpluses. Welfare gains to producers are thus measured by the expected change in producers' surplus and welfare gains to consumers are measured by the expected change in consumers' surplus. The model measures both the incremental gains from a policy, given certain price policies that are already practiced, as well as the total gains from a given combination of policies.

## Data and Parameters

The parameters of the model are not representative of any particular country but they were deliberately chosen to approxi-

*Food Security Alternatives* 191

mate orders of magnitude of a country like India. In the simulation experiments, a time horizon of 30 years has been used. This was found to be "long enough" in the sense that succeeding events had only small effects on the outcomes. Each simulation experiment involved 300 iterations, each using a different 30-year sequence of world and country production as drawn from the specified distributions. The specific parameters used were as follows:

*World grain market.* One main objective is to explore the trade opportunities of the LDCs. The primary food grain traded by them is wheat. World grain prices are assumed to be best represented by the world price of wheat. World wheat production is assumed to be normally distributed with an annual mean and standard deviation of 350 million and 14 million metric tons, respectively.

World demand for wheat is assumed to be kinked linear. The elasticities, calculated at the mean level of world production (i.e., in the vicinity of $125 per metric ton), are:

$$\eta = .2 \text{ for } P > \$125$$
$$\eta = .4 \text{ for } P < \$125$$

Taken together, these assumptions imply that the median world price is $125 per metric ton.

*Country grain market.* Country production is assumed to be normally distributed with annual mean and standard deviation of 110 million metric tons and 7 million metric tons, respectively.

Domestic consumers were divided into three groups: low-income urban consumers, other urban consumers, and rural consumers. Table 9.1 shows the assumed elasticities and median consumptions for the three groups and the country as a whole. The assumed demand parameters when the price is in the vicinity of $125 per metric ton are summarized.

*Subsidy to the low-income urban population.* With this policy the government maintains consumption of the low-income population in the urban areas above what it would otherwise be in years of high prices. The policy is active when $P \geq \$125$ per metric ton and effectively changes both the demand of low-

192                              *Shlomo Reutlinger and David Bigman*

Table 9.1 Country Demand Parameters

|  | Low income urban | Other urban | Rural | Aggregate |
|---|---|---|---|---|
| Quantity consumed (mmt) | 33 | 33 | 44 | 110 |
| Price elasticity: | | | | |
| P > $125/mt | .35 | .20 | .15 | .225 |
| P < $125/mt | .35 | .30 | .20 | .275 |

income urban consumers and aggregate demand. The decision parameter of the program is the elasticity of the subsidy schedule. Table 9.2 summarizes the price elasticities of the beneficiary group and of all consumers in the vicinity of $125 per metric ton with and without the subsidy.

*Price support program.* With this policy the government maintains a constant price floor of $100 per metric ton.

*Buffer stock operations.* The buffer stock is operated using a quantity trigger band. The lower limit is 108 million metric tons, while the upper limit is 112 million metric tons. Grain moved into and out of storage is subject to a $5 per ton loading/ unloading charge. The interest rate for grain held in storage is 8 percent. Construction costs are assumed to be $100 per metric ton capacity and the storage facilities are assumed to be amortized over a period of 30 years.

*Trade policies.* The transportation charge for imports or exports of grain is $25 per metric ton. For the calculations reported in this chapter, the excess demand adjustment—whereby the country's demand for imports or supply of exports alters the world food grain price—is not effective.

Three alternative trade policies are examined, all of which are enforced by tariffs or subsidies. With "no-trade," the government sets import/export tariffs so high that there is no incentive for trade. Under the free trade policy, imports and exports are not taxed, with two exceptions. The government

# Food Security Alternatives

Table 9.2 Price Elasticities of Demand With and Without Subsidy Payments

| Beneficiary group | | All consumers | |
|---|---|---|---|
| Without subsidy | With subsidy | Without subsidy | With subsidy |
| .350 | .075 | .225 | .143 |

does not allow exports to lower supply in the country below 108 million metric tons, nor does it allow imports to lower the price below 0.95 of the median price. This rule is enforced by setting tariffs of an appropriate size.

Stabilizing trade policy is determined by the elasticities of the country's demand schedule. Table 9.3 summarizes the price elasticities in the vicinity of $125 per metric ton of the country's demand with the stabilizing trade policy and of the original demand schedules with and without the internal price subsidy program.

## Stabilization Effects

As noted earlier, the main instruments for stabilization available to a government are internal food price subsidy and support policies, buffer stock operations, and trade policies. The effects of implementing a wide range of these policies for the stability of major food policy-related variables are summarized in Table 9.4, in terms of the probabilities of encountering specified, undesirable events.

The most noteworthy result of the simulation experiments is the stabilizing effects of international trade. Contrary to a rather widely held belief, self-reliance, or the avoidance of trade, is the worst enemy of stability.[2] Without trade, instability in domestic production leads to a high degree of instability in foodgrain prices that in turn translates into high probabilities that the consumption of the low-income population will fall below minimally adequate levels and that farmers' income will

Table 9.3 Country's Price Elasticities of Demand With and Without Stabilizing Trade

| | Aggregate market demand | | Stabilizing trade |
| | Without subsidy | With subsidy | |
|---|---|---|---|
| P > $125 | .225 | .143 | .075 |
| P < $125 | .275 | .275 | .130 |

be put into jeopardy. Free trade alone can reduce the probability of an extreme shortfall in the quantities available to low-income consumers and fluctuations in prices to an extent that no reasonably sized buffer stock can achieve. For instance, when no other price policy is active, the probability that grain prices will be 20 percent above the median price is reduced with free trade from 23.6 percent to 11.8 percent. A buffer stock of 6 million metric tons (nearly one standard deviation of production) in the closed economy will reduce this probability to only 14.3 percent.[3] Yet, free trade is seen to be only partially effective in reducing the probability of foodgrain consumption curtailment among the low-income population.

Against the option of isolating the domestic market from the world market, which enhances rather than diminishes instability, the stabilizing trade policy insulates the country from external disturbances with compensating subsidies and taxes, thereby increasing the flow of trade in and out of the country. The effects of this policy on the stability of the domestic market are indeed far-reaching. The probability of an extreme shortfall in the quantity available for low-income consumers is reduced from over 30 percent in the closed economy to less than 4 percent with the stabilizing trade policy. The probability of having high grain prices (20 percent above median) is reduced from over 23 percent to less than 1 percent. The probability of farmers' income falling to 10 percent below the median is reduced from 29 percent to 4 percent.

Although it is clear that food security for consumers and stability of farmers' income can be achieved by various combina-

Table 9.4  Stability of Food Policy-Related Variables: Probability (in percent) of Specified Event

| Policy | Consumption of low-income consumers less than 95% of median /a | Market price in excess of 20% above median price /b | Market price in excess of 40% above median price | Market price less than 20% of median price | Farmers' gross income less than 90% of median /c | Food import bill in excess of $700 million /d | Fiscal cost of food policies in excess of $700 million |
|---|---|---|---|---|---|---|---|
| — — — — — — — — — — — — Without Internal Price Subsidy and Support Program — — — — — — — — — — — — | | | | | | | |
| No trade | 30.4 | 23.6 | 7.2 | 18.8 | 28.9 | 0 | 0 |
| No trade + stocks | 19.2 | 14.3 | 4.2 | 10.7 | 15.3 | 0 | 1.6 |
| Free trade | 22.1 | 11.8 | 1.2 | 8.8 | 16.5 | 8.4 | 0 |
| Free trade + stocks | 12.3 | 6.2 | .6 | 5.5 | 9.9 | 7.7 | 2.2 |
| Stabilizing trade | 3.9 | .6 | 0 | .8 | 4.1 | 16.9 | 0 |
| Stabilizing trade + stocks | 2.2 | .3 | 0 | .5 | 2.6 | 11.6 | 3.3 |
| — — — — — — — — — — — — With Internal Price Subsidy and Support Program — — — — — — — — — — — — | | | | | | | |
| No trade | 6.2 | 32.5 | 16.9 | 18.8 | 26.6 | 0 | 44.9 |
| No trade + stocks | 3.6 | 20.9 | 10.0 | 10.7 | 13.0 | 0 | 25.2 |
| Free trade | 0 | 16.4 | 2.9 | 8.8 | 15.4 | 12.1 | 19.0 |
| Free trade + stocks | 0 | 8.6 | 1.4 | 5.8 | 9.3 | 10.9 | 11.8 |
| Stabilizing trade | 0 | 5.9 | 0 | .8 | 3.6 | 16.9 | 6.8 |
| Stabilizing trade + stocks | 0 | 3.1 | .1 | .6 | 2.3 | 13.0 | 6.2 |

/a  The median is 33 million tons.

/b  The median is $125/ton.

/c  The median is 13.75 billion dollars.

/d  $700 million is approximately 5% of the median value of food grain consumed.

tions of trade and buffer stock policies, Table 9.4 clearly illustrates that these stabilizing effects cannot be achieved without destabilizing other accounts of major consequence: the balance of payments and the government's budget. Trade that acts to stabilize prices and supplies results in unstable foreign exchange transactions. With free trade, there is an 8.4 percent probability that foreign exchange to finance an import bill in excess of $700 million will be needed for food alone (nearly 5 percent of the value of food grain consumption). A stabilizing trade policy will double this probability. Buffer stock operations, in turn, make unstable demands on the government's budget.

The internal price policies are aimed at specific groups or sectors. They are very effective in reducing instability for the beneficiary groups but, at the same time, they increase substantially the instability for other groups or sectors. The effect of the price subsidy program is to reduce the probability of an extreme shortfall in the quantity available for low-income consumers from 30.4 percent to 6.2 percent in the closed economy and from 22.1 percent to almost zero in the open economy. Other consumers, however, will suffer from greater instability due to this program. The probability of having high prices (i.e., 20 percent above median) in the market, increases from 23.6 percent to 32.5 percent in the closed economy and from 11.8 percent to 16.4 percent in the open economy.

Several conclusions are warranted at this point. First, stability on any particular food-related objective can be achieved by any number or combinations of interventions. However, each intervention will affect differently the stability of other policy objectives. One consideration in choosing among interventions is this trading off of stability on different objectives. Second, the stabilizing effects of each individual policy depend on the other forms of interventions (or absence of interventions) that are already practiced. Thus, buffer stocks will significantly increase the stability both of food grain prices and farmers' income in the closed economy, but will affect only marginally those parameters in an open economy. On the other hand, when internal subsidy programs are in effect, stocks will be particularly effective in reducing the instability of financial parameters, such as the food import bill and the government budget. Third,

*Food Security Alternatives* 197

free trade in general and stabilizing trade policy in particular are very powerful and very efficient for achieving the main stabilization targets. They will destabilize foreign exchange transactions, however, to an extent that few developing countries would be able to meet the large amounts of foreign exchange required during unfavorable years.

### Expected Benefits and Costs

Table 9.5 shows the incremental expected (long-run) gains and losses for the overall economy, consumer groups, producers, and the government from employing a single or combination of policies in comparison with the closed economy case. Several interesting observations can be noted.

First, if we were to follow in the path of most of the writings in the economic literature, namely, that the sole criterion by which stabilization policies are to be judged is the overall effect on the economy (the combined consumer and producer surplus), the only justifiable intervention would be free trade (see column 1, Table 9.5). In the presence of free trade, the incremental benefits for all other interventions are negative.

Second, if as argued earlier the concern of governments with unstable food supplies goes far beyond considerations of long-run economic welfare, none of the interventions specified in the simulation experiments can be ruled out on the basis of overall economic gains. To the contrary it is noteworthy that the incremental total welfare gain or loss for any single or combination of policies is small,[4] whereas as noted previously, the stabilization consequences differ a great deal. The aggregate welfare loss from introducing a price subsidy and payments program, for instance, is only a few million dollars, whereas the food security effect has been shown to be very large. In this context, the economic welfare loss might be best regarded as an insurance premium paid by the country in return for reducing the risk of scarcity and famine.

Third, the distribution of gains and losses accruing to different groups and sectors is much more sensitive to the choice of intervention policy than the overall welfare effect on the economy. A price subsidy and support program superimposed

Table 9.5 Expected Annual Gains and Losses from Different Policies

($ million)

| Policy | Economy | Consumers | | Producers | Government | | Total |
| | | Low income | Other | | Storage operation | Other | |
|---|---|---|---|---|---|---|---|
| | | | — Without Domestic Price and Subsidy Program — | | | | |
| No trade | 0 | 0 | 0 | 0 | 0 | 0 | 0 |
| No trade + stocks | −43 | −32 | −56 | 104 | −59 | 0 | −59 |
| Free trade | 49 | −58 | −106 | 209 | 0 | 4 | 4 |
| Free trade + stocks | −20 | −50 | −81 | 184 | −76 | 3 | −73 |
| Stabilizing trade | 30 | 20 | 91 | −35 | 0 | −46 | −46 |
| Stab. trade + stocks | −33 | 10 | 71 | −4 | −81 | −29 | −110 |
| | | | — With Domestic Price and Subsidy Program — | | | | |
| No trade | −25 | 301 | −617 | 1283 | 0 | −992 | −992 |
| No trade + stocks | −60 | 201 | −533 | 973 | −51 | −650 | −701 |
| Free trade | 41 | 186 | −275 | 537 | 0 | −407 | −407 |
| Free trade + stocks | −33 | 150 | −244 | 464 | −79 | −324 | −403 |
| Stabilizing trade | 27 | 127 | −129 | 271 | 0 | −242 | −242 |
| Sta. trade + stocks | −40 | 113 | −127 | 271 | −82 | −215 | −297 |

*Food Security Alternatives*   199

on a closed economy, for instance, results in large gains for farmers and a high cost to nonbeneficiary consumers and to the government. Here it suffices to note that the selection of appropriate interventions requires a careful trade-off on diverse objectives. Calculations of the kind shown in Table 9.5 illustrate also why some remedies may not be feasible within the political structure of certain countries.

The marginal gains or losses from an individual policy will be completely different depending on what other policies a country has already adopted. Table 9.6 illustrates the expected gains and losses from a 6 million metric ton buffer stock under alternative sets of existing policies. The more open the economy is to international trade, the less frequently are buffer stocks used to stabilize supply. As a consequence, the expected gains or losses to the various groups and sectors from the storage operation (as well as its stabilizing effect) are significantly smaller in the open economy. At the same time, since the rate of utilization of the storage facility falls, expected annual storage costs—which include variable costs (including interest) and amortization—rise in relation to the gains from buying grain when prices are low and selling when prices are high. Consequently, net welfare gains from buffer stocks that are negative in all cases are somewhat more attractive in the closed economy.

An intriguing result to be observed in Table 9.6 is that while

Table 9.6  Expected Annual Gains and Losses Due to Buffer Stocks

($ million)

| Policy | Economy | Consumers | | Producers | Government | | Total |
|---|---|---|---|---|---|---|---|
| | | Low income | Other | | Storage operation | Other | |
| — — — — — — — Without Internal Price Subsidy and Support Program — — — — — — — — | | | | | | | |
| No trade | −43 | −32 | −56 | 104 | −59 | 0 | −59 |
| Free trade | −69 | 8 | 25 | −25 | −76 | −1 | −77 |
| Stabilizing trade | −62 | −9 | −20 | 31 | −81 | 17 | −64 |
| — — — — — — — — With Internal Price Subsidy and Support Program — — — — — — — | | | | | | | |
| No trade | −34 | −100 | 85 | −310 | −51 | 342 | 291 |
| Free trade | −72 | −36 | 32 | −73 | −79 | 84 | 5 |
| Stabilizing trade | −67 | −14 | 2 | 0 | −82 | 27 | −55 |

the overall costs of stocks are small and do not vary much with the incidence of other policies, the expected gains or losses among some groups can vary significantly. For instance, in the closed economy without internal price subsidy and support policies, low-income consumers will lose on average $32 million, other consumers will lose $56 million, and producers will gain $104 million from a 6 million metric ton buffer stock. If, however, internal price subsidy and support programs are implemented, low-income consumers will lose, on average, $100 million while other consumers will gain $85 million and producers will lose $310 million. It should be emphasized, however, that these gains and losses manifest the marginal effects of the buffer stock. Thus, for example, producers' losses from stocks when internal price subsidy programs prevail are, in effect, only a reduction of their gains from the subsidy program. Producers lose from stocks only in the sense that they reduce the windfall gain accruing to them from the government's decision to subsidize consumption of low-income consumers. If we compare consumers' total gains from all the policies summarized in Table 9.6 we observe that in the closed economy producers gain on average $104 million from stocks alone whereas they gain $973 million from a combination of stocks and the internal price programs.

Similarly low-income consumers do not gain from buffer stocks when a subsidy program exists because they do not benefit from stock-induced price reductions, whereas they pay higher prices, like all consumers, when grain is stored up for the future. On the other hand, buffer stocks perform a more significant price stabilizing role when an internal price subsidy program destabilizes the price. Hence, nonbeneficiary consumers gain more from a buffer stock (or regain some of the losses accruing to them from having to pay higher prices) when the government is committed to uphold consumption among low-income consumers.

Clearly, with a stabilizing trade policy in effect, buffer stocks have only a marginal effect on stabilization and therefore generate only small gains or losses to consumers and producers. One important conclusion from these results is that the benefits and costs of buffer stocks cannot be evaluated without taking into

# Food Security Alternatives

201

account the policy environment in which the buffer stock is operated. Disregarding otherwise prevailing policies that have stabilization effects may lead to serious errors in judging the desirability of buffer stocks.

Another intriguing result is the effect of storage on the government's budget and the balance of trade. When the government is implementing subsidy and support price programs, buffer stocks yield large savings in government expenditures for these programs that far outweigh the cost of operating the buffer stock. These significant savings on the government's account could justify buffer stocks in spite of "negative" effects on low income consumers and on producers, particularly when the losses incurred by these groups from stocks consist merely of reductions in their gains from other policies.

Buffer stocks may also have some justification on account of their stabilizing effects on foreign exchange requirements. With trade and no internal price policies, the probability of encountering a trade deficit in foodgrains in excess of $100 million is 19.6 percent without stocks, but only 13.7 percent with stocks. When the stabilizing trade policy is implemented, the probability of having such a deficit is reduced from 35.2 percent without stocks to 26.1 percent with stocks.

The marginal gains and losses from the stabilizing trade policy are summarized in Table 9.7. Quite remarkably, despite the very strong stabilizing effects of this policy, the expected economic and financial gains and losses to the various groups and sectors are relatively small. Even more interesting is the effect of this policy on government accounts. Without internal price policies, the cost of implementing this policy is no more than $50 million per year—undoubtedly a miniscule amount compared with the size of the national income on the one hand, and the strong stabilizing effect of the policy on the other. If, in addition, the government is already committed to the maintenance of minimally adequate grain consumption by the low-income population and a minimum price for producers, the stabilizing trade policy will be very attractive for reducing the fiscal burden.

With this policy the government more than doubles the probability of running a deficit on the food foreign exchange account in excess of $500 million from 11.1 percent in free trade to 22.3 percent. Over the long run, the government will have a food import bill above $100 million more than 35 percent of the time if this policy is carried out compared with less than 20 percent of the time under free trade. Obviously, not all governments are able to commit or mobilize foreign exchange in a sufficient amount to carry out this policy. The possibility of stabilizing prices and supplies in the domestic market by implementing such a policy illustrates, however, the monetary and foreign exchange dimensions of the food security problem.

Finally, Table 9.8 summarizes the expected gains and losses from the internal price subsidy program. Although implementation of the program involves a very small net loss to the economy as a whole—and therefore possibly a price worth paying for securing a minimally adequate level of nutrition for the weaker groups in the population—the transfer of income involved is quite substantial. The essence of the program, in effect, is a redistribution of the quantity of grain available for consumption via the price system. By subsidizing the price of grain to low-income consumers, the government forces other consumers to pay a higher price. If, as assumed in the study, the demand of the other consumers is price elastic, the end result will be a

Table 9.7 Expected Annual Gains and Losses Due to Stabilizing Trade Policy

| Economy | Consumers | | Producers | Government | | Total |
| | Low income | Other | | Storage operation | Other | |
|---|---|---|---|---|---|---|
| ($ millions) | | | | | | |
| Without internal price subsidy and support program | | | | | | |
| -18 | 78 | 197 | -243 | 0 | -50 | -50 |
| With internal price subsidy and support program | | | | | | |
| -11 | -59 | 147 | -256 | 0 | 166 | 166 |

# Food Security Alternatives

transfer of foodgrain from high- and middle-income to low-income consumers.

In the closed economy with the parameters of our model, the low-income consumers gain from the subsidy program $301 million. The other 70 percent of the population suffer losses that on average total $617 million. Since the transfer of income and of grain is carried out through the price system, the big gainers from the program will be the producers, which in the closed economy gain on average $880 million. For the government this program is very expensive relative to the other options considered in our study; the government's expected cost in the closed economy is close to $600 million. Not less worrisome is the destabilizing effect of the program on the budget as reflected by the large number of times in which, over the long-run, government expenditures for the program will be above $1 billion. When the country engages in active trade and/or holds buffer stocks, the income transfer payments are much lower and the destabilizing effects of the program on the government budget are substantially reduced.

## What Can Be Expected from International Stabilization Initiatives?

Major international initiatives have been undertaken in recent years to induce massive investments in stocks sufficiently large to buffer future shortfalls in production. These initiatives

Table 9.8 Expected Annual Gains and Losses of Program to Subsidize Consumption of Low-Income Consumers

| Policy | Economy | Consumers | | Producers | Government | | |
|---|---|---|---|---|---|---|---|
| | | Low income | Other | | Storage operation | Other | Total |
| ($ million) | | | | | | | |
| No trade | -25 | 301 | -617 | 880 | 0 | -589 | -589 |
| Free trade | -9 | 244 | -170 | 244 | 0 | -327 | -327 |

have borne little success. The recent buildup of stocks must be primarily attributed to national governments' concerns over depressed grain prices and farm incomes.

In our view, the stabilization of world grain supplies and prices is neither a realistic nor a cost-effective undertaking in terms of achieving food security. The underlying causes of instability in international food markets are complex. Economists have rightly pointed out that under conditions of free trade the global supply of food and hence international food prices would be much more stable than the supply and prices in individual countries in the absence of trade (Johnson, Chapter 12). But political and short-run economic interests often lead to trade interventions that destabilize the international market. The frequently advocated buffer stocks are an expensive remedy. Moreover, the benefits from stabilization accruing to different countries differ widely and the major beneficiaries are often either unwilling or unable to bear the costs. Therefore, it is unlikely that food importing and exporting countries can look forward to anything but continuing high instability in the international food market.

Foodgrain supply and price stabilization on a worldwide scale is an expensive undertaking relative to the social gains likely to be perceived. Although the benefit from price stabilization for grain imported by developing countries whose populations live at the margin of minimum subsistence and who cannot cope with a rise in their import bill is beyond question, it is not at all clear that stabilization of food consumption by the population of the rich countries has social benefits beyond satisfying their consumers' whims and preferences. In fact, there is now a lot of discussion of the issue of whether it would be physically and socially healthier if people in the rich countries were to eat less than their accustomed diets. For the consumers of most of the world's grain, fluctuating grain prices affect primarily their level of consumption of livestock products. This causes variability in the palatability of their diet, but hardly qualifies to be considered a food security problem.

In our context, the crucial question is how much food security developing countries could gain from stabilization of international prices. Assuming that all the conflicts of interests could

*Food Security Alternatives*

be resolved and an agreement could be reached to institute large international buffer stocks, how cost effective a remedy would it be? Or would it be possible, for a fraction of the cost of what it would take to stabilize international prices, to achieve greater food security for the developing countries by some other means?

To investigate these questions, one can gain instruction from another simulation experiment on our hypothetical country, with the world price held constant at $125 per metric ton. Under free trade and without foreign exchange constraints, a stable import price, say at 20 percent above the median price, would yield a zero probability of price ever rising above this level. Whereas we have seen that with an unstable world price, the probability of the price rising above this level is about 12 percent. In the more likely event, however, that the country's foreign exchange reserves put a constraint on trade, the potential beneficial effect of a stable world price might be only partially realized. Table 9.9 shows that the probability of importing grain during times of domestic production shortfalls is about the same with or without a stable world price if the country were, for instance, unable to pay for a food grain import bill in excess of $700 million.[5] Similarly, a stable world price would not improve the country's capacity to pursue a stabilizing trade policy, when there is a financial constraint on the size of the

Table 9.9 Foreign Exchange Instability: Probability of Import Bill Exceeding $700 Million

|  | No stock | 6 mmt stock |
|---|---|---|
|  | (percent) | |
| Free Trade |  |  |
|    Unstable World Price | 8.4 | 7.7 |
|    Stable World Price | 8.0 | 7.1 |
| Stabilizing Trade |  |  |
|    Unstable World Price | 16.9 | 11.6 |
|    Stable World Price | 17.7 | 11.4 |

import bill. In contrast, a modest 6 million metric ton buffer stock does effectively reduce the probability of requiring foreign exchange in excess of $700 million dollars.

Elsewhere, reporting on simulation experiments with countries that normally import food and whose capacity to import is financially constrained, one of us (Reutlinger, 1978) also showed that food security is only marginally improved by a drastic stabilization of the world's grain supply.

## Food Security: A Financial Problem

Thus far we have seen that stabilization on food policy-related objectives can be achieved by any number of policy interventions. However, each intervention has its undesirable side effects. Buffer stocks sufficiently large to achieve satisfactory levels of stabilization would have unacceptably high costs. Target group-oriented internal stabilization policies would involve excessive destabilization of food prices in the unprotected, open market and extremely large explicit and implicit transfer payments. And trade policy-oriented solutions destabilize the foreign exchange account on food trade.

Although no single policy can be regarded, therefore, as being completely satisfactory, we believe that trade-oriented solutions may be the least objectionable among the lot. In essence, trade-oriented solutions transform the problem of instability on food policy-related objectives into a problem of instability in the foreign exchange account. We believe that realistically feasible remedies can be found for this financial instability problem, while remedies precluding stabilizing trade policies are likely to expose countries to insurmountable difficulties. We would go so far as to predict that, without adequate financial arrangements, food security—as defined for the purpose of this discussion—will remain nearly as elusive as it has been in the past, except perhaps in normally food-surplus countries.

Table 9.10 illustrates how trade-oriented policies transform the problem of an unstable food supply in a country into a financial instability problem.[6] The "moderately stabilizing" trade policy is the one described earlier in this chapter whereby trade is moderately responsive to external prices. The "com-

*Food Security Alternatives* 207

Table 9.10  Stability of Country's Foodgrain Supply and
Foreign Exchange Account

| Policy | Country's foodgrain supply within range of $\pm$ 2.5 million tons of median /a | Foreign exchange account within range of $\pm$ $300 million |
|---|---|---|
| | probability (percent) | |
| **Without buffer stock** | | |
| No trade | 28 | 100 |
| Free trade | 45 | 67 |
| Moderately stabilizing trade | 70 | 48 |
| Completely stabilizing trade | 100 | 28 |
| **With buffer stock** | | |
| No trade | 54 | 100 |
| Free trade | 65 | 75 |
| Moderately stabilizing trade | 80 | 65 |
| Completely stabilizing trade | 100 | 44 |

/a  The median is 110 million tons.

pletely stabilizing" trade policy is added to describe a scenario
whereby a deviation in domestic food production (adjusted for
stock operations, where applicable) would be offset by equivalent changes in the volume of trade.

Clearly, an active trading policy can stabilize the food supply
in an individual country to any degree desired. However, the
destabilizing effect of such trade policies on the foreign exchange
account for food trade can be very significant. For instance,
for a normally self-sufficient country with the parameters
assumed in our analysis, a policy that completely stabilizes
the food supply would result in a 72 percent chance of the
foreign exchange account being outside the range of $\pm$ $300 mil-
lion  when there are no buffer stocks and a 66 percent chance
of a similarly unstable foreign exchange account when the
country has a 6 million metric ton buffer stock.

Table 9.11 gives additional statistics to describe the destabilizing effect of stabilizing trade policies. The probability of having high import bills in some years and large export earnings in other years is large when trade becomes the major instrument of stabilization.

This is not the place to go into the whole range of possible financial arrangements that could be made to cope with financial instability on account of food-stabilizing trade policies. First, a country would wish to determine how difficult it would be to have a more-or-less stable foreign exchange account for food trade. Would there be any correlation between foreign exchange earnings and a food import bill consistent with food security? Similarly, there may not be a serious problem if the value of food trade is a small proportion of total foreign trade (see Valdés and Konandreas, Chapter 2, Table 2.3).

Remedies may range from bilateral trade agreements to international insurance schemes. The country may enter into agreements to take deliveries in accordance with fluctuating requirements, but spread payments at more-or-less equal increments over the years. Another approach would be for the country to

Table 9.11  Stability of Foreign Exchange Account from Food Trade with Alternative Policies

| Foreign Exchange ($ million) | Free trade | | "Moderately" Stabilizing trade | | "Completely" Stabilizing trade | |
|---|---|---|---|---|---|---|
| | N.S. | W.S.[1] | N.S. | W.S. | N.S. | W.S. |
| | Probability (%) | | | | | |
| <  -900 | 6 | 6 | 13 | 9 | 20 | 13 |
| -900 to -100 | 14 | 8 | 23 | 17 | 26 | 33 |
| -100 to  100 | 57 | 67 | 32 | 48 | 9 | 9 |
| 100 to  900 | 17 | 15 | 25 | 21 | 34 | 38 |
| >  900 | 6 | 4 | 7 | 5 | 11 | 7 |
| Expected import bills in excess of $100 million: $million: | 136 | 112 | 276 | 195 | 401 | 316 |
| Expected export earnings in excess of $100 million: $million: | 157 | 115 | 206 | 143 | 286 | 214 |

1/  N.S.  =  no stocks

W.S.  =  with 6 million ton buffer stock.

*Food Security Alternatives* 209

provide for greater liquidity in its investment portfolio. Any financial arrangements of this kind are likely to involve a real cost to the economy. If, for instance, one billion dollars would have to be put into liquid assets having a return that is 3 percent less than what the same investment could earn in less liquid assets, the annual cost would be $30 million. Beyond a small level of physical buffer stocks, such an arrangement is still likely to cost less and give greater food security than an equivalent expenditure in additional buffer stocks.

The most satisfactory remedy, in our view, is an international food-import-bill insurance scheme by and/or in behalf of the developing countries that could take advantage of risk pooling and would be tied in with development assistance.

## Conclusions

A basic premise underlying the work presented in this chapter has been that food security has many dimensions and that countries have many policy options by which to address all or some of the undesirable consequences of unstable food production within and outside their boundaries. Our main purpose has been to define in operational terms various aspects of food security and to illustrate that proposed remedies may address effectively some food security–related concerns, but do little or even have negative implications for other concerns. This suggests that there are no simple solutions applying uniformly to all countries. In some countries, the prevention of near-famine conditions for some segments of the population is the predominating objective. In other countries, instability in food prices, in the government's budget, or in the balance of payments is the main problem. Moreover, in the final analysis, difficult political choices have to be made, when resources are inadequate to remedy effectively all the ills associated with food production instability.

A first requirement for dealing wisely with food security issues is, therefore, to estimate quantitatively various aspects of the problem and the implications flowing from various remedies. It has been our major purpose to show that a stochastic simulation model is a powerful method for transforming reasonably available information about instability in food production in a country and in world food prices into otherwise unavailable quantitative estimates of the instability of variables associated with food security and the expected long-run benefits and costs of remedial policies.

The numerical estimates presented in this chapter are, of course, applicable only within the constraints of the particularly specified model and parameters. In general, however, the estimates are sufficiently robust to illustrate orders of magnitude and particularly the direction of the effects flowing from adopting a wide range of policy options.

Thus, we could cautiously conclude that most developing countries could achieve a modest reduction in the instability of their domestic food prices by operating a small buffer stock and by permitting nearly free trade. Such policies would benefit nearly all segments of their population. The extent to which these remedies can be implemented may be constrained by the government's capacity to cope with budgetary and balance-of-payment constraints. Stock operations make unstable demands on the government's budget and trade makes unstable demands on foreign exchange.

In addition, governments are confronted with the reality that, even with modest stabilization of the aggregate food supply, uneven income and wealth distribution means that there may be large segments of the population unable to maintain their normal minimally adequate levels of food consumption when food prices rise in the market. Only financial assistance in the form of subsidized food rations can achieve this kind of food security. To the extent that large transfer payments are not feasible, the only other option for the country is to resort to a stabilizing trade policy, i.e., the importation of food in sufficient quantities to maintain the aggregate food supply at a sufficiently high level.

Countries would then need to finance occasionally an import bill exceeding manyfold its normal size. Just like the reallocation of existing food supplies within a country, the reallocation of the world food supply between countries requires appropriate financial arrangements. Fortunately, the analogy is far from complete. Whereas reallocation within a country could

# Food Security Alternatives

involve drastic increases in prices and reductions in the amount of food available to the unprotected consumers, occasional, even manifold, increases in the imports of individual low-income countries would only marginally decrease the amount of foodgrains available to the rest of the world. Moreover, the financial arrangements required for reallocating food between countries by way of international grants, loans, or self-financed insurance schemes are much less demanding than the financial demands on poor and middle-income countries of schemes designed to assist their lowest income population to maintain adequate levels of consumption in times of general scarcity and high food prices.

It has long been recognized that random fluctuations in food production require crop insurance schemes to protect farm incomes. Concern for food security focused on the individual or the country as a consumer should make us think about food bill insurance schemes to protect the level of food consumption of those who would be otherwise subjected to excessive risks.

## Notes

Research on which this paper is based is part of a study undertaken by the World Bank (RPO 671-24) on various aspects of food stabilization policies in developing countries. Previous papers include: S. Reutlinger, D. Eaton and D. Bigman (1976); S. Reutlinger (1978); D. Bigman and S. Reutlinger (1979a); and D. Bigman and S. Reutlinger (1979b).

The authors wish to express their gratitude to David Eaton, Keith Knapp, and Yony Levy, who participated in various stages of this study. The views expressed in this paper are those of the authors and are not to be attributed to the organizations with which they are affiliated.

1. The former policy is essentially the one implemented in Indonesia whereas the latter is closely related to the trade activities of the Indian government.

2. The extent to which trade acts to stabilize the country's supply depends, of course, on the relative stability of domestic production and foreign supply. For most if not all developing countries, trade is likely to have a strong stabilizing effect (Bigman and Reutlinger, 1979b).

3. Experiments with higher stock levels show rapidly diminishing incremental stabilization effects and increasing costs.

212                                    Shlomo Reutlinger and David Bigman

4. Seventy million dollars represents approximately one half of one percent of the value of annual grain consumption in the hypothetical country.

5. Price stabilization is about as likely to increase as it is to decrease the price, hence the effect on the probability of a large import bill is small.

6. The calculations in Table 9.10 assume that no special subsidy program to the low-income population is in effect. For the case of free trade, a subsidy program would have the effect of increasing the stability of the country's foodgrain supply while decreasing the stability of the foreign exchange account.

## References

Bigman, D., and S. Reutlinger. "National and International Policies Toward Food Security and Price Stabilization." *American Economic Review* (May 1979a).

___. "Food Price and Supply Stabilization: National Buffer Stocks and Trade Policies." *American Journal of Agricultural Economics* 61 (November 1979b):657–667.

Reutlinger, S. "Food Insecurity: Magnitude and Remedies." *World Development* 6 (1978):797–811.

Reutlinger, S., D. Eaton, and D. Bigman. "Should Developing Countries Carry Grain Reserves?" *Analysis of Grain Reserves: A Proceeding.* Economic Research Service, U.S. Department of Agriculture, Report No. 634, August 1976.

10

# The International Wheat Agreement and LDC Food Security

*Daniel Morrow*

The FAO International Undertaking on World Food Security, endorsed by the World Food Conference of 1974, emphasized the need for international coordination of nationally held food-grain reserve stocks as a major element of world food security. Since 1975, a new International Wheat Agreement (IWA) has been regarded as the vehicle to achieve a meaningful reserve stock system. But after several years of preliminary discussions and a year-long UNCTAD negotiating conference, agreement could not be reached on a new IWA with reserve stock provisions. The UNCTAD Conference on the IWA adjourned in February 1979 with no immediate prospects for reconvening. This chapter analyzes principal issues on which agreement could not be reached and considers briefly the implications of the collapse of the IWA negotiations for the food security of developing countries.

## Recent Negotiations on a New International Wheat Agreement[1]

Following preparatory work within the International Wheat Council, an UNCTAD Conference held its first session in February and March 1978 and worked on an international agreement with three parts: the Wheat Trade Convention, the Coarse Grains Trade Convention, and the Food Aid Convention. The Wheat Trade Convention (WTC) included the system of internationally coordinated, nationally held wheat stocks, and subsequent discussion is limited to the issues of the WTC. The

*213*

Conference held a second session in November 1978 and a third session in January and February 1979. By the end of the last session, the basic structure of the new WTC had been fairly well established. There would be three "rising action points" and three "falling action points" on a price indicator scale. The price indicator would be an average of current export prices for several major wheats of specified quality and location. In both rising and falling price situations, the action points would trigger consultations as follows:

First action point: review of the market situation before reserve stock action is taken.

Second action point: agreement on a program of obligatory accumulation or release of WTC reserve stocks; if no agreement were reached within a specified period, reserve action would be taken automatically under a program stipulated in advance.

Third action point: agreement on a joint program of measures (e.g., production adjustments) to be adopted to prevent further outward price movement.

Thus, reserve stock accumulation and release at specific levels of the price indicator (i.e., the second action point) would be the primary obligation of the agreement and the primary mechanism for price stabilization. No obligatory actions were specified at the first and third action points.

However, when the Conference adjourned there were substantially different views on the price levels for reserve stock action. Developing importers generally supported accumulation and release prices of $130 and $160 per metric ton respectively, and major exporters generally supported $140 and $210. Furthermore, the size of reserve stock obligations was not resolved; the total of individual country commitments was reported to be 18 to 19 million metric tons. The major exporters and developing importers considered 25 to 30 million metric tons as the minimum necessary to meet the objectives of the Convention, while the EEC and others apparently considered the smaller figure acceptable.[2]

## Analysis of WTC Price Levels and
## Reserve Stock Size

The proposed WTC reserve stock system is intended to reduce price variability in the international market. This section considers how the level of the accumulation and release prices and the size of the reserve stock obligations affect the realization of that objective. First, the nature of the reserve stock mechanism is examined in order to clarify the logic and the likely qualitative impact of the price-triggered system of nationally held reserve stocks. Then data on world wheat prices and stocks are analyzed in order to evaluate the alternative positions taken at the Conference. As a supplement to this analysis, the results of a detailed simulation model by A. Sarris (1976) are considered.[3]

### Nature of the Reserve Stock Mechanism

The WTC reserve stock is only that stock that is held according to the rules for accumulation and release set out in the Convention. The draft text specified that the reserve stock must be in excess of "minimum working stocks." Thus, following any period of accumulation, ending stocks of wheat for a participating country would have to be at least its declared minimum working stock plus its accumulated WTC reserve stock. A country could hold other stocks not subject to the WTC price band rules. The reserve stock obligation of each member country is a maximum obligation, i.e., the upper limit on the reserve stock that the member is required to accumulate when the WTC price indicator reaches the second falling action point. Thus, the sum of individual reserve stock obligations is the capacity of the system, not the level of WTC reserve stocks held at any given time. The actual size of WTC reserve stocks at any time depends on past market price movements relative to the specified accumulation and release prices. Given this definition of the WTC reserve stock, the relevant question is: What is the maximum size of stocks that should be subject to the accumulation and release rules of the Convention?

In contrast, the term "reserve stock" is often used to refer to all ending stocks in excess of working stocks, and emphasis is then placed on the minimum desired level of stocks. For example, the FAO has estimated the "minimum safe level" of stocks to maintain world food security. For wheat, the "total safe level" is 25 to 26 percent of annual world utilization (104 to 108 million metric tons based on 1978/79), including 17 percent (71 million metric tons) for "working stocks," and an 8 to 9 percent (33 to 37 million metric tons) "reserve element" (FAO, 1974). These estimates appear to be based on two observations about the historical behavior of the world wheat economy. In recent decades, the lowest observed level of ending stocks as a percent of utilization was 16.9 percent in 1972/73 (USDA, 1979). This could be regarded as the base level of working stocks. The largest observed shortfall from a linear trend of world production (for 1960/61 to 1978/79) was 8.3 percent (in 1963/64). Thus, "reserve stocks" at or above this level are very unlikely to be depleted by a single year's shortfall.

The FAO is correct to emphasize the relationship between total stocks and the degree of price stability. But this definition of reserve stock is not appropriate for the WTC because it is not desirable that all world stocks in excess of minimum working stocks should be subject to accumulation and release based on international price band rules. Some countries may wish to hold stocks that are accumulated and released in response primarily to fluctuations in national production, not the price in international markets. For example, India now holds a large foodgrain stock primarily to protect against its own crop failures. It would not be rational to expect India to hold all of its stocks until the international market price (which is not highly correlated with Indian production) reaches a high level. Also, it is reasonable for exporters to hold commercial stocks that are available to respond to marginal shifts in domestic production or foreign import demand. If all stocks in excess of minimum working stocks were subject to WTC rules, the ending stock levels could not adjust marginally in response to price movements within that price band.

The problem in designing the WTC reserve stock system is to effect an increase in total stockholding even though the WTC

*The International Wheat Agreement* 217

does not—and should not—control all stock decisions. The purpose must be to shift the pattern of stockholding that would otherwise occur so that the sum of the WTC and other stocks will be larger than otherwise and thus provide greater international price stability.[4]

The qualitative shifts among the key variables of the world wheat economy which the WTC should attempt to bring about are illustrated in Figures 10.1–10.4. The relationships shown with solid lines are a model of the simultaneous determination of price and ending stocks in the world market in the absence of a WTC.[5] In Figure 10.1, the quantity supplied $S_O$ includes the new harvest plus beginning stocks. At the equilibrium price $P_O$ in that year, this quantity is divided between demand for current consumption and demand for ending stocks. The demand for ending stocks could include both stocks held in the expectation of profitable resale and stocks held as the result of government price-support programs. When quantity supplied is at $S_M$, the demand for ending stocks is equal to minimum working stocks ($MWS$) and price equals $P_M$. As $S$ increases above $S_M$, ending stocks also increase and price falls. This relationship between total supply (production plus beginning stocks) and ending stocks is illustrated in Figure 10.2 and the corresponding relationship between ending stocks and price in Figure 10.3. Figure 10.4 illustrates the probability distribution of price that results from interaction between weather-induced production fluctuations and this model of price determination.

The purpose of the WTC is to reduce the variability of price, as represented by the dashed line in Figure 10.4. The dashed lines in Figures 10.1–10.3 show the qualitative shifts in the other relationship that would be necessary to bring about this reduction in price variability. For all but low levels of total supply, ending stocks would be larger. Thus, there would be a higher probability that ending stocks would be above "minimum safe levels" and a lower probability that ending stocks would be drawn down to minimum working stock levels. In periods of very large supply, the price would be higher than otherwise, which would benefit producers and exporters. Because these larger stocks are available to offset production shortfalls, the probability of very small supplies and high prices

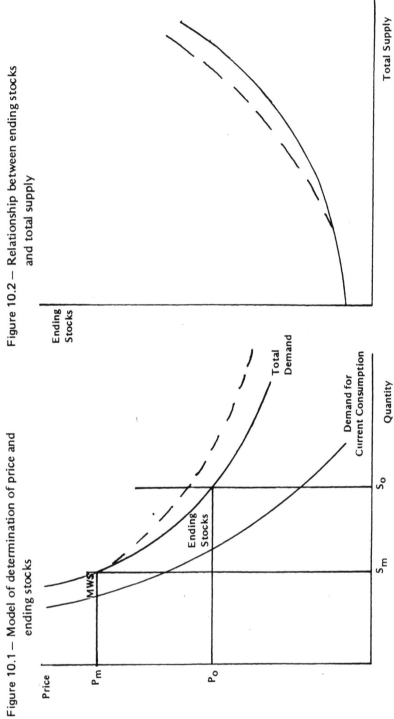

Figure 10.1 – Model of determination of price and ending stocks

Figure 10.2 – Relationship between ending stocks and total supply

Figure 10.3 — Relationship between price and ending stocks

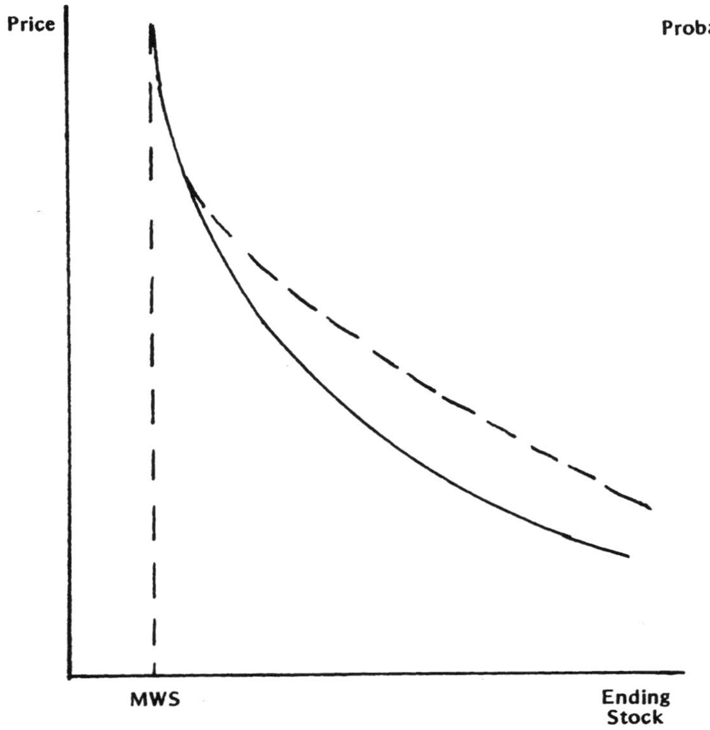

Figure 10.4 — Probability distribution of price

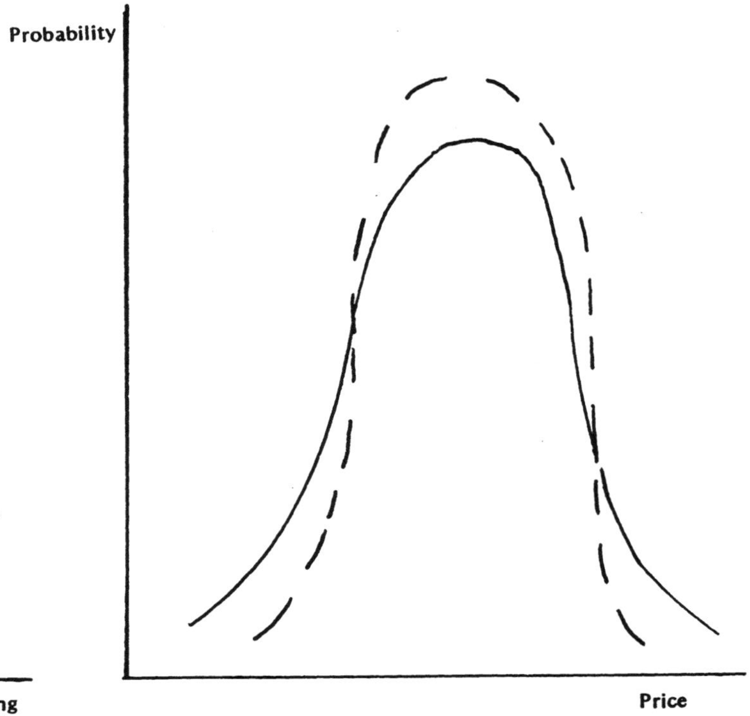

is reduced, which would benefit consumers and importers.

The proposed WTC reserve stock system is a necessarily crude instrument for bringing about these desired shifts. For the reasons already mentioned, the WTC could not feasibly attempt to control all stocks in the world. The marginal adjustments that should be made in the total stock level and the distribution of that total among countries in response to the distribution of production fluctuations among countries are far too complex and competitive to subject to rules imposed either by the text of a Convention or by a committee meeting at the IWC in London. Instead, the WTC should seek to supplement the stockholding activities that are likely to be undertaken independently of itself.

The key question is how to ensure that WTC reserve stocks bring about a net increase in world ending stocks. As D. Gale Johnson (1978, p. 297) notes:

> Most discussions of international grain reserve schemes ignore the extent to which the reserve so held or controlled simply substitute for reserves that would otherwise have been held. Thus, if an agreement were reached that a group of countries would agree to create a reserve of a given size, say 50 million tons, the increase in world grain reserves would only be a fraction of this. American and Canadian experience indicates that governmentally-held reserves replace most privately-held stocks. Stocks held pursuant to an international agreement would substitute quite directly for stocks held by at least some governments. Consequently, the size of reserves that resulted from an international agreement might add relatively little to world grain stocks until the amount of such reserves became very large.[6]

In order to ensure that the WTC reserve stock system brings about a net addition to world ending stocks, the parameters of the system must meet two criteria. First, the range between accumulation and release prices must be rather wide, and the accumulation price must not be too far below the mean price (i.e., the longer run average price). Second, the WTC reserve stock obligation must be sufficiently large to compensate for the fact that not all WTC reserve stocks will actually be additional to what would otherwise be held. In a general sense, these two criteria are based on the principle that the management

*The International Wheat Agreement* 221

rules for the WTC reserve stock must be different from the rules for managing stocks that countries are likely to pursue independently. If they are not different, then countries can participate in the WTC system without behaving differently than they otherwise would, and the world wheat economy, including its price variability, would not behave differently than otherwise. The more specific rationale for these two criteria follows.

By establishing a wide price range, the WTC reserve stocks will clearly be unavailable for meeting contingencies other than a very high world price. An exporter could not expect to use the WTC reserve as part of its commercial stock to maintain export volumes in years of national production shortfalls or to increase export volumes in years of somewhat higher foreign import demand. An exporter who desires stocks for these commercial purposes would have to rely primarily on stocks other than his WTC reserve stock. Similarly, an importer who desires to hold stocks to offset national production shortfalls could not rely primarily on his WTC reserve. More generally, if any market participant wished to hold stocks because it appeared profitable to do so—i.e., because the expected future price exceeds the current price by more than carrying costs—he could not use his WTC reserve stocks for this purpose. The WTC reserve stock must be subject to rules that are not expected to be financially profitable, since it is reasonable to believe that market participants will take advantage of expected profit opportunities in any case.[7] The wide price band would leave room for such profit-seeking stockholding. Furthermore, the WTC reserve stock should be accumulated before prices fall to a level at which many market participants and countries will be holding stocks anyway either as a result of domestic price support programs or because it seems profitable to do so. Thus, the accumulation price should not be too far below the mean price.

By establishing a WTC reserve stock obligation larger than the net addition to stockholding that is actually desired, the system will compensate for the fact that, even with a wide price range centered above the mean, the WTC reserve stocks will not be fully additional to what would otherwise be held. Some countries already have substantial stocks, as shown below, and would probably be willing to subject some of these existing

222  *Daniel Morrow*

stocks to WTC rules. Furthermore, it must be expected that some part of WTC reserve stock obligations will not be fulfilled at all. Some members would be granted temporary "relief of obligations" due to lack of adequate storage facilities or special circumstances in their national market, and others may be able to avoid their full WTC obligation without detection since stock data are so inadequate for some countries.[8]

Before turning to the specific proposals on price levels and reserve stock size, it is useful to note several other key relationships between the price levels for accumulation and release, the size of the WTC reserve stocks, and other variables of the system.[9] First, for a given release price, the average size of the WTC reserve stocks (i.e., the average which would be expected over many years of operation of the system) increases as the accumulation price increases. If the accumulation price is set low (relative to the mean price), it is unlikely that a large reserve stock will be accumulated. Similarly, for a given accumulation price, the average size increases as the release price increases. Also, the probability that the reserve stock will be fully depleted decreases as the release price increases. If the depletion of the reserve stock has a destabilizing psychological impact on the market, it may be risky to set the release price (or accumulation price) too low. These relationships strengthen the argument that the price band should be centered above the mean price.[10] Finally, the expected net cost of the reserve stocks (i.e., expected financial loss) increases as the release price increases because the average time the stocks are held increases. Thus, the probability of reserve stock depletion can only be reduced at greater financial cost.

## Prices and Reserve Stock Size

With this conceptual framework in mind, consider the proposals for accumulation and release prices and for the WTC reserve stock size. In order to estimate the consequences of particular price levels and reserve stock capacity, a simulation model of the world wheat economy is most useful. But before examining the results of one such model, considerable insight can be gained from the historical data on wheat price,

# The International Wheat Agreement 223

ending stocks, and production fluctuations.

*Price levels.* The annual averages for the WTC price indicator from 1960 to 1978 in both nominal and real terms are displayed in Figure 10.5.[11] In 1978 dollars, the average price during this period was $181 per metric ton, but there appears to be a slight downward trend. It is reasonable, therefore, to assume a long-run average price in 1978 dollars of $150 to $180. This is consistent with the projection of mean price by others.[12]

In considering the fluctuations of past prices, it is necessary to examine weekly or monthly, not annual, averages since the WTC price indicator would be calculated weekly or daily and action would be triggered on this basis. In nominal dollars, the price indicator rose from a monthly average of about $60 in early 1972 to a peak of $226 in February 1974 and then fell to $100 in August 1977. In 1978 dollars, the prices were $137 in early 1972, $324 in February 1974, and $108 in August 1977. Thus, from its stable level in 1972, the price indicator increased about 270 percent in nominal terms and 136 percent in real terms to its 1974 peak.

At the time of the negotiating conference in late 1978 and early 1979, the WTC price indicator stood at about $145. Based on the relationship between spot and futures prices in the U.S. market at that time, it appeared as if the price indicator would fall to about $135 in July 1979 as the Northern Hemisphere harvest began and would rise thereafter reflecting normal carrying charges.

Based on these data, the following observations can be made regarding the proposals for accumulation and release prices:

1. The proposal for accumulation and release prices of $140 and $210 respectively (in nominal terms) would have been centered at or somewhat above the apparent long-run average price. The 50 percent range (in nominal terms) would have established a much narrower range of fluctuations than observed during the early 1970s but may have been wide enough to ensure that the WTC reserve stocks were at least partly additional to stocks that would otherwise have been held. If inflation eroded the real value of the release price relative to the accumulation price, as appears likely, the center of the band and

the range would be lower in real terms.

2. In contrast, the proposal for a 23 percent range from $130 to $160 would have placed the release price near, if not below, the long-run average price. Many countries, especially the major exporters, could probably have fulfilled their WTC reserve stock obligations, if any accumulation were ever required, with stocks that would have been held in any case.

3. Even if the accumulation price were $140, it would have been reasonable to expect only modest reserve stock accumulation during the first year of the Convention.[13] Full accumulation of the reserve stock would have required harvests well above average in 1979/80 and probably 1980/81. If there were

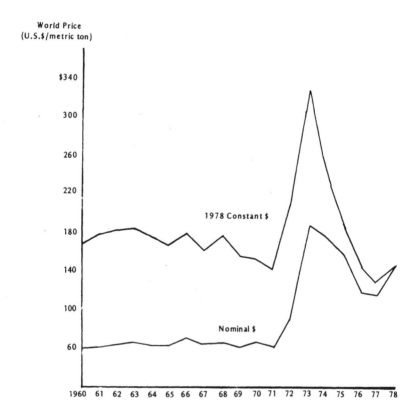

Figure 10.5  WTC Price Indicator (annual average)

*The International Wheat Agreement* 225

continuing inflation in those years (without corresponding adjustment of the accumulation price) and average harvests, there might have been little or no accumulation during the life of the agreement. The probability of significant accumulation would have been even lower if the accumulation price had been $130. As it turns out, due largely to poor crop conditions in the Soviet Union during May 1979, the WTC price indicator in early July was over $180 so that no accumulation would have taken place during the first year. According to these observations, it seems that the proposal for a price band of $140 to $210 would be more likely to achieve the objective of reduced price variability than a lower or narrower price band.

*Size of WTC reserve stock obligations.* There is no simple criterion for determining the desirable maximum size for the WTC reserve stock, but as a first approach it is reasonable to argue that the maximum WTC reserve stock should be able to offset a very large shortfall in world wheat production.[14,15] Then, in a year of large supplies and low prices, total ending stocks in excess of minimum working stocks would be larger than the WTC reserve stock itself to the extent that the WTC reserve stock was additional to what would otherwise be held. Thus, if the WTC reserve stock alone were large relative to possible single-year production shortfalls, the total ending stocks would offer considerable protection against two consecutively poor harvests. Or, in a year of reduced supplies in which prices began to approach the WTC release price and other stocks were largely depleted, the WTC reserve stock alone would offer considerable protection against a single very bad harvest. On this simple basis, which does not take into account the cost-effectiveness of the reserve stock, the maximum WTC reserve stock should be equal to the "minimum safe level" estimated by the FAO. As noted above, this level is 33 to 37 million metric tons for 1978/79.

As a second approach, the WTC reserve stocks for those countries who historically carry stocks in excess of minimum working stocks should be a significant fraction of the stocks that they would otherwise carry in a low price situation. If this is not the case, the WTC reserve stocks are unlikely to bring about a net increase in their total ending stocks. Table 10.1 shows the ending stocks in excess of estimated minimum working stocks for major countries and the world as a whole as estimated by the author based on U.S. Department of Agriculture stock data.[16] There is no empirical basis for estimating the extent to which these countries would place part of these stocks under the control of the WTC price band rules rather than build additional stocks for that purpose. But it is plausible that until WTC reserve stocks reached perhaps one third of existing stocks, no net increase in stock holding would occur.[17] Assuming accumulation would occur in 1978/79, this would suggest that about 20 million metric tons of the world's 63 million metric tons of ending stocks in excess of minimum working stocks would have to be placed in the WTC reserve stock before any net increase in ending stocks was achieved among those now holding stocks.[18] And, if it is intended that major countries such as the EEC, Japan, and Brazil that have not held substantial stocks should begin to do so, then the maximum WTC obligation should be correspondingly larger than 20 million metric tons.

*Results of the Sarris simulation model.* The most detailed attempt to simulate the impact of a reserve stock system on the world wheat economy is the model developed by Alexander Sarris (1976). The model disaggregates the world wheat economy into 19 regions and specifies excess demand and supply functions for each region, taking into account existing trade restrictions and incorporating the fact that domestic production fluctuations in many countries are only partially transmitted to the world market. The model assumes that an international Buffer Stock Agency (BSA) buys and sells wheat at specified accumulation and release prices up to a specified maximum buffer stock capacity. However, the model does not include any other stockholding activity by market participants.

Sarris concludes that the buffer stock capacity for wheat should be 10 to 15 million metric tons and that the accumulation and release prices should be about $108.9 and $180 per metric ton (basis Hard Red Winter Ordinary, f.o.b., U.S. Gulf) in 1974 dollars. The $108.9-$180 price band and 15 million metric ton capacity results in a 30 to 35 percent reduction in

Table 10.1     Ending Stocks of Wheat in Excess of Minimum Working Stocks

| Year | U.S. | Canada | Australia | Argentina | Four major Exporters[a] | EEC | India | Soviet Union | Rest of world[b] | World | World excluding Soviet Union |
|------|------|--------|-----------|-----------|------------------------|-----|-------|--------------|------------------|-------|------------------------------|
| 1960/61 | 32.38 | 10.23 | 0.57 | 0.40 | 43.58 | 3.40 | 1.66 | 3.00 | 0.51 | 52.15 | 49.15 |
| 1961/62 | 29.75 | 4.21 | 0.37 | 0.00 | 34.33 | 3.13 | 1.50 | 0.00 | 0.72 | 39.68 | 39.68 |
| 1962/63 | 26.10 | 6.72 | 0.51 | 0.14 | 33.47 | 4.92 | 2.23 | 1.00 | 1.65 | 43.27 | 42.27 |
| 1963/64 | 17.89 | 5.85 | 0.42 | 1.84 | 26.01 | 2.81 | 1.16 | 4.00 | 2.28 | 36.26 | 32.26 |
| 1964/65 | 18.13 | 7.20 | 0.52 | 2.96 | 28.81 | 2.04 | 0.39 | 14.00 | 1.04 | 46.28 | 32.28 |
| 1965/66 | 10.88 | 4.55 | 0.29 | 0.00 | 15.72 | 3.32 | 1.62 | 5.00 | 1.83 | 27.49 | 22.49 |
| 1966/67 | 6.66 | 8.56 | 2.02 | 0.00 | 17.24 | 1.73 | 0.64 | 32.00 | 1.78 | 53.39 | 21.39 |
| 1967/68 | 9.60 | 11.19 | 1.23 | 0.62 | 22.64 | 1.72 | 0.56 | 31.00 | 2.66 | 58.58 | 27.58 |
| 1968/69 | 16.84 | 15.94 | 7.07 | 0.46 | 40.31 | 3.68 | 2.07 | 33.00 | 2.60 | 81.66 | 48.66 |
| 1969/70 | 18.74 | 20.10 | 7.01 | 0.38 | 46.22 | 0.06 | 2.08 | 14.00 | 1.30 | 63.66 | 49.66 |
| 1970/71 | 14.07 | 12.49 | 3.12 | 0.27 | 29.95 | 0.33 | 2.98 | 6.00 | 0.07 | 39.33 | 33.33 |
| 1971/72 | 18.24 | 8.27 | 1.02 | 0.00 | 27.53 | 1.72 | 4.88 | 9.00 | 2.26 | 45.39 | 36.39 |
| 1972/73 | 7.40 | 2.20 | 0.00 | 0.00 | 9.60 | 0.41 | 2.78 | 11.00 | 2.72 | 26.51 | 15.51 |
| 1973/74 | 0.12 | 2.21 | 1.39 | 0.61 | 4.33 | 1.75 | 0.46 | 24.00 | 2.74 | 33.28 | 9.28 |
| 1974/75 | 2.41 | 0.03 | 1.18 | 0.29 | 3.91 | 4.06 | 0.05 | 13.00 | 4.53 | 25.55 | 12.55 |
| 1975/76 | 8.36 | 0.08 | 2.15 | 0.32 | 10.91 | 1.73 | 3.93 | 2.00 | 5.21 | 23.78 | 21.78 |
| 1976/77 | 20.21 | 5.02 | 1.46 | 0.97 | 27.66 | 1.11 | 9.30 | 10.00 | 10.11 | 58.18 | 48.18 |
| 1977/78 | 21.63 | 3.68 | 0.14 | 0.07 | 25.50 | 0.02 | 7.16 | 1.00 | 6.90 | 40.59 | 39.59 |
| 1978/79 | 14.49 | 6.44 | 3.82 | 0.66 | 25.41 | 2.57 | 4.52 | 19.00 | 11.40 | 62.90 | 43.90 |

a/ Includes U.S., Canada, Australia, and Argentina.

b/ World minus U.S., Canada, Australia, Argentina, Soviet Union, EEC and India.

price variability and an expected net profit close to zero (not greater than -$200 million). Because the reduction in price variability decreases sharply and expected costs increase sharply for each additional ton of capacity beyond 15 million metric tons, this appears to be the upper limit for a cost-effective buffer stock operation. Sarris notes that, as the price band is narrowed, the conflicts of interest among countries increase (i.e., expected gains for importers and losses for exporters both increase). Also, as the price band is narrowed, the average size of the buffer stock decreases and the probability of depletion increases.

Sarris's preferred price band is wider (65 percent) than those proposed for the WTC. If the long-run average price in terms of the price indicator in 1978 dollars is $165, then his preferred band is equivalent to $128 to $212.[19] Because his preferred price band is centered very close to, rather than above, the long-run average price, the average stock size is only a fraction of the capacity: in the third year of operation, the average size is 4.5 million metric tons, rising slowly thereafter.[20] In that year, the standard deviation of stock size is 4.9 million metric tons, indicating a significant probability of depletion. In order to increase the average stock size and reduce the probability of depletion, the accumulation price should be raised. In that case, the Sarris results would tend to support the WTC proposal for a price band of $140 to $210.

Sarris's preferred buffer stock capacity (10 to 15 million metric tons) is smaller than a reasonably cost-effective WTC reserve stock maximum for three reasons. First, Sarris's model assumes that the buffer stock is entirely additional to what would otherwise be held. If this is not the case, the capacity would have to be substantially increased.[21] Second, his buffer stock is internationally held and must compensate only for those fluctuations in supply and demand that reach the international market.[22] But the WTC would be nationally held and therefore must compensate also for some fluctuations in domestic production among major importers that would not have caused equivalent shifts in effective demand in the international market. Third, Sarris's model assumes that buffer stock depletion has no special impact on the international price, i.e., it

# The International Wheat Agreement

does not assume that depletion might trigger panic buying and price increases greater than indicated by the model's excess demand and supply functions. However, if it is believed that there is a high penalty associated with reserve stock depletion due to panic buying and very sharp price increases, then a larger reserve stock is warranted.[23] For these reasons, the total WTC reserve stock obligation for the price band similar to that proposed by Sarris should probably be much larger than the 10 to 15 million metric ton buffer stock capacity advocated by Sarris.

## Problems in Reaching Agreement

Even if countries were able to agree on the price levels and reserve stock size that were most appropriate for reducing world price variability, the problem of how to share the costs of the reserve stock would be extremely difficult to solve for two reasons. First, there is considerable uncertainty about the distribution of benefits from greater international price stability.[24] Sarris's model indicates that, in terms of expected social surplus and/or expected trade costs or revenues, exporting countries would lose and importing countries would gain from greater price stability. But importing countries might believe that the major exporters will need to undertake stockholding anyway as a result of their domestic price support programs and that the WTC would simply shift part of the exporter's burden onto importers. Some may argue that exporters also benefit because world price stability encourages importers to rely on the world market and thus stability is conducive to the long-term growth in import demand. Finally, it may be that many countries are unconcerned about the degree of world price stability because they can easily absorb the impact of world price changes in their foreign exchange balances and thus insulate their consumers and producers from world price fluctuations. For all of these reasons, the distribution of benefits from greater world price stability is uncertain, and countries are probably not sure how much they should be willing to pay to achieve greater stability. Second, even if a country believes that it would benefit from greater stability, it would like to minimize its own contribution to the reserve stock system and rely on stockholding efforts by others. The price stability produced by a reserve stock system is like a public good: it cannot practically be withheld from a country that has not contributed to it. Thus, each country would prefer to remain a "free rider," hoping to benefit from the efforts by others without bearing much of the costs itself.

### Consequences for LDC Food Security

The new WTC and its reserve stock system was regarded by many as critical to the food security of developing countries. Assuming that almost all of the WTC reserve stock would be held or financed by developed countries, it is almost certainly true that the developing countries could have benefited from the proposed WTC. But the WTC itself would have made only a modest contribution to food security of developing countries as a whole, and the collapse of the negotiations does not mean that substantial contributions to the food security of poorer countries cannot be achieved by other means.

The contribution of the proposed WTC to LDC food security would have been modest for two reasons. First, even if the mechanisms envisioned for the WTC functioned well, the world wheat price would still fluctuate rather widely compared to the very stable prices before 1972. The reduction in price variability attributable to the WTC would not be very large. Second, the major source of instability of food consumption in many developing countries is their own production fluctuations, not the world wheat price. Food security for these countries—measured as it should be in terms of stability of consumption—is not substantially increased by stabilizing the world price of wheat.

### Reduction in World Wheat Price Variability

A reserve stock system with a wide price band and limited capacity necessarily has limited impact on world price variability. This is illustrated by the results of Sarris's model.[25] Under his preferred policy, Sarris found that price variability was reduced about 35 percent: the standard deviation of the annual average price decreased from about $60 per metric ton without the buffer stock system to about $40 per metric ton. Although

# The International Wheat Agreement

this is a substantial reduction, the degree of variability is much greater than observed before 1972.[26]

In addition to the inherent limitations of the reserve stock itself, the WTC would not have imposed any significant new disciplines on three potential sources of world market instability. The Soviet Union, which produces and consumes about one fourth of the world's wheat and which has accounted for a substantial part of the variability of world trade, could continue to impose highly variable, unanticipated demands on wheat supplies in the rest of the world. Any WTC reserve stock that the Soviets might have accepted would have been small relative to their production fluctuations. No other features of the WTC would have required the Soviet Union to move toward stock or trade policies that would have stabilized their import demand and helped other countries to efficiently anticipate that import demand. Second, the WTC would not have imposed any explicit disciplines on the use of production controls by major exporters. Vigorous production cutbacks between 1969 and 1972 contributed significantly to the reduction in world stocks that led to the high, unstable prices of the early 1970s.[27] Although the new WTC would have required the major exporters to consult with other member countries about such policies, it would not have imposed any limits on them. Third, the new WTC would not have limited the degree to which countries can insulate their own consumers from world scarcity and high prices. Because of such insulation, the world market is much more inelastic and the world price is much more variable than would otherwise be the case.[28] So that the burden of world production shortfalls does not fall disproportionately on a few countries, especially on a few poor countries that cannot afford to compete in the world market, it is imperative that countries share responsibility for consumption restraint (especially of wheat for livestock feed) more equitably than in the past. The proposed WTC would have required consultations only on policies affecting consumption.

Despite these inherent limitations and weaknesses, the new WTC would have been a step forward toward greater international cooperation. It would have had a modest, but positive, impact on world price stability.

## LDC Food Security and World Price Stability

However, world price stability would not solve the problem of food security for developing countries. In their chapter in this volume, Reutlinger and Bigman conclude that for the developing countries as an aggregate, "food security is only marginally improved by a drastic stabilization of the world's grain supply." In an earlier work, Reutlinger (1977) also demonstrates that the major source of food insecurity for developing countries as a whole is domestic production variability and the consequent import volume instability, not world price instability. For some individual developing countries, however, world price stability is very important. Valdés and Konandreas, in this volume, consider the sources of variability in the food import bill for a large set of developing countries during 1961–1976. For most developing countries their results are consistent with Reutlinger's analysis: The variability of food import cost has been caused primarily by variability of import volumes due to domestic production fluctuations. But for some countries (the Philippines, Sri Lanka, Egypt, Libya, Ghana, Nigeria, Senegal, Zaire, Guatemala, and Peru), world price fluctuations have accounted for over 30 percent of the variability of food import costs during 1961–1976 (Table 2.5). More importantly, world prices were generally quite stable during the period observed. If future prices are less stable than prices during 1961–1976, as seems likely, then world price variability would be a more important source of food import cost variability. In fact, it would likely contribute at least 50 percent of the food import cost variability for a significant number of countries. Because the importance of world price stability increases as a country becomes more dependent on imports, these developing countries that are most dependent could have benefited significantly from an effective WTC reserve stock system and its consequent price stabilization.

## Conclusion

Recent conditions for the 1979/80 world wheat crop have not been very favorable and it is very unlikely that this year's

*The International Wheat Agreement*   233

wheat harvest will match the record harvest of 1978/79. Thus, prices have rebounded to levels well above those proposed for WTC reserve stock accumulation. For the time being, therefore, it seems unlikely that a reserve stock system as proposed by the WTC could be implemented even if the major difference in views on key issues could be resolved. What then can be done at the international level to improve the food security of poor people in developing countries? Several authors in this volume have analyzed the benefits and costs of financial mechanisms such as a Food Import Bill Insurance Scheme. As Reutlinger and Bigman argue (Chapter 9), such schemes could take advantage of "opportunities in today's world for reallocating existing food supplies within and between countries." Although they may be more difficult to negotiate and more costly to implement in the absence of greater world price stability, these schemes could be operated despite the lack of a world reserve stock system for price stabilization. Indeed, the importance of such financial mechanisms for developing countries is greater in the absence of new measures for world price stabilization.

### Notes

1. This discussion is based on FAO Committee on World Food Security (1979) and World Food Council (1979).

2. Also, there were unresolved differences on special provisions for developing country members. See FAO (1979).

3. The results from Sarris (1976) are also reported in detail in Taylor, Sarris, and Abbott (1977).

4. The premise of this analysis is that the WTC should attempt to bring about a net increase in world stockholding. However, there are three alternative premises that should be noted. First, it could be argued that the WTC should be regarded as a "fail-safe" mechanism only: As there is uncertainty about how much stockholding would take place without the .WTC, the WTC should be instituted to assure that at least its stockholding program will be achieved. But it is the author's view that, given a wide price band and a sufficiently large WTC obligation, the WTC could induce increased stockholding and reduced price variability and that it should be designed to do so. Second, it could be argued that the purpose of the WTC

234 *Daniel Morrow*

is to shift part of the responsibility for stockholding from those countries such as the United States and Canada that have traditionally held stocks to other major countries that have not. It is the author's view that increased responsibility for stockholding by other countries is important primarily as a means to increase total world stockholding and that the WTC should be designed so that the United States and Canada also do more stockholding than they otherwise would. Third, it could be argued that the WTC should not necessarily increase total stockholding during periods of large supplies but should improve the management of those stocks during periods of shortage, e.g., to ensure that existing stocks are not released prematurely in a rising market. It is the author's view that unless additional stockholding is undertaken in situations of large supplies, the rules for managing those stocks in short supply situations will not significantly influence the degree of price variability. Furthermore, a WTC mechanism that is intended to isolate stocks from a low price market for release only in a high price market will necessarily induce some increase in stockholding during the period of WTC accumulation.

5. Such a theoretical model is developed fully in Gardner (1979) and Morrow (1980). For an early application of this basic model to the United States, see Meinken (1955). Morrow shows that the model can usefully describe the recent behavior of the world wheat economy.

6. For an analysis of the U.S. experience, see Peck (1978). For a detailed attempt to model the interaction between government and private stocks in the U.S. market, see Holland and Sharples (1978).

7. However, the financial returns to any buffer stock are highly variable: even if the expected profit is negative, the actual profit may be positive depending on the sequence of production deviations.

8. The proposed WTC would have granted temporary "relief" from the obligations to accumulate, hold, or release reserve stocks under certain conditions. It is clear that the WTC reserve stock would more likely be additional to what would otherwise be held if such relief, especially relief from the obligation to hold, could not be obtained easily.

9. These intuitive relationships are demonstrated by several simulation models of buffer stocks such as Sarris (1976) and Cochrane and Danin (1976).

10. Gardner (1979) presents a detailed analysis of the desirability of a price band centered above the mean assuming that there are large penalties associated with very high prices and the buffer stock is designed to supplement profitable stockholding.

11. The WTC price indicator would be the simple average of several f.o.b. prices. The price indicator used here is based on the proposal for an indicator including No. 2 Canadian Western Red Spring (CWRS), 13.5 per-

# The International Wheat Agreement 235

cent protein, f.o.b. St. Lawrence and f.o.b. Vancouver; U.S. No. 2 Hard Red Winter Ordinary, f.o.b. Gulf; No. 2 Soft Red Winter, f.o.b. Gulf; No. 2 Dark Northern Spring 14 percent, f.o.b. Lakes; No. 2 Western White, f.o.b. Pacific; and Australian Standard White, f.o.b. East Coast. Prices are from International Wheat Council, *World Wheat Statistics*, and U.S. Department of Agriculture, *Wheat Situation*, various issues. Note that there can be substantial differences in the price of individual wheats and that the level of the price indicator changes somewhat depending on which wheats are included. Nominal prices are deflated using the developed countries' indices of U.S. dollar unit values of manufactured exports to developing countries (cif index), which is the deflator used by the World Bank, *Commodity Trade and Price Trends*, 1978. Real prices are somewhat lower using other deflators.

12. In terms of the WTC price indicator in 1978 constant dollars, the World Bank's projected wheat price for 1980, 1981, 1985, and 1990 are $147.9, $151.9, $156.8, and $162.8, respectively. The U.S. Department of Agriculture (1978) Grains-Oilseeds-Livestock model projects 1985 wheat prices under the base scenario of $170.0. A recent study by Mitchell and Heady (undated) at Iowa State University projects a 1985 wheat price of $169.

13. Although there was a provision for initial accumulation at prices above the second falling price point, it is assumed that no significant accumulation would take place under such a provision.

14. This analysis does not consider the possible interaction between wheat and feedgrain markets for two reasons. First, as argued by Taylor, Sarris, and Abbott (1977), it appears to be empirically realistic to analyze the two markets separately (pp. 28–30). Second, and most importantly, it is assumed that substantial feedgrain stocks will be held as a result of unilateral policies, primarily by the United States, and thus the WTC reserve stock of wheat need not bear the burden of fluctuations in the feedgrain market.

15. It may be argued that, in order to stabilize the international market price, the WTC reserve stock needs to be large relative to fluctuations in trade volume, which are less than half as large as fluctuations in world production. But this is incorrect for two reasons. First, the WTC reserve stocks will be nationally held, and some of the reserves would presumably be in major importing countries such as the Soviet Union and India. In the event that these importing countries have a large production shortfall in the same year that the world price reaches the WTC release price, they will both draw upon their own WTC reserves for internal use and increase their import demand. Thus, their potential demand on the total WTC reserve stocks, including their own, could correspond more closely to their

potential production shortfalls than their potential change in import demand. Second, in the past, exporters have held stocks that have been used to stabilize their trade volumes even in years of their own production shortfalls. Given that WTC reserve stocks will partially substitute for these other stocks, they must be large relative to possible production shortfalls, not past fluctuations in trade volumes.

16. Minimum working stocks for each country/region are assumed to equal the lowest observed level of ending stocks as a percentage of production or consumption, whichever is larger. Minimum working stocks for the world as a whole are assumed to be the sum of minimum working stocks for the individual countries. Note that, by this estimate, the world did not reach minimum stock levels in 1973/74. For details, see Morrow (1980).

17. Of the 16.58 million metric tons shown for the United States, about 11 million metric tons were held in the Farmer-Owned Reserve Program. Thus, any WTC obligation assumed by the United States would have drawn upon the remaining 5.5 million metric tons of free stocks.

18. The net increase in the cost of stockholding to the economy as a whole and to public treasuries would depend on the net increase in stocks. But, to the extent that WTC stocks held by the government substituted for private stocks, the risks borne by public treasuries would increase greatly.

19. Sarris (1976) determines his accumulation and release prices as a function of the assumed equilibrium (long-run average) price of $140 (HRW, f.o.b. Gulf, in 1974 dollars). The accumulation price is $p \cdot e^{-b}$ and the release price is $p \cdot e^{b}$, where $p$ = equilibrium price and, for the preferred price band, $b = 0.2513$ ($e$ is the exponential constant). See pp. 155 and 196.

20. See Table 7.12c, p. 275, Sarris (1976). By the tenth year the average size levels off at about 10 million metric tons with a standard deviation of about 5 million metric tons.

21. It may be reasonable to argue that the net addition to stockholding due to the WTC should be 10 to 15 million metric tons. Then, if each ton of WTC reserve stock increases total stockholding by 0.5 million metric tons, the WTC reserve stock obligations should total 20 to 30 million metric tons. In defense of the model's failure to explicitly incorporate other stockholding activity, it could be argued that the empirically based demand and supply functions already capture this stockholding activity. But, in that case, these functions should shift in response to BSA activity.

22. The model explicitly assumes that only a fraction of national production fluctuations are registered in the international market through a shift in excess demand. For example, the fractions for the Soviet Union,

*The International Wheat Agreement* 237

India, and Brazil are 0.29, 0.24, and 0.49, respectively. See Sarris (1976, p. 189).

23. In an earlier paper, Sarris himself had argued that the primary purpose of a reserve stock must be to prevent panic buying such as occurred in 1973/74; for this purpose, he supported a 15 million metric ton reserve. But this argument was omitted in his consideration of the desirable buffer stock capacity. See Sarris and Taylor (1976).

24. On this general issue, see Morrow (1980).

25. Other simulation models also indicate the interest limitations of such a buffer stock system. See Reutlinger (1976) and Cochrane and Danin (1976).

26. Sarris's model probably overstates the contribution of the buffer stock to price stability for three reasons. First, Sarris's results are based on simulations over a 20-year period so that the initial conditions do not affect the results significantly. But, as already noted, it is very unlikely that the WTC with the price levels proposed would have led to significant reserve stock accumulation and thus would have had little effect on upward price fluctuations over the 3-to-5-year life of the agreement. Second, because it neglects the extent to which the buffer stock would substitute for rather than add to other stocks and because it considers international rather than nationally held stocks, the Sarris model of a 15-million-metric-ton buffer stock probably has more effect on the simulated market than WTC reserves of 20 or even 30 million metric tons would have had on the actual market. Finally, Sarris does not consider the run-up in prices that would likely accompany reserve stock depletion and panic buying. For all of these reasons, the WTC would probably reduce world price variability by less than the 35 percent reduction estimated for Sarris's buffer stock.

27. On this point, see World Food Council (1979, pp. 12–14).

28. The extent to which national policies that insulate domestic markets from the international markets contribute to international price instability is considered in the chapters by Josling and Johnson in this book.

# References

Cochrane, Willard W., and Yigal Danin. *Reserve Stock Grain Models, The World and the United States, 1975–1985.* Technical Bulletin 305, University of Minnesota, Agricultural Experiment Station, 1976.

FAO. *World Food Security: Draft Evaluation of World Cereal Stock Situation.* CCCP: GR 74/11, July 1974.

\_\_\_. Committee on World Food Security. *Outcome of the Negotiating Conference for a New International Grains Arrangement: Implications*

238                                                           *Daniel Morrow*

*for World Food Security and Proposals for Implementing the International Undertaking.* CFS: 79/8, March 1979.

Gardner, Bruce L. *Optimal Stockpiling of Grain.* Lexington, Mass.: Lexington Books, 1979.

Holland, Forrest D., and Jerry A. Sharples. *WHEATSIM: Description and Computer Program Documentation.* Station Bulletin No. 191, Department of Agricultural Economics, Agricultural Experiment Station. West Lafayette, Ind.: Purdue University, May 1978.

International Wheat Council. *World Wheat Statistics.* London, various issues.

Johnson, D. Gale. "Limitations of Grain Reserves in the Quest for Stable Prices." *World Economy* (June 1978).

Meinken, Kenneth W. *The Demand and Price Structure for Wheat.* Technical Bulletin No. 1136. Washington, D.C.: USDA, 1955.

Mitchell, Donald D., and Earl O. Heady. *U.S. Exports, Farm Employment, and Income Simulated Under Alternative Export Demands.* CARD Report No. 81, Iowa State University (undated).

Morrow, Daniel T. *The Economics of International Stockholding of Wheat.* International Food Policy Research Institute, Research Report 18, Sept. 1980.

Peck, Anne. "Implications of Private Storage of Grains for Buffer Stock Schemes to Stabilize Prices." *Food Research Institute Studies* 16, no. 3 (1978).

Reutlinger, Shlomo. "A Simulation Model for Evaluating Worldwide Buffer Stocks of Wheat." *American Journal of Agricultural Economics* 58 (February 1976).

____. "Food Insecurity: Magnitude and Remedies." World Bank Staff Working Paper No. 267, July 1977.

Sarris, Alexander H. *The Economics of International Grain Reserve Systems.* Massachusetts Institute of Technology, unpublished Ph.D. dissertation, 1976.

Sarris, Alexander H., and Lance Taylor. "Cereal Stocks, Food Aid and Food Security for the Poor." *World Development* 4 (December 1976).

Taylor, Lance; Alexander Sarris; and Philip Abbott. *Grain Reserves, Emergency Relief, and Food Aid.* Washington, D.C.: Overseas Development Council, 1977.

U.S. Congress, House Committee on International Relations. "The U.S. proposal for an International Grain Reserves System—II." Washington, D.C.: U.S. Government Printing Office, 97-747, October 1978.

U.S. Department of Agriculture. *Alternative Futures for World Food in 1985.* Washington, D.C.: USDA, 1978.

____. *Foreign Agriculture Circular: Grains.* FG-9-79. Washington, D.C.: USDA, June 22, 1979.

# The International Wheat Agreement

239

___. *Wheat Situation.* Washington, D.C.: USDA, various issues.

World Bank. *Commodity Trade and Price Trends.* Washington, D.C., 1978.

World Food Council. *World Food Security for the 1980's: Report by the Executive Director.* WFC/1979/5, April 1979.

# 11
# Insurance Approach to Food Security: Simulation of Benefits for 1970/71-1975/76 and for 1978-1982

*Barbara Huddleston*
*Panos Konandreas*

Many developing countries are marginal actors in world grain markets and their needs are not likely to receive priority attention when supplies are tight. Therefore, an international food insurance scheme designed specifically to help such countries over supply shortfalls in high-price years could provide a cost-effective approach to food security for them. This was the premise upon which a recent study published by the International Food Policy Research Institute was based (Konandreas et al., 1978). The IFPRI report evaluates an insurance scheme that would permit developing countries to stabilize cereal consumption at a relatively stable cost. It draws on earlier work by Johnson (1976), Reutlinger (1977), and Hathaway (1976), but adds a number of refinements, particularly in its analysis of supply variability and probable food insurance requirements at individual country level.

There are two sources of food insecurity in food-deficit developing countries: first, a temporary reduction in their own food production and, second, a temporary increase in international foodgrain prices. The Johnson proposal deals only with the first source of food insecurity and implicitly assumes that developing countries will be able to handle the second source by varying their foreign exchange expenditure on food imports. Even if such variable spending of scarce foreign exchange were possible, it would severely hamper the overall economic development of many developing countries. Therefore, a food security scheme that would protect developing countries from both sources of food insecurity must deal with fluctuations in their food import expenditures.

Reutlinger has redefined food insecurity of developing countries by recognizing the importance of fluctuating foreign exchange requirements. His study estimates the cost of financing food imports needed to maintain consumption when the aggregate food import bill of developing countries exceeds its normal level.

The study summarized in this chapter follows Reutlinger's approach in principle but adds a number of refinements. First, rather than treating developing countries as a group, this study estimates the level and variability of grain production and the import requirements of each country individually, taking production and consumption growth into account. Second, it clearly specifies operating rules at the country level, allowing an objective estimate of benefits received by each country. Finally, it estimates the cost of an insurance scheme for a period of five consecutive years rather than for a single independent year.

The food insurance approach developed at IFPRI assumes that countries will attempt to stabilize consumption within a fairly narrow range above and below projected demand, if they can do so at reasonable cost. As will be seen later on, this assumption is not always borne out by the historical record of countries' behavior during periods of tight supply; nevertheless, we considered it a rational and appropriate basis for conducting the analysis.

The consumption level defended by the system varies between 95 and 100 percent of the projected cereal demand for each country.[1] The system operates on the assumption that a country will allocate foreign exchange to cereal imports at a level sufficient to cover their trend cost, and that in high-price years it will be prepared to spend somewhat in excess of trend in order to prevent excessive downward adjustments in consumption. How much in excess of trend the country will spend of its own accord determines the level of insurance it will need to defend the assumed consumption objectives. In practice the desired level of insurance would probably vary from country to country. For purposes of the discussion in this chapter, the insurance level is fixed at 130 percent of the trend cereal import bill.[2] Each year its actual import bill is calculated as if

*Insurance Approach to Food Security* 243

the country were importing the quantity required to defend the target consumption level. For any year in which the actual import bill exceeds 130 percent of trend, the system will compensate the country for the amount of the excess.

An international food insurance scheme could operate in either of two ways: (1) it could serve as a purely financial mechanism that provides participating countries with funds to cover overruns in their cereal import bills; or (2) it could operate with a limited grain reserve in addition to the financial mechanism. In the latter case, the IFPRI analysis assumes that grain would be released only to countries experiencing a cereal production shortfall greater than 5 percent below trend, and that it would be released only when the world wheat price exceeds $200 per metric ton.

To evaluate the proposed scheme a model was built that simulates cereal demand, trend production, and production variability on a country by country basis, as well as the variability of the world price of wheat (see Appendix).

Price considerations have an important bearing on the evaluation of the merits of combining a grain reserve with a compensatory financing scheme to insure against high food import bills. The world wheat price distribution generated by the model indicates that there is about a 20 percent probability of world price falling below $105 per ton (expressed in 1977 dollars), and an equal chance of it exceeding $200 per ton over the next five years. Since this would mean that the scheme could expect to acquire grain in one year out of five, and to release grain in one year out of five, IFPRI assumed that a grain reserve could be created with a one-time acquisition in a low-price year such as 1977, and that no further acquisitions would be made during the five-year period under study. Reserves of 4, 8, 12, 16, and 20 million tons were evaluated as to cost effectiveness in attaining the scheme's objectives and compared with the operation of the scheme without reserves.

The simulation model generates 275 five-year (1978 to 1982) cereal production sequences for each country, and 275 corresponding five-year world wheat price sequences. For each year the model determines which countries are eligible for compensation and the amounts for which they are eligible, based on the rules specified previously. The summation of compensations to countries for a given year constitutes the cost of the scheme for that year. The cost for a five-year sequence is expressed in present value by discounting future expenditures. The outcomes of the 275 sequences are summarized by probability distributions.

If the scheme operates with a grain reserve facility, then in addition to compensatory payments there are three additional components that must be taken into account when computing the scheme's total cost: first, the acquisition cost (a one-time acquisition at the beginning of the five-year period was assumed); second, the carrying cost for the grain stored on behalf of the scheme, which is assumed to equal $10 per ton annually; and finally, the salvage value of the grain remaining in the scheme at the end of five years, which is assumed to equal the residual quantity multiplied by the prevailing market price of the final year.

Results showed that, as expected, the larger the grain reserve held, the lower the cost of the compensatory financing component of the scheme.[3] The striking finding is that the expected costs of operating the scheme with various grain reserve levels are not significantly different. Varying the carrying cost and the discount rate have some effect,[4] but again the differences are relatively unimportant. This indicates that criteria other than expected cost should determine the choice of the appropriate size of the grain reserve, if any.

Under all scenarios at an insurance level of 110 percent the present value (in 1977 dollars) for the expected cost of the scheme over the five-year period is roughly $5.1 billion, and the average annual cost equals $1.18 billion.[5] Comparable values for a scheme operating at an insurance level of 130 percent are approximately $3.7 billion and $750 million respectively. The larger the grain reserve, the less skewed the cost distribution becomes, meaning that extremely high compensatory payments are less likely. Thus, at an insurance level of 110 percent there is a 95 percent probability that total compensatory payments of a scheme with 20 million metric tons of grain will be less than $12 billion. Adding the $1.1 billion cost for the grain reserve still yields a figure well below the comparable cost of about

*Insurance Approach to Food Security* 245

$16 billion for a scheme operating solely as a compensatory financing mechanism. At the 130 percent insurance level, a scheme with the same probability of meeting its objectives would cost $9.1 billion with a 20-million-ton grain reserve and $12 billion without a reserve.

Aside from reducing the cost variability, a scheme operating with a grain reserve facility provides supply guarantees during high price years. The analysis shows important differences in how well various reserve levels fulfill the objective of attaining supplies equal to 95 percent of trend production during high price years. For example, with a grain reserve of 8 million tons there is a 77.5 percent probability that every member country will attain this objective during the first year of operation, whereas by 1982 this probability falls to about 19.5 percent. A grain reserve of 20 million tons provides much greater guarantees, satisfying this objective with a probability of 98.5 percent in 1978 and 62.5 percent in 1982.

In order to obtain a better understanding of the practicality of such a scheme, the model was applied to the actual situation during the early 1970s, a period when the scheme should have provided significant benefits to developing countries had it been in operation. The methodology employed was the same as that used to obtain the results for the simulation exercise, with trend consumption extrapolated backward from the 1975 per-capita base.[6]

For this historical analysis trend imports were valued at the average U.S. price for soft red winter wheat, f.o.b. Atlantic ports, 1960–1975. This price equals $134.2 per metric ton in 1975 dollars, or $158.7 per metric ton in 1977 dollars. The stability of nominal prices for the period 1960–1972 reflects a gradual decline in real prices as the cost of production per unit of output dropped, but this decline was more than offset by the sharp increase in the cost of production inputs that accompanied the high world wheat prices in 1973 and 1974. Thus, in 1977 dollars the constant price for the period 1960–1975 as a whole is almost $10.0 per ton greater than the $148.0 average for the period from 1960–1972, and approximately equals the equilibrium price of $155.8 per metric ton generated for the future period 1978–1982.

A comparison of the results obtained for the historical period 1970/71–1975/76 with the hypothetical cost and distribution of benefits by country for the operation of a comparable scheme during the period 1978–1982 is shown in Table 11.1. The total value of the compensation that would have been paid during the historical period is somewhat higher than the expected cost for the scheme as simulated for 1978–1982 (4.1 compared to 3.7 billion in 1977 dollars), and had a probability of less than 15 to 20 percent of being required (Table 11.2). India, Morocco, Mexico, and Turkey are the top four beneficiaries in both periods, though in slightly different order and with somewhat less disparity among them for the historical period than for the future operation of the scheme. Other countries receiving more than 2 percent of the benefits in 1970/71–1975/76 would have included Brazil, Syria, Bangladesh, the Philippines, Ethiopia, Egypt, Indonesia, Algeria, Iraq, and Korea. Of these, all but Iraq and the Philippines could also be expected to rank among the leading beneficiaries in the future. In addition, Nigeria, Sudan, Zambia, and Iran could also expect to obtain significant benefits.

In considering these results, one must remember that according to the rules of this scheme, compensation would be paid for in the form of grain only in years when world price exceeds $200 per ton. For the historical period, prices in constant 1977 dollars reached this level in only two years: 1972/73 and 1973/74. Assuming that all of the compensation in those years were given in grain, the total would have amounted to 16.3 million tons. The total grain equivalent of the monetary compensation that countries would have received in other years would have come to only 6.4 million tons. This grain would have been purchased by recipient countries on the open market.

As the scheme's rules specify that the grain reserve could be drawn upon only in high price years, a 20-million-ton reserve would not have been fully utilized in the 1972–1974 crisis; in fact, the skewedness of the price distribution for 1978–1982— with a relatively large number of price outcomes falling in the lower range and a relatively few scattered in the extreme upper range—suggests that the full amount of the grain reserve would very rarely be needed. Yet the fact that over three quarters of

247

Table 11.1 Distribution of Value of Benefits of Insurance Scheme, by Country, 1978-82 and 1970/71-1975/76

| | 1978-82 | | 1970/71-1975/76 | |
|---|---|---|---|---|
| Country[a] | Share of Benefits | Expected Compensation[b] | Share of Benefits | Estimated Actual Compensation Required[b] |
| **LOW INCOME** | | | | |
| India | 24.07 | $900.2 | 7.24 | $271.3 |
| Indonesia | 3.63 | 135.8 | 2.40 | 89.8 |
| Nigeria | 3.23 | 120.8 | 0.75 | 28.3 |
| Egypt | 3.07 | 114.8 | 2.91 | 108.9 |
| Bangladesh | 2.67 | 99.9 | 4.84 | 181.5 |
| Sudan | 2.34 | 87.5 | 0.37 | 13.8 |
| Sri Lanka | 1.31 | 49.0 | 0.76 | 28.6 |
| Malawi | 1.03 | 38.5 | 1.67 | 62.7 |
| Philippines | 1.00 | 37.4 | 3.17 | 118.8 |
| Burma | .95 | 35.5 | 0.70 | 26.2 |
| Tanzania | .72 | 26.9 | 1.35 | 50.5 |
| Upper Volta | .72 | 26.9 | 0.69 | 25.8 |
| Afghanistan | .63 | 23.6 | 1.84 | 68.9 |
| Senegal | .51 | 19.1 | 1.76 | 65.9 |
| Cameroon | .35 | 13.1 | 0.45 | 16.8 |
| Zaire | .29 | 10.8 | 0.27 | 10.3 |
| Bolivia | .28 | 10.5 | 0.23 | 8.7 |
| Uganda | .28 | 10.5 | 0.58 | 21.6 |
| Mali | .26 | 9.7 | 0.18 | 6.6 |
| Angola | .23 | 8.6 | 0.15 | 5.7 |
| Malagasy | .23 | 8.6 | 0.72 | 27.1 |
| Niger | .23 | 8.6 | 0.75 | 28.1 |
| Honduras | .13 | 4.9 | 0.22 | 8.4 |
| Guinea | .11 | 4.1 | 0.22 | 8.1 |
| Haiti | .09 | 3.4 | 0.15 | 5.8 |
| Rwanda | .09 | 3.4 | 0.01 | 0.4 |
| Sierra Leone | .06 | 2.2 | 1.12 | 42.0 |
| Benin | .05 | 1.9 | -- | -- |
| Chad | .03 | 1.1 | 0.14 | 5.3 |
| Gambia | .02 | 0.7 | 0.01 | 0.3 |
| Burundi | N.A. | N.A. | 0.18 | 6.6 |
| Ethiopia | N.A. | N.A. | 3.31 | 124.0 |
| Kenya | N.A. | N.A. | -- | -- |
| Mozambique | N.A. | N.A. | 0.96 | 35.8 |
| Nepal | N.A. | N.A. | -- | -- |
| Pakistan | N.A. | N.A. | 0.39 | 14.8 |
| **MIDDLE INCOME** | | | | |
| Morocco | 9.72 | $363.5 | 8.28 | $310.3 |
| Turkey | 4.87 | 182.1 | 10.64 | 398.7 |
| Syria | 3.44 | 128.7 | 5.23 | 195.9 |
| Korea, Rep. of | 3.27 | 122.3 | 2.02 | 75.9 |
| Algeria | 2.44 | 91.3 | 2.22 | 83.1 |
| Zambia | 2.31 | 86.4 | 1.28 | 48.1 |
| Tunisia | 1.85 | 69.2 | -- | -- |

248

Table 11.1 (continued)

| Country a/ | 1978-82 | | 1970/71-1975/76 | |
|---|---|---|---|---|
| | Share of Benefits | Expected Compensation b/ | Share of Benefits | Estimated Actual Compensation Required b/ |
| MIDDLE INCOME | | | | |
| Cuba | 1.46 | 54.6 | 1.07 | 40.0 |
| Peru | 1.31 | 49.0 | 0.96 | 36.1 |
| Malaysia | .58 | 21.7 | 0.89 | 33.4 |
| Colombia | .54 | 20.2 | 0.66 | 24.7 |
| Jordan | .47 | 17.6 | 0.59 | 22.3 |
| El Salvador | .30 | 11.2 | 0.66 | 24.6 |
| Ecuador | .29 | 10.8 | 0.37 | 13.8 |
| Dominican Rep. | .27 | 10.1 | 0.50 | 18.6 |
| Ghana | .27 | 10.1 | -- | -- |
| Ivory Coast | .22 | 8.2 | 0.36 | 13.5 |
| Nicaragua | .18 | 6.7 | 0.53 | 19.8 |
| Paraguay | .21 | 7.9 | 0.21 | 7.9 |
| Guatemala | .12 | 4.5 | 0.07 | 2.7 |
| Liberia | .07 | 2.6 | 0.02 | 0.7 |
| Guyana | N.A. | N.A. | 0.01 | 0.5 |
| HIGH INCOME | | | | |
| Mexico | 5.74 | 214.7 | 8.51 | 319.0 |
| Brazil | 2.56 | 95.7 | 5.80 | 217.4 |
| Iran | 2.29 | 85.6 | 1.00 | 37.4 |
| Iraq | 1.62 | 60.6 | 2.20 | 82.3 |
| Venezuela | 1.49 | 55.7 | 1.90 | 71.2 |
| Chile | 1.11 | 41.5 | 1.84 | 69.1 |
| Lebanon | .63 | 23.6 | 0.46 | 17.3 |
| Cyprus | .28 | 10.5 | 0.61 | 22.8 |
| Jamaica | .27 | 10.1 | 0.16 | 6.1 |
| Trinidad & Tobago | .19 | 7.1 | 0.17 | 6.5 |
| Costa Rica | .15 | 5.6 | 0.11 | 4.3 |
| Panama | .11 | 4.1 | 0.19 | 7.0 |
| Uruguay | N.A. | N.A. | -- | -- |
| TOTAL | | $3,711.5 | | $3,748.4 |

a/ A number of countries projected to become food deficit countries in the 1980's were net exporters in the 1970's. In some years these countries experienced production shortfalls such that their loss in potential export earnings exceeded 30% below trend. In such cases compensation has been calculated so as to cover this excess foreign exchange loss as well as to cover the cost of any imports required to meet target consumption. Countries which experienced such losses in the 1970/71-75/76 period include: Asia - Burma; North Africa/Middle East - Afghanistan, Sudan, Turkey; Sub-Saharan Africa - Angola, Ethiopia, Mali, Niger, Nigeria, Rwanda, Uganda; Latin America - Guyana. Countries having a per capita income in excess of $3,000 per year were excluded. Low income is considered less than $400 per capita as of mid-1975; middle income $400-$950; and high income more than $950.

b/ Values are expressed in 1977 dollars for 1978/82 and in 1975 dollars for 1970/71-1975/76, and apply to operation of a scheme without grain reserves.

*Insurance Approach to Food Security* 249

Table 11.2  Comparison of expected compensation for historical and future periods and probability associated with estimated actual compensation required for 1970/71-1975/76

| | 1970/71-1975/76 | 1978-82 |
|---|---|---|
| Expected Compensation<br>1977 dollars (billion) | 2.7 | 3.7 |
| Associated Probability[a/]<br>With 20 million ton reserve (%)<br>Without reserve (%) | 75-80<br>70-75 | 75-80<br>70-75 |
| Estimated Actual Compensation<br>Required<br>1977 dollars (billion) | 4.1 | 5.6[b/] |
| Associated Probability[a/]<br>With 20 million ton reserve (%)<br>Without reserve (%) | 85-90<br>80-85 | 85-90<br>80-85 |
| Average Annual Cost<br>1977 dollars (billion)<br>Expected<br>Estimated Actual:<br>Minimum (1970/71)<br>Maximum (1973/74) | .450<br><br>.068<br>1.643 | .750 |

a/  Represents probability that amount of compensation indicated would be sufficient or more than sufficient to cover target consumption under all circumstances, where target consumption equals trend consumption except in cases of production shortfall when it is adjusted downward to a minimum not less than 95% of trend.

b/  Equivalent to actual amount required in historical period if 1972-74 crisis were to recur in future period.

the available reserve might have been called upon, had 20 million tons been available, indicates the magnitude of the contribution a large reserve could make to food security for those countries that from time to time experience severe domestic production shortfalls coinciding with tight world markets. To obtain a comparable degree of security without a reserve would require a financial capacity of $8.7 billion rather than the $6.1 billion total cost of the scheme with a 20-million-ton reserve. Further, in an extreme year, if countries were funded so as to enable them to purchase the equivalent of 20 million tons of grain, the effect of this additional market demand would undoubtedly place further upward pressure on prices.

Much of the requirement for a large reserve in extreme years comes from a few large countries where a serious production shortfall can make a significant difference in world markets. This suggests that such countries should pursue domestic reserve programs of some size so that the skewedness of the cost distribution for the scheme as a whole and the size of the required reserve could be reduced. However, low-income countries should not, on this account, be required to pay a higher cost for their food security than other beneficiaries of the scheme. Separate consideration should therefore be given to offering subsidies to such countries to cover all or part of the cost of their domestic reserves. If this were done, a reserve of 6 million tons would cover the expected release of grain for the hypothetical period 1978-1982. Six million tons is probably an appropriate size to use for purposes of further analyzing possible relationships between a financial food import facility and a grain reserve restricted for use in high price years.

## Notes

1. Throughout this chapter, the term "cereal" refers to wheat, rice, and feedgrains. The composition of cereal imports varies from country to country and even within countries. For purposes of this study, wheat is taken as the basic staple commodity and the value of cereal imports is computed as if these imports were composed entirely of wheat. The term "grain" is used in the context of discussions on physical reserves, which could be comprised either of wheat only or of wheat and rice. The grain reserve discussed in this chapter is assumed to be a wheat reserve.

2. The analysis contained in *IFPRI Research Report No. 4* also considered insurance levels of 110 and 120 percent.

3. In evaluating the cost and effectiveness of various size grain reserves, an insurance level of 110 percent was used. Comparison with other insurance levels was made only for the scheme operating without reserves and with a reserve of 20 million metric tons.

4. A carrying cost of $10 per metric ton, reflecting the storage payment

*Insurance Approach to Food Security* 251

received by U.S. farmers for holding reserves, and a discount rate of 8 percent were assumed.

5. The average annual cost represents an equal annual expenditure of $1.183 billion in each of the scheme's five years that would yield a present value equal to the scheme's expected cost of $5.1 billion.

6. In addition to simulating the expected cost of the scheme for the historical period in 1975 dollars, the operation of the scheme for the crop years 1970/71–1975/76 was calculated using actual crop year production data and actual prices for calendar years 1971–1976, expressed in constant 1975 dollars, as follows:

| 1971 | $110.7 per ton | 1974 | $201.1 per ton |
| 1972 | 113.3 per ton | 1975 | 138.4 per ton |
| 1973 | 189.2 per ton | 1976 | 120.9 per ton |

*Source:* World Bank (1977).

## References

FAO. *Agricultural Commodities Projections 1970–1980.* Vol. 2. 1971.

Hathaway, Dale E. "Grain Stocks and Economic Stability: A Policy Perspective." *Analysis of Grain Reserves, a Proceedings.* ERS-634. Washington, D.C.: U.S. Department of Agriculture and the National Science Foundation, 1976.

Johnson, D. Gale. "Increased Stability of Grain Supplies in Developing Countries: Optimal Carry-overs and Insurance." *World Development* 4, no. 12 (1976):977–987.

Konandreas, Panos; Barbara Huddleston; and Virabongsa Ramangkura. *Food Security: An Insurance Approach.* Research Report No. 4. Washington, D.C.: International Food Policy Research Institute, September 1978.

Reutlinger, Shlomo. "Food Insecurity: Magnitude and Remedies." World Bank Working Paper No. 267. Washington, D.C., July 1977.

World Bank. *Commodity Trade and Price Trends.* Report No. EC-166/77. Washington, D.C., 1977.

## APPENDIX: METHODOLOGY

1. Trend consumption for total cereals for each country is obtained on the basis of population growth, GNP growth, and income elasticities. The expression used is as follows:

$$\overline{C}_{it} = N_{it} \left[ c_{oi\ 1975} \cdot (1 + r_i \cdot g_{oi})^{t-1975} + c_{ei\ 1975} \cdot (1 + r_i \cdot g_{ei})^{t-1975} \right]$$

where

$\overline{C}_{it}$ = trend cereal demand of the $i$th country in year $t$;

$N_{it}$ = projected population of the $i$th country in year $t$. (Population data were obtained from the World Bank midyear estimates, 1960–1975 [1977 World Bank Atlas].)

$c_{oi\ 1975}, c_{ei\ 1975}$ =

per-capita trend foodgrain and feedgrain consumption, respectively, of the $i$th country in 1975, which was obtained by fitting logarithmic time trends to actual per-capita data for the period 1960/61–1975/76 (provided by USDA [Foreign Agricultural Service]).

$r_i$ = annual growth rate of real per-capita GNP of the $i$th country. (A low income growth rate assumption was made here. Growth rates were arrived at from the 1976 *World Bank Atlas* and other World Bank materials.)

$g_{oi}, g_{ei}$ = income elasticities of foodgrains and feedgrains, respectively, of the $i$th country. (These were largely derived from FAO [1971] adjusted to accommodate the low growth assumption.)

2. Production trends for total cereals have been estimated for each country by fitting a logarithmic time trend to actual production data for the period 1960/61–1975/76 (provided by USDA [FAS]). The trend equations are in the form of

$$\overline{Q}_{it} = \overline{Q}_{io} e^{b_i(t-1960)} \quad t = 1960, 1961, \ldots,$$

where $\overline{Q}_{it}, \overline{Q}_{io}$ are trend production for the $i$th country of year $t$, and the base year 1960/61, respectively; and $b_i$ is the annual rate of growth of cereal production for the $i$th country. The variability of cereal production above and below trend has been analyzed for each country. Actual produc-

*Insurance Approach to Food Security* 253

tion levels for each year from 1960 to 1975 have been expressed as a percentage deviation from trend, as

$$Q_{it} = \frac{Q_{it} - \overline{Q}_{it}}{\overline{Q}_{it}} \; 100$$

where $Q_{it}$ is the actual production level in the year $t$. For the simulation analysis the generation of production levels for each country took into consideration the observed regional correlation in production by jointly generating production deviation vectors. Production variability as specified above is multiplicative in nature, which means that although production deviations from trend expressed as a percentage do not grow over time, the absolute levels of production fluctuations increase with time.

3. Adjusted target consumption in the $i$th country during a particular year $(C_{it}^*)$ is determined on the basis of actual grain production level in the country for that year. It is set lower than projected demand $(\overline{C}_{it})$ when a country experiences a production shortfall. Thus, if actual production for a particular year $(Q_{it})$ is below 95 percent of trend production $(\overline{Q}_{it})$ then:

$$C_{it}^* = 0.95 \; \overline{C}_{it}$$

If $Q_{it}$ is between 95 percent and 100 percent of $\overline{Q}_{it}$, then $C_{it}^*$ is set at the same level, i.e.,

$$C_{it}^* = \frac{Q_{it}}{\overline{Q}_{it}} \; \overline{C}_{it}$$

and finally, if $\overline{Q}_{it}$ is above $Q_{it}$, then $C_{it}^* = \overline{C}_{it}$.

4. The trend price $(\overline{P}_t)$ used in the application of the simulation model to the historical period was derived from a simple average of actual prices for the period 1960–1975, expressed in 1975 dollars. The trend price used in the simulation itself was generated from the following equation:

$$\log_e \frac{P_t}{p^*} = -0.89028 + 0.96268 \; \frac{M_t}{\overline{M}_t} \; +$$

$$(2.0)$$

$$0.86181 \; \log_e \; \frac{P_{t-1+u_t}}{p^*}$$

$$(4.6)$$

$$\text{SE} = 0.17378 \qquad R^2 = 0.75$$

where $P_t$ is world wheat price in year $t$ (in constant 1972 dollars); $p^*$ is the average world wheat price for the pre-1972 period ($74.1/MT), which is assumed to approximate the cost of production in exporting countries; $M_t$, $\overline{M}_t$ are total food deficit developing countries' actual and trend cereal imports, respectively, in year $t$; and $u_t$ is the random component of the price generating function in year $t$. The log-linear specification used above is meant to reflect the nonlinear price behavior ascribed to the international wheat market.

The price generating function used in the simulation was based on the estimated relationship. $p^*$ was adjusted to reflect current production costs in exporting countries. Thus, $p^*$ is set at \$85.0 per metric ton (about \$2.31 per bushel), which is approximately the current level of the U.S. government's wheat loan rate and thus reflects current production costs. As an initial value for the lagged price $(P_{t-1})$, the average wheat price for the last three years (1975–1977) is used. This price, a simple average of U.S. and Canadian wheat prices expressed in 1977 dollars, equals \$137.0 per metric ton.

5. Trend imports represent the difference between trend consumption $(\overline{C}_{it})$ and trend production $(\overline{Q}_{it})$. Target imports represent the difference between target consumption $(C_{it}^*)$ and actual production $(Q_{it})$.

6. The target import bill was calculated as:

$$(C_{it}^* - Q_{it}) \cdot P_t$$

and the uninsured import bill was calculated as:

$$(\overline{C}_{it} - \overline{Q}_{it}) \cdot \overline{P}_t \cdot 1.3.$$

# 12
# Grain Insurance, Reserves, and Trade: Contributions to Food Security for LDCs

*D. Gale Johnson*

World economic growth and its associated technological changes have greatly increased international food security over the past century. Substantial—one might say revolutionary—improvements in the speed of communication, the almost universal availability of rapid means of communication, and the reductions in the costs of and time required for transportation have significantly decreased the hardships and suffering resulting from shortfalls in food production in specific geographic areas. These dramatic changes in communication and transportation have enormously expanded the extent of the market from which food supplies could be drawn for almost any local community or region in the world. For many parts of the world a century ago, food 100 miles away was no more available to relieve the impacts of crop failure than if the food were on another planet. There remain a few areas of the world that are so isolated that relief in case of need may be delayed due to limited communication facilities and high transport costs. But such areas involve but a tiny fraction of the world's population, and even in these cases, if an early warning system were created, most of the suffering from food insufficiency due to natural causes could be avoided.

Two other factors have operated to improve international food security, though both together are probably much less important than the changes in communication and transportation. The first is that the variability of grain production for the world has declined significantly during the past century. This statement cannot be proven beyond a reasonable doubt

*255*

because of data inadequacies, but we do know that in specific regions of the world variability of grain production has been substantially reduced. The second is that increases in per-capita incomes for a considerable fraction of the world's population have created reserves of food that could be and have been drawn upon. I refer to the substantial increase in the amount of cereals fed to livestock, other than draft animals, that has occurred primarily in the twentieth century. In recent years more than a third of the world's grain production has been fed to livestock and most of this to animals other than draft animals. If farmers receive the appropriate price signals, some of the grain usually fed to livestock will be made available for human consumption. This is exactly what happened in the United States in 1974-1975 when the feed use of grain declined by a fourth. As a part of the same change in the structure of food production and consumption, the inventories of animals also provide a significant food reserve.

It is true that during the past century the world's population has almost trebled. But the changes referred to have been of such significance as to improve the food security for the much larger population of the world. Instead of the incidence of famine having increased over the past century, it has declined substantially.[1] This is a remarkable achievement that appears to have gone largely unrecognized in recent and current discussions of world food security.

But the changes that have occurred in technology and the world economy have a potential positive impact on world food security greater than has so far been realized. The means now exist to prevent nearly all deaths and most of the hardships due to food production shortfalls in any and all parts of the world. This may seem like an extreme statement, but it should be noted that it addresses only one part of the problem of food insufficiency and malnutrition. The statement does not refer to the interrelationships between poverty and the inability to acquire adequate food for good health and normal work activity. But I am serious in saying that it is no longer necessary for food production shortfalls in any part of the world to result in serious human hardship due to food insufficiency.

## Causes of International Food Insecurity

The primary reason why we have failed to achieve the degree of international food security that is now possible is not nature but man. And the aspect of man that is responsible for our failure is not man as a farmer or scientist or extension worker or grain marketer or food retailer but man as a politician. I use the term *politician* very broadly to include all who influence decisions that affect production, prices, and trade of food. Variability in the world's production of grain may be used, I believe, to give an approximate indication of variability of world food production. Since 1970-1971, when there has been so much concern expressed about climatic variability, the maximum negative deviation from trend in grain production appears not to have been in excess of 3 percent. The positive deviations may have been rather larger, perhaps as much as 5 percent in two of the last six years.[2]

With any reasonable assumption concerning the price elasticity of demand for grain for use or consumption the negative deviations from trend cannot be considered to be large. A negative deviation of 3 percent and a price elasticity of demand of –0.1 would result in a price change of 30 percent—assuming that stocks remained unchanged. Even if the price elasticity of demand for grain in the world were as low as –0.05, it would have required only a 35-million-ton reduction in stocks to have held price increases during recent years to 30 percent. But the price changes in international markets for grains between 1972/73 and 1973/74 and 1974/75 were substantially larger than this in real terms.

In two previous publications I have argued that the substantial increases in international grain prices in the years following 1971/72 could not be explained primarily by production shortfalls plus a variety of other factors such as the decline in fishmeal production, the Russian grain purchases, increased affluence (including business cycle effects), and the devaluation of the dollar (Johnson, 1975a, Chapter 3; and 1975b). After the effects of these variables upon international grain prices were taken into account there remained a substantial part of the rise

258                                                                 D. Gale Johnson

in grain prices between mid-1972 and 1973/74 that had to be attributed to other factors.

The conclusion that much of the international price instability, and thus the need for a large percentage of optimal carry-overs, is due to governmental policies has been supported by two recent articles that are independent of our work. Shei and Thompson (1977), using a model in which empirical estimates were made of excess demand functions for importing countries and excess supply functions for exporting countries, estimated the effects of various trade restrictions upon the international price of wheat in 1972/73. They conclude: "The most significant result of this study is the demonstration that greater world market price variability results as more countries prevent world price signals from being reflected across their borders into the domestic market through some form of trade control (p. 637)."

Paul Johnson, Grennes, and Thursby (1977) estimated the effect of national wheat price policies of Canada, Australia, Argentina, Europe, and Japan upon the increase in the international and U.S. price of wheat between 1972/73 and 1973/74. In their estimate they assumed that wheat exports to the rest of the world were exogenous. Between 1972/73 and 1973/74 the increase in the real price of wheat in the United States was 59.1 percent. If 1972/73 policies, such as the size of the European Community (EC) variable levy, had remained unchanged, the estimated real price of wheat would have increased 19.9 percent. The actual policy changes in the countries specified were responsible for an additional increase in the price of wheat of 20.9 percent or somewhat more than a third of the actual increase between 1972/73 and 1973/74. Approximately a third of the price increase was not explained by their model.

There is considerable resistance to accepting the view that it was man and not nature that was responsible for a large fraction of the substantial increases in international grain prices that occurred after mid-1972. To accept this view is to conclude that much of the human suffering that occurred in the low-income countries of the world due to higher food prices in international markets was the result of human action and not the inevitable consequence of the adversities imposed by nature. I am not arguing that the adversities imposed upon poor people were intended to be the effects of the policies followed. In other words, the decision makers in the Soviet Union or the European Community did not intend to reduce the food supplies available to South Asia or Central Africa. But I do hope that the point that national policies that insulate domestic prices and consumption from the effects of world variations in demand and supply have inevitable and at times adverse effects upon others has been made. Often those who are adversely affected are much, much less capable of coping with the consequences than those who are being protected by the policies.

## Alternatives for International Food Security

There are numerous approaches that could contribute to improved international food security. The approaches can be classified under three major headings: liberalization of barriers to trade in agricultural products, grain and food reserves, and insurance schemes for developing countries. These approaches should not be considered as competitive. It can easily be shown that liberalizing international trade would reduce the size of grain reserves required to achieve a given degree of food security. Further, if international trade were conducted under more liberal terms than is now the case, any of the suggested several insurance proposals would be less costly than with current trade policies.

At the Conference four different proposals were presented for food insurance for the developing countries. I shall here present one of them, namely a grain insurance proposal. The basic idea of the grain insurance proposal is very simple: Each developing country in the world would be assured that any deficit in its annual grain production in excess of a given percentage of trend production would be made available. This proposal could be underwritten by the United States alone, by the United States and the other major grain exporting countries, or by a group of high-income industrial countries. A premium could be established ranging from zero or near zero to a substantial fraction of the actuarial value of the insurance. The premium, if any were charged, should be varied with percapita income.

## Trade Liberalization

The conventional argument for a grain reserve is to offset uncontrolled variations in production. Although this argument may be valid for an individual country that does not engage in international trade, it is not a valid justification for the holding of reserves significantly in excess of working stocks for the world as a whole.

We have made estimates of optimal reserves for individual countries, for regions, and for the world as a whole and these estimates will be used to indicate the effect of free trade upon the appropriate size of grain reserves.[3] As these results depend upon the assumptions that we have made, let me first briefly describe what we have done.

Optimal grain reserves are defined according to a storage rule in which the expected gain from adding an amount to reserves equals the expected cost of holding that amount of grain until it would be withdrawn.[4] In other words, the amount of storage is based upon the expectation that investment in holding reserves would yield a normal or usual rate of return on that investment. As with all other investments, there is no certainty that when grain is added to a reserve the investment will yield the expected return. However, over a period of time the actual return should approximate the expected return. In our estimates we have assumed that the physical costs of storage were $7.50 per ton-year and that the real rate of interest was 5 percent.

The estimates of optimal grain reserves presented below are based on two assumptions that must be borne in mind. One is that only production variability has been taken into account; demand variability can also affect the size of optimal reserves and has not been taken into account. For foodgrains, however, demand variability is very small and would have little effect on the estimates. This is not true for feedgrains. The second assumption is that for country and region estimates, free trade in grain within the country or region is assumed but net grain trade among countries or among regions is held constant at the 1970 level. As changes in imports and exports of grain are alternatives to storage for a given country or region, the assumption of constant net trade results in an overestimate of optimal

*Grain Insurance, Reserves, and Trade* 261

reserves for all countries and regions except possibly North America.[5]

Estimates of optimal reserves (in excess of working stocks) are given in Table 12.1 for individual countries, certain regions, and the world as a whole. The top part of the table indicates

Table 12.1

Optimal Carryovers For Selected Countries And Regions, 1975

| Country or Region | 1975 Trend Production | Cumulative Probability Levels | | |
|---|---|---|---|---|
| | | 0.50 | 0.75 | 0.95 |
| | (million tons) | | | |
| A. Demand elasticity $\eta$ = -.10 | | | | |
| Burma | 6 | 0.3 | 0.7 | 1.2 |
| India | 100 | 6.5 | 9.5 | 13.5 |
| Indonesia | 16 | 1.6 | 2.9 | 4.4 |
| Pakistan-Bangladesh | 23 | 1.4 | 2.4 | 4.2 |
| Philippines | 6 | 0.1 | 0.2 | 0.3 |
| Thailand | 13 | 3.5 | 4.7 | 6.2 |
| Other Far East | 19 | 1.4 | 2.1 | 3.1 |
| Africa | 46 | 1.5 | 3.0 | 5.0 |
| Far East | 184 | 3.0 | 7.5 | 12.5 |
| Latin America | 78 | 2.5 | 5.0 | 8.5 |
| Near East | 48 | 2.5 | 4.5 | 8.5 |
| All Developing Regions | 353 | 2.5 | 7.5 | 15.0 |
| Europe | 231 | 1.3 | 5.5 | 9.5 |
| North America | 270 | 10.0 | 18.0 | 33.0 |
| Oceania | 18 | 8.0 | 10.5 | 15.4 |
| USSR | 199 | 28.0 | 41.0 | 49.0 |
| World | 1,304 | 0.0 | 2.0 | 18.0 |
| B. Demand elasticity $\eta$ = -.20 | | | | |
| India | | 2.0 | 4.0 | 7.5 |
| Africa | | 0.0 | 0.5 | 2.5 |
| Far East | | 0.0 | 1.0 | 7.0 |
| Developing Regions | | 0.0 | 1.0 | 7.0 |
| North America | | 1.5 | 8.5 | 22.0 |
| USSR | | 13.0 | 24.0 | 37.0 |
| World | | 0.0 | 0.0 | 7.0 |

262                                                    D. Gale Johnson

the optimal reserves for six individual countries and all other developing countries of the Far East (except China). The sum of the optimal carryover levels for the individual countries at a probability level of 0.50 for the Far East is 14.8 million tons.[6] However, if there were free trade within the Far East the optimal carryover at the same probability level would be just 3.0 million tons. It may also be noted that if there were free trade among all developing regions (excluding China) the optimal carryovers would be very small. Thus the developing countries could achieve a remarkable degree of food security by trading freely among themselves. It should be noted that if transportation costs were included in the model, optimal carryovers for the developing regions would be increased somewhat for regions and countries that are both net importers and net exporters. However, the effects of this modification would be small.

The estimates of optimal carryover levels for the world indicate the striking effects of free trade upon food security. At least half of the time optimal carryovers would be nil; in only one year out of twenty would such reserves (in excess of working stocks) equal or exceed 18 million tons. Thus a low cost means of achieving a significant degree of supply and price variability would be free trade; for the developing countries the free trade would not have to be with all countries but only the other developing countries.[7]

The previous discussion has been in terms of free trade in grains in the world or within large regions. Actually the assumption of free trade is not necessary for meeting the objective of increased stability of international grain prices. It is not trade interferences per se that increase instability of international prices, but the forms of trade interferences. The Common Agricultural Policy results in a high average degree of protection for grains produced in the European Community but it is not the degree of protection that increases the instability of international grain prices. The EC-induced instability of international grain prices results from the implementation of a policy of internal price stability that results in variable degrees of protection for domestic production. The protection is high when international prices are low and increases as international prices decline; the protection is low (or negative) when inter-

# Grain Insurance, Reserves, and Trade 263

national prices are high and decreases further as international prices increase. If the same average degree of protection over a period of time were achieved by the use of constant ad valorem (fixed percentage) tariffs, producer and consumer prices in the EC would reflect changes in international grain prices. Net grain trade of the EC would thus be responsive to international prices while under the current policy it shows little or no responsiveness. Consequently it would be possible to achieve a high degree of international food security with substantial degrees of protection to domestic agriculture if the form of the protection were appropriate.[8]

## Grain Reserves

There is no question that grain reserves could be managed to reduce the variability in available supplies and prices of grain for the world. One needs only to review the behavior of international grain prices from the late 1950s to the early 1970s to find proof of this conclusion (Johnson, 1975a, pp. 51-55). The remarkable price stability for that period was due primarily to large stocks held by the major grain exporters, primarily the United States and Canada, as an unwanted consequence of their domestic price policies. The rates of return on stockholding were negative and large; the stocks were not held in response to an investment criterion.

The combination of negative economic returns from stockholding and the political liability of large stocks in the three major grain exporters resulted in efforts to dispose of the stocks as rapidly as possible in 1972/73, and was partly responsible for the subsequent sharp price increases.

In our research at The University of Chicago we have estimated optimal grain reserves for North America. In these estimates we have assumed that both production and demand were subject to variability. North America has traditionally carried most of the world's grain reserves in excess of working stocks. The production and demand variability were based upon actual variability for the period from 1950 through 1976. Although the carryover estimates presented in Tables 12.2 and 12.3 are said to be for 1977, two caveats are in order. First, the supply estimates for 1977 did not take into account the actual carryin

# 264 D. Gale Johnson

Table 12.2

Supply And Optimal Carryovers, 1977

| 1977 Income per Capita | Cumulative Probability Level of Carryover [a] | | | Cumulative Probability Level of Supply [a] | | |
|---|---|---|---|---|---|---|
| | 0.5 | 0.75 | 0.95 | 0.5 | 0.75 | 0.95 |
| | | (million tons) | | | | |
| | U.S.: | Trend Production for 1977 = 244.3 | | | | |
| $3115 | 9 | 19 | 34 | 253 | 267 | 286 |
| $3461 | 10 | 20 | 36 | 255 | 269 | 288 |
| $3872 | 12 | 22 | 38 | 256 | 269 | 290 |
| | North America: | Trend Production for 1977 = 279.4 | | | | |
| $3115 | 21 | 33 | 50 | 301 | 317.5 | 338 |
| $3461 | 26 | 38 | 53 | 304 | 321 | 342 |
| $3872 | 28 | 41 | 56 | 306 | 323 | 344 |
| | | Australia[b] | | | | |
| | a) Trend Production for 1977 = 15.8 | | | | | |
| Using II.a.4 a) | 4 | 7 | 11 | 19.5 | 23 | 28 |
| Using II.a.4 b) | 7.5 | 10 | 13 | 22.5 | 26 | 31 |
| | b) Trend Production for 1977 = 17 | | | | | |
| Using II.a.4 a) | 2 | 4.5 | 9 | 18.5 | 21.5 | 26 |
| Using II.a.4 b) | 5.5 | 8 | 11.5 | 21.5 | 24.5 | 29 |

[a]Storage Cost = $7.50/ton and r = 2 percent.  Prices and costs are in 1967 dollars.

[b]See Appendix (Table 12.9) for demand functions.

for the 1977 year and, second, the demand variability based on 1950 through 1976 probably underestimated the demand variability that actually existed in the late 1970s. Demand variability in the 1970s was almost certainly greater than for 1950–1970 due to the policy modifications in numerous countries that influence the demand for North American grain.[9] More countries were capable of and willing to stabilize their domestic

*Grain Insurance, Reserves, and Trade*  265

Table 12.3

Supply and Optimal Carryovers, 1977a

| 1977 Income per Capita | Cumulative Probability Level for Carryovers[a] | | | Cumulative Probability Level for Supply[a] | | |
|---|---|---|---|---|---|---|
| | 0.5 | 0.75 | 0.95 | 0.5 | 0.75 | 0.95 |
| | (million tons) | | | | | |
| | U.S.: Trend Production for 1977 = 244.3 | | | | | |
| $3115 | 5 | 13 | 26 | 250 | 262 | 280 |
| $3461 | 6 | 14 | 27 | 252 | 263 | 281 |
| $3872 | 7 | 15 | 28 | 253 | 264 | 282 |
| | North America: Trend Production for 1977 = 279.4[b] | | | | | |
| $3115 | 16 | 26 | 40 | 296 | 310 | 330 |
| $3461 | 20 | 32 | 47 | 299 | 314 | 336 |
| $3872 | 23 | 34 | 51 | 302 | 318 | 340 |
| | Australia[c] | | | | | |
| | Trend Production for 1977 = 15.8 | | | | | |
| Using II.a.4 a) | 3 | 5 | 9 | 18 | 21 | 27 |
| Using II.a.4 b) | 6 | 9 | 12 | 21.5 | 25 | 30 |
| | Trend Production for 1977 = 17 | | | | | |
| Using II.a.4 a) | 1 | 3 | 6.5 | 17.5 | 20 | 24.5 |
| Using II.a.4 b) | 4 | 6.5 | 10.5 | 20 | 23 | 28 |

[a]Storage cost = $10/ton; r = 5 percent. Prices and costs are in 1967 dollars.

[b]To make a comparison with the case where the variability comes only from the production side, the optimal carryovers were computed with the same production as above and a non-stochastic demand equal to trend for North America.

| 1977 Income per Capita | Cumulative Probability Level for Carryovers | | | Cumulative Probability Level for Supply | | |
|---|---|---|---|---|---|---|
| | 0.5 | 0.75 | 0.95 | 0.5 | 0.75 | 0.95 |
| | (million tons) | | | | | |
| $3115 | 7 | 12 | 22 | 288 | 299 | 316 |
| $3461 | 10 | 16 | 28 | 290 | 302 | 320 |
| $3872 | 13 | 19 | 32 | 293 | 305 | 324 |

[c]See Appendix (Table 12.9) for demand functions.

supplies and prices of grain during the 1970s than during the 1950s and 1960s. This meant that more of their domestic instability was absorbed by international markets and less by internal market adjustments.

If the optimal carryover levels in Table 12.2 are to be compared to actual carryover levels, working stocks need to be added. We have estimated that working stocks of grain for North America are approximately 33 million tons.

The actual 1977 grain supply, including a carryin of 46 million tons (excluding working stocks), was 348 million tons. This would place the 1977 supply at a probability level of somewhat more than 0.95; in other words, 95 percent of the time it would be expected that the supply would be less than that amount. Assuming a per-capita income of approximately $3,500, the optimal carryover would have been approximately 57 million tons (including working stocks, 90 million tons). The actual carryover from the 1977 crop was 60 million tons (including working stocks, 93 million tons). But it should be noted that these are very high carryover levels and are expected less than one year out of twenty. Grain production in 1977 was some 23 million tons in excess of 1977 trend production, based on the log-linear trend from 1950 through 1976. If production had been at trend level in 1977, optimal 1977 carryover stocks would have been approximately 40 million tons (including working stocks, 73 million tons). Since 1978 North American grain production now also appears to be significantly above trend level for that year, it may well be that there has been a shift in the production curve not caught by our analysis.

My main point in presenting the results of our analysis of North American optimal grain reserves is to show that recent and current levels of grain reserves in North America are at or above the optimal level. In addition, given the fact that North America bears a large fraction of the world's variability in production and demand for grains, these results indicate that further increases in reserves will not occur in response to investment criteria but will instead be the result of political decisions related to price support levels in North America and, perhaps, in Australia.

Table 12.3 is included for two reasons. First, the optimal carryovers in Table 12.3 assume higher costs of storage than were used in Table 12.2. In Table 12.3 annual physical storage costs (in 1967 dollars) are $10.00 per ton compared to $7.50 per ton in Table 12.2 and an interest rate of 5 percent is assumed instead of 2 percent. It should be noted that these seemingly

# Grain Insurance, Reserves, and Trade 267

low rates of interest are real rates since all monetary variables are in terms of prices of constant purchasing power. Counting both storage and interest costs, the annual cost of holding a ton of grain in Table 12.3 is approximately $15.00 per ton compared to $9.50 in Table 12.2. As a result the optimal carryover levels in Table 12.3 are smaller than those in Table 12.2 by approximately 5 million tons for both the United States and North America at the 0.5 percent probability level. This is what one would expect since the gain from the last ton of grain stored must be greater when costs are higher.

Second, Footnote b to Table 12.3 gives an indication of the role of demand variability for the grain supply of North America upon the level of optimal carryovers. The optimal carryover levels in Footnote b assume that only production is stochastic; demand is stable though growing. At the 0.50 and 0.75 probability levels and the lower per-capita income levels, optimal carryovers when demand variability is ignored are only half as large as the carryovers when demand variability is included.

There are several sources of demand variability for North American grain: internal factors—business cycles, variations in livestock production, variability of production in importing and other exporting regions, and the policies of other nations. It is quite obvious from Table 12.3 that analyses of grain reserves, if such analyses are to serve as policy guides, must include a stochastic demand function.

We have not estimated the probability distribution of prices that would be generated by a system of optimal carryovers. Such calculations could be made and it is fairly obvious what they would show. There would be some small probability that prices could be double or treble the long-run expected price. This is inevitable given that optimal carryover levels are based on the expectation that marginal gains from storage will equal the marginal cost of storage. If there is a probability of 1 percent in any given year that the market price will be three times the expected (average) price of $100 per ton, the impact of this expectation, compared to a nil expectation of such a high price, would be to add less than $2 to the expected marginal gain from storing a ton of grain. Obviously stocks would be increased by a greater probability of such an event, but the increase in

268                                            D. Gale Johnson

stocks would be small. In Table 12.3 the costs of storage are
approximately $5.50 per ton greater than in Table 12.2 and
optimal carryovers are reduced by approximately 20 percent.
Therefore, it could be expected that an increase in the expected
marginal gain of a little less than $2 would increase optimal
carryover level by about 8 percent or about 2 million tons at
the 0.5 probability level for North America.

*A Grain Insurance Program*

The proposal for a grain insurance program is a simple one:
the United States, either alone or in cooperation with other
industrial countries, guarantees to each developing country
that in any year in which grain production declines more than
a given percentage of trend production that the shortfall in excess of that amount would be supplied. This would foster in
each developing country a high degree of stability in its domestic supply of grain and such stability could be achieved at a
relatively low cost to the donor nations. If the developing nations were willing and able to adopt a modest storage program
of their own, year-to-year variability in grain supplies could be
held to levels within 3 or 4 percent of trend production. Thus a
substantial degree of internal price stability could be achieved
at low cost for each developing country.

The selection of percentage shortfall from trend production
that would trigger the transfer of grain should reflect two considerations: the incentive for holding reserves in the developing countries and the effect of the insurance payments on the
output behavior of the producers in those countries. If the percentage is too low, say between 1 and 2 percent, there would
be no economic incentive for holding reserves and the magnitude of the grain transfers would be large enough to significantly
reduce the average expected return to local producers and thus
lower the rate of growth of domestic grain production. By a
process of trial and error, I have concluded that the most
appropriate criterion would be 6 percent—all production shortfalls in excess of 6 percent would be met.

However, as later comparisons will indicate, criteria of either
4 or 5 percent have rather modest effects upon the total payments under the insurance program and relatively little effect

*Grain Insurance, Reserves, and Trade* 269

upon optimal carryovers. One possibility would be to vary the criterion from country to country. The 4 percent criterion might be used for countries with very low per-capita incomes and relatively poor transportation and communication. In such countries it is quite possible that the response of prices to production variability is greater than in developing countries with somewhat higher per-capita incomes and better marketing systems.

The primary objective of the proposal is to assist the developing countries to hold year-to-year variations in grain consumption to a reasonable or acceptable level. In my opinion, this is the most meaningful definition of food security. The proposal should constitute the primary form of food aid provided by the countries that participate in the provision of grain insurance. If nothing else, I believe that the insurance feature of the proposal constitutes the most reasonable rationale for food aid to the developing countries.[10] The proposal provides a solution to an important problem confronting many developing countries: variability of food availability at times so extreme that significant hardship results. I know of no similarly important objective that has been met by most of the food aid that has been distributed over the past two decades.

The proposal is not put forward as a solution to the long-run objective of expanding per-capita food production and consumption in the developing countries. Neither this proposal nor any other form of food aid can make a significant contribution to the expansion of food production. But I am confident that the insurance proposal will not have significant negative effects upon the growth of food production and the same cannot be said about other methods of distributing food aid.

Table 12.4 presents estimates of the annual payments that would have been made under the insurance program for 1955 through 1973. The countries included in the estimates are all developing countries that produce more than a million tons of grain annually. Developing countries are defined to include all the countries of Latin America, Africa, and Asia excluding Japan, South Africa, Argentina, China, North Korea, and North Vietnam. The limitation of the analysis to countries producing more than a million tons of grain was done to limit data

270

Table 12.4

Insurance Payments To Developing Countries For Different Programs, 1955-1973

| Year | 6 percent | 5 percent | 4 percent |
|------|-----------|-----------|-----------|
| | (million tons) | | |
| 1955 | 2.2 | 2.4 | 2.8 |
| 1956 | 1.0 | 1.2 | 1.6 |
| 1957 | 4.5 | 5.8 | 7.3 |
| 1958 | 3.0 | 3.6 | 4.4 |
| 1959 | 2.8 | 3.1 | 3.4 |
| 1960 | 3.3 | 3.7 | 4.1 |
| 1961 | 2.9 | 3.2 | 3.6 |
| 1962 | 0.1 | 0.2 | 0.3 |
| 1963 | 2.1 | 2.4 | 2.7 |
| 1964 | 1.0 | 1.1 | 1.3 |
| 1965 | 8.1 | 9.3 | 10.5 |
| 1966 | 14.8 | 16.3 | 18.1 |
| 1967 | 2.2 | 2.5 | 2.8 |
| 1968 | 2.2 | 2.3 | 2.5 |
| 1969 | 0.6 | 0.9 | 1.2 |
| 1970 | 1.2 | 1.5 | 1.9 |
| 1971 | 3.6 | 4.4 | 4.9 |
| 1972 | 7.9 | 8.7 | 10.3 |
| 1973 | 13.4 | 14.5 | 15.7 |
| Total | 76.9 | 87.1 | 99.4 |

*Grain Insurance, Reserves, and Trade* 271

collection and processing and has little effect on the results. Some countries, such as Iran and Chile that no longer merit the classification of developing countries, are included if the concept of "developing countries" is taken to be synonymous with "low-income countries."

The average annual payment for the nineteen-year period would have been 4.0 million tons if the insurance payment covered all shortfalls in excess of 6 percent for each developing country producing more than 1.0 million tons. The largest payments would have been 14.8 million tons in 1966 and 13.4 million tons in 1973. The average annual payments under 5 percent and 4 percent programs would have been approximately 13 and 30 percent larger, respectively.

The grain insurance proposal requires reasonably accurate data on annual grain production for the current year and for enough prior years to permit the calculation of the trend level of production for the current year. The proposal does not require data on stocks held in the recipient countries.

The accuracy of data on grain production in many developing countries leaves something to be desired, to put it mildly. The existence of the insurance program could provide an incentive to a government to minimize its estimates of grain production in a given year in order to increase the grain actually transferred. Over time this practice would be self-defeating since estimates of trend production for future years would be affected by such underestimates. However, since many governments are short-lived, the self-correcting feature may not be of much value in some cases. It might be necessary for the insurance agency to have the right to obtain grain production estimates from an organization independent of both the developing country and the countries providing the grain. It should be noted that for most countries there will be time within any crop year to adjust and revise production estimates. The insurance payments would normally be spread out over the crop year and in most cases would not be required in the months immediately following the harvest as long as it was known that the shipments were to be forthcoming.

It should be recognized that there are populations in developing countries that rely on food products other than grains for a significant part of their caloric intake. The grain insurance proposal could be adapted to these circumstances and probably should be. It would be possible to translate manioc and potato production, for example, into grain equivalents and include such products in the production data. Unfortunately, the production data for such products are less reliable than for grains. In addition, some recognition should be given to the small populations that depend upon livestock products for a major source of calories. The malnutrition and deaths that occurred in the Sahel were due primarily to the devastation of the livestock herds and not to a reduction in grain production.

I have so far said nothing about the composition of the grain transfers under the insurance proposal. Obviously wheat would be the major component of the transfers. It dominates world trade in foodgrains. Obtaining corn and grain sorghum would not be difficult since adequate supplies would be available. Rice is the most difficult of the major grains to supply since only a small percentage of the total world supply is traded internationally and consumer preferences for rice vary considerably. However, both the United States and Japan could contribute substantial quantities of rice to a reserve to meet contingencies arising when rice production is adversely affected in some part of the world and a substitute grain, such as wheat, would be inadequate to replace all of the shortfall. Also, rice might be purchased when prices are low and used to build a special reserve. There are other grains that are primarily local in their production and consumption. Special consideration should be given to acquiring modest stocks of such grains to meet particular local production shortfalls.

## Some Illustrative Results

The remainder of this section consists of several tables that illustrate some of the effects of the grain insurance program upon optimal carryovers and stability of consumption. Table 12.4 above has presented the annual payments for three criteria for 1955 through 1973 while Table 12.1 gave the optimal carryovers for 1975 assuming a constant level of international trade in grains.

Table 12.5 repeats the calculations of optimal carryovers

273

Table 12.5

Optimal Carryover Levels For Selected Developing Countries And Regions,
1975, Alternative Insurance Programs In Effect

| Country or Region and Insurance Program | Probability Levels for Carryovers[a] | | |
|---|---|---|---|
| | 0.5 | 0.75 | 0.95 |
| | (million tons) | | |
| **A. 6 Percent** | | | |
| Burma | 0.1 | 0.3 | 0.7 |
| India | 1.5 | 3.5 | 7.5 |
| Indonesia | 0.7 | 1.5 | 2.9 |
| Pakistan-Bangladesh | 0.3 | 1.5 | 2.7 |
| Philippines | 0.0 | 0.1 | 0.3 |
| Thailand | 0.6 | 1.2 | 2.1 |
| Other Far East[b] | 0.3 | 0.7 | 1.5 |
| Africa[b] | 0.0 | 1.0 | 3.0 |
| Far East[b] | 2.0 | 5.0 | 10.0 |
| Latin America | 0.5 | 2.5 | 5.5 |
| Near East | 0.5 | 1.5 | 5.0 |
| All Developing Regions[b] | 2.0 | 6.0 | 14.0 |
| **B. 5 Percent** | | | |
| Burma | 0.0 | 0.2 | 0.7 |
| India | 1.0 | 2.5 | 7.0 |
| Indonesia | 0.5 | 1.3 | 2.7 |
| Pakistan-Bangladesh | 0.3 | 1.3 | 2.5 |
| Philippines | 0.0 | 0.1 | 0.3 |
| Thailand | 0.3 | 1.0 | 1.8 |
| Other Far East[b] | 0.2 | 0.6 | 1.5 |
| Africa[b] | 0.0 | 1.0 | 3.0 |
| Far East[b] | 2.0 | 5.0 | 9.0 |
| Latin America | 0.5 | 2.5 | 5.0 |
| Near East | 0.5 | 1.5 | 5.0 |
| All Developing Regions[b] | 0.0 | 6.0 | 13.5 |
| **C. 4 Percent** | | | |
| Burma | 0.0 | 0.2 | 0.6 |
| India | 0.5 | 2.5 | 6.0 |
| Indonesia | 0.5 | 1.1 | 2.6 |
| Pakistan-Bangladesh | 0.2 | 1.0 | 2.2 |
| Philippines | 0.0 | 0.0 | 0.2 |
| Thailand | 0.3 | 0.8 | 1.8 |
| Other Far East[b] | 0.0 | 0.6 | 1.3 |
| Africa[b] | 0.0 | 1.0 | 3.0 |
| Far East[b] | 1.0 | 4.0 | 8.0 |
| Latin America | 0.5 | 2.0 | 4.5 |
| Near East | 0.0 | 1.5 | 4.5 |
| All Developing Regions[b] | 0.0 | 3.5 | 12.0 |

[a]Price elasticity of demand equals -0.1.
[b]Excludes China.

presented in Table 12.1 but under the assumption that the grain insurance program was in effect and shows the optimal carryovers for each of three criteria. A comparison of the results given in Tables 12.1 and 12.5 indicates that the insurance program, given any of the criteria for making payments, would substantially reduce optimal carryover levels. The results are most striking for the six individual countries in the Far East. For India the optimal carryover level at the 0.5 probability level would be reduced from 6.5 million tons to 1.5, 1.0, and 0.5 million tons, respectively, for the 6, 5, and 4 percent insurance criteria. For Pakistan-Bangladesh the relative reduction in optimal carryovers would be 80 percent or more. In the case of Indonesia the relative effect of the insurance program on optimal carryovers would be relatively small (50 to 70 percent) due to the characteristics of the probability distribution of production.

Tables 12.6, 12.7, and 12.8 provide estimates of optimal carryovers for India and Africa with no insurance program, a 6 percent program, and a 4 percent program. In these tables we have used only the information that would be available at the time carryover decisions were made. Thus the optimal carryover for 1968 for India reflects the production variability experienced from 1948 through 1967. It was assumed for India that there was no carryover at the end of the 1967 marketing year since 1965 and 1966 were poor crop years and 1967 grain production was somewhat below trend level. For Africa a beginning carryover of 1.0 million tons was assumed.

Table 12.6, which assumes no insurance program, indicates that for India with two relatively poor crop years since 1967 (1972 and 1974) an optimal carryover program would have resulted in relatively small deviations of available supply around the trend. The available supply in 1972 would have been almost exactly at the trend level, while in 1974 with production approximately 11 percent below trend, consumption would have been 4.2 million tons or approximately 4.3 percent below trend. With a price elasticity of −0.1 grain prices in 1974 would have been approximately 40 percent above those in 1973. Added imports of 2 million tons of grain would have held the price increase to approximately 20 percent.

Table 12.6

Effects Of Carryover Program On Available Supply Based On Actual Production, India And Africa, 1968-1975

| Year | Actual Production | Optimal Carryover | Available Supply | Trend |
|------|-------------------|-------------------|------------------|-------|
| | | (million tons) | | |
| | | India | | |
| 1968 | 81.6 | 3.0 | 78.6 | 80.7 |
| 1969 | 85.1 | 5.0 | 83.1 | 83.2 |
| 1970 | 91.7 | 10.0 | 86.7 | 85.8 |
| 1971 | 90.2 | 10.0 | 90.2 | 88.5 |
| 1972 | 86.6 | 5.5 | 91.1 | 91.2 |
| 1973 | 95.4 | 7.0 | 93.9 | 94.0 |
| 1974 | 86.7 | 1.0 | 92.7 | 96.9 |
| 1975 | | | | 99.9 |

at probability level

$$\text{Carryover} < \frac{0.5}{4.0} \quad \frac{0.75}{4.5} \quad \frac{0.95}{6.5}$$

| Year | Actual Production | Optimal Carryover | Available Supply | Trend |
|------|-------------------|-------------------|------------------|-------|
| | | Africa | | |
| 1967 | | (1.0) | | |
| 1968 | 40.5 | 2.5 | 39.0 | 38.2 |
| 1969 | 41.3 | 3.0 | 40.8 | 39.3 |
| 1970 | 40.2 | 2.0 | 41.2 | 40.4 |
| 1971 | 40.9 | 1.0 | 41.9 | 41.5 |
| 1972 | 44.4 | 2.0 | 43.4 | 42.7 |
| 1973 | 37.1 | 0.0 | 39.1 | 43.9 |
| 1974 | 42.2 | 0.0 | 42.2 | 45.1 |
| 1975 | | | | 46.4 |

at probability level

$$\text{Carryover} < \frac{0.5}{1.0} \quad \frac{0.75}{1.5} \quad \frac{0.95}{3.0}$$

Table 12.7

Effects Of Carryover Program On Available Supply Based On Actual Production, 6 Percent Insurance Policy, India And Africa, 1968-1975

| Year | Actual Production | Optimal Carryover | Insurance Payment | Available Supply |
|------|-------------------|-------------------|-------------------|------------------|
| | | (million tons) | | |
| | | India | | |
| 1968 | 81.6 | 0.5 | 0.0 | 81.1 |
| 1969 | 85.1 | 1.5 | 0.0 | 84.1 |
| 1970 | 91.7 | 5.0 | 0.0 | 88.2 |
| 1971 | 90.2 | 4.0 | 0.0 | 91.2 |
| 1972 | 86.6 | 0.0 | 0.0 | 90.2 |
| 1973 | 95.4 | 1.0 | 0.0 | 94.4 |
| 1974 | 86.7 | 0.0 | 4.3 | 92.0 |
| 1975 | | | | |

at probability levels

$$\text{Carryover} < \frac{0.5}{1.0} \quad \frac{0.75}{2.0} \quad \frac{0.95}{4.0}$$

| Year | Actual Production | Optimal Carryover | Insurance Payment | Available Supply |
|------|-------------------|-------------------|-------------------|------------------|
| | | Africa | | |
| 1968 | 40.5 | 2.5 | 0.0 | 39.5 |
| 1969 | 41.3 | 3.0 | 0.0 | 40.8 |
| 1970 | 40.2 | 2.0 | 0.0 | 41.2 |
| 1971 | 40.9 | 1.0 | 0.0 | 41.9 |
| 1972 | 44.4 | 2.0 | 0.0 | 43.4 |
| 1973 | 37.1 | 0.0 | 4.2 | 43.3 |
| 1974 | 42.2 | 0.0 | 1.2 | 43.4 |
| 1975 | | | | |

at probability level

$$\text{Carryover} < \frac{0.5}{0.5} \quad \frac{0.75}{1.0} \quad \frac{0.95}{2.0}$$

# 276 D. Gale Johnson

Table 12.8

Effects Of Carryover Program On Available Supply Based On Actual Production, 4 Percent Insurance Policy, India And Africa, 1968-1975

| Year | Actual Production | Optimal Carryover | Insurance Payment | Available Supply |
|------|------|------|------|------|
| | | (million tons) | | |
| | | India | | |
| 1968 | 81.6 | 1.0 | 0.0 | 80.6 |
| 1969 | 85.1 | 1.0 | 0.0 | 85.1 |
| 1970 | 91.7 | 4.0 | 0.0 | 88.7 |
| 1971 | 90.2 | 3.0 | 0.0 | 91.2 |
| 1972 | 86.6 | 0.0 | 0.7 | 90.3 |
| 1973 | 95.4 | 0.0 | 0.0 | 95.4 |
| 1974 | 86.7 | 0.0 | 6.4 | 93.1 |
| 1975 | | at probability levels | | |

Carryover < $\frac{0.5}{1.0}$ $\frac{0.75}{2.0}$ $\frac{0.95}{4.0}$

| | | Africa | | |
|------|------|------|------|------|
| 1968 | 40.5 | 2.0 | 0.0 | 39.5 |
| 1969 | 41.3 | 2.0 | 0.0 | 41.3 |
| 1970 | 40.2 | 1.0 | 0.0 | 41.2 |
| 1971 | 40.9 | 0.0 | 0.0 | 41.9 |
| 1972 | 44.4 | 1.0 | 0.0 | 43.4 |
| 1973 | 37.1 | 0.0 | 5.0 | 43.1 |
| 1974 | 42.2 | 0.0 | 1.0 | 43.2 |
| 1975 | | at probability level | | |

Carryover < $\frac{0.5}{0.5}$ $\frac{0.75}{1.0}$ $\frac{0.95}{2.0}$

The reader may be somewhat surprised to discover that for India in 1974 the 6 percent insurance program would not have provided as high a level of grain availability as did the optimal grain carryover without an insurance program (Table 12.7). The insurance program would have encouraged higher levels of consumption from 1969 through 1973 and very low levels of carryover at the end of 1973. Obviously the results for 1974 are due to the "accidents" of the production levels in the years immediately before 1974. The 4 percent program would have provided for a somewhat higher level of available supply in 1974.

The bottom part of each table gives similar calculations for

*Grain Insurance, Reserves, and Trade* 277

Africa. In this case there are no surprises—the insurance program would have provided increased stability of available supplies. The stability of available supply for Africa would have been greater with any one of the three insurance programs than with optimal carryovers alone. The major difference would have been in 1973 when an optimal carryover program alone would have resulted in available supply of 4.8 million tons below trend; this would have been a shortfall of 11 percent. With the 6 percent insurance program the shortfall below the trend would have been only 0.6 million tons; with a 4 percent program the shortfall would have been 0.2 million tons.

For the seven-year period the 6 percent insurance program would have reduced total carryovers in India to 12.0 million ton-years from 41.5 million ton-years without the insurance program. The savings in interest and storage costs would have been approximately $450 million if the price of grain were $150 per ton. This saving would have required the delivery of 4.3 million tons of grain with a value of $650 million. With the 4 percent insurance program the savings on holding carryovers would be increased, but not by as much as the increased value of the delivered grain. The 4 percent insurance program would have reduced the total ton-years of carryovers to 9 million tons and payments would have been increased by 2.9 million tons. However, over the seven-year period grain consumption in India would have been increased by approximately the amount of the payment under the insurance program and this needs to be considered in any cost-benefit calculation.

For Africa the 6 percent insurance program would not have reduced the optimal carryover by very much since production variability for the years prior to 1973 implied a very low probability of a production shortfall equal to or greater than 6 percent. Only if the 4 percent insurance program were in effect would there have been any significant reduction in optimal carryover levels.

The illustrations presented here indicate that if the developing nations provided for optimal carryovers within the framework of an insurance program that covered all grain production shortfalls from trend in excess of 6 percent, grain consumption variability would be held to low and manageable levels. By low

278  D. Gale Johnson

and manageable levels I mean that in most years (nine out of ten, approximately), and in almost all developing countries, negative deviations of consumption from trend would be held to 3 percent or less. This could be achieved by holding relatively modest levels of carryover stocks in the developing countries of the order of 4 million tons.

It might be noted that with the insurance program in effect some developing countries might well find it more economical to use trade to offset the remaining consumption variability rather than to hold grain carryovers. This probably will be true when the costs of holding reserves in a developing country are substantially above such costs in the major exporting countries, though other factors such as probability distributions of international grain prices and freight rates need to be taken into account.

### Grain Reserves and the Insurance Proposal

Would grain reserves be required to augment or support the grain insurance proposal? Here I refer to reserves that might be held in the donor countries rather than in the recipient countries. In a world in which governments interfered relatively little with market prices the answer would be that a special or separate reserve would not be required because the anticipated effect of the insurance program upon the demand for grain would be fully reflected in the storage decisions made by private agencies. However, we do not live in a world in which governments interfere relatively little with market prices (in the case of grain, the interferences seem designed to maximize instability in international markets). Consequently, if the insurance program had been in operation in 1973 with the expectation that the 13 million tons would be required under the 6 percent criterion, the market price increase required to provide the grain would probably have been so great as to result in a failure to deliver the full amount.

Consequently it would be desirable to have a separate grain reserve of sufficient size to meet a substantial fraction of the insurance payments in excess of the average annual level of such payments. Unfortunately this would add to the cost of the insurance proposal, but it may be required if the commitments of the donor countries are to be believed.

*Grain Insurance, Reserves, and Trade* 279

### Insurance Quantities and Not Price

The grain insurance proposal is designed to cover only one contingency, namely that of quantities required to offset grain production shortfalls. Other proposals, including those presented in this book, include variations in prices or the import bill and thus cover more than quantity variations. My decision to restrict the insurance to quantity variability rests on the assumption that there is a high correlation among the prices of agricultural products imported and exported by the developing countries. Thus when the prices of imported grain are high, the prices of other agricultural products will be high. Since, on balance, the developing countries are net exporters of agricultural products, a high import bill will be offset by an increase in the value of exports of agricultural products.[11]

These presumptions, which were based upon somewhat impressionistic comparisons of the price indexes of developing country agricultural exports and imports and the 1973–1975 changes in export earnings and import costs of agricultural products, are supported by the results presented by Valdés and Konandreas in Table 2.5 of Chapter 2. For the period from 1961 through 1976 they found that only a quarter of the annual variability in the food import bills of 24 developing countries was due to price variations. The remaining variability was due to quantity variations.[12]

It is true that if a country imports a large fraction of its grain and has an excess of the value of agricultural imports over agricultural exports, that country might not gain much added security from the grain insurance proposal. But of the 31 developing countries referred to earlier, there were but five countries during 1973–1975 that had an excess of agricultural imports over agricultural exports of more than 10 percent: these countries were Bangladesh, Egypt, Korea, Syria, and Chile. For Egypt the excess was only 12 percent and the last three countries in the list are probably properly considered to be middle-income developing countries. Thus most developing countries, at least those with populations of 7 million or more, are likely to achieve significant food security if only quantity variations are taken into account.

## Benefits of the Insurance Proposal

If it were not for the existence of civil strife and war, I believe it is now possible to essentially eliminate all deaths due to the direct effects of food production variability. If achieved, this would be a remarkable accomplishment, one that could not have been imagined as recently as the beginning of this century or even as recently as a quarter century ago.

This important objective cannot be reached solely through the efforts of the United States and other high-income countries. It requires the cooperation of the governments of the developing countries. Specifically, it requires greater investment by developing countries in crop forecasts during growing seasons and the willingness to participate in early warning efforts of actual or possible crop failures. Although communication difficulties can now be overcome at modest cost, there are still some areas where transport is slow and costly. Where transport facilities are limited, it is essential, if hardship due to weather hazards is to be minimized, that early warning be obtained of pending difficulties. Such advance warning would permit preparations for grain transfer if required.

The grain insurance proposal does not require, except in cases of extreme crop disasters, that the grain be transferred immediately after the harvest. It *is* essential that there be full confidence that the grain would arrive in sufficient time during the marketing year so that supplies can be rationed by the market on a relatively even basis throughout the year. A production shortfall of 10 percent, for example, means that local or domestic supplies are adequate for meeting consumption requirements for as many as six months of the year if it is certain that the insurance payment will be available by the end of the sixth month. The period of adequate supplies from domestic sources is not as long as might be inferred from a production shortfall of 10 percent. The reason is that local regions suffering the largest production shortfalls will reduce their outshipments of grain. To do otherwise means that grain would later have to be transported back into the local regions with the severest production shortfalls.

It was pointed out at the Conference that the programs of

Grain Insurance, Reserves, and Trade    281

some governments may require that the insurance payments actually arrive in a country even earlier. Such need may arise if a government procures substantial quantities of grain, either for its urban population or for particular disadvantaged or low-income groups as done in Pakistan and India. If a government acquires a relatively small percentage of the total supply, say 10 percent, the production shortfall could approach the amount of grain procured in an average year. In such instances, an early receipt of the insurance payments would .reduce domestic procurements and prevent transfers back to the producing regions later in the year.

Although domestic storage would solve this difficulty, the insurance program would be able to assist most adequately if additional resources were devoted to improving the accuracy of forecasts of crop production. If this were done, plans could be made for shipments even before the harvest were completed. Certain costs would be incurred if it later turned out that payments were not required. But these costs could be considered as a reasonable part of foreign economic assistance by the participating countries.

My statement that it is now possible to prevent nearly all deaths and most of the hardships caused by production shortfalls assumes that governments will use part of the insurance payment to directly benefit those agricultural producers whose output is adversely affected. Unless this is done, limiting price increases in the national market could reduce the average incomes of many food producers, especially of those suffering a shortfall. Food production shortfalls can be very great in limited areas of a country and hardship—perhaps even starvation—could be due to loss of income suffered by agricultural producers. If the affected area is relatively small, the probability is substantial that the rural population will make sufficient adjustments to prevent starvation.[13]

The grain insurance proposal is not intended as a panacea or solution to long-run problems of food insufficiency. The proposal would assist in minimizing hardship from fluctuations in food production in low-income countries. It is important that the great progress the world has made in this century in reducing famine be continued. The grain insurance proposal, ac-

# 282                                    D. Gale Johnson

companied by greater emphasis on crop forecasts and early warning systems and further improvements in communication and transportation, would contribute to that important end.


## Notes

Some of the research for this paper was supported by grants to the University of Chicago by the National Science Foundation (Grant No. 51A75-13889) and the Rockefeller Foundation. The opinions and views expressed in this paper are those of the author and do not necessarily reflect the views of the National Science Foundation or the Rockefeller Foundation. I wish to acknowledge the important contributions of Daniel Sumner, Chung Ming Wong and Gabrielle Brenner to the research on which this paper is based.

This paper draws heavily upon the following articles by the author: Johnson and Sumner (1976), Johnson (1978a), Johnson (1978b), and Johnson (1978c).

1. See "Famine" in the *Encyclopedia Britannica*, 1973 edition. The article is not in the most recent revision.

2. These estimates are derived from world grain production estimates of the USDA. The deviations are estimated from a linear trend line and thus may underestimate the absolute magnitude of the negative deviations and overestimate the positive deviations. However, it is highly unlikely that the maximum negative deviation from trend exceeded 4 percent. Due to variations in stocks of grains, the deviations of world grain consumption from trend levels were smaller than for grain production.

3. For a presentation of the theory, empirical assumptions and some estimates of reserves, see Johnson and Sumner (1976).

4. Put another way, the assumption is that the change in price for the grain from the time the grain is added to the reserve to when it is removed from the reserve equals the cost of holding the grain for the period of time.

5. North America may be an exception due to the great importance of net exports in total use of grain produced. Our research is now concentrating on the effects of variability of export demand on the optimal size of reserves.

6. The optimal carryover levels for 1975 indicated for that year are not meant to imply carryover levels for a specific year. The carryover levels given are based on the distribution of possible supplies (carryin and production) at the beginning of a year. In an actual case the available supply would be known at the beginning of the year and the optimal carryover level could be estimated. All references are to metric tons.

# Grain Insurance, Reserves, and Trade 283

7. Perhaps a word of explanation is in order about the implications of estimates of nil or low optimum stocks to price stability and food security. If optimal carryover levels are nil half the time, this means there is a very small probability that the price increase from one year to the next is expected to exceed the cost of storage. With grain at $100 per ton this would mean that price increases from one year to the next are likely to be less than 12.5 percent in real terms. As reserves become larger the probability of price increases being greater than the marginal costs or storage for one year increases. However, when the optimal reserves for the world are equal to or less than 1.5 percent of world production in 19 years out of 20, price variability would be held to plus or minus 25 percent with a very high degree of probability.

8. The conclusion that fixed ad valorem tariffs do not contribute to international price instability is exactly correct only if the grain demand function has a constant elasticity. With other types of demand functions the conclusion would be affected somewhat.

9. For example, a policy change made in the Soviet Union, probably in 1971, resulted in both higher average grain imports and larger variance of imports. The net effect of this policy change, induced by the objective of expanding livestock production, was to increase the variability of grain demand in international trade.

10. I do not mean to imply that the insurance program should be the only form of food aid but only that it should be the primary form. There are natural disasters, such as the earthquake in Guatemala, that can be partially alleviated by food aid. And some food aid can be effectively utilized in particular development projects or in special nutrition programs. By being "effectively utilized" I mean that the food aid would approximate the effectiveness of an unrestricted cash transfer. It should be noted, for those who believe more food aid is appropriate than is implied by the previous sentences, that the grain insurance program has an advantage in that it would permit more effective planning of food aid for objectives other than national food security. This would be true for both the recipient and donor countries. If food aid is considered desirable as support for rural development or for a significant expansion of the available food supply, these forms of aid could be planned in advance and for a significant period of time without fear of a major disruption due to grain production shortfalls.

11. See Johnson (1978d, pp. 199–201, especially Table 1). Of the 31 developing countries with populations of 7 million or more, the value of agricultural exports in 1973–1975 exceeded the value of agricultural imports by $11.6 billion or by almost 100 percent. Only four countries had an excess of agricultural imports over exports during 1969–1971 and only eight countries during 1973–1975. For the 31 countries the annual average value of the excess of agricultural exports over imports increased by

284          D. Gale Johnson

$4.3 billion from 1969-1971 to 1973-1975.
12. See Valdés and Konandreas, Chapter 2 of this volume. Goreux's chapter (Chapter 14) supports the view that there are significant intercorrelations between the prices of imports and exports of developing countries and that these intercorrelations tend to provide substantial price insurance for such countries.
13. I especially commend a remarkable article by David M. Morris (1974). He provides an excellent analysis of the means used by Indian farmers to adjust to famine conditions, especially in areas subject to a high probability of drought. These range from choice of crops, storage of water, accumulation of gold and silver (often in the form of jewelry), to migration. Morris quite rightly points out that great care must be exercised in designing relief efforts for areas subject to periodic rain deficiency in order that the local mechanisms designed to preserve life and activity not be destroyed.

## References

Johnson, D. Gale. *World Food Problems and Prospects*. Washington, D.C.: American Enterprise Institute, 1975a. Chapter 3.
___. "World Agriculture Commodity Policy and Price Variability." *American Journal of Agricultural Economics* 57, no. 5 (1975b):823-828.
___. "International Food Security: Issues and Alternatives." In *International Food Policy Issues, A Proceedings*, Foreign Agricultural Economics Report No. 143. Washington, D.C.: Economic Research Service. U.S. Department of Agriculture, January 1978a.
___. "World Food Supply and Demand: How They Can be Linked—Potential Role of Humanitarian Efforts." Presented at a symposium sponsored by the Federal Reserve Bank of Kansas City, World Agricultural Trade: The Potential for Growth, May 18-19, 1978b.
___. "Estimating Appropriate Levels of Grain Reserves for the United States: A Research Report." Office of Agricultural Economic Research, The University of Chicago, Paper No. 77, revised. February 10, 1978c.
___. "International Prices and Trade in Reducing Distortions of Incentives." In T. W. Schultz, ed., *Distortions of Agricultural Incentives*. Bloomington: Indiana University Press, 1978d.
Johnson, D. Gale, and Daniel Sumner. "An Optimization Approach to Grain Reserves for Developing Countries." *Analyses of Grain Reserves, A Proceeding*, compiled by David J. Eaton and W. Scott Steele, U.S. Department of Agriculture, Economic Research Service Report No. 634, August 1976, pp. 56-76.
Johnson, Paul; Thomas Grennes; and Marie Thursby. "Devaluation, Foreign

Trade Controls and Domestic Wheat Prices." *American Journal of Agricultural Economics* 59, no. 4 (November 1977):619–627.

Morris, David M. "What is Famine?" *Economic and Political Weekly* 9, no. 44 (November 1974):1855–1864. New Delhi.

Shei, Shun-Yi, and Robert L. Thompson. "The Impact of Trade Restrictions on Price Stability in the World Wheat Market." *American Journal of Agricultural Economics* 59, no. 4 (November 1977):628–638.

# APPENDIX

Table 12.9

Estimates Of Total Demand Functions, Log Linear Form

| Equation | Country | | Constant Term (C) | ln $Inc_t$ | ln $P_t$ | t | Observation Years | Instrumental Variables |
|---|---|---|---|---|---|---|---|---|
| II.a.1 | United States | | 11.5238 [a] (4.23) $R^2$ = 0.89 | 0.1066 (0.29) D.W. = 1.49 | -0.1286 (1.68) | 0.0184 (2.09) | 1950 to 1975 | ln (carryover-stocks) |
| II.a.2 | Canada | | -10.7161 (1.75) $R^2$ = 0.68 | 2.25 (3.12) D.W. = 1.6 | 0.451 (1.45) | -0.0307 (1.50) | 1951 to 1972 | Carryover Stocks |
| II.a.3 | North America | | 10.0831 (4.04) $R^2$ = 0.9 | 0.2736 (0.80) D.W. = 1.59 | -0.0829 (1.22) | 0.01483 (1.81) | 1950 to 1975 | ln (carryover-stocks) |
| II.a.4 | Australia | a) | 8.85 (3.59) $R^2$ = 0.36 | | -0.340 (1.68) D.W. = 2.24 | 0.0416 (3.17) | 1961 to 1974 | Price of Wool |
| | | b)[b] | 6.56 (3.8) $R^2$ = 0.65 | | -0.1826 (1.32) D.W. = 2.6 | 0.0445 (4.31) | 1961 to 1974 | ln (price of wool) |

a/ t-statistics in parenthesis.

b/ For this estimate, we introduced a dummy variable whose value is 1 in 1972, when the Russians entered the market for the first time, and 0 elsewhere.

# 13
# Responsiveness of Food Aid to Variable Import Requirements

*Barbara Huddleston*

Since 1954, when the U.S. Congress enacted the Agricultural Trade and Development and Assistance Act (PL480), supply availability and policy considerations in the United States have dominated the international food aid picture. Although the role of other donors has become increasingly important during the past decade, on average the United States still provides around two-thirds of the total amount of cereals food aid. Many of the principles discussed in this chapter pertain regardless of which countries are the major donors. However, the United States would play a crucial part in any international consideration of the responsiveness of food aid to variable food security requirements because of its prominence as a source of supply. The special significance of the following analysis for U.S. food aid policy is thus developed explicitly where it seemed important to do so. Throughout this chapter, discussion is limited to cereals food aid, since cereals are the primary commodity required to offset periodic harvest failures in developing countries.

## Food Aid Convention and International Emergency Food Reserve

In 1967 a Food Aid Convention was attached to the new International Wheat Agreement. This convention ensured that a certain minimum flow of cereals food aid would be made available through bilateral food aid programs, regardless of the supply situation. It was thought that ensuring a minimum flow would provide for the food security needs of developing countries when markets tightened but the 4.2 million ton minimum that was in force during the crisis years of 1972–1974 did not prove adequate, and the World Food Conference, the World Food Council, and the FAO have all endorsed a higher minimum of 10 million tons.

The proposed increase in the minimum level of cereals food aid does provide more assurance that food aid supplies will be adequate, even in years when supply availability is tight. But as food security requirements are by nature variable, and as they are likely to be greatest in years when food aid flows drop close to the internationally agreed minimum, a flat minimum commitment by itself will not be enough to ensure that food security needs are met.

Without special assistance, many low-income countries must make a difficult choice in years of poor harvest and/or high world prices. Yet only one initiative to improve the responsiveness of food aid flows to variable recipient requirements has thus far met with international acceptance. This was the creation of the 500,000-ton International Emergency Food Reserve (IEFR) under the auspices of the World Food Programme (WFP), under which donor countries pledge in advance to make grain available when the WFP alerts them that such aid is necessary to avert starvation in the face of nonrecurring natural disasters or wars.

Although famine relief efforts will clearly require priority attention for some years to come, the kind of food aid that is given as general balance of payments support also needs to vary in amount from year to year in accordance with fluctuations in a country's capacity to supply its consumption requirements from domestic resources. Although such food aid has been variable, the primary considerations in the past have been supply availability and political objectives in donor countries rather than recipient country requirements.

### Food Aid Flows and the Probable Magnitude of Food Security Requirements

What is the line between localized calamities that require emergency relief and generalized production shortfalls and high

*Food Aid and Variable Import Requirements* 289

market prices that require food security assistance? Several estimates have by now become available that suggest the orders of magnitude involved. Sarris, Abbott, and Taylor (1979, p. 192) suggest, for example, that for the 45 countries identified by the UN as "most severely affected" by the oil price increases and recession of 1974-1975, an annual flow of 1 million metric tons would meet emergency requirements in most years. This rather crude estimate is substantiated by FAO's 1978 assessment of food aid requirements, in which countries accounting for over three fourths of total emergency and other nonproject food aid in 1976/77 indicated that "about 80 percent of the aid was absorbed in 'variable' uses to meet needs which may vary greatly in intensity from year to year." Of this, 73 percent of total aid in cereals was used to maintain current consumption levels in the face of domestic crop shortfalls, and 7 percent was used in emergency situations due to natural disasters or political upheavals. If applied to all aid-receiving countries in that year, these percentages give 5.3 and 0.5 million tons as the amounts provided to all developing countries to give balance-of-payments relief and cover emergency needs. FAO goes on to estimate that emergency relief requirements will continue to range from half a million to a million tons a year, but makes no attempt to quantify the amount required for balance-of-payments relief, noting simply that in years of critical crop shortages the emergency element would need to be substantially larger, and that potential food aid requirements for creating national food reserves in developing countries have not been taken into account (World Food Programme, 1978, pp. 15 and 21).

Another independent estimate of the tonnages required to offset domestic crop shortfalls is contained in the chapter by D. Gale Johnson (Chapter 12) in this book. Johnson's results, which estimate the tonnages required to meet production shortfalls greater than 5 percent below trend for all developing countries producing more than a million tons of grain annually, are presented in Table 13.1 along with the results obtained by Huddleston and Konandreas (Chapter 11 in this book), which also use a 5 percent production shortfall trigger but impose downward consumption adjustments and an additional payments burden before relief is provided.

Table 13.1   Insurance Payments to Developing Countries for Different Programs,
Cereal Food Aid, Actual and Food Security Imports

| Year | | Johnson 5 percent shortfall rule | IFPRI 5 percent short-fall/130 percent cost overrun rule | Cereal food aid | Actual imports | Food security imports[a/] |
|---|---|---|---|---|---|---|
| | | (million metric tons) | | (thousand metric tons) | | |
| 1955 | | 2.4 | | | | |
| 1956 | | 1.2 | | | | |
| 1957 | | 5.8 | | | | |
| 1958 | | 3.6 | | | | |
| 1959 | | 3.1 | | | | |
| 1960 | | 3.7 | | | | |
| 1961 | | 3.2 | | | | |
| 1962 | | 0.2 | | | | |
| 1963 | | 2.4 | | | | |
| 1964 | | 1.1 | | | | |
| 1965 | | 9.3 | | | | |
| 1966 | | 16.3 | | | | |
| 1967 | | 2.5 | | | | |
| 1968 | | 2.3 | | | | |
| 1969 | | 0.9 | | | | |
| 1970 | | 1.5 | | | | |
| 1971 | (1970/71) | 4.4 | 0.6 | 8,154 | 29,909 | 22,840 |
| 1972 | (1971/72) | 8.7 | 1.2 | 7,947 | 32,753 | 30,950 |
| 1973 | (1972/73) | 14.5 | 6.8 | 5,643 | 35,564 | 39,823 |
| | (1973/74) | | 9.5 | 3,681 | 41,146 | 36,753 |
| | (1974/75) | | 3.1 | 5,865 | 45,094 | 46,263 |
| | (1975/76) | | 1.5 | 4,017 | 45,944 | 36,893 |
| Total | | | 22.7 | 35,307 | 230,410 | 213,522 |

a/  Food security imports equal trend consumption ($\overline{C}$) minus actual production ($P_a$) for all developing countries in which $P_a < \overline{C}$.

# Food Aid and Variable Import Requirements 291

Although Johnson's numbers are higher than IFPRI's because fewer constraints are imposed, both approaches clearly show the difference in the amount of compensation required in normal years and the considerably larger amount required in those occasional years when production shortfalls are relatively severe and widespread. Johnson shows a range of 1 to 4 million tons as covering food security requirements roughly 50 percent of the time. But in just four of the nineteen years observed, the amounts required come to between 9 and 16 million tons, accounting for nearly half of the total over the entire period. IFPRI's results show an even greater disparity, with the grain equivalent of the food security payments in the two high-price years 1972/73 and 1973/74 amounting to nearly 75 percent of the total over the six years 1970/71-1975/76. Looking to the future, IFPRI's work shows that on average about 4.7 million tons or less per year could be expected to satisfy the requirements called for by its approach for the period 1978-1982.[1] There would be about a 25 percent chance that larger amounts would be needed, however, and these amounts could be quite high in any given year.

In Chapter 2 of this volume, Valdés and Konandreas discuss the volume and value of food security imports for 67 developing countries for the period 1961-1976. They do not break down their results by year, although they do conclude that under the more liberal of their two decision rules, the difference between the total volume of food imports required to maintain trend consumption in 1976 and the trend value of actual imports for that year would have amounted to 11.1 million tons. Their approach makes no downward adjustment in consumption in shortfall years. Also in estimating the volume of food security requirements, they make no adjustment for the financing of a portion of this requirement by the country itself, although they do impose this constraint when estimating the potential cost of a food security scheme. Thus, if worked out in unaltered form, the yearly requirements implied by their approach would probably be considerably higher than those presented in the other two chapters, and would overestimate the annual volumes that the international community could reasonably be expected to provide.

In working out their analysis of the variation of consumption around trend, Valdés and Konandreas bring out another point that bears noting, however. They find that the consumption of major staples in their study countries displays a high positive correlation with production, implying that imports have in general not been used to offset production shortfalls. This finding is borne out by the yearly data shown in Table 13.2, but it should not be interpreted to mean that countries saved foreign exchange as a result of their lack of immediate import response to production shortfalls. In fact, the data for the period 1970/71 through 1975/76 show that in the aggregate, the sum of actual cereal imports of developing countries exceeded by a considerable amount the imports required to make up the difference between trend consumption and actual production. The numbers suggest that what may have happened is that countries tended to import in excess of trend requirements in years of low world prices and good domestic harvests at the beginning and end of the period, but that in 1972/73 when requirements rose sharply and prices were starting up, countries chose to draw down stocks rather than increase imports significantly. In the following year when prices were substantially higher, requirements were lower, but countries apparently imported more than they needed in order to rebuild stocks. The pattern of import policies that these numbers reflect suggests that not only did a number of countries fail to maintain trend consumption in the face of domestic production shortfalls, but they simultaneously incurred excessively high foreign exchange bills for their food imports over the six-year period. This double-barreled adverse effect of food insecurity makes the rationalization of the international response all the more important.

Although not all countries include food aid in their recorded imports, most of the larger shipments probably are included, so that the cost implications of the actual import data can be reduced somewhat on that account. Nevertheless, the aggregate data show that the lack of correspondence between food aid flows and food security import requirements clearly aggravated the cost burden of actual imports in high-price years.

Although it is frequently assumed that supply availability in donor countries, particularly in the United States, explains the

*Food Aid and Variable Import Requirements* 293

changes in magnitude of food aid flows from one time period to another, regression analysis shows world market price and aggregate developing country demand to be far more significant than supply variables.[2] Supply variables might prove to be more significant if lagged relationships were introduced, but this finding is nevertheless consistent with the U.S. practice of determining actual quantities of food aid shipments in accordance with the dollar amounts appropriated annually for PL480 rather than the supply availability determination that the Secretary of Agriculture makes at the beginning of each marketing year. Thus, it seems fair to suggest that in the aggregate food aid is quite responsive to production fluctuations in developing countries except when constrained by tight world markets and high prices.

On a country-by-country basis, there are only a few cases in which food aid flows actually matched the variable requirement represented by the hypothetical compensation for which IFPRI estimated a country to be eligible in a given year during the historical period 1970/71-1975/76.[3] Including cases in which food aid was responsive but not adequate in amount, and cases in which food aid was responsive in some but not all years, only 16 of the 71 countries could look to food aid for security. In far more cases the total food aid flow for the six-year period roughly matched the total compensation for which a country was eligible according to IFPRI's rules, even though it was poorly distributed in relation to fluctuations in yearly requirements (Table 13.2). A few large countries received substantially more food aid than needed to meet variable requirements; thus, the aggregate food aid flow to this group of countries amounted to 35 million tons of cereals, whereas the aggregate compensation required amounted to about 23 million tons.

These figures indicate that better management of variable food aid could make an important contribution to an international food security system for developing countries without jeopardizing the ability of donor countries to program substantial quantities of food aid for other purposes, including stable, development-oriented multiyear programs. The ready availability of grain in donor countries in most years makes the proposal that food aid be used to cover food security requirements

294

Table 13.2  Cereals Food Aid and Hypothetical Compensation Under IFPRI
Insurance Scheme, 1970/71-1975/76 Totals, by Country

|  | Food Aid | Compensation |
|---|---|---|
| ASIA | (thousand metric tons) | |
| **Low Income** | | |
| Bangladesh | 5,611.0 | 957.0 |
| Burma | 41.0 | 138.5 |
| India | 5,267.0 | 1889.2 |
| Indonesia | 2,104.0 | 474.6 |
| Nepal | 46.0 | --- |
| Pakistan | 4,462.0 | 99.4 |
| Philippines | 541.0 | 627.9 |
| Sri Lanka | 902.0 | 145.8 |
| **Middle Income** | | |
| Korea, Rep. of | 5,645.0 | 385.8 |
| Malaysia | 3.0 | 170.1 |
| NORTH AFRICA/MIDDLE EAST | | |
| **Low Income** | | |
| Afghanistan | 389.0 | 437.5 |
| Egypt | 1,492.0 | 551.9 |
| Sudan | 68.0 | 86.2 |
| **Middle Income** | | |
| Algeria | 222.0 | 413.2 |
| Jordan | 358.0 | 110.9 |
| Morocco | 1,234.0 | 1,938.6 |
| Syria | 39.0 | 1,328.9 |
| Tunisia | 765.0 | --- |
| Turkey | 763.0 | 2,282.0 |
| **High Income** | | |
| Cyprus | 39.0 | 113.4 |
| Iran | 383.0 | 188.3 |
| Iraq | --- | 409.2 |
| Lebanon | 239.0 | 87.9 |
| SUB-SAHARA AFRICA | | |
| **Low Income** | | |
| Angola | --- | 37.3 |
| Benin | 10.0 | --- |
| Burundi | 8.0 | 51.6 |
| Cameroon | 10.0 | 96.9 |
| Chad | 62.0 | 18.9 |
| Ethiopia | 130.0 | 718.2 |
| Gambia | 14.0 | 1.5 |
| Guinea | 150.0 | 41.0 |
| Kenya | --- | --- |
| Malagasy | 16.0 | 135.6 |

295

Table 13.2 (continued)

|  | Food Aid | Compensation |
|---|---|---|
| **NORTH AFRICA/MIDDLE EAST** | | |
| Malawi | --- | 434.9 |
| Mali | 751.0 | 33.3 |
| Mozambique | --- | --- |
| Niger | 277.0 | 140.8 |
| Nigeria | 14.0 | 233.1 |
| Rwanda | 13.0 | 2.9 |
| Senegal | 151.0 | 343.0 |
| Sierra Leone | 7.0 | 209.1 |
| Tanzania | 129.0 | 364.9 |
| Uganda | 1.0 | 153.7 |
| Upper Volta | 139.0 | 128.6 |
| Zaire | 74.0 | 52.3 |
| **Middle Income** | | |
| Ghana | 364.0 | --- |
| Ivory Coast | 18.0 | 69.8 |
| Liberia | 16.0 | 5.6 |
| Zambia | 6.0 | 280.7 |
| **LATIN AMERICA** | | |
| **Low Income** | | |
| Bolivia | 213.0 | 44.1 |
| Haiti | 28.0 | 48.1 |
| Honduras | 42.0 | 61.1 |
| **Middle Income** | | |
| Colombia | 410.0 | 130.5 |
| Cuba | --- | 202.7 |
| Dominican Republic | 254.0 | 94.7 |
| Ecuador | 100.0 | 68.6 |
| El Salvador | 7.0 | 126.7 |
| Guatemala | 19.0 | 13.6 |
| Guyana | 4.0 | 4.4 |
| Nicaragua | 16.0 | 103.7 |
| Paraguay | 92.0 | 41.1 |
| Peru | 102.0 | 182.6 |
| **High Income** | | |
| Brazil | 449.0 | 1,145.4 |
| Chile | 715.0 | 356.9 |
| Costa Rica | 4.0 | 22.0 |
| Jamaica | 25.0 | 30.8 |
| Mexico | --- | 1,804.1 |
| Panama | --- | 36.8 |
| Trinidad & Tobago | --- | 32.8 |
| Uruguay | 214.0 | --- |
| Venezuela | --- | 365.9 |
| TOTAL | 35,667.0 | 21,297.6 |

attractive. However, as in fact food aid availability would have been higher than average in the years of least need, it seems highly unlikely that a donor country commitment to provide production shortfall assistance could be met from current supplies in the occasional bad years that are bound to recur from time to time. In combination with other food security programs, however, food aid has an important complementary role to play.

**Food Aid and Grain Reserves**

Government spokesmen for both developed and developing countries have attached considerable importance to the negotiation of a new International Wheat Agreement (IWA) as an instrument for assuring food consumption in developing countries in high-price years. As Morrow points out, however, the primary purpose of such an agreement would have been to stabilize world prices within a band of roughly $140 to $210 per ton (see Chapter 10 in this volume). Although developing countries could generally expect the agreement to contain the price of their wheat imports within this range, the upper limit is nearly as high as the peaks reached during the 1972–1974 crisis. Further, the agreement would not have prevented prices from rising above that limit in times of real stress.

Under these conditions, the balance of payments relief that the new IWA would have provided might not have proved very significant. Also, in years of rising prices, when the $210 price trigger for releasing reserves had not yet been reached, developing countries would still have to bid competitively with other importers to obtain needed supplies. In such years developing countries with exceptionally poor harvests, foreign exchange constraints, and relatively smaller orders to place compared to large developed country importers, would be relatively weak bidders. Thus, they might still have no choice but to pay excessively high food import bills in order to avoid curtailing consumption. Further, the operation of a price stabilization reserve would not take into account differences among countries' ability to be flexible in making transport and handling arrangements for substantially increased imports. On this account also such a reserve would tend to be biased in favor of developed importers.

*Food Aid and Variable Import Requirements* 297

For all these reasons an International Wheat Agreement, even if successfully negotiated, would not be sufficient to meet the special food security needs of developing countries. In the absence of such an agreement, consideration of alternative mechanisms becomes all the more important. One alternative would involve using food aid commitments to guarantee adequacy of supply to developing countries. As noted above, the United States put forward a proposal for incorporating variable food aid commitments in a new Food Aid Convention, but this was not accepted by other donors. This approach could be implemented unilaterally by the United States, however.

Food aid granted to meet food security requirements would vary in accordance with recipient country needs rather than supply availability in the United States. As the numbers given in the previous section show, a relatively small amount would be required in most years. But in years of widespread production shortfalls and high world prices, when the need would be substantially greater, a grain reserve would probably be required to back up a food security commitment given by one or more food aid donors. Such a reserve has been proposed by the U.S. administration. It calls for 4 million tons to be set aside for use when necessary "to provide emergency food assistance to developing countries at any time that the domestic supply of wheat in the United States is so limited that quantities of the commodity cannot be made available . . . for disposition under the Agricultural Trade and Development and Assistance Act of 1954 (PL480) except for urgent humanitarian purposes."[4]

These rather loose release provisions do not constitute a true food security commitment, however. If the United States is to create a reserve, the proper method is to earmark it. Otherwise its alleged purpose will not be served. This could be done either by amending PL480 so that the definition of emergency food assistance explicitly includes all situations in which balance-of-payments support is needed to cover variable food import requirements or by including more explicit release provisions in the reserve legislation itself. In either case, such a reserve can be no more than a limited tool in relation to the total food security needs of developing countries.

## Food Aid and Domestic Food Reserves
## in Developing Countries

In the wake of the apparent failure of the Wheat Agreement negotiations, FAO's Committee on World Food Security reaffirmed the importance of the International Undertaking on World Food Security by adopting a Five-Point Program of Action set forth by FAO's Director-General Edouard Saouma. The Undertaking calls for the adoption of national stock policies and the establishment of targets sufficient to ensure continuity of supply and provide for emergency situations.

Although more than 75 governments have subscribed to it since it was endorsed by the World Food Conference in 1974, far fewer have actually proceeded to implement such policies (FAO, 1979). A number of important developing country importers of grain and rice have formulated national stock policies in accordance with the principles of the Undertaking, and a number of others are working toward this goal. Yet, in order for developing countries to participate effectively in the International Undertaking, many of them will need financial assistance to establish domestic food storage programs. As a follow-up to the World Food Conference, the FAO created a Food Security Assistance Scheme in early 1975. Since its inception, the scheme has provided assistance to at least 28 low-income, food-deficit countries.

Government procurement agencies in developing countries maintain bulk storage facilities in ports and at major distribution points, but according to one estimate 70 to 90 percent of all grain produced in developing countries is stored on the farm until needed for home consumption or distribution through the local trading network (Kansas State University, 1975). Although private traders function in rural areas in almost all countries, lack of an integrated national transport system frequently prevents them from moving grain stored on farms in one region to another food-deficit region during the course of a marketing year. Countries with this kind of intrayear distribution problem are more likely to suffer from interyear problems, since grain coming in from outside cannot flow smoothly to needy areas. If the internal market is consistently characterized by wide price

*Food Aid and Variable Import Requirements* 299

variation within a year, this probably indicates that the country also has a lower expected carry-out than would be desirable for the coming marketing year.

The Food Security Assistance Scheme was intended to help countries design storage programs that would provide for reserves held against the occasional bad year when local production fails and imports are very costly. However, the relative benefits of spending scarce financial resources on year-to-year storage when intrayear storage and distribution facilities do not adequately serve a country's population have been questioned by some. The Food Security Assistance Scheme provides help in three phases and could be adapted to meet both needs. The first phase consists of a review of the current status of food security planning in the country receiving assistance. On the basis of this review, the FAO team conducting the study may recommend stocking policy options, including improvements in intrayear grain handling as well as creation of security reserves. If a plan is adopted, the FAO will then offer the country technical assistance in implementing it. At present there is, however, no assurance that donor countries will provide the necessary financial aid, and funds for each plan must be obtained on a case-by-case basis. Creation of a Food Security Assistance Fund such as the LDCs proposed during the course of the International Wheat Agreement negotiations would facilitate implementation of this scheme and creation of a network of strategically located in-country reserves.

Bilateral aid can also contribute to the improvement of food storage and distribution programs in developing countries. The financing of local storage improvement programs, farm-to-market roads, and intermediate collection points are already key features in the agricultural development assistance programs of major donors, and further research to identify the problems and recommend investment priorities is underway. In a number of countries, food aid can be effectively used to build up reserve stocks if it is provided in ways that complement donor country support for the improvement of storage and distribution facilities.

Most research suggests that developing countries do not need to build sizeable domestic stocks as a hedge against bad years, since the international market can be counted on to provide a substantial portion of their needs in most years, at lower long-run costs than those associated with domestic reserves. But the idea is gaining acceptance that most countries should fix their stocks targets at a level high enough to provide for some carry-over at the end of a good harvest year, and maintain that surplus in reserve until a bad harvest year.

If consumption levels are not adequate to provide proper nutrition to a country's entire population, even in good years the country may wish to direct all of its surplus production into consumption and look to concessional or grant imports to create its reserve stocks. For the donors, providing food aid for this purpose does not mean that the flow must be continuous year after year. Like an international buffer stock, domestic food security reserves once created will be called upon only occasionally if they are to serve their true purpose of buffering against years of extreme shortage or extreme world prices or both. Thus, donors could designate extra amounts of food aid for building up food security reserves in developing countries in years when world market prices are relatively low, with the expectation that developing countries would not call on these reserves except in accordance with the principles of the International Undertaking and/or a new International Wheat Agreement if one is eventually concluded. This approach to the use of food aid for food security would permit donor countries to provide variable food aid in accordance with developing country requirements, and yet to do so in the years when their own supply situations make it easiest to offer supplementary assistance.

As with any form of insurance, if participants agree to pool their risks, the amount of money (and/or grain) that has to be kept in reserve against a rainy day is much less than if each one insures himself. Proliferation of national reserve stock programs in many parts of the world could lead to an overall accumulation considerably in excess of the amount needed to provide reasonable food security. But most reserve plans being considered by developing countries do not involve these kinds of amounts; rather, most offer only partial protection and are intended to complement rather than supplant other international mechanisms for providing food security.[5]

## Food Aid and an Insurance Facility

A number of researchers have suggested that because of the special food security requirements of developing countries, due to their relatively inelastic demand for grain, a special insurance facility should be created that would provide financial compensation or credit whenever the cost of food imports rises significantly above trend. Work done at IFPRI (see chapters by Huddleston and Konandreas and by Valdés and Konandreas in this volume) explores various alternative approaches and demonstrates their implications for the recent past. In this work, as well as in an earlier study of the subject by Reutlinger (1977), the crucial element in determining the value of a country's potential call on a financial facility has been the calculation of trend imports and their trend cost. Two of the studies (Huddleston and Konandreas; and Reutlinger) calculate trend imports by estimating trend consumption independently and assuming trend imports to equal the difference between actual trend production and estimated trend consumption. The other study (Valdés and Konandreas) uses historical trends for all pertinent variables.

Either approach would pose some problems for the implementation of an insurance scheme. If trend consumption is estimated independently, political judgments will be involved in fixing the per-capita consumption minimum that these estimates would imply. If historical trends are used, they may not provide equitable coverage for all participating countries. Countries that have sacrificed other objectives in order to maintain trend consumption with additional imports or that may have obtained food aid in larger amounts than they would have paid for commercially would have established higher trend consumption lines than those that permitted consumption to drop sharply when harvests were poor. Thus the scheme would be biased at least initially against countries in which food insecurity has had the most serious adverse effects in the past.

An alternative would be to project trend imports independently on the basis of historical trends, on the assumption that countries would make their own judgments each year as to the level of consumption they wanted to maintain, and that with the scheme in effect they could afford to push up imports to whatever level they needed to achieve their internal consumption objectives. By calculating trend imports directly rather than as a residual, the problem of obtaining an appropriate figure for trend production would also be avoided. This approach would be affected by the same initial bias as the use of historical trend consumption data, but the bias would tend to disappear the longer the life of the scheme.

If this approach were followed, the level of imports considered would include commercial imports only, and the cost would be valued at a long-term average world market price. Food aid would not be included in this calculation, as its cost to the recipient country is substantially less than its true market value.

A possible way of implementing this approach would be to adapt the rules for determining normal imports that already operate within the framework of the FAO Consultative Sub-Committee on Surplus Disposal (CSD). The FAO has established a set of procedures that govern the establishment of "usual marketing requirements" (UMRs) whenever a bilateral food aid agreement is being negotiated between a supplier and a receiving country. UMRs are usually based on the average of commercial imports for the preceding five years, but a number of other factors may also be taken into account.[6]

At the present time, UMRs are calculated only when a developing country requests food aid; after the calculations have been completed, the supplying and the receiving country agree bilaterally on the amount of concessional or grant food aid to be supplied and the receiving country must then meet its residual consumption requirement with commercial imports in excess of the UMR or permit consumption to fall. If an insurance facility were also operating, the country could obtain financing to meet some of this residual consumption requirement in years when foreign exchange constraints might otherwise result in a decision not to maintain consumption.

The rules for calculating UMRs provide for flexibility in estimating trend imports. To adapt the determination of UMRs to the needs of an insurance facility, countries would have to agree to an automatic annual determination at the beginning of each crop year, and that determination would have to be made for

*Food Aid and Variable Import Requirements* 303

all supplying countries, perhaps through a consultative procedure with the CSD acting as the coordinating body. If during the course of that year a country contracts for imports with a value significantly above the expected value of its UMR (say 110 percent of that value), it would be entitled to draw on the facility to finance the excess. Apart from its technical advantages, adaptation of the UMR rule may be preferred over other approaches, since the rule is already operational and its use would allow the insurance facility to be created without requiring any change in existing procedures for administering ongoing food aid programs.

Earlier analysis at IFPRI suggested that the quantities and true import cost of food aid to the recipient country would be included explicitly in the calculation of the country's eligibility for compensation from the facility. This assumed that the insurance facility would be self-financing and that the food aid would be used to subsidize the premium payments owed by low-income developing countries as their contribution to the scheme. The method outlined above assumes that developing countries would in effect borrow from the facility when eligible for compensation, and that they would be required to reimburse the facility only for the amounts actually borrowed, plus appropriate interest. This avoids the necessity of calculating the premium payments; if the funders of the facility wish to subsidize the participation of low-income countries, this can be done by offering below market interest rates to such countries. The relationship between food aid and an insurance facility described here presumes that food aid would be offered on more concessional terms than insurance payments and that recipient countries would prefer food aid to compensation from the financial facility if they could get it. The combined effect of continued bilateral food aid programs and an insurance facility should, however, make the aggregate distribution of food security benefits to developing countries more equitable.

The importance of taking some action is graphically described in a recent essay by Michalopoulos (1975) on the overall financial problems facing many low-income developing countries in light of oil price increases and continuing worldwide inflation. Although the character of the problem has to do with

304                                                              *Barbara Huddleston*

a lack of liquidity in hard currencies, he considers that for the poorer countries, traditional monetary and credit mechanisms will be insufficient to resolve it. An enlarged food assistance program, combining more responsive concessional food transfers with an innovative financing mechanism administered under international auspices, could do much to bring food security within reach for large numbers of people who will otherwise be at risk.

## Notes

1. Obtained by dividing the $3.7 billion expected cost for the scheme operating with an insurance level of 130 percent by the expected world wheat price of $155.8 per metric ton to get a grain equivalent of the expected cost of 23.7 million tons, and then using one fifth of that amount as the annual average for the period 1978–1982. See *IFPRI Research Report No. 4*, pp. 26 and 50.

2. Simple and logarithmic forms of the equation

$$PL = a_1 + a_2 P + a_3 S + a_4 USQ + a_5 LDCQ$$

where

| | | |
|---|---|---|
| $PL$ | = | U.S. food aid flows in crop year $t$, |
| $P$ | = | world price of wheat in calendar year $t$, |
| $S$ | = | world ending stocks for crop year $t$-1, |
| $LSQ$ | = | U.S. production for crop year $t$, and |
| $LDCQ$ | = | LDC production for crop year $t$. |

The results for the simple form were considered to be more reliable than the logarithmic form, which exhibited signs of autocorrelation. The regression equation is

$$PL = 49.912 - .036620P + .008954S - .010824USQ - .093201LDCQ$$
$$(-2.7) \qquad (.4) \qquad (-.3) \qquad (-4.2)$$

3. IFPRI's data file contains country-by-country results upon which this statement is based.

4. From "A bill to authorize the establishment of a food security reserve of wheat and for other related purposes."

5. See Reutlinger and Bigman, and Johnson in this book for discussion of the calculation of optimum domestic reserves for individual developing countries.

# Food Aid and Variable Import Requirements 305

6. These factors include:

- a substantial change in production in relation to consumption of the commodity concerned in the recipient country;
- a substantial change in the balance-of-payments position or general economic situation of the recipient country;
- evidence of a significant trend in the reference period in the commercial imports of the commodity concerned of the recipient country;
- the level of the relevant UMR negotiated according to the procedures laid down in the present paragraph by the interested countries in the nearest previous period;
- any exceptional features affecting the representativeness of the reference period for the recipient country;
- any other special considerations, including those which the government of the recipient country may raise in its request, or otherwise. (FAO, 1979).

## References

Austin, James E., and Mitchel B. Wallerstein. *Toward a Development Food Aid Policy.* Massachusetts Institute of Technology, INP Discussion Paper No. 11, C/77, December 1977.

Baker, Janice E. *Food for Peace, 1954-1978: Major Changes in Legislation.* Library of Congress, Congressional Research Service, Food and Agriculture Section, January 4, 1979.

Food and Agriculture Organization of the United Nations. *FAO Principles of Surplus Disposal and Consultative Obligations of Member Nations.* July 1979.

_____. *World Food Programme: A Story of Multilateral Aid.* Third edition, revised, 1973.

FAO Committee on World Food Security. "Action Taken to Adopt National Cereal Stock Policies and Targets in Accordance with the International Undertaking on World Food Security." CFS: 79/4, February 1979.

Huddleston, Barbara. "The Use of Food as a Tool for International Diplomacy." Lecture presented to the Symposium on Food Production, Population Growth, and Human Values, Coker College, Hartsville, South Carolina, November 30, 1978.

_____. "Approaches to World Food Security." Paper prepared for the Presidential Commission on World Hunger. Washington, D.C., June 27, 1979.

Jones, David. *Food and Interdependence*. London: Overseas Development Institute, 1976.

Kansas State University, Food and Feed Grain Institute. *Status of Grain Storage in Developing Countries*. Special Report No. 3, July 1975.

Konandreas, Panos; Barbara Huddleston; and Virabongsa Ramangkura. *Food Security: An Insurance Approach*. IFPRI, Research Report No. 4, September 1978, Washington, D.C.

Mellor, John S., and Barbara Huddleston. "Programming United States Food Aid to Meet Humanitarian and Developmental Objectives." Working Paper 78/4/PUB. Washington, D.C.: International Food Policy Research Institute, May 30, 1978.

Michalopoulos, Constantine. *Financing Needs of Developing Countries: Proposals for International Action*. Department of Economics, Princeton University, Essays in International Finance, No. 110, June 1975.

Organization for Economic Co-operation and Development. *Food Aid*. Paris, 1974.

Reutlinger, Shlomo. *Food Insecurity: Magnitude and Remedies*. World Bank Working Paper No. 267. Washington, D.C.: World Bank, July 1977.

Sarris, Alexander H.; Phillip C. Abbott; and Lance Taylor. "Grain Reserves, Emergency Relief, and Food Aid." Chapter 2 in William R. Cline, ed., *Policy Alternatives for a New International Economic Order*. New York: Praeger Publishers, for the Overseas Development Council, 1979.

Taylor, Lance. *Rich Country Policy and Food Security of the Less Developed World*. Paper prepared for the Agricultural Development Council Seminar on LDC Food Security: The International Response. Reston, Va., August 1978.

Timmer, C. Peter. "Food Aid and Malnutrition." *International Food Policy Issues, A Proceedings*. USDA/ESCS Foreign Agricultural Economic Report No. 143, January 1978, pp. 29–35.

U.S. Senate, Committee on Agriculture, Nutrition, and Forestry. *New Directions for U.S. Food Assistance*. A Report of the Special Task Force on the Operation of Public Law 480, December 18, 1978. Washington, D.C.: U.S. Government Printing Office, 1978.

Wallerstein, Mitchel B. *Multilateralizing International Food Aid: The Nature of the Debate*. Massachusetts Institute of Technology, unpublished draft, September 1978.

World Food Programme. "Assessment of Food Aid Requirements and of Food Aid Targets for Cereals—Possible Approaches." WFP/CFA: 3/7-B, March 1977.

_____. "Interim Report on the Assessment of Food Aid Requirements Including the Question of Food Aid Targets." WFP/CFA: 5.5-B, March 1978.

# 14
# Compensatory Financing for Fluctuations in the Cost of Cereal Imports

*Louis M. Goreux*

This chapter considers whether a compensatory financing scheme protecting its members against fluctuations in the cost of cereal imports could improve food security. It analyzes the relative costs of establishing a separate scheme dealing with fluctuations in the cost of cereal imports only and of merging such a scheme into a broader one dealing with fluctuations in total export earnings. The comparison is made without any presumption that one or the other solution is likely to be adopted.

The chapter is divided into two sections. The first summarizes the issues and the broad findings, the second presents the statistical analysis.

## Food Security and Compensatory Financing

### The Problem of Food Security

When a country experiences a shortage in its production of cereals, the country could maintain its supply for domestic consumption at satisfactory levels by importing more, provided it had the foreign exchange to pay for the higher import bill. Developing countries with weak balance-of-payments positions and for which the cost of cereal imports is a substantial part of their total export earnings may, however, be unable to do so. For such countries, there is a problem of food security, and two methods have been advocated for solving this problem. One is to establish a food aid program that would provide developing countries with the amount of cereals needed to offset their domestic production shortage. The other is to establish a compensatory financing scheme that would provide developing countries with the financial means of importing the quantities needed to offset their production shortages.

D. Gale Johnson argues that food security could be insured by modifying the distribution pattern of food aid without increasing substantially the average amount of food aid given in the long term. Food aid would be given to the developing countries experiencing shortfalls in their production of cereals, and the aid would be tailored to the amount of the production shortfall. By defining the shortfall as the downward deviation from a given fraction, say 95 percent, of the trend value of production, the scheme would operate as an insurance for losses subject to a deductible amount. If the deviation from the production trend were small, say less than 5 percent, the country would not receive anything. If the deviation were large, the country would receive the difference between 95 percent of the trend value and the current value of production. Such a scheme could provide adequate food security to developing countries, but it would require a change in the policies followed by the countries providing food aid. In the past, food aid has resulted from the existence of surplus stocks that had been accumulated as a consequence of domestic policies aiming at supporting agricultural prices and farm incomes. Moreover, variations in the amounts of stock available for food aid have mostly reflected changes in domestic price policies. Under the proposed scheme, aid-giving countries would have to program their production so as to have enough grain available to offset the production shortfalls experienced by developing countries. They would also have to store the grain until these shortfalls occurred, and they would have to dissociate the criteria for eligibility to food aid from any political considerations.

Konandreas, Valdés, and others favor multilateral schemes and argue that food security would be more likely if an international compensatory financing scheme was established to protect developing countries against fluctuations in the cost of their cereal imports. The proposed scheme would compensate countries not only in the case of production shortfalls, but also in the case of abnormally high import prices. In the case of

*Compensatory Financing* 309

countries with weak balance-of-payments positions and for which the cost of cereal imports is a substantial part of the total import bill, the scheme would be attractive. It might not, however, be particularly attractive for countries that can cushion fluctuations in the cost of their cereal imports without too much difficulty by drawing on their external reserves or by borrowing on commercial markets. For the latter group of countries, it is not obvious that the cost of cereal imports would need to be treated differently from the cost of other import items, such as oil or capital goods.

Another way to provide protection against fluctuations in the cost of cereal imports would be to enlarge the scope of existing compensatory financing schemes now dealing only with fluctuations in the value of export earnings. The cost of enlarging the scope of existing schemes, such as the one administered by the IMF, would be considerably lower than that of establishing a new scheme dealing only with cereal imports, since countries would not need to be compensated for an increase in the cost of cereal imports if the latter was offset by an increase in export earnings. In 1974, for example, it would not have been necessary to compensate most primary exporting countries for the sharp increase in the cost of cereal imports because, with the commodity boom, most of these countries had exceptionally high export earnings in that year.

*Compensatory Financing*

Three facilities aim at protecting their members against fluctuations in their export earnings. The International Monetary Fund facility is by far the largest one. From 1976 to 1978, the amount disbursed under the Fund facility was approximately 20 times larger than the amount transferred under STABEX, the facility administered by the European Community (EC) for some 50 associated states belonging to the African, Caribbean, and Pacific regions (ACP). The facility recently established by the Arab Monetary Fund is complementary to the Fund facility. It could provide additional financial assistance to those members of the Arab Monetary Fund experiencing export shortfalls or having to pay abnormally high bills for their imports of agricultural products. At the end of March 1979, however, no disbursement had been made under that facility.[1]

Under STABEX, ACP members are compensated by the EC when their earnings derived from exports of specified commodities to the EC fall. The amount of compensation is calculated commodity by commodity, and the member can receive compensation for a commodity shortfall even if this shortfall is offset by excess exports of other commodities included in the STABEX scheme. The compensation is intended to assist the commodity sector where the shortfall occurred. However, the government is not constrained to use the assistance received exclusively for that sector. By contrast, Fund members can draw under the compensatory financing facility only if they experience a net shortfall in their earnings from all merchandise exports to all destinations. Suppose, for example, that a Fund member derives all of its export earnings from coffee and sugar. In 1977, that member would have experienced a shortfall in its earnings from sugar, but an excess in its earnings from coffee, and it would have been able to draw under the Fund facility only if, and to the extent that, the shortfall from sugar would have been larger than the excess from coffee. There is good reason for this Fund practice because the Fund provides general balance-of-payments assistance to its members and because the responsibility for allocating the funds among sectors rests with the member.

Fund members experiencing shortfalls in their export earnings can draw under the compensatory financing facility only if they have a balance-of-payments need and several conditions are fulfilled. The member must cooperate with the Fund in an effort to find, where required, appropriate solutions for its balance-of-payments difficulties. The shortfall must be of a temporary character and due to circumstances largely beyond the member's control. Moreover, the amount that the member can draw on the facility cannot exceed a given percentage of the member's quota in the Fund. The purpose of this chapter is to assess the effect of enlarging the scope of the facility on the size of the net shortfalls.

The Fund facility now covers earnings from all merchandise exports, but it has been suggested to extend the scope of the facility by including export earnings from services (in par-

# Compensatory Financing

ticular, tourism and remittances from workers abroad). If a country had a shortfall in services only when it had a shortfall in merchandise, the net shortfall in earnings from merchandise and services would be identical to the sum of the merchandise and service shortfalls. However, shortfalls in merchandise are sometimes offset by excesses in services and vice versa. For a sample of 46 countries, the correlation coefficient between shortfalls in merchandise and shortfalls in services averages .46 for the 13-year period 1963-1975.[2] Assuming costs are proportional to the sum of shortfalls, the cost of expanding the scope of the facility to include services would be only 70 percent of the cost of operating a separate facility dealing with services only.

Instead of protecting members only against shortfalls in export earnings, a facility could also protect members against excesses in the cost of their imports. This could be done by subtracting the cost of imports from the value of export earnings before calculating the net shortfall. When shortfalls (excesses) are defined as the downward (upward) deviation from a five-year average, this would be equivalent to adding (subtracting) the import excess (shortfall) to the export shortfall.[3] For the same sample of 46 countries and the same 13 years, there is a positive correlation between exports and imports, and therefore a negative correlation (-.44) between export shortfalls and import excesses. Because a decline in export earnings is more often than not offset by a decline in the cost of imports, the cost of expanding the scope of the facility would be only 27 percent of the cost that would have been incurred by establishing a separate facility dealing with fluctuations in the cost of merchandise imports only.[4]

If it was considered desirable to give a special treatment to the cost of cereal imports, the net shortfall could be calculated by subtracting only the cost of cereal imports from the value of export earnings. For the same statistical sample, export earnings and cost of cereal imports are positively correlated; excesses in the cost of cereal imports are negatively correlated (-.30) with shortfalls in export earnings. During the observation period (1963-1975), excesses in the cost of cereal imports were more often than not offset by excesses in export earnings,

312                                              Louis M. Goreux

and the coverage of the facility could have been expanded at very little cost. A number of countries would have received more, but some would have received less.

## Need for Additional Research

Extending the coverage of the compensatory financing facility (CFF) of the Fund by including the cost of cereal imports could improve food security at little extra cost. If serious consideration were given to this possibility, the analysis should be extended in several directions, namely: the measurement of additional import costs; the effect of quota limitations; and the complementarity between compensatory and stock financing.

*Measurement of additional import costs.* The statistical analysis reported above was based on actual export earnings and actual import costs. Although this method has the obvious advantage of simplicity, actual needs are greater than the increase in the cost of imports as measured from historical series; with greater food security, members should be able to consume more when a production shortage occurs. An alternative solution would be to measure excesses in the cost of cereal imports by applying a food security norm, such as one of the norms proposed by Valdés and Konandreas (Chapter 2).

*Quota limits.* The amount that a member can draw under the CFF cannot exceed the amount of its shortfall in export earnings and cannot exceed either given percentage of the member's quota in the Fund. The amounts drawn by members under the 1975 CFF decision were in the majority of cases constrained by the quota limits specified in that decision. These quota limits could, however, be modified if the scope of the facility were to be expanded so as to protect members against fluctuations in both earnings from merchandise exports and costs of cereal imports.

*Complementarity between compensatory financing and stock financing.* Providing additional financial resources to importers in periods of supply shortages would merely contribute to raised prices if the physical supply could not be raised at the same time. Proposals for the International Wheat Agreement, adjourned in February 1979, contained provisions for the international coordination of national reserve stocks and possible ways of

*Compensatory Financing* 313

providing financial assistance to developing countries for holding reserve stocks. Fund members maintaining special stocks of sugar under the terms of the 1977 International Sugar Agreement can receive financial assistance under the Fund buffer stock facility, and several of them have already received such assistance. A similar arrangement could be considered for wheat if the negotiations of an international wheat agreement were reconvened.

## Statistical Analysis

Members can draw under the Fund compensatory financing facility when they experience shortfalls in their earnings from all merchandise exports. It has been proposed by some to restrict the coverage of the facility to commodity earnings only, and by others to extend it so as to cover services and the cost of cereal imports. The object of this analysis is to assess the effect of a modification in the scope of the facility on the size of shortfalls and to compare the additional resources required to expand the scope of the facility to the resources that would be required to establish a separate facility dealing with services only or with the cost of cereal imports only.

The statistical analysis is divided into three sections. The first defines the model in algebraic terms, the second describes the statistical sample, and the third summarizes the results.

### Model

Call $S_1$ the net shortfall in earnings from all items belonging to group 1, $S_2$ the net shortfall in earnings from all items belonging to group 2, and $S_{1+2}$ the net shortfall in earnings derived from all of the items belonging to either group 1 or group 2. Assuming the cost of a compensatory financing scheme is proportional to the sum of net shortfalls, the cost of expanding the scope of a scheme from group 1 to group 1+2 in relation to that of establishing a separate scheme for group 2 is given by $(S_{1+2} - S_1)/S_2$. This ratio $\gamma$ depends on the values of two coefficients. The first is the correlation coefficient $r_{12}$ between the fluctuations in earnings from all items belonging to group 1 and those from all items belonging to group 2. The second is the

314        *Louis M. Goreux*

relative size of the fluctuations for each group, $\alpha = \sigma_2/\sigma_1$. The function $\gamma(r_{12}, \alpha)$ is given below as Equation 7 for country $i$, and as Equation 10 for a group of countries. For convenience, the notations used in this section are summarized below:

Subscripts:

| | |
|---|---|
| $i$ | country |
| $k = 1, 2, 1 + 2$ | group of items covered by the facility |
| $t = 1, \ldots, n$ | year |

Variables:

| | |
|---|---|
| $x_{ikt}$ | earnings derived by country $i$ from group $k$ exports in year $t$ |
| $u_{ikt}$ | deviation from trend |
| $-u_{ikt} > 0$ | shortfall in export earnings |
| $S_{ik} = \sum\limits_{t=1}^{t=n}(-u_{ikt} > 0)$ | sum of shortfalls |

Parameters:

| | |
|---|---|
| $\sigma_{ik}$ | standard deviation of error term $u_{ikt}$ |
| $c_{ik} = \sigma_{ik}/x_{ik}$ | coefficient of variation with $x_{ik} = \dfrac{1}{n}\sum\limits_{t=1}^{t=n} x_{ikt}$ |
| $r_i$ | coefficient of correlation between error terms $u_{i1t}$ and $u_{i2t}$ |
| $\alpha_i = \sigma_{i2}/\sigma_{i1}$ | fluctuation ratio |
| $\beta_i = S_{i2}/S_2$ | country $i$'s share in sum of shortfalls relating to group 2 |
| $\gamma_i = \dfrac{S_{i,\,1+2} - S_{i1}}{S_{i2}}$ | cost ratio for countries defined as the additional cost of expanding coverage from 1 to 1 + 2 over cost of establishing a separate facility to cover 2 only |
| $\gamma = \dfrac{S_{1+2} - S_1}{S_2}$ | cost ratio for all countries that can draw under the scheme |

Export earnings derived from commodity group $k$ by country $i$ are assumed to fluctuate randomly from a linear trend. Ignoring subscripts $i$ and $k$ at this stage, the export earnings can be written

$$x_t = a + bt + u_t, \tag{1}$$

# Compensatory Financing

where $u_t$ is a random disturbance normally distributed with

$$E(u_t) = 0 \text{ and } E(u_t^2) = \sigma^2.$$

In the Fund facility, the shortfall is defined as the downward deviation from a medium-term trend measured as the five-year average centered on the shortfall year. Its value is calculated as

$$S_t = \left( .2 \sum_{T=-2}^{T=2} x_{t+T} \right) - x_t \text{ for } S_t > 0.$$

For the purpose of this analysis, it is more convenient to measure the shortfall in relation to the least squares trend value $a + bt$ and, therefore, to measure it as $-u_t$. The expectancy of the sum of the negative values of the random disturbance (taken here as the shortfalls) is proportional to the standard deviation of the random disturbances if the latter are normally distributed, and can be written as[5]

$$E(S) = E\left( \sum_{t=1}^{t=n} (-u_t > 0) \right) = \frac{n}{2\sqrt{2\pi}} \sigma. \qquad (2)$$

Let us now introduce a distinction between groups 1 and 2 and call $\sigma_1$ and $\sigma_2$ the standard deviations of the random terms $u_{1t}$ and $u_{2t}$ of Equation 1. Subscripts 1 and 2 identify the source of export earnings; for example, group 1 could cover merchandise exports, and group 2 service exports. Call $\sigma_{1+2}$ the standard deviation of random term $u_{1+2,t}$ of Equation 1, when this equation relates to earnings derived from the two groups together, that is to say from merchandise and service exports in the previous example. The relation between $\sigma_{1+2}$, $\sigma_1$ and $\sigma_2$ is given by

$$\sigma_{1+2}^2 = \sigma_1^2 + \sigma_2^2 + 2 r\sigma_1\sigma_2, \qquad (3)$$

where $r$ is the correlation coefficient between random disturbances $u_{1t}$ and $u_{2t}$. For selected values of $r$, this relation takes the simplified forms

$$\sigma_{1+2} = \sigma_1 + \sigma_2 \qquad \text{for } r = 1,$$
$$\sigma_{1+2} = \sqrt{\sigma_1^2 + \sigma_2^2} \qquad \text{for } r = 0,$$
$$\sigma_{1+2} = \sigma_1 \qquad \text{for } r = -.5\sigma_2/\sigma_1,$$
$$\sigma_{1+2} = |\sigma_1 - \sigma_2| \qquad \text{for } r = -1.$$

Suppose an existing facility deals with shortfalls in export earnings from all merchandise exports. Expanding the coverage of the existing facility from group 1 (merchandise exports) to group 1 + 2 (merchandise and service exports) would increase the sum of shortfalls by $S_{1+2} - S_1$. Instead, creating a new facility to deal with shortfalls in service exports would increase the sum of shortfalls by $S_2$. Assuming drawings are proportional to shortfalls, the cost ratio between the two different ways of covering shortfalls in service exports would be given by

$$\gamma = \frac{S_{1+2} - S_1}{S_2}. \tag{4}$$

As many countries are eligible to draw under the facility, variable $S_k$ ($k = 1,2,1+2$) of Equation 4 is the sum of the shortfalls in earnings from group $k$ experienced by all countries $i$ for all years $t$:

$$S_k = \sum_{it} (-u_{ikt} > 0) = \sum_i S_{ik}.$$

Equation 4 can therefore be rewritten as

$$\gamma = \frac{\sum_i S_{i,1+2} - \sum_i S_{i1}}{\sum_i S_{i2}} = \sum_i \left(\frac{S_{i2}}{S_2}\right) \left(\frac{S_{i,1+2} - S_{i1}}{S_{i2}}\right)$$

or

$$\gamma = \sum_i \beta_i \gamma_i, \tag{5}$$

where $\beta_i = S_{i2}/S_2$ is country $i$'s share of total shortfalls in earnings from group 2, and $\gamma_i$ is the cost ratio for country $i$. In view of Equation 2, the latter may be rewritten as

$$\gamma_i = \frac{S_{i,1+2} - S_{i1}}{S_{i2}} = \frac{\sigma_{i,1+2} - \sigma_{i1}}{\sigma_{i2}}. \tag{6}$$

*Compensatory Financing* 317

Replacing $\sigma_{i,1+2}$ by its value from Equation 3 and calling $\alpha_i = \sigma_{i2}/\sigma_{i1}$, Equation 6 can be rewritten as

$$\gamma_i = \frac{(1 + 2r_i\alpha_i + \alpha_i^2)^{\frac{1}{2}} - 1}{\alpha_i}. \tag{7}$$

Consider, first, the relationship between $\gamma_i$ and $r_i$ by taking three particular values for $r_i$:

For $r_i = 1$, Equation 7 gives $\gamma_i = 1$. In this case, expanding the facility so as to cover both groups 1 and 2 would cost as much as establishing an independent facility for group 2, as shortfalls in group 2 would be always associated with and, therefore, added to shortfalls in group 1.

At the other extreme, for $r_i = -1$, and $\sigma_{i1} > \sigma_{i2}$, Equation 7 gives $\gamma_i = -1$, which leads to maximum savings. Expanding the facility to cover groups 1 and 2 would save an amount equivalent to the cost of creating an independent facility for group 2.

For $r_i = 0$, Equation 7 gives $\gamma_i = (\alpha_i^{-2} + 1)^{\frac{1}{2}} - \alpha_i^{-1}$, which is always non-negative; when $\alpha_i$ is small, $\gamma_i$ is also small since $\gamma_i \simeq 0.5 \, \alpha_i$. In other words, when shortfalls in groups 1 and 2 are not correlated, there is an additional cost in expanding the coverage of the facility. This additional cost is, however, small in relation to that of establishing a new facility for group 2, if fluctuations in group 2 are small in relation to those in group 1.

Turn now to the relationship between $\gamma_i$ and $\alpha_i$ and start with the case when the sizes of fluctuations are the same for the two groups:

$$\alpha_i = 1 \text{ gives } \gamma_i = \sqrt{2(1 + r_i)} - 1, \tag{8}$$

and for $r_i = 0$, $\gamma_i = \sqrt{2} - 1$.

When fluctuations in group 2 are small in relation to those in group 1, a small $\alpha_i$ implies

$$(1 + 2r_i\alpha_i + \alpha_i^2)^{\frac{1}{2}} \simeq 1 + r_i\alpha_i + .5\alpha_i^2,$$

hence

$$\gamma_i \simeq r_i + .5\alpha_i. \tag{9}$$

318                                                      *Louis M. Goreux*

The differentiation of Equation 7 with respect to $\alpha_i$ gives in the general case

$$\frac{d\gamma_i}{d\alpha_i} = \frac{(1 + 2r_i\alpha_i^{-1} + \alpha_i^{-2})^{\frac{1}{2}} - (r_i + \alpha_i^{-1})}{\alpha_i^2(1 + 2r_i\alpha_i^{-1} + \alpha_i^{-2})^{\frac{1}{2}}}$$

which is always non-negative since $-1 \leqslant r_i \leqslant 1$. Consequently, when $\alpha_i$ falls from $+\infty$ to 0, $\gamma_i$ declines monotonically from 1 to $r_i$, as can be seen from Equations 7 to 9.

Equation 7 or 9 shows the cost ratio for each country as a function of $r_i$ and $\alpha_i$. Cost ratio $\gamma$ for all countries $i$ is obtained by weighting each country cost ratio $\gamma_i$ by share coefficient $\beta_i$:

$$\gamma \simeq \sum_i \beta_i r_i + .5 \sum_i \alpha_i \beta_i, \text{ where } \sum_i \beta_i = 1. \tag{10}$$

Cost ratio $\gamma$ critically depends on the values of coefficients $r_i$ and $\alpha_i$ for those countries $i$ that account for a large share of shortfalls in earnings from group 2. The cost ratio declines with the correlation coefficients $r_i$ and with the variance ratios $\alpha_i = \sigma_{i2}/\sigma_{i1}$.

The coverage of the facility might be expanded either by using a broader basis in the calculation of export shortfalls, for example, by adding export services to total merchandise exports or by including the cost of cereal imports. In the first case, earnings from export services would be added to earnings from merchandise exports before calculating the combined shortfall. In the second case, the cost of cereals imports would be subtracted from the value of export earnings before calculating the combined shortfall. What was said in terms of the shortfall in export earnings from group 2 could be repeated in terms of the excess (taken as the negative shortfall) in the cost of cereal imports.

### Statistical Sample

Neither the 14 members classified in the International Financial Statistics (IFS) as industrial countries nor the 12 members classified as oil exporters have made use of the compensatory financing facility under the 1975 decision. The sample was, therefore, selected among the 108 other Fund members. The 46 countries selected were those for which reliable yearly data on total merchandise exports and on export

*Compensatory Financing* 319

services and cereal imports could be collected since 1961. For a number of these 46 countries, export data were not available for 1977 and estimates were used instead. The sample countries may be divided into three groups that reflect their level of economic development: (a) countries eligible for IMF's Trust Fund Loans, which are also the countries eligible for International Development Association (IDA) credits from the World Bank; (b) other nonoil developing countries; and (c) more developed primary producing countries.

Export earnings from services are those reported in categories 3 through 8 of the IMF Balance of Payments Manual.[6] They include, in particular, earnings from tourism and remittances from workers abroad. Service exports are on the average equal to 43 percent of total merchandise exports (Table 14.1). They represent less than 10 percent for Liberia and Zambia; between 50 and 100 percent for Kenya, Mexico, Jamaica, Tunisia, and Portugal; and over 100 percent for Jordan, Panama, Barbados, and Cyprus.

Costs of cereal imports are measured both on a gross and a net basis. On a gross basis, import volumes (as recorded in FAO statistics) are valued at prevailing market prices. On a net basis, the aid content associated with cereal imports is deducted from the gross value.

The cost of cereal imports averages 7.3 percent of earnings from all merchandise exports, but only 6.0 percent of it when the aid content of cereal imports is deducted (Table 14.2). The dependence on cereal imports is the highest for Trust Fund countries (Group A) and the lowest for more developed countries (Group C). The cost of cereal imports is less than 5 percent of earnings from merchandise exports for 22 of the 46 sample countries. It is between 10 and 20 percent for The Gambia, Haiti, Morocco, Pakistan, Upper Volta, Cyprus, and Tunisia. It is above 20 percent for India, Jordan, Mali, and Somalia. It should be noted that India, which had by far the largest import bill during the sample period, has recently reduced its dependence on cereal imports and now has large stocks of cereals. For each country group, the index of fluctuations in the cost of cereal imports is higher when a deduction is made for the aid content of such imports and, in both cases, is considerably

Table 14.1  Service Exports: Dependence and Variability, 1963-75
(IFS Data, 46 Countries)

| | Service exports averages (1961-77) | Service exports to merchandise exports | Index of fluctuation[1] |
|---|---|---|---|
| | (Millions of SDRs) | (Percent) | |
| **All countries: Mean** | 225.93 | 43.04 | 5.34 |
| (SD)[2] | | (58.90) | (3.43) |
| **Group A: Mean** | 92.42 | 36.88 | 6.30 |
| (SD)[2] | | (57.19) | (4.40) |
| Burundi | 2.7 | 10.9 | 3.9 |
| Cameroon | 69.5 | 28.5 | 6.0 |
| El Salvador | 32.5 | 11.2 | 4.8 |
| Ethiopia | 61.9 | 43.6 | 2.4 |
| Gambia, The | 4.0 | 21.0 | 4.3 |
| Haiti | 15.0 | 29.5 | 5.9 |
| Honduras | 20.5 | 10.9 | 2.6 |
| India | 428.9 | 18.1 | 3.8 |
| Jordan | 170.5 | 278.3 | 18.9 |
| Kenya | 217.2 | 62.4 | 4.7 |
| Liberia | 11.6 | 5.4 | 4.9 |
| Mali | 10.8 | 34.1 | 6.4 |
| Mauritania | 10.4 | 11.5 | 7.4 |
| Morocco | 239.9 | 36.7 | 1.7 |
| Pakistan | 155.7 | 22.9 | 5.3 |
| Rwanda | 2.8 | 11.1 | 14.3 |
| Somalia | 12.7 | 31.7 | 5.0 |
| Thailand | 392.7 | 36.1 | 3.4 |
| Upper Volta | 9.4 | 41.8 | 4.5 |
| Afghanistan | 25.2 | 22.0 | 15.0 |
| Zambia | 46.9 | 6.7 | 7.0 |
| **Group B: Mean** | 260.56 | 52.64 | 4.92 |
| (SD)[2] | | (67.17) | (2.19) |
| Argentina | 371.3 | 18.6 | 9.3 |
| Brazil | 481.8 | 13.2 | 6.1 |
| Chile | 128.9 | 12.6 | 5.4 |
| Costa Rica | 53.1 | 22.1 | 3.6 |
| Dominican Republic | 50.3 | 16.5 | 4.0 |
| Mexico | 1,500.6 | 91.4 | 2.1 |
| Nicaragua | 46.0 | 21.7 | 4.9 |
| Panama | 339.3 | 293.4 | 5.5 |
| Peru | 184.1 | 21.0 | 3.9 |
| Uruguay | 69.8 | 28.4 | 4.5 |
| Barbados | 64.4 | 135.4 | 2.3 |
| Guyana | 18.2 | 12.6 | 2.6 |
| Jamaica | 183.3 | 55.0 | 1.9 |
| Cyprus | 127.3 | 114.3 | 5.3 |
| Syria | 156.1 | 45.7 | 3.8 |
| Malaysia | 207.9 | 10.1 | 9.3 |
| Singapore | 934.3 | 39.5 | 4.8 |
| Gabon | 37.5 | 13.1 | 8.6 |
| Tunisia | 190.4 | 68.2 | 4.1 |
| Guatemala | 66.5 | 20.0 | 6.4 |
| **Group C: Mean** | 648.18 | 30.52 | 3.02 |
| (SD)[2] | | (19.74) | (0.30) |
| Ireland | 495.1 | 36.5 | 2.8 |
| Portugal | 611.8 | 62.4 | 3.3 |
| Australia | 1,144.0 | 20.8 | 2.8 |
| New Zealand | 195.4 | 13.6 | 3.4 |
| South Africa | 794.6 | 19.3 | 2.8 |

[1] Sum of shortfalls (arithmetic nominal) to sum of service exports.
[2] SD = standard deviation.

*Compensatory Financing* 321

greater than the index of fluctuations in service exports (last two columns of Table 14.2 compared with last column of Table 14.1).

*Results*

The effects on country shortfalls of enlarging the coverage of the facility are summarized in Tables 14.3, 14.4, and 14.5. The effect of adding service exports to merchandise exports is shown in Table 14.3. The effects of expanding further the coverage in order to protect members also against fluctuations in the cost of cereals imports are shown in Table 14.4 where costs are valued at market prices, and in Table 14.5 where the aid content of food imports is deducted from the market value.

Consider first the effect of including service exports (Table 14.3). Shortfalls in services and in merchandise exports are positively correlated for 38 countries and negatively correlated for the remaining 8 countries. For the 46 countries together, the weighted fluctuation ratio ($\alpha = \sum_i \beta_i \alpha_i = .68$) and correlation coefficient ($r = \sum_i \beta_i r_i = .46$) are relatively high. As a result, including services raises the sum of shortfalls by SDR (Special Drawing Rights) 3,126 million,[7] which represents 70 percent of the sum of the shortfalls in earnings from services (SDR 5,126 million).[8] This percentage is lower for Trust Fund countries (60 percent) than for more developed primary exporters (80 percent), because the correlation between shortfalls in earnings from export services and from merchandise exports is weaker for Trust Fund countries (.10) than for the other group (.59).

When the scope of the facility is further extended by also protecting members against fluctuations in the cost of cereals imports, the sum of net shortfalls for the 46 countries is marginally reduced from SDR 24,891 million to SDR 24,771 million (Table 14.4). This occurs because the weighted fluctuation ratio is relatively low ($\alpha = .35$), while the weighted correlation coefficient is negative ($r = -.30$). The negative correlation between excesses in the cost of cereal imports and shortfalls in export earnings reflects the fact that, during the sample period, prices of cereal imports and prices of exports moved more often in the same direction than not. As can be noted, Trust Fund

Table 14.2 Cereal Imports: Dependence and Variability, 1963-75
(IFS Data, 46 Countries)

| | Cereal imports | Cereal imports net of aid | Cereal imports to merchandise exports | Cereal imports net of aid to merchandise exports | Index of fluctuation[1] | |
|---|---|---|---|---|---|---|
| | | | | | Cereal imports | Cereal imports net of aid |
| | Average (1961-77) | | | | | |
| | (Millions of SDRs) | | | (Percent) | | |
| All countries: Mean[2] (SD)[2] | 39.22 | 30.27 | 7.32 (6.99) | 6.01 (5.85) | 15.50 (12.04) | 17.26 (13.02) |
| Group A: Mean[2] (SD)[2] | 38.90 | 23.71 | 10.14 (9.00) | 7.83 (7.74) | 13.60 (7.87) | 15.73 (9.16) |
| Burundi | 1.14 | 0.87 | 4.61 | 3.53 | 7.9 | 9.9 |
| Cameroon | 7.12 | 6.95 | 2.92 | 2.85 | 8.9 | 10.0 |
| El Salvador | 9.03 | 8.56 | 3.11 | 2.95 | 9.8 | 10.4 |
| Ethiopia | 5.54 | 2.00 | 3.90 | 1.41 | 19.8 | 22.0 |
| Gambia, The | 2.62 | 2.35 | 13.72 | 12.29 | 4.8 | 4.9 |
| Haiti | 8.11 | 6.66 | 15.95 | 13.09 | 4.4 | 9.1 |
| Honduras | 5.80 | 5.21 | 3.08 | 2.77 | 13.5 | 12.5 |
| India | 536.12 | 309.09 | 22.65 | 13.06 | 11.0 | 16.7 |
| Jordan | 20.86 | 15.43 | 34.05 | 25.19 | 5.2 | 9.9 |
| Kenya | 5.27 | 4.04 | 1.51 | 1.16 | 30.7 | 25.7 |
| Liberia | 9.25 | 8.88 | 4.29 | 4.12 | 6.1 | 5.6 |
| Mali | 7.28 | 5.76 | 22.92 | 27.72 | 25.6 | 29.8 |
| Mauritania | 8.63 | 7.45 | 9.54 | 8.24 | 4.6 | 4.9 |
| Morocco | 69.37 | 52.60 | 10.62 | 8.05 | 16.4 | 22.0 |
| Pakistan | 82.41 | 32.79 | 12.11 | 4.82 | 18.0 | 23.6 |
| Rwanda | 0.87 | 0.59 | 3.50 | 2.38 | 20.1 | 23.5 |
| Somalia | 8.31 | 6.49 | 20.82 | 16.27 | 18.4 | 13.6 |
| Thailand | 7.60 | 7.41 | 0.70 | 0.68 | 6.1 | 7.4 |
| Upper Volta | 3.20 | 2.20 | 14.23 | 9.76 | 10.4 | 10.7 |
| Afghanistan | 8.48 | 3.03 | 7.42 | 2.65 | 25.0 | 39.1 |
| Zambia | 9.83 | 9.60 | 1.41 | 1.38 | 18.9 | 19.1 |

| | | | | | | |
|---|---|---|---|---|---|---|
| Group B: Mean[2/] | 40.46 | 36.23 | 5.48 | 4.93 | 17.01 | 18.70 |
| (SD)[2/] | | | ·(3.11) | (2.74) | (16.14) | (17.30) |
| | | | | | | |
| Argentina | 7.52 | 7.52 | 0.38 | 0.38 | 66.6 | 66.6 |
| Brazil | 223.10 | 178.33 | 6.10 | 4.88 | 9.1 | 13.8 |
| Chile | 62.12 | 50.56 | 6.09 | 4.96 | 21.8 | 26.2 |
| Costa Rica | 10.06 | 9.81 | 4.19 | 4.08 | 6.9 | 7.1 |
| Dominican Republic | 17.09 | 13.94 | 5.60 | 4.57 | 18.9 | 21.5 |
| Mexico | 92.49 | 91.39 | 5.63 | 5.56 | 33.5 | 33.9 |
| Nicaragua | 6.28 | 6.06 | 2.96 | 2.85 | 9.5 | 9.4 |
| Panama | 5.03 | 4.91 | 4.35 | 4.24 | 12.0 | 12.6 |
| Peru | 68.85 | 65.14 | 7.86 | 7.44 | 8.4 | 8.6 |
| Uruguay | 3.90 | 2.94 | 1.59 | 1.20 | 49.9 | 61.1 |
| Barbados | 4.37 | 4.37 | 9.19 | 9.19 | 6.3 | 6.3 |
| Guyana | 5.67 | 5.59 | 3.93 | 3.88 | 3.1 | 3.1 |
| Jamaica | 31.82 | 30.76 | 9.55 | 9.23 | 6.0 | 6.7 |
| Cyprus | 11.17 | 10.58 | 10.03 | 9.50 | 19.1 | 20.3 |
| Syria | 32.06 | 26.15 | 9.38 | 7.65 | 22.7 | 22.7 |
| Malaysia | 104.86 | 104.62 | 5.09 | 5.08 | 10.2 | 10.3 |
| Singapore | 81.28 | 81.26 | 3.43 | 3.43 | 6.9 | 6.9 |
| Gabon | 2.12 | 2.07 | 0.74 | 0.72 | 13.0 | 14.4 |
| Tunisia | 29.47 | 19.60 | 10.55 | 7.01 | 8.4 | 13.9 |
| Guatemala | 9.94 | 9.07 | 2.98 | 2.72 | 7.9 | 8.6 |
| | | | | | | |
| Group C: Mean[2/] | 35.59 | 33.92 | 2.85 | 2.69 | 17.42 | 17.96 |
| (SD)[2/] | | | (3.95) | (3.62) | (6.98) | (6.55) |
| | | | | | | |
| Ireland | 44.27 | 43.52 | 32.6 | 3.20 | 8.9 | 9.0 |
| Portugal | 93.72 | 86.14 | 9.56 | 8.79 | 12.3 | 14.9 |
| New Zealand | 10.64 | 10.64 | 0.74 | 0.74 | 18.1 | 18.1 |
| Australia | 0.58 | 0.58 | 0.01 | 0.01 | 26.3 | 26.3 |
| South Africa | 28.74 | 28.74 | 0.70 | 0.70 | 21.5 | 21.5 |

1/ Ratio of sum of excess (nominal arithmetic) to sum of corresponding imports.
2/ SD = standard deviation.

Table 14.3  Extending the Scope of the Facility to Cover Fluctuations in Earnings from Services Exports
  1 = Earnings from all merchandise exports
  2 = Earnings from services exports
  1+2 = Earnings from all merchandise and service exports

| Country | Sums of shortfalls $S_1$ | $S_2$ | $S_{1+2}$ | Variance ratio $\alpha = S_2/S_1$ | Country share $\beta_i = S_{i2}/S_2$ | Correlation coefficient r | Cost ratio $\gamma = \dfrac{S_{1+2} - S_1}{S_2}$ |
|---|---|---|---|---|---|---|---|
| | (millions of SDRs) | | | | (Percentage) | | |
| **Group A:** | | | | | | | |
| Burundi | 47 | 1 | 48 | 0.03 | 0.000 | 47.24 | 0.84 |
| Cameroon | 184 | 46 | 193 | 0.25 | 0.009 | -38.75 | 0.19 |
| El Salvador | 181 | 18 | 194 | 0.10 | 0.004 | 40.82 | 0.70 |
| Ethiopia | 77 | 20 | 87 | 0.26 | 0.004 | 54.90 | 0.48 |
| Gambia, The | 20 | 2 | 21 | 0.10 | 0.000 | 22.19 | 0.41 |
| Haiti | 36 | 10 | 40 | 0.28 | **0.002** | -5.93 | 0.32 |
| Honduras | 109 | 6 | 114 | 0.06 | 0.001 | 43.07 | 0.87 |
| India | 1011 | 198 | 1190 | 0.20 | 0.039 | 59.71 | 0.90 |
| Jordan | 65 | 269 | 302 | 4.13 | 0.052 | -32.59 | 0.88 |
| Kenya | 209 | 124 | 284 | 0.59 | 0.024 | -5.72 | 0.60 |
| Liberia | 86 | 7 | 85 | 0.08 | 0.001 | -34.91 | -0.22 |
| Mali Republic | 26 | 9 | 30 | 0.36 | 0.002 | -0.86 | 0.47 |
| Mauritania | 41 | 9 | 42 | 0.22 | 0.002 | 51.84 | 0.08 |
| Morocco | 423 | 51 | 465 | 0.12 | 0.010 | 30.85 | 0.81 |
| Pakistan | 252 | 98 | 265 | 0.39 | 0.019 | 15.36 | 0.13 |
| Rwanda | 41 | 4 | 43 | 0.09 | 0.001 | 75.15 | 0.65 |
| Somalia | 21 | 8 | 27 | 0.37 | 0.001 | 38.24 | 0.80 |
| Thailand | 823 | 179 | 874 | 0.22 | 0.035 | 15.59 | 0.28 |
| Upper Volta | 18 | 5 | 22 | 0.25 | 0.001 | 23.07 | 0.71 |
| Afghanistan | 62 | 32 | 85 | 0.52 | 0.006 | 49.26 | 0.72 |
| Zambia | 852 | 42 | 864 | 0.05 | 0.003 | 15.18 | 0.30 |
| Subtotal | 4594 | 1140 | 5275 | 1.19 | 0.222 | 10.24 | 0.60 |

Group B:

| | | | | | | | |
|---|---|---|---|---|---|---|---|
| Argentina | 1715 | 392 | 1903 | 0.23 | 0.077 | 69.57 | 0.43 |
| Brazil | 1940 | 346 | 2206 | 0.18 | 0.068 | 63.71 | 0.77 |
| Chile | 1100 | 86 | 1164 | 0.08 | 0.017 | 29.92 | 0.75 |
| Costa Rica | 116 | 22 | 131 | 0.19 | 0.004 | 45.55 | 0.67 |
| Dominican Republic | 190 | 24 | 207 | 0.13 | 0.005 | 71.72 | 0.71 |
| Mexico | 844 | 402 | 1206 | 0.48 | 0.078 | 86.69 | 0.90 |
| Nicaragua | 114 | 27 | 128 | 0.24 | 0.005 | 28.50 | 0.52 |
| Panama | 43 | 213 | 248 | 4.41 | 0.042 | 72.82 | 0.94 |
| Peru | 457 | 90 | 487 | 0.20 | 0.018 | 33.99 | 0.33 |
| Uruguay | 182 | 37 | 213 | 0.21 | 0.007 | 66.75 | 0.98 |
| Barbados | 24 | 19 | 38 | 0.76 | 0.004 | 24.61 | 0.75 |
| Guyana | 110 | 6 | 107 | 0.06 | 0.001 | -39.16 | -0.39 |
| Jamaica | 212 | 45 | 224 | 0.21 | 0.009 | 71.12 | 0.26 |
| Cyprus | 95 | 88 | 174 | 0.93 | 0.017 | 82.83 | 0.90 |
| Syria | 270 | 73 | 325 | 0.27 | 0.014 | 61.72 | 0.76 |
| Malaysia | 1707 | 227 | 1924 | 0.13 | 0.044 | 53.16 | 0.96 |
| Singapore | 1917 | 496 | 2134 | 0.26 | 0.097 | 8.79 | 0.44 |
| Gabon | 242 | 37 | 254 | 0.15 | 0.007 | 3.05 | 0.31 |
| Tunisia | 197 | 91 | 283 | 0.46 | 0.018 | 90.71 | 0.95 |
| Guatemala | 212 | 47 | 257 | 0.22 | 0.009 | 74.84 | 0.96 |
| Subtotal | 11691 | 2770 | 13620 | 0.60 | 0.540 | 55.93 | 0.70 |

Group C:

| | | | | | | | |
|---|---|---|---|---|---|---|---|
| Ireland | 413 | 167 | 541 | 0.40 | 0.033 | 36.10 | 0.76 |
| Portugal | 344 | 280 | 592 | 0.82 | 0.055 | 80.40 | 0.88 |
| Australia | 1731 | 402 | 2105 | 0.23 | 0.078 | 56.96 | 0.93 |
| New Zealand | 921 | 81 | 963 | 0.09 | 0.016 | -16.71 | 0.53 |
| South Africa | 1598 | 286 | 1799 | 0.18 | 0.056 | 62.06 | 0.70 |
| Subtotal | 5007 | 1216 | 5999 | 0.37 | 0.237 | 59.11 | 0.82 |
| Total | 21282 | 5126 | 24893 | 0.68 | 0.999 | 46.48 | 0.71 |

N.B. Subtotals and totals are obtained by simple summation for $S_1$, $S_2$, $S_{1+2}$ and $\beta$. They are obtained for $\alpha$, r and $\gamma$ by applying weights $\beta_1$. Thus, for all 46 countries, $\alpha = \sum_i \alpha_i \beta_i$. For Group A countries (Trust Fund), $\alpha_A = \beta_A^{-1} \sum_{i \in A} \alpha_i \beta_i$ with $\beta_A = \sum_{i \in A} \beta_i$. Minor differences in the summation are due to computer rounding errors.

Table 14.4  Extending the Scope of the Facility to Cover Fluctuations in the Cost of Cereals Imports
1 = Earnings from merchandise and service exports
2 = Cost of cereals imports
1-2 = Earnings from merchandise and service exports minus cost of cereals imports

| Country | Sums of shortfalls | | | Variance ratio $\alpha = S_2/S_1$ | Country share $\beta_i = S_{i2}/S_2$ | Correlation coefficient r | Cost ratio $\gamma = \dfrac{S_{1-2} - S_1}{S_2}$ |
|---|---|---|---|---|---|---|---|
| | $S_1$ | $S_2$ | $S_{1-2}$ | | | | |
| | (millions of SDRs) | | | | (Percentage) | | |
| **Group A:** | | | | | | | |
| Burundi | 48 | 1 | 48 | 0.02 | 0.000 | 43.35 | 0.40 |
| Cameroon | 193 | 8 | 190 | 0.04 | 0.003 | -36.18 | -0.27 |
| El Salvador | 194 | 10 | 191 | 0.05 | 0.003 | -21.82 | -0.32 |
| Ethiopia | 87 | 13 | 81 | 0.15 | 0.004 | -54.45 | -0.42 |
| Gambia, The | 21 | 1 | 19 | 0.05 | 0.000 | 23.02 | -1.65 |
| Haita | 40 | 3 | 34 | 0.08 | 0.001 | -56.06 | -1.76 |
| Honduras | 114 | 10 | 118 | 0.08 | 0.003 | 76.94 | 0.43 |
| India | 1190 | 783 | 1321 | 0.66 | 0.250 | -4.73 | 0.17 |
| Jordan | 302 | 12 | 293 | 0.04 | 0.004 | -32.46 | -0.77 |
| Kenya | 284 | 20 | 284 | 0.07 | 0.007 | 24.09 | -0.01 |
| Liberia | 85 | 7 | 84 | 0.09 | 0.002 | -11.07 | -0.13 |
| Mali Republic | 30 | 28 | 55 | 0.95 | 0.009 | 46.89 | 0.91 |
| Mauritania | 42 | 4 | 41 | 0.11 | 0.001 | -26.35 | -0.12 |
| Morocco | 465 | 135 | 454 | 0.29 | 0.043 | -44.60 | -0.03 |
| Pakistan | 265 | 178 | 328 | 0.67 | 0.057 | -17.75 | 0.35 |
| Rwanda | 43 | 2 | 43 | 0.05 | 0.001 | 4.25 | -0.22 |
| Somalia | 27 | 19 | 21 | 0.72 | 0.006 | -77.48 | -0.29 |
| Thailand | 874 | 5 | 866 | 0.01 | 0.002 | -96.27 | -1.50 |
| Upper Volta | 22 | 4 | 23 | 0.19 | 0.001 | -6.59 | 0.31 |
| Afghanistan | 85 | 33 | 101 | 0.39 | 0.011 | -24.49 | 0.47 |
| Zambia | 864 | 23 | 881 | 0.03 | 0.007 | 52.64 | 0.73 |
| | 5272 | 1302 | 5476 | 0.57 | 0.416 | -10.66 | 0.16 |

Group B:

| | | | | | | | |
|---|---|---|---|---|---|---|---|
| Argentina | 1903 | 83 | 1848 | 0.04 | 0.027 | -35.84 | -0.66 |
| Brazil | 2206 | 254 | 2087 | 0.12 | 0.081 | -83.85 | -0.47 |
| Chile | 1164 | 177 | 1039 | 0.15 | 0.056 | -82.50 | -0.71 |
| Costa Rica | 131 | 9 | 129 | 0.07 | 0.003 | -12.29 | -0.30 |
| Dominican Republic | 207 | 36 | 189 | 0.18 | 0.012 | -43.86 | -0.49 |
| Mexico | 1206 | 455 | 1292 | 0.38 | 0.145 | -10.00 | 0.19 |
| Nicaragua | 128 | 8 | 129 | 0.06 | 0.002 | 29.47 | 0.08 |
| Panama | 248 | 8 | 245 | 0.03 | 0.002 | -8.77 | -0.41 |
| Peru | 487 | 72 | 505 | 0.15 | 0.023 | -8.15 | 0.26 |
| Uruguay | 218 | 31 | 227 | 0.14 | 0.010 | 15.87 | 0.29 |
| Barbados | 38 | 3 | 35 | 0.09 | 0.001 | -72.80 | -0.88 |
| Guyana | 107 | 2 | 105 | 0.02 | 0.001 | -41.35 | -0.82 |
| Jamaica | 224 | 24 | 208 | 0.11 | 0.008 | -84.91 | -0.67 |
| Cyprus | 174 | 27 | 162 | 0.15 | 0.009 | -59.97 | -0.46 |
| Syria | 325 | 95 | 320 | 0.29 | 0.030 | -63.85 | -0.06 |
| Malaysia | 1924 | 137 | 1873 | 0.07 | 0.044 | -73.98 | -0.37 |
| Singapore | 2134 | 72 | 2113 | 0.03 | 0.023 | -78.86 | -0.29 |
| Gabon | 254 | 3 | 252 | 0.01 | 0.001 | -61.84 | -0.57 |
| Tunisia | 283 | 28 | 295 | 0.10 | 0.009 | 19.52 | 0.42 |
| Guatemala | 257 | 9 | 255 | 0.04 | 0.003 | 10.20 | -0.16 |
| | 13620 | 1532 | 13308 | 0.20 | 0.489 | -45.93 | -0.20 |

Group C:

| | | | | | | | |
|---|---|---|---|---|---|---|---|
| Ireland | 541 | 49 | 536 | 0.09 | 0.016 | -43.50 | -0.09 |
| Portugal | 592 | 137 | 562 | 0.23 | 0.044 | -61.26 | -0.22 |
| Australia | 2105 | 2 | 2105 | 0.00 | 0.001 | -13.93 | 0.34 |
| New Zealand | 963 | 23 | 978 | 0.02 | 0.007 | 87.80 | 0.67 |
| South Africa | 1799 | 87 | 1808 | 0.05 | 0.023 | -29.50 | 0.10 |
| Subtotal | 5999 | 297 | 5990 | 0.14 | 0.095 | -37.39 | -0.03 |
| Total: | 24891 | 3131 | 24773 | 0.35 | 1.000 | -30.45 | -0.03 |

N.B. Subtotals and totals are obtained by simple summation for $S_1$, $S_2$, $S_{1-2}$ and $\beta$. They are obtained for $\alpha$, r and $\gamma$ by applying weights $\beta_1$. Thus, for all 46 countries, $\alpha = \sum_i \alpha_i \beta_i$. For Group A countries (Trust Fund) $\alpha_A = \beta_A^{-1} \sum_{i \in A} \alpha_i \beta_i$ with $\beta_A = \sum_{i \in A} \beta_i$. Minor differences in the summation are due to computer rounding errors.

Table 14.5  Extending the Scope of the Facility to Cover Fluctuations in the Cost of Cereals Imports Net of
Aid Content
1 = Earnings from merchandise and service exports
2 = Costs of cereals imports net of aid content
1-2 = Earnings from merchandise and services exports minus cost of cereals imports net of aid content

| | Sums of shortfalls | | | Variance ratio $\alpha = S_2/S_1$ | Country share $\beta_i = S_{i2}/S_2$ | Correlation coefficient r | Cost ratio $\gamma = \dfrac{S_{1-2} - S_1}{S_2}$ |
|---|---|---|---|---|---|---|---|
| | $S_1$ | $S_2$ | $S_{1-2}$ | | | | |
| | (millions of SDRs) | | | (Percentage) | | | |
| **Group A:** | | | | | | | |
| Burundi | 48 | 1 | 49 | 0.02 | 0.000 | 45.78 | 0.62 |
| Cameroon | 193 | 9 | 189 | 0.05 | 0.003 | -45.00 | -0.38 |
| El Salvador | 194 | 11 | 191 | 0.05 | 0.004 | -21.31 | -0.29 |
| Ethiopia | 87 | 5 | 87 | 0.06 | 0.002 | -12.30 | 0.00 |
| Gambia, The | 21 | 1 | 19 | 0.05 | 0.000 | 33.92 | -1.49 |
| Haiti | 40 | 6 | 36 | 0.15 | 0.002 | -54.65 | -0.66 |
| Honduras | 114 | 8 | 118 | 0.07 | 0.003 | 72.60 | 0.43 |
| India | 1190 | 641 | 1211 | 0.54 | 0.221 | 0.62 | 0.03 |
| Jordan | 302 | 17 | 290 | 0.06 | 0.006 | -34.94 | -0.71 |
| Kenya | 284 | 13 | 288 | 0.05 | 0.004 | 53.96 | 0.34 |
| Liberia | 85 | 6 | 84 | 0.08 | 0.002 | -17.37 | -0.20 |
| Mali Republic | 30 | 25 | 47 | 0.84 | 0.009 | 32.92 | 0.69 |
| Mauritania | 42 | 4 | 42 | 0.10 | 0.001 | -2.70 | 0.02 |
| Morocco | 465 | 131 | 433 | 0.28 | 0.005 | -49.42 | -0.25 |
| Pakistan | 265 | 84 | 240 | 0.32 | 0.009 | -61.96 | -0.30 |
| Rwanda | 43 | 1 | 42 | 0.03 | 0.000 | -74.37 | -1.08 |
| Somalia | 27 | 11 | 25 | 0.42 | 0.004 | -59.66 | -0.18 |
| Thailand | 874 | 6 | 865 | 0.01 | 0.002 | -91.85 | -1.35 |
| Upper Volta | 22 | 3 | 21 | 0.13 | 0.001 | -13.85 | -0.34 |
| Aghanistan | 85 | 19 | 94 | 0.22 | 0.006 | -15.50 | 0.51 |
| Zambia | 864 | 23 | 881 | 0.03 | 0.008 | 52.27 | 0.73 |
| Subtotal | 5272 | 1026 | 5251 | 0.43 | 0.354 | -11.00 | -0.02 |

Group B:

| | | | | | | | |
|---|---|---|---|---|---|---|---|
| Argentina | 1903 | 83 | 1848 | 0.04 | 0.029 | -35.84 | -0.66 |
| Brazil | 2206 | 299 | 2126 | 0.14 | 0.103 | -71.97 | -0.27 |
| Chile | 1164 | 170 | 1037 | 0.15 | 0.059 | -83.67 | -0.75 |
| Costa Rica | 131 | 9 | 128 | 0.07 | 0.003 | -15.90 | -0.31 |
| Dominican Republic | 207 | 31 | 191 | 0.15 | 0.011 | -36.20 | -0.54 |
| Mexico | 1206 | 455 | 1289 | 0.38 | 0.157 | -9.99 | 0.18 |
| Nicaragua | 128 | 7 | 128 | 0.06 | 0.003 | 30.47 | 0.03 |
| Panama | 248 | 8 | 245 | 0.03 | 0.003 | -7.08 | -0.41 |
| Peru | 487 | 70 | 508 | 0.14 | 0.024 | -6.55 | 0.31 |
| Uruguay | 218 | 29 | 222 | 0.13 | 0.010 | -6.63 | 0.13 |
| Barbados | 38 | 3 | 35 | 0.09 | 0.001 | -72.80 | -0.88 |
| Guyana | 107 | 2 | 105 | 0.02 | 0.001 | -41.68 | -0.80 |
| Jamaica | 224 | 26 | 208 | 0.12 | 0.009 | -85.34 | -0.60 |
| Cyprus | 174 | 27 | 161 | 0.15 | 0.009 | -60.58 | -0.51 |
| Syria | 325 | 83 | 332 | 0.25 | 0.029 | -53.90 | 0.08 |
| Malaysia | 1924 | 137 | 1874 | 0.07 | 0.047 | -73.81 | -0.37 |
| Singapore | 2134 | 72 | 2113 | 0.03 | 0.025 | -78.89 | -0.29 |
| Gabon | 254 | 3 | 252 | 0.01 | 0.001 | -68.34 | -0.61 |
| Tunisia | 283 | 29 | 282 | 0.10 | 0.010 | 16.85 | -0.03 |
| Guatemala | 257 | 9 | 254 | 0.04 | 0.003 | -9.57 | -0.24 |
| Subtotal | 13620 | 1552 | 13339 | 0.20 | 0.536 | -44.64 | -0.18 |

Group C:

| | | | | | | | |
|---|---|---|---|---|---|---|---|
| Ireland | 541 | 49 | 538 | 0.09 | 0.017 | -45.05 | -0.05 |
| Portugal | 592 | 159 | 576 | 0.27 | 0.055 | -58.41 | -0.09 |
| Australia | 2105 | 2 | 2105 | 0.00 | 0.001 | -13.93 | 0.34 |
| New Zealand | 963 | 23 | 978 | 0.02 | 0.008 | 87.80 | 0.67 |
| South Africa | 1799 | 87 | 1808 | 0.05 | 0.030 | -29.50 | 0.10 |
| Subtotal | 5999 | 320 | 6006 | 0.16 | 0.110 | -37.91 | 0.02 |
| Total | 24891 | 2898 | 24596 | 0.28 | 1.000 | -31.99 | -0.10 |

N.B.  Subtotals and totals are obtained by simple summation for $S_1$, $S_2$, $S_{1-2}$ and $\beta$.  They are obtained for $\alpha$, r and $\gamma$ by applying weights $\beta_i$.  Thus, for all 46 countries, $\alpha = \sum_i \alpha_i \beta_i$.  For Group A countries (Trust Fund) $\alpha_A = \beta_A^{-1} \sum_{i \varepsilon A} \alpha_i \beta_i$ with $\beta_A = \sum_{i \varepsilon A} \beta_i$.  Minor differences in the summation are due to computer rounding errors.

countries would have gained from the inclusion of cereal imports while the other two groups would have lost. This occurs because, for Trust Fund countries, the relative importance of fluctuations in the cost of cereals imports was greater (.57 compared with .20 and .14), while the negative correlation between excesses in cereals imports and shortfalls in export earnings was weaker (-.11 compared with -.46 and -.39).

Deducting the aid content from the market value of cereals imports affects mainly the Trust Fund countries. The sum of the net shortfalls of these countries is raised marginally by taking into account the gross value of cereals imports (Table 14.4). But this modest gain disappears when a deduction is made for the aid content of cereals imports (Table 14.5).

To conclude, the effects of changes in the scope of the Fund facility on the sum of the shortfalls of the 46 sample countries are summarized in Table 14.6. In rows (1) and (2), coverage is restricted to the primary commodities, which account for at least 5 percent of total merchandise exports. In row (1), shortfalls are calculated, as in STABEX, by adding up all the commodities shortfalls without taking account of commodity excesses. In all other cases, shortfalls are calculated instead, as in the Fund facility, by netting out commodity excesses from commodity shortfalls. This netting out reduces the sum of shortfalls from SDR 21.0 billion in row (1) to SDR 13.8 billion in row (2). Enlarging coverage to all merchandise exports (as in the Fund facility) raises the sum of shortfalls from SDR 13.8 billion in row (2) to SDR 21.3 billion in row (4). Enlarging the present scope of the Fund facility to cover export services raises the sum of shortfalls to SDR 24.9 billion. Enlarging coverage to protect members against fluctuations in the cost of cereal imports does not, however, raise the sum of shortfalls any further.

The index of fluctuations is greater for primary commodities (6.0 percent) than for other merchandise exports (5.2 percent) and service exports (4.0 percent). But the highest value of the index of fluctuations is for the cost of cereals imports net of aid content (17.1 percent).

## Compensatory Financing 331

Table 14.6 Simulated Shortfalls in Export Earnings by Commodity Groups[1]/
(1963-75, IFS Data, 46 Countries)

| | Sum[3]/ of | | Index of fluctuation |
|---|---|---|---|
| | Export earnings | Short-falls | Sum of shortfalls as percentage of sum of earnings |
| | (billions of SDRs) | | |
| (1) Individual primary commodities[2]/ | 230 | 21.0 | 9.1 |
| (2) All primary commodities as a group[2]/ | 230 | 13.8 | 6.0 |
| (3) Other merchandise exports | 211 | 11.0 | 5.2 |
| (4) All merchandise exports | 441 | 21.3 | 4.8 |
| (5) Service exports | 127 | 5.1 | 4.0 |
| (6) All merchandise & services | 568 | 24.9 | 4.4 |
| (7) Cost of cereal imports | 23 | 3.1[4]/ | 13.5[4]/ |
| (8) (All merchandise & services) - (Cost of cereal imports) | 545 | 24.8 | 4.5 |
| (9) Aid content of cereal imports | 6 | 0.8 | 13.3 |
| (10) (Cost of cereal imports) - (Aid content) | 17 | 2.9[4]/ | 17.1[4]/ |
| (11) (All merchandise & services) - (Cost of cereal imports - aid content) | 551 | 24.6 | 4.5 |

[1]/ Shortfalls are calculated, as for the purpose of the compensatory financing facility, as downward deviations from the five-year moving average centered on the shortfall year. Calculations are made in nominal terms and using an arithmetic average, according to current practices.

[2]/ The primary commodities selected are those for which export earnings account for, at least, 5 percent of the country's earnings from all merchandise exports, since the IFS coverage of commodity exports is available only on this basis. Row (1) gives the sum of commodity shortfalls calculated, as for the purpose of STABEX, without taking into account commodity excesses. Row (2) gives the sum of all net country excesses from commodity shortfalls for each year.

[3]/ Sums of shortfalls and sums of earnings for all countries and all years.

[4]/ Excesses in the cost of cereals imports measured as upwards deviations from a five-year moving average centered on the excess year.

## Notes

1. *IMF Survey*, March 6, 1978, pp. 69-71.

2. See the section entitled "Statistical Sample" under the heading "Statistical Analysis," p. 318.

3. When an arithmetic average is used to calculate the trend value, the

332 Louis M. Goreux

net shortfall is equal to the sum of the shortfalls minus the sum of the excesses, but it is not so when the geometric average is used.

4. Assuming again costs are proportional to the sum of the net short-falls.

5. See demonstration in L. M. Goreux (1977).

6. They cover: freight and insurance on international shipments; other transportation such as passenger fares, time charters, port disbursements, mail fees, etc.; travel; investment income both direct and other; other government not included elsewhere—embassies and consulates; and other services—construction, technical services, nonmerchandise insurance, workers' earnings, etc.

7. $3,126 = 24,891 - 21,282 = S_{1+2} - S_1$.

8. This percentage may be calculated in two different ways since

$$\gamma = \frac{S_{1+2} - S_1}{S_2} = \sum_i \beta_i \gamma_i.$$

# References

Goreux, L. M. "Compensatory Financing: The Cyclical Pattern of Export Shortfalls." IMF Staff Papers No. 24 (November 1977), p. 633.

Johnson, D. G. "Increased Stability of Grain Supplies in Developing Countries: Optimal Carryovers and Insurance." *The New International Economic Order: The North-South Debate*, ed. by J. N. Bhagwati. Cambridge, Mass.: MIT Press, 1977.

Valdés, Alberto, and Panos Konandreas. "Assessing Food Insecurity Based on National Aggregates in Developing Countries." Chapter 2 of this book.

# Participants:
# IFPRI-CIMMYT Conference on Food Security for Developing Countries

## November 1978

R. Glenn Anderson
Centro Internacional de
  Mejoramiento de Maíz y Trigo
Mexico

Edgardo Barandiaran
Universidad Católica
Chile

Randolph Barker
Cornell University
U.S.A.

David Bigman
International Monetary Fund
U.S.A.

Ahmad Birowo
Ministry of Agriculture
Indonesia

Norman Borlaug
Centro Internacional de
  Mejoramiento de Maíz y Trigo
Mexico

Raoul Branco
Food and Agriculture Organization
Italy

Derek Byerlee
Centro Internacional de
  Mejoramiento de Maíz y Trigo
Mexico

Wilfred V. Candler
International Bank for
  Reconstruction and Development
U.S.A.

Ricardo Castillo-Arronte
Compañía Nacional de
  Subsistencias Populares
Mexico

Ralph Kirby Davidson
Rockefeller Foundation
U.S.A.

Jorge García García
Universidad de los Andes
Colombia

Arturo Goetz
World Food Council
Italy

Ahmed A. Goueli
Zagazig University
Egypt

Barbara Huddleston
International Food Policy
  Research Institute
U.S.A.

D. Gale Johnson
The University of Chicago
U.S.A.

*333*

334                                                    *Participants*

Timothy Josling
Stanford University
U.S.A.

Dilawar Ali Khan
Economic Research Institute
Pakistan

Panos Konandreas
International Food Policy
  Research Institute
U.S.A.

Uma Lele
International Bank for
  Reconstruction and Development
U.S.A.

Kighoma Malima
University of Dar es Salaam
Tanzania

Charles Mann
Rockefeller Foundation
U.S.A.

John W. Mellor
International Food Policy
  Research Institute
U.S.A.

Juan Carlos Martinez
Centro Internacional de
  Mejoramiento de Maíz y Trigo
Mexico

Dharm Narain
International Food Policy
  Research Institute
U.S.A.

Shlomo Reutlinger
International Bank for
  Reconstruction and Development
U.S.A.

Alexander Sarris
University of California
U.S.A.

Ammar Siamwalla
International Food Policy
  Research Institute
U.S.A.

Kutlu Somel
University of Ankara
Turkey

Peter Svedberg
University of Stockholm
Sweden

Stephen Tangermann
Goethe University
West Germany

Alberto Valdés
International Food Policy
  Research Institute
U.S.A.

Harry Walters
International Bank for
  Reconstruction and Development
U.S.A.

Donald Winkelmann
Centro Internacional de
  Mejoramiento de Maíz y Trigo
Mexico

# Index

Abbott, Phillip C., 289
Accumulation price, 224–225
ACP. *See* African, Caribbean, and Pacific regions
Actual values, 42–43
Adabia port (Egypt), 156
ADB. *See* Asian Development Bank
Afghanistan, 27
Africa, 274, 275(tables), 276(table), 277. *See also* East Africa; Production fluctuations, African; Southern Africa; Sub-Sahara Africa; individual countries
African, Caribbean, and Pacific (ACP) regions, 309, 310
Agricultural Trade and Development and Assistance Act (PL480) (1954), 287, 293, 297
Agriculture, 3–4, 10, 19–20, 299. *See also* Cereals; Crop yield variability; Production fluctuations; Technological change, and crop yields
Agronomic practices, 11, 62, 65–66, 68–70
Alexandria (Egypt), 156
Algeria, 29, 30(table), 246, 247–248(table)
Animal feed. *See* Livestock feed

Arab Food Security Declaration, 155
Arab League, 155
Arab Monetary Fund, 17, 309
Arbitrage, 170, 177
Argentina, 258
ASEAN. *See* Association of Southeast Asian Nations
Asia. *See* East Asia; South Asia; Southeast Asia; individual countries
Asian Development Bank (ADB), 54, 85
Asian Rice Trade Fund, 89
Association of Southeast Asian Nations (ASEAN), 12
and cereal calorie supply, 95(table)
countries of, 79
and food and energy security, 89, 91
rice imports and exports, 83(table), 92, 95
Australia, 258, 266

Balance of payments, 20, 128, 156, 179, 196, 289, 307, 308, 310. *See also* Balance of Payments Manual
Balance of Payments Manual, 319
Bananas, 111. *See also* Plantains

*335*

Bangladesh, 3
food import/export ratio, 31, 32(table), 279
food imports and export earnings, 43, 44, 45(table), 46
and grain insurance program, 274
as insurance scheme beneficiary, 246, 247-248(table)
production stability in, 33, 34(table)
and rice trade, 89
Barbados, 319
Barker, Randolph, 11, 54
Barley, 144
Barter, 102, 103(figure)
Benefit-cost ratios, 70, 197-203
Bigman, David, 12, 14, 83, 85, 137, 232
Bihar (India), 63
Bimas Program. *See* Indonesia, Bimas Program
Blast disease, 70
Brazil, 226, 246, 247-248(table)
Brown planthopper, 70, 73
BSA. *See* Buffer Stock Agency
Budget. *See* Government budget
Buffer Stock Agency (BSA), 226
Buffer stocks, 14, 75, 82, 90, 91, 92, 136-137, 185, 300
and food security model, 189, 192, 193, 194, 196, 199(table), 200, 201, 203, 205, 206, 209
and Sarris model, 226, 228-229
BULOG. *See* National Logistics Agency

Calorie consumption calculations, 129-130
Cambodia, 3
Canada, 56, 258, 263
Candler, Wilfred, 12, 13
Capital market, 8, 9
mechanism, 5
Carryover. *See* Optimal grain reserves

Cash balances, 5
Cash flows, 169
Cassava, 106, 111, 115
Central Luzon (the Philippines), 70
Central-plan countries, 170
Centro Internacional de Mejoramiento de Maíz y Trigo (CIMMYT), 2. *See also* Conference on Food Security for Developing Countries
Cereals
consumption of, 54, 111-112, 201, 202, 241, 257
defined, 250(n1)
domestic prices of, 8, 188, 189
drought-resistant, 106, 115. *See also* Millet; Sorghum
exports, 178, 189
imports, 178, 189, 202, 307, 322-323(table), 326-329(tables), 330. *See also* Compensatory financing schemes, and food security
and infrastructure, 62, 64
international prices of, 1, 35-37, 178, 190, 194, 204, 205, 241, 257, 258, 262-263, 279
models, 187-188, 189-190, 206, 258
production, 35, 53, 54, 56, 105, 112, 232, 243, 257. *See also* Food aid, requirements
proportion of, in total food consumption, 27-29, 35
reserves of, 116-117, 178, 243, 263-268. *See also* Food aid, and reserves; Grain insurance program; international grain reserve system; Optimal grain reserves
stocks of, 172, 178
surplus of, 190, 204-206, 308
*See also* Crop yield variability; International food insurance

# Index

337

scheme, model; Livestock feed; Noncereal foods; Storage; individual cereals and countries

CFF (compensatory financing facility). *See* Compensatory financing schemes, compensatory financing facility

Chile, 30, 271, 279

China. *See* People's Republic of China

CIMMYT. *See* Centro Internacional de Mejoramiento de Maíz y Trigo

Climatic change, 3-4, 55-56, 57, 257

Closed market, 161, 162-163, 164, 171(table), 194, 196, 200, 203

Coarse Grains Trade Convention, 213

Colombia
calorie consumption in, 129, 130, 131(table), 133, 135
calorie output, supply, and consumption, 126(table)
cereal production in, 127-128
food consumption in, 13, 123-124, 125-126
as food exporter, 124
food import/export ratio, 31, 32(table)
food imports of, 128(table), 134, 137
food insecurity in, 127, 128, 133, 136, 138
food prices in, 134-135
food production in, 125(table), 126-129, 134-135, 137, 138
and foreign exchange, 125, 127, 128, 137, 138
infrastructure, 129, 137
and malnutrition, 123, 129, 130, 133
nutritional status in, 123,

125-126, 129-133, 135
policy options of, 136-138
population, per-capita income, and expenditure, 132(table), 133-135, 136(table)
rural poverty, 136, 137
wheat imports of, 128

Committee on World Food Security, 298

Common Agricultural Policy, 262

Communication, 255, 269, 280

Compensatory financing schemes, 17, 181, 188, 233, 301
compensatory financing facility (CFF), 312, 313
and food security, 307-313
and grain reserve, 243
statistical analysis, 313-330

Conference on Climate Change, Food Production, and Interstate Conflict, 57-58

Conference on Food Security for Developing Countries, 2, 171, 259, 280-281
papers introduced, 10-20
participants, 333-334

Consultative Sub-Committee on Surplus Disposal (CSD), 302, 303

Consumer food prices, 172, 179

Consumer goods, 113, 146

Consumption adjustments, 14, 177, 179, 180, 204, 231

Consumption stability. *See* Food consumption, stability

Cooling trend. *See* Climatic change

Corn. *See* Maize

Credit, 181, 301

Crop insurance, 9-10, 211

Crop yield stability, 65-66, 69, 71, 74

Crop yield variability, 55-60, 62-76, 106
coefficient of variation, 55, 58, 59(tables), 68, 69(table). *See*

338 Index

*also* Production fluctuations, and coefficient of variation
CSD. *See* Consultative Sub-Committee on Surplus Disposal
Cyprus, 319

DANE. *See* Departamento Administrativo Nacional de Estadística
Day, R. H., 66
Demand variability, 267, 286(table)
Departamento Administrativo Nacional de Estadística (DANE), 135
Department of Agriculture. *See* United States, Department of Agriculture
Developed countries
and consumer price stabilization, 170
exports, 178
national policy options, 171-176
wheat production, 165, 166(table), 167
*See also* Consumption adjustments; individual countries
Developing countries. *See* Less-developed countries
Disease. *See* Plant diseases
Distribution. *See* Food reallocation; Public food distribution
Domestic grain reserves, 18, 19, 150. *See also* individual countries
Downy mildew, 70, 71-72
Drainage, 60, 62, 154, 155. *See also* Water control
Drought, 60, 63, 64
Drought-resistant crops. *See* Cereals, drought-resistant; Millet; Sorghum
Dry season, 69

Dual price system, 137

East Africa, 12, 101, 102, 116
and cereal consumption, 111
food crisis in (1973-1974), 106
marketing channels in, 102, 103(figure), 114
and national food security policies, 105, 106, 117-118
*See also* individual countries
East Asia, 64, 65, 262. *See also* Japan; Korea
EC. *See* European Community
Economists, international agencies', 105. *See also* Statistics
EEC (European Economic Community). *See* European Community
Egypt
and Arab cooperation, 155
calorie intake in, 144
economy of, 150, 156
exports of, 146, 147-148(tables)
feddans, 143
Five-Year Plan, 156
food consumption in, 50, 144-146
food import/export ratio, 31, 32(table), 279
and food imports, 13, 36, 37(table), 40(table), 41
food insecurity in, 154, 156
food price policy of, 151, 152, 153, 154
food rationing in, 153
and food security, 143, 148, 154-157
and France, 150
as insurance scheme beneficiary, 246, 247-248(table)
maize consumption in, 144, 146, 153(figure)
maize production in, 149-150, 152
population of, 143

*Index*

production stability in, 33, 34(table), 151, 232
rice consumption in, 144, 146, 150
rice exports of, 152-153
sorghum consumption in, 144
subsidized commodities in, 151, 153-154
and United States, 150, 151(table)
wheat consumption in, 144, 146, 152(figure), 154, 156
wheat production in, 151, 156
Emergency food assistance. *See* Food aid
Ending stock. *See* Minimum working stock
ESCAP. *See* United Nations Economic and Social Commission for Asia and the Pacific
Ethiopia, 28, 101, 102, 246, 247-248(table)
European Community (EC), 150, 172, 214, 226, 258, 262-263, 309, 310
Evenson, R. E., 71
E-V frontier, 69
Export earnings. *See* Real export earnings
Exports. *See* Food export; Merchandise exports; Service exports

Famine, 256
relief, 115, 288
*See also* Food aid
FAO. *See* Food and Agriculture Organization
Far East. *See* East Asia
Farm income, 172, 193-194, 204, 308
Feddans. *See* Egypt, feddans
Fertilizer, 54, 66, 68-69, 70, 75, 87
crisis, 75

Financing, 304. *See also* Compensatory financing schemes
Five-Point Program of Action, 298
Floods, 60, 63, 64
Food aid, 7, 14, 15-18, 36-37, 111, 150, 269, 287-288, 307-308
and foreign exchange, 177, 180-181
and insurance facility, 301-304
requirements, 288-289, 291-293, 296, 301
and reserves, 296-300
and surpluses, 180
Food Aid Convention (1967), 213, 287, 297
Food and Agriculture Organization (FAO), 26, 50, 89, 107, 213, 216, 225, 288, 289, 298. *See also* Committee on World Food Security; Consultative Sub-Committee on Surplus Disposal
Food assistance. *See* Food aid
Food consumption, 5, 38-39, 111, 301
in calorie equivalents, 28(table)
downward adjustment of, 20, 25, 30-31, 38
and nutritional requirements, 29
and prices, 25
and production, 25, 33, 38, 211
rural, 111-112, 191, 192(table)
stability, 9, 11, 12, 13, 19, 33, 48, 164, 169, 230. *See also* Food security, decision rules
staple, 28(table), 29-31, 35
urban, 112, 191, 192(table)
variability, 39-40, 50
*See also* Consumption adjustments; Historical trend; Target consumption levels
Food crises, 38
1965, 76

1972-1974, 1, 76, 288
1973/1974, 106
Food export, 36, 112, 115, 260.
  *See also* Cereals, exports;
  Subsidies, export; individual
  crops and countries
Food for work program, 10
Foodgrains. *See* Cereals;
  individual cereals
Food Import Bill Insurance
  Scheme, 233
Food imports, 7, 33, 260
  and consumption stability,
    39-41
  and export earnings, 42-47,
    51(table)
  financing, 20, 31
  and prices, 35-37, 38
  ratio to total export receipts,
    11, 31, 32(table)
  and rice stocks, 87-88
  *See also* Cereals, imports;
    Cereals, international prices
    of; Import costs; Price
    fluctuations; Stabilization of
    Export Receipts; Trend,
    imports; individual countries
Food insecurity, 4-6, 9, 10, 18-19,
    101-102
  causes, 25, 33-37, 163, 257-259
  defined, 42, 242
  and national policy options,
    168-170, 171
  reduction of, 38-44, 46-47
  sources, 241
  *See also* Less-developed
    countries, and food
    insecurity; individual
    countries
Food markets, 4, 101, 161. *See
  also* Closed market; Marketed
  surpluses; Marketing
  parastatal; Open market
Food production. *See* Marketed
  production; Production
  fluctuations

Food rationing. *See* Egypt, food
  rationing in
Food reallocation, 186, 210-211,
  233
Food reserves, 101, 105-106,
  116-117, 155. *See also*
  Cereals, reserves of; Food
  aid, and reserves; Wheat
  reserve stock system
Food security
  alternatives, 187-211, 259-279
  and Association of Southeast
    Asian Nations, 89-91
  assumptions about, 102
  commodity requirements for,
    112-113
  concepts of, 3-4, 5
  decision rules, 38-39, 40(table),
    41, 45(table), 46, 51(table),
    187, 188-190
  defined, 1, 2-3, 38
  and developed countries, 167,
    172, 299. *See also* Food aid
  and distribution, 161
  and domestic trade, 8
  and international market,
    143, 156
  international scheme
    planning, 33, 111, 116-117,
    118, 177-182, 203-206,
    230-233
  issues, 12, 75
  national models, 66, 70, 111
  policies, 2, 14, 16, 115-116,
    136-137, 154-157. *See also*
    Developed countries, and
    national policy options;
    National food security
    policies
  rural, 111, 114-115. *See also*
    Food consumption, rural
  and technology, 256
  urban, 116. *See also* Food
    consumption, urban
  *See also* Capital market;
    Compensatory financing

*Index*                                                341

schemes, and food security;
Food insecurity; Food
reserves; National food
security policies; individual
countries
Food Security Assistance Fund,
299
Food Security Assistance Scheme
(1975), 298, 299
Food supplies, 4, 7, 53, 101, 116,
197, 206–207, 299–300
urban, 109, 118
*See also* Staple food supplies;
individual countries
Foreign exchange, 20, 41, 113,
170, 171, 190, 196, 197,
205(table), 208, 210
assistance, 179–181
constraints, 11, 31, 48, 206–207
reserves, 5, 6
and rice, 79
*See also* Colombia, and foreign
exchange; Food aid, and
foreign exchange; Less-
developed countries, and
foreign exchange
France, 150
Free trade policy, 192–193, 194,
196, 197, 202, 205, 210, 262

Gabler, Eric C., 11
Gambia, The, 319
Gap analyses, 54
García García, Jorge, 13
General Agency for Commodities'
Supplies, 149
Ghana, 232
Goldman, R. H., 83
Goreux, Louis M., 17
Government budget, 196, 201,
203, 210
Grain. *See* Cereals; Livestock
feed; individual cereals
Grain insurance program, 16–17,
259, 268–274, 276–282

Green leafhopper, 73
Green Revolution, 57, 149
Grennes, Thomas, 258
Groundnuts, 29
Guatemala, 232

Haiti, 319
Hathaway, Dale E., 241
Herdt, R. W., 54
Historical trend, 39, 41, 48,
245–246, 249(table), 301
Huddleston, Barbara, 16, 17, 18,
289

IBRD. *See* International Bank for
Reconstruction and
Development
ICBF. *See* Instituto Colombiano
de Bienestar Familiar
IDA. *See* International
Development Association
IEFR. *See* International
Emergency Food Reserve
IFPRI. *See* International Food
Policy Research Institute
IFS. *See* International Financial
Statistics
IMF. *See* International Monetary
Fund
Import costs, 169, 178, 179–180,
181, 189, 193, 208, 232, 279,
307–309, 312, 319
Imports. *See* Food imports;
Import costs; Nonfood
imports; Target import
volume
Income
redistribution, 136, 137
transfer mechanisms, 9–10, 138,
202, 203
*See also* Farm income; Per-
capita income
India
dry-season cropped area, 69

342 Index

food aid to, 37
food import/export ratio, 31,
 32(table)
food imports, 40(table), 41, 319
food imports and export
 earnings, 43, 44, 45(table), 46
as insurance scheme beneficiary,
 246, 247-248(table)
irrigation in, 62, 63
millet, 74
as model for food security
 alternatives, 190-193
optimal carryover in, 274,
 275(tables), 276(table), 277
production stability in, 33,
 34(table)
rice-growing areas of, 71
rice stocks in, 87
rice trade, 89
and self-sufficiency, 7
wheat growing in, 72
Indian Council of Agricultural
 Research, 71
Indonesia
Bimas Program, 80, 87
brown planthopper damage in,
 70
food imports and export
 earnings, 45(table), 46
grain insurance program, 274
inflation in, 84
as insurance scheme beneficiary,
 246, 247-248(table)
irrigation in, 62, 63
maize market of, 94
production stability in, 33,
 34(table)
ragged stunt disease in, 73
as rice exporter, 82, 91, 92, 95
rice policy of, 83, 84-85, 87
rice prices in, 85-86, 87, 93
rice production in, 59(table)
rice stocks in, 87
and rice supplies, 12
and technology, 80

See also National Logistics
 Agency
Inflation, 84, 172, 223, 225
Informal markets. See Traditional
 production sector
Infrastructure. See Cereals,
 and infrastructure; Colombia,
 infrastructure;
 Communication; Transport
Insect damage, 60, 70
Insecticides, 70. See also
 Pesticides
Instituto Colombiano de Bienestar
 Familiar (ICBF), 123, 130
Insurance. See Crop insurance;
 Food aid, and insurance
 facility; Food aid,
 requirements; Food Import
 Bill Insurance Scheme; Grain
 insurance program;
 international food insurance
 scheme; Rice, insurance
International Bank for
 Reconstruction and
 Development (IBRD), 54,
 154, 319
International Center for Maize
 and Wheat. See Centro
 Internacional de
 Mejoramiento de Maíz y
 Trigo
International Development
 Association (IDA), 319
International Emergency Food
 Reserve (IEFR), 288
International Financial Statistics
 (IFS), 318
International food insurance
 scheme, 18, 106, 208, 241,
 242, 243, 290(table)
model, 243-250, 301
methodology, 252-254
See also Food aid, requirements
International Food Policy
 Research Institute (IFPRI), 2,

54, 241, 243, 291, 293, 294–295(table), 303
See also Conference on Food Security for Developing Countries
International grain reserve system, 14, 19, 177, 213, 220. See also Domestic grain reserves; Food reserves; Wheat reserve stock system
International Monetary Fund (IMF), 17, 18, 309, 310–311, 313, 315, 318, 319
International Rice Research Institute (IRRI), 71
International Sugar Agreement (1977), 313
International Undertaking on World Food Security, 213, 298, 300
International Wheat Agreement (IWA), 14, 296, 297, 298, 299, 300
1967, 287
1975, 213
1978 negotiations, 213–214, 312–313
International Wheat Council (IWC), 14, 220
Investment, 6, 25
Iran, 36, 37(table), 246, 247–248(table)
Iraq, 246, 247–248(table)
IRRI. See International Rice Research Institute
Irrigation, 54, 60, 62–63. See also Water control
IRRI Reporter, The, 73
IWA. See International Wheat Agreement
IWC. See International Wheat Council

Jamaica, 319

Japan, 172, 226, 258, 272. See also East Asia
Johnson, D. Gale, 16–17, 91, 220, 241, 289, 291, 308
Johnson, Paul, 258
Jordan, 319
Josling, Timothy, 13

Kenya, 101, 106, 116, 319
Konandreas, Panos, 6, 11, 14, 18, 232, 279, 289, 291–292, 308, 312
Korea, 246, 247–248(table), 279. See also East Asia
Kurtosis. See Standard deviation

Land
amelioration, 60, 62, 74, 154–155
classes, 60, 61(figure), 62
reclamation, 155
Large-scale production sector, 102, 103(figure)
LDCs. See Less-developed countries
Lele, Uma, 12, 13
Lesotho, 101
Less-developed countries (LDCs), 2, 4
and capital market, 9
countries included as, 269, 271
crop forecasts of, 280, 282
crop yield variability of, 66
export earnings, 47, 279
financial resources, 46, 47(table), 210
food consumption in, 28(table), 169, 242, 269, 278
food insecurity, 11–13, 19, 25–27, 41, 186, 210, 241
food production, 271
food supplies, 25, 54
and foreign exchange, 41, 241, 242

as importers, 6, 7, 25, 39, 48, 178, 204, 206, 229, 243, 296. *See also* Import costs
investments, 25–26
production stability in, 33, 54
trade opportunities, 191, 262
and Wheat Trade Convention, 230–233
*See also* Balance of payments; Food aid; Price fluctuations; Production fluctuations; individual countries
Liberia, 319
Libya, 31, 32(table), 232
Livestock feed, 112, 117, 149, 231, 256, 260
Livestock products, 27–28, 204

Marketed surpluses, 113–114, 115
Market identities, 171(table)
Marketing parastatal, 102, 103, 104–105, 116. *See also* Large-scale production sector; Namboard; National Milling Corporation; Traditional production sector
Masagana 99 Program. *See* Philippines, the, Masagana 99 Program
Merchandise exports, 321, 324–329(tables), 330, 331(table)
Mexico
export earnings of, 319
food import/export ratio, 31, 32(table)
as insurance scheme beneficiary, 246, 247–248(table)
wheat yields in, 70
*See also* Puebla Project; Yaqui Valley
Michalopoulos, Constantine, 303–304
Milled products, 105, 110(table), 116, 117, 152, 153

Millet, 12, 74, 107, 111
bulrush, 115
finger, 115
Minhas, B. S., 7
Minimum daily requirements level, 3, 210, 256
Minimum working stock (MWS), 216, 217, 218–219(figures)
excess, 225–226, 227(table)
Models. *See* Compensatory financing schemes, statistical analysis; Food security, national models; International food insurance scheme, model; Open economy model; Sarris, Alexander H., and world wheat economy simulation model
Macroeconomic stabilization policies, 8, 20, 90, 190, 193–197, 199, 200, 204–206
Maize
consumption, 111, 144, 146
diseases of. *See* Downy mildew; Streak virus; Stunt disease
as dominant commodity, 53, 115
as insurance compensation, 92–93
as insurance proposal grain, 272
international market in, 94
as livestock feed, 149
as source of energy and protein, 53
storage, 117
U.S. yields, 55
wheat and rice as substitutes, 112
*See also* Milled products; Tanzania, maize production in; United States, as maize exporter; Zambia, maize production in
Malawi, 101
Malaysia, 79, 80, 82–83, 91

# Index

Mali, 28, 319
Malnutrition, 3, 256, 272. *See also*
Colombia, and malnutrition
Manioc production, 272
Mann, Charles K., 58, 74
Market economies, 167, 168. *See also* Open economy model
Marketed production, 107,
109-111
Moisture
control, 54
stress, 62, 63, 72, 75
Monetary reserve, 106
Monoculture, 106
Monopsonistic parastatal, 102
Moorman, F. R., 60
land-class model, 61(figure)
Morocco
cereal imports, 319
food insecurity, 28
as insurance scheme beneficiary,
246, 247-248(table)
production stability in, 33,
34(table)
staple food consumption in, 29,
30(table)
Morris, David M., 9
Morrow, Daniel T., 15, 296
Most seriously affected (MSA)
countries, 18, 47, 289
MSA. *See* Most seriously affected
countries
Multilines, 72
Multilocation testing, 72
Multiplier process, 5
MWS. *See* Minimum working
stock

Namboard (Zambia), 103-104,
110-111
National food security policies, 7,
19, 55, 66, 105, 109, 114,
168-170, 171. *See also* Policy
options model

National Grains Authority (NGA)
(the Philippines), 84-85
National Logistics Agency
(BULOG) (Indonesia), 84-85
National Milling Corporation
(NMC) (Tanzania), 105, 109,
112, 116
Nebraska, 58-59, 63
NGA. *See* National Grains
Authority
Nigeria, 31, 40(table), 41, 232,
246, 247-248(table)
NMC. *See* National Milling
Corporation
Noncereal foods, 35, 123-124,
145(tables), 149, 153,
271-272. *See also* Livestock
products; Root crops;
Staples; Sugar
Nonfood imports, 43
Nonfood security, 181
NPK (nitrogen, phosphorus,
potassium), 68
Nutrition, 202. *See also* Minimum
daily requirements level

Oil. *See* Petroleum
Open-economy model, 187-193,
196, 210
Open market, 162(table), 163-164,
171(table)
Optimal grain reserves, 260-263,
264(table), 265(table), 266,
267-268, 273(table), 274,
275(tables)

Pakistan, 59(table), 60, 62, 274,
319
Panama, 319
Parastatal. *See* Marketing
parastatal; Monopsonistic
parastatal
People's Republic of China, 8, 62,
91, 94
Per-capita income, 256, 269

346                                *Index*

Peru, 29, 30(table), 232
Pesticides, 73. *See also*
    Insecticides
Petroleum
    and Association of Southeast
        Asian Nations, 89
    exporters, 318
Philippines, the
    drought in, 60
    floods in, 60
    food imports and export
        earnings, 44, 45(table)
    inflation in, 84
    as insurance scheme beneficiary,
        246, 247–248(table)
    and irrigation, 62, 63
    maize market of, 94
    Masagana 99 Program, 80, 87
    production stability in, 33,
        34(table), 232
    ragged stunt disease in, 73
    rice policy of, 83, 84–85, 87, 89,
        91
    rice prices in, 85, 86(table), 87
    rice production in, 59(table).
        *See also* Insect damage
    rice stocks in, 87
    staple food consumption in, 29,
        30(table)
    and technology, 80
    tungro virus in, 70
    *See also* National Grains
        Authority
Plant adaptability, 71
Plantains, 29. *See also* Bananas
Plant breeding, 11, 62, 70–74
Plant diseases, 70, 71–72, 73
Plant stability, 71. *See also* Crop
    yield stability
PL480. *See* Agricultural Trade
    and Development and
    Assistance Act
Policy options model, 187. *See*
    *also* Developed countries, and
    national policy options; Food
    insecurity, and national policy

    options; Food security,
    international scheme
    planning; Food security,
    policies; National food
    security policies
Portfolio management, 5–6
Port Said (Egypt), 156
Portugal, 319
Potato production, 272
Poverty, 256. *See also* Colombia,
    and rural poverty
Price elasticities, 192, 193(table),
    194(table), 202, 257
    negative, 36
Price fluctuations, 5, 7, 12, 25,
    35–37, 91, 113, 114, 178, 308.
    *See also* Consumer food
    prices; Farm income; World
    price model
Price insulation, 8, 259, 262–263
Price stability, 14, 37, 154, 169,
    170, 176, 200, 202, 204–206,
    229, 230, 231, 232, 233, 262,
    268. *See also* Macroeconomic
    stabilization policies
Price support programs, 174, 175,
    188, 192, 193, 197, 200, 201,
    229
Production fluctuations, 5, 8, 9,
    15, 25, 31, 33–35, 38, 48, 50,
    53, 54, 102, 113, 185, 207,
    231, 241, 255–256
    African, 106–107, 116
    and coefficient of variation, 33
    and food aid, 180, 308. *See also*
        Food aid, requirements
    and imports, 205
    and market instability, 161–165,
        168, 170
    and optimal grain reserves, 260
    and technology, 255
    *See also* Cereals, production;
        Compensatory financing
        schemes, statistical analysis;
        Marketed production;
        individual countries

*Index*

347

Public food distribution, 10, 38, 109, 110, 118, 129
  rural, 112, 137
  systems, 104
  urban, 112
  *See also* Storage; Transport
Public good, 230
Puebla Project (Mexico), 66, 67(figure, table), 68
Pulses, 29, 149

Ragged stunt disease, 73
Rainfall. *See* Climatic change
Real export earnings, 6, 20, 310-311, 312, 331(table). *See also* Compensatory financing schemes, statistical analysis
Real income, 133-135, 136(table)
  fluctuation, 5, 6, 8, 9, 19
Reserves. *See* Cereals, reserves of; Domestic grain reserves; Food reserves; International grain reserve system; Monetary reserve; Wheat reserve stock system
Reutlinger, Shlomo, 12, 14, 83, 85, 137, 232, 241, 242, 301
Rice
  breeding, 73-74
  consumption, 79, 111, 144
  diseases. *See* Blast disease; Brown planthopper; Ragged stunt disease; Tungro virus
  and domestic stabilization, 82
  as dominant commodity, 53, 115
  exporters, 91
  and infrastructure, 64
  insurance, 89-90, 91, 92
  as insurance proposal grain, 272
  international trade in, 79-80, 81(tables), 91-92
  and irrigation, 63, 64(table)
  IR26, 73

marketing structures. *See* National Grains Authority; National Logistics Agency
  milled, 79, 105
  paddy, 108(table)
  policies, 82-95
  prices, 80, 85-86, 90
  production, 54, 58, 59(table), 60, 62, 68, 69(table), 79, 80, 81(tables), 91
  quality, 90-91
  rain-fed, 71
  reserve, 89
  semidwarf variety, 60
  as source of energy and protein, 53
  stocks, 87-88, 95
  as substitute for maize, 112
  supplies, 7, 12, 79, 83
  technological dynamism in, 85
  varieties, 80, 82(table)
Rice Committee of the Board of Trade (Thailand), 90
Rockefeller Foundation, 57, 70
Root crops, 29
Roumasset, J., 66
Rust resistance, 70, 72

Sadat, Anwar, 148
Safaga (Egypt), 156
Sahel, 272
Salinity, 63
Saouma, Edouard, 298
Sarris, Alexander H., 39, 226, 289
  and world wheat economy simulation model, 226, 228-229, 230
SDCs. *See* Selected developed countries
SDRs. *See* Special Drawing Rights
Seedbeds. *See* Vinyl seedbeds
Selected developed countries (SDCs), 165, 166(table), 167, 173(table), 175
Self-sufficiency, 7, 112-113, 115, 148

348

Senegal, 30, 31, 32(table), 232
Service exports, 319, 320(table),
  321, 324–329(tables),
  331(table)
Shei, Shun-Yi, 258
Shortfalls. *See* Food imports, and
  export earnings; Production
  fluctuations
Siamwalla, Ammar, 12
Sinai utilization program, 155
Skewness. *See* Standard deviation
Slow rusting, 72. *See also* Rust
  resistance
Soil conservation, 60
Somalia, 319
Sorghum, 12, 107, 111, 115, 144,
  272
South America, 72. *See also*
  individual countries
South Asia, 62, 63, 65
Southeast Asia, 62, 63, 65, 72, 80.
  *See also* Association of
  Southeast Asian Nations
Southern Africa, 101
South Vietnam, Republic of, 89
Soviet Union
  wheat consumption, 231
  as wheat importer, 175
  wheat market, 14, 165,
    166(table), 168, 173(table),
    174, 176
  wheat production, 165, 167, 225
Special Drawing Rights (SDRs),
  321, 330
Sri Lanka
  drought in, 60
  food import/export ratio, 31,
    32(table)
  food imports and export
    earnings, 43, 232
  and irrigation, 63
  rice production in, 59(table)
  rice trade in, 89
STABEX. *See* Stabilization of
  Export Receipts

Stabilization of Export Receipts
  (STABEX), 17, 309, 310, 330
Stabilization policies. *See*
  Macroeconomic stabilization
  policies
Standard deviation, 55, 66, 68,
  69(table), 315
Staple food supplies, 3, 34(table),
  54, 161. *See also* Cereals
Staples, 27–28, 29
Statistics, 107, 313–318
Stock
  accumulation, 165, 167, 176,
    204, 300
  changes, 167, 168, 173(table),
    174, 257
  domestic, 169
  holding, 177–178, 180, 263, 313
  levels, 174, 177, 181–182,
    267–268
  prices, 177, 200
  purchases, 169
  sales, 161–162, 163, 168–169
  stabilizing, 172
  *See also* Buffer stocks; Cereals,
    reserves of; International
    grain reserve system; Optimal
    grain reserves; Wheat reserve
    stock system; Working stocks
Storage, 161, 163, 186, 189, 192,
  201, 260, 266, 267, 268, 281
  facilities, 75, 109, 115–116,
    155–156, 177, 192, 222, 298
  programs, 298, 299
  and trade activities, 190
Streak virus, 71
Stunt disease, 72
Sub-Sahara Africa, 45(table), 46,
  101, 102
Subsidies
  consumer, 144, 188, 191, 192,
    193, 196, 197, 199, 200, 201,
    202–203
  export, 112, 169
  input, 88

# Index

tax-subsidy system, 189
*See also* Price support programs
Subsistence farmers, 114, 118
Sudan, 101, 246, 247-248(table)
Sugar, 27-28, 149, 153. *See also*
International Sugar
Agreement
Sukhatme, P. V., 130
Surplus. *See* Cereals, surplus of;
Food aid, and surpluses;
Marketed surpluses;
Wheat, surplus
Swaminathan, M. S., 57
Syria
food import/export ratio, 31,
32(table), 279
food imports and export
earnings, 45(table), 46
as insurance scheme beneficiary,
246, 247-248(table)

Tamil Nadu (India), 63
Tanta (Egypt), 156
Tanzania
crop subsidies in, 115
food consumption in, 30
food crisis (1973/1974) in, 106
food distribution in, 109
food import/export ratio, 31,
32(table)
food imports and export
earnings, 44, 45(table)
food production in, 107,
108(table)
food reserve in, 106, 110, 116
and food security, 101
maize production in, 107,
108(table)
milled products, 110(table)
millet production in, 107,
108(table)
rice production in, 108(table)
sorghum production in, 107,
108(table)
state farms in, 102

wheat production in, 108(table)
*See also* National Milling
Corporation
Target consumption levels, 2, 3,
25
Target import volume, 41
Tariffs. *See* Import costs
Taylor, Lance, 289
Taylor Series, 35
Te, A., 54
Technological change, 11, 256
and crop yields, 53, 54, 55,
56-60, 62
high use, 66, 67(figure)
and land, 60, 62
low use, 66, 67(figure)
and policy implications, 74-76
and rice production, 54, 60
Temperature. *See* Climatic change
Thailand
as rice exporter, 7, 12, 79, 82,
91, 92, 95
rice policy of, 83, 88, 94
rice prices in, 85, 86(table), 88,
90
rice as war reparations, 84
Thompson, L. M., 55, 57
Thompson, Robert L., 258
Thursby, Maria, 258
Tourism earnings, 311, 319
Trade barriers. *See* Food security,
and domestic trade;
Transport, cost
Trade policy, 164, 169, 170, 186
model, 187, 189-190, 192-193,
201-202, 205-208, 210
Traditional production sector,
102-103, 105
Transport, 115, 137, 269, 296, 299
cost, 8, 13, 27, 75, 189, 192,
255, 262
Trend
cost, 301
imports, 301-302
levels, 38, 40

output, 127–129, 134–136, 268
*See also* Historical trend; Trend values
Trend values, 38, 40(table), 41, 42–43, 308
Trust Fund Loans, 319, 321, 330
Tungro virus, 70, 73
Tunisia, 319
Turkey, 58, 74, 246, 247–248(table)

UMRs. *See* Usual marketing requirements
UNCTAD. *See* United Nations Conference on Trade and Development
United Nations Conference on Trade and Development (UNCTAD), 14
IV, 89, 213, 214
United Nations Economic and Social Commission for Asia and the Pacific (ESCAP), 89
United States
crop yields in, 56–57
Department of Agriculture (USDA), 50, 56, 107, 110
as exporter, 263
and food aid, 16, 150, 151(table), 287, 292–293, 297
and grain insurance program, 268, 272
and livestock feed, 256
as maize exporter, 91. *See also* Maize, U.S. yields
as rice exporter, 91
as wheat exporter, 91
wheat price policy, 258
wheat production, 223. *See also* Nebraska
University of Chicago, 263
Upper Volta, 40, 45(table), 46, 319
USDA. *See* United States, Department of Agriculture
Usher, Dan, 90

USSR (Union of Soviet Socialist Republics). *See* Soviet Union
Usual marketing requirements (UMRs), 302–303

Valdés, Alberto, 6, 11, 14, 18, 232, 279, 291–292, 308, 312
Values. *See* Actual values; Trend values
Vinyl seedbeds, 62

Warming trend. *See* Climatic change
Water control, 11, 62–65, 80
Weather. *See* Climatic change
Welfare gain and loss, 190, 197
Wet season, 69
WFP. *See* World Food Programme
Wheat
consumption, 144, 165
diseases of. *See* Rust resistance
as dominant commodity, 53, 115
exports, 165, 167, 221
Hard Red Winter Ordinary, 226
imports, 39
as insurance compensation, 92–94
as insurance proposal grain, 272
1978/1979 crop, 233
1979/1980 crop, 232
policies, 15, 173(table)
prices, 175, 176, 191, 231, 243, 258, 296. *See also* Wheat Trade Convention, price indicator
production, 58–59, 62, 74, 165, 176, 191, 225
as representing world grain prices, 197
reserves, 154. *See also* Wheat reserve stock system
and Sarris simulation model, 226, 228–229
semidwarf variety, 60

*Index*

Soft Red Winter, 245
as source of energy and protein, 53
spring, 72
stocks, 174. *See also* Wheat reserve stock system
storage, 155–156, 222
as substitute for maize, 112
supplies, 7, 12
surplus, 167, 175
trade volume, 173(table)
*See also* International Wheat Agreement; International Wheat Council; Milled products; Multilines; individual countries
Wheat reserve stock system, 213–226, 229, 230, 231, 232, 233
Wheat Trade Convention (WTC), 14, 15, 213–214, 215, 216–217, 220, 221, 222, 223, 228, 229, 231, 233
price indicator, 214, 218–219(charts), 223, 224(figure), 225
*See also* Wheat reserve stock system
Winkelmann, Donald, 11
Workers' remittances, 311, 319

Working stocks, 4, 19, 261, 262. *See also* Minimum working stock
World Bank. *See* International Bank for Reconstruction and Development
World Food Conference (Rome, 1974), 1, 213, 288, 298
World Food Council, 288
World Food Programme (WFP), 288
World price model, 187, 188, 192, 205–206
. and median grain price, 191
WTC. *See* Wheat Trade Convention

Yaqui Valley (Mexico), 58–59, 63

Zaire, 27, 232
Zambia
export earnings, 319
and food security, 101
as insurance scheme beneficiary, 246, 247–248(table)
and large-scale expatriate production, 102
maize production in, 104(figure)
*See also* Namboard